STM

Peacemaking in a Troubled World

Edited by Tom Woodhouse

Peace studies and peace research are flourishing in a number of international centres as the people of the world seek solutions to the dangers and threats of a range of potentially lethal conflicts. The Bradford Department of Peace Studies is the largest centre of its kind in the UK. Its founding Professor is Adam Curle, pioneer in peace education, to whom this volume is dedicated. It presents the first account of Curle's work and ideas and sets it in the context of a range of work currently being pursued in peace studies.

Tom Woodhouse, Senior Lecturer in the Department of Peace Studies and Chairman of Postgraduate Studies, University of Bradford.

Peacemaking in a Troubled World

Edited by
Tom Woodhouse

BERG

New York / Oxford

Distributed exclusively in the US and Canada by
St. Martin's Press, New York

First published in 1991 by
Berg Publishers Limited
Editorial Offices:
150 Cowley Road, Oxford OX4 1JJ, UK
165 Taber Avenue, Providence RI 02906, USA

Library of Congress Cataloging-in-Publication Data
Peacemaking in a troubled world / edited by Tom Woodhouse.
     p.   cm.
    Includes bibliographical references.
    ISBN 0–85496–594–7
    1. Peace—Study and teaching. 2. Peace—Research. 3. Conflict
management. 4. Pacific settlement of international disputes.
    I. Woodhouse, Tom.
    JX1904.5.P426   1991   90–369
    327.1′72′07—dc20   CIP

British Library Cataloguing in Publication Data
Woodhouse, T. (Tom), *1950–*
   Peacemaking in a troubled world.
   1. Peacemaking
   I. Title
   327.172

ISBN 0–85496–594–7

Printed in Great Britain by
Billing & Sons Ltd, Worcester

Contents

Contents

Figures and Tables

Figures

Tables

Abbreviations

ANZUS	Security treaty between Australia, New Zealand and the United States of America
CDE	Conference on Disarmament in Europe
CND	Campaign for Nuclear Disarmament (UK)
COPRED	Consortium on Peace Research, Education and Development
ILP	Independent Labour Party
IMEMO	Moscow Institute of World Economy and International Relations
INF	Intermediate Nuclear Forces
IPRA	International Peace Research Association
ISKAN	Institute of the USA and Canada (USSR)
NGO	Non-Governmental Organisation
NMWM	No More War Movement
OAU	Organisation of African Unity
UNESCO	United Nations Educational, Scientific and Cultural Organisation
PRIO	Peace Research Institute, Oslo
PRS(I)	Peace Research Society (International)
QCEA	Quaker Council for European Affairs
SDI	Strategic Defense Initiative
START	Strategic Arms Reduction Treaty
UNITAR	United Nations Institute for Training and Research
WILPF	Women's International League for Peace and Freedom
WPI	World Policy Institute

Introduction

Tom Woodhouse

Now in his mid-seventies, Adam Curle has had more than thirty years' experience as an unofficial mediator in violent conflicts. He also served as the first Professor of Peace Studies at the University of Bradford in England, between 1973 and 1978, and his academic work has been influential in the emergence of peace studies as a legitimate field of educational endeavour. He has produced a coherent and challenging philosophy of peace in a series of studies which have focused on the transcendence of violence through the unfolding of the potential for good in human relationships; and this focus has in turn been the product of insights gained from a diverse academic formation tempered with experience of the pain of human conflict in many settings.

This book is divided into five parts: the first is devoted to 'Adam Curle and Peace Studies', beginning with a short essay by Curle himself which distils the essence of his philosophy of peace and peacemaking. In 'Peacemaking – Public and Private' Curle explores the roles of the peacemakers, and the importance of revealing the 'inner' (personal awareness) and 'outer' (political–structural) dimensions of peacemaking; 'public peacemaking is what we do; private peacemaking is what we are, the two being interpenetrating'. Structural and personal or subjective and objective factors are interconnected in a complex manner in all conflicts, and in all conflicts the common factor is the human one: 'Although the structure of a relationship may have been built up over centuries, eight of them in the case of Northern Ireland, it is the men and women of today who maintain that structure.' It is also the case that only people can break established patterns of behaviour, and transform their relationships from violence to tolerance.

This volume is presented in recognition of Curle's work in

establishing peace studies at Bradford and of his leading role as a peace educator. Equally importantly it is presented to acknowledge the achievements of a man whose wisdom, good humour, and humanity have led him to seek to apply his knowledge as a peacemaker in a range of international and social conflicts from Northern Ireland to Sri Lanka with a quiet courage, a deep strength of spirit, and a voracious appetite for justice and reconciliation.

It is not the purpose of this book simply to indulge in a demonstration of respect for Curle's work. The efforts which have been made worldwide to establish the legitimacy of peace education have met with scepticism and on occasion with hostility, especially from some quarters in the United Kingdom. But in general, in this nuclear age, in a world dangerously divided and rapidly changing, it is clear that peace studies is not a 'soft' educational pastime, but a vital and expanding area of knowledge. The widespread extent of peace research and education may be gauged from a glance at some of the directory guides to the area which have appeared in recent years.[1] As Kenneth Boulding has put it:

> if I were to nominate the activity which is now open to mankind and which would increase most dramatically the prospects of his survival, I would nominate a massive intellectual effort in peace research – that is in the application of the social sciences to the study of conflict systems and especially of conflict systems in their international aspect.[2]

Though there is some way to go, the investments to which Boulding referred in 1982 are now being made. In 1984 the United States Institute of Peace was established and has a variety of grant-aid schemes to support research, training and education in the area of international peace and conflict management. In the United Kingdom efforts are under way to establish a Chair of Peace Studies at the University of London and the Richardson Institute at Lancaster University has both a taught Master of Arts degree and a group of doctoral research students. The University of Ulster at its Magee campus in Derry has a BA and an MA degree, and the Irish School of Ecumenics in Dublin also offers an MA degree validated

1. *See, for example, T. Woodhouse, The International Peace Directory*, Plymouth, 1988; Robert Rudney, *Peace Research in Western Europe; A Directory Guide*, Washington, DC, 1989; and the *Peace Resource Book*, ed. C. Conetta, Cambridge, Mass. 1988
2. K. Boulding, 'The War Trap', in *Towards a Just World Order*, eds. R. Falk, S. Kim and S. Mendelovitz, Boulder, Colo., 1982, p. 238.

by Trinity College, Dublin. Meanwhile, the department of Peace Studies in Bradford, now in its seventeenth year, has survived and prospered through what has been a difficult period for British universities in general; it has attracted a large group of postgraduate students (currently twenty-five full-time doctoral research students and twenty postgraduates following a taught MA course). In addition, between seventy and eighty undergraduates are in residence in any one year.

Adam Curle is one of that group of innovators who saw the need for this kind of investment in higher education, and now, thirty years after the formation of Johan Galtung's influential Peace Research Institute in Oslo (PRIO), and fifteen years into the life of the Bradford Department, it is appropriate to bring together the work of peace educators and researchers to demonstrate some of the key approaches of peace studies. The essays presented in this book are not intended to constitute a comprehensive coverage of concepts and issues in peace research. Nor will the reader find a history of the development of peace studies at Bradford. The purpose, rather, is to present a selection of work from within the Bradford Department, and from eminent people in the field worldwide, so that the reader may get an impression of the range of peace research and education and of some of its findings.

Curle's work in peace studies can best be understood in the context both of the intellectual revolution (in effect an attempt to come to terms with the nuclear age), which began in the 1950s and which is still proceeding, and of the traditional pacifist beliefs and actions of the Quakers or the Religious Society of Friends, with whom he has been involved since the late 1950s.

The detonation of nuclear weapons over Hiroshima and Nagasaki brought a new urgency to the problem of understanding warfare and its avoidance. Peace as an academic pursuit emerged in a number of centres in Europe and North America as academics began to realise that the traditional formation of disciplines could not by themselves adequately develop the knowledge and skills necessary to deal with the conditions of conflict in the later years of the twentieth century.

Peace studies is built on the foundations laid by the formation of peace research centres in Northern Europe and the USA, amongst which the University of Michigan's Centre for Research on Conflict Resolution and the PRIO in Norway, were important early ventures. From 1957, the Michigan Centre published the *Journal of*

3

Conflict Resolution and Kenneth Boulding's editorial in its first issue clearly spelled out the need for a transformation of approach:

> The reasons which have led us to this enterprise [the launch of the *Journal*] may be summed up in two propositions. The first is that by far the most important practical problem facing the world today is that of international relations – more specifically the prevention of global war. The second is that if progress is to be made in this area, the study of international relations must be made an interdisciplinary enterprise, drawing its discourse from all the social sciences and even further.[3]

While peace research is young, attempts at a lifestyle guided by the values of peace have a long history. In Britain the Quaker peace testimony runs back into the seventeenth century and still carries the injunction of George Fox 'to live our lives so as to take away the occasion for war'. This tradition of Quaker concern had a direct bearing on the establishment of a School of Peace Studies at Bradford because it was within the Monthly Meeting of the Society of Friends in Cheshire in the north west of England that a 'concern' first emerged that resources should be devoted to the study of peace. This concern was recognised and supported by the Meeting for Sufferings, the 'executive committee' of the Society of Friends. Meanwhile the University of Bradford under the leadership of its Vice-Chancellor E. G. Edwards and his deputy Robert McKinlay had accepted in its charter a commitment not only to the pursuit of knowledge, but to 'the application of knowledge to human welfare'. The fusion of Quaker concern with the progressive attitudes of the executive of the new university proved to be fertile ground for the endowment of a Chair in Peace Studies. Staff began work in 1973, the first students arrived in October 1974, and the School was guided through its formative years by Adam Curle. Now well into its second decade, the Bradford Department is established internationally as a vigorous centre of both education and research.

My chapter, 'Making Peace: The Work of Adam Curle', provides a profile of the development of Curle's ideas through the disciplines of anthropology and psychology to the emergence of his innovatory ideas in peace studies. Curle's academic interest in peace has been characterised by a deep desire to seek practical solutions to the world's problems, and his academic work has been only part of a broader experience gained from involvement in a range of develop-

---

3. K. Boulding, *Journal of Conflict Resolution*, vol. 1, no. 1, March 1957, p. 1.

ment projects in the 1950s and 1960s. This work in the field in turn brought him into contact with people involved in major violent conflicts in Africa and Asia and his role as a mediator in these conflicts, together with his subsequent writings on mediation as a part of peacemaking, are seen to provide key insights into the practical tasks of peacemaking in a contemporary world troubled by conflict.

This chapter is followed by Robert McKinlay's account of the way in which the Chair in Peace Studies came to be established at Bradford. As one of the younger British universities, Bradford added to the standard objectives of universities (to seek advances in knowledge) the principle that such knowledge should also be applied to human welfare. Under its first Vice-Chancellor, Ted Edwards, the University established a reputation for innovation guided by an internationalist outlook. This outlook has also long been cherished by the Religious Society of Friends, whose activities were so decisive in the formation of the School.

The second part of the book, 'Peace Research and Education', brings together the contributions of Mack, O'Connell, Rank, Green and Galtung in a set of essays which explore the debates about the approaches and priorities of peace studies.

Peace education has on occasion been criticised for being value laden, even propagandistic, and indeed this has been the subject of the most heated debates between its opponents and advocates. As Johan Galtung has remarked, peace research quite explicitly upholds a value: it is for peace and against war, just as medical science is biased in favour of health and against disease. Undoubtedly important questions remain to be clarified about the role of scholarship and academic professionalism in peace research and education and these questions are taken up in the chapters by Andrew Mack and James O'Connell.

Mack's 'Objectives and Methods of Peace Research' explores the development of the area in the form of a general review of its institutional growth and its evolution as an area of academic study. Peace research was influenced in its early years by the new social sciences developing in the 1950s and 1960s. Its 'growth poles' were in Europe and North America (especially in the Michigan Center for Research in Conflict Resolution, in Johan Galtung's International Peace Research Centre, which in 1964 began publishing the *Journal of Peace Research*, and in the Polemological Institute in Holland which opened in 1962). Debates emanating from these and other institutes which opened subsequently are described by Mack who identifies the formative controversies (about positive and negative conceptions of peace, structural violence and the relationship between values, academic objectivity and political commitment).

These latter issues are further examined in James O'Connell's chapter 'Approaches to the Study of Peace in Higher Education: The Tensions of Scholarship'. O'Connell recognises the paradox that while all are in favour of peace it is nonetheless a controversial term. Yet despite resistance to recognising peace as a proper area of study, the academic study of peace has now been accepted, not least because the issues which it raises cannot be avoided in the modern age: the technical development of weapons and the failure to develop co-operative relations between states has meant that we will all be destroyed if peace breaks down. For this reason alone the conditions of peace must be studied.

O'Connell's chapter identifies the core approaches of peace research, its 'architectonic ideas' and the ways in which they are specifically applied in the work of the Bradford Department. He considers the responsibilities of scholarship as well as the relevant concerns of peace studies as an academic area: 'Its contribution is to provide a longer term perspective to looking at peace as well as providing the detachment and breadth that are sometimes missed out in practical concentration or in ideologically committed orientations.' In essence, O'Connell is arguing for the opportunity for people to think creatively, systematically and rigorously about problems of human conflict. Meeting this opportunity will ultimately provide the greatest resource for peacemaking in troubled times.

Carol Rank explores the development of peace studies programmes in the United States' university system and reviews a sample of courses from some of the main sectors of higher education (religious colleges, liberal arts colleges and public and private universities) including the first to emerge, at Manchester College, Indiana, in 1948. The infrastructure which supports the evolution of peace studies as a distinct and coherent area of study is also identified by Rank, that is, the professional associations, academic journals and administrative arrangements which are necessary to establish peace studies as part of the academic community. In this respect the work of the Consortium on Peace Research, Education, and Development (COPRED) has been stimulating, and there is a good range of peace journals which provide an indispensable medium for debate and dissemination of knowledge. The field, then, is developing rapidly, although there are a number of tensions which need to be addressed: these include the identification of a 'substantive core' for peace studies; the question of interdisciplinarity and the problems of academic territoriality; the role of values, the charges of bias and the tension between scholarship and activism. Rank points to the tendency to gravitate towards traditional modes of research and thinking (for example, the security problems of nation states) rather than towards firmly establishing globalism and integrative processes in the world community, studied in an interdisciplinary manner, at the heart of the peace-studies core. This chapter concludes with a discussion of how peace studies might develop, so that the values, policies and social processes which support a 'global' civic literacy and a non-violent world order may be better understood.

Kevin Green's contribution looks at 'Peace Education in Great Britain', and comments on the controversies which have accompanied the spread of peace studies into the secondary-school system. His research and experience suggest that peace studies as a separate and distinct subject does not exist to a significant degree in British schools and much of the controversy about its alleged bias is therefore misplaced. Green does, however, make a distinction between peace studies as a subject and education for peace as a process which is cross-curricular, which is present in many schools and which raises vital questions about education for world citizenship. This chapter, then, concentrates on the acquisition of knowledge, the development of values and attainment of skills appropriate to peace education at the secondary level.

The section is concluded with a short essay, 'Peace Research, Peace Studies and Peace as a Profession: Three Phases in the Emergence of a New Discipline', by Johan Galtung, who suggests that after thirty years of organised peace research, the time has come to further the application of knowledge through the development of vocational expertise and the launching of new courses for peace professionals.

This has been for some time a characteristic of the Bradford approach, with an emphasis on the application of research to enhance policy formation. The newly established Centre for Conflict Resolution, a venture of the Department of Peace Studies, has initiated a programme which concentrates on the design of training and educational modules for groups involved or interested in the process of conflict resolution. The programme has three general objectives:

1. To research conflict resolution and mediator training schemes and to evaluate the theoretical assumptions and content in the various programmes and approaches.
2. To research and develop training and educational materials which will service the development of knowledge and skill in the areas of conflict resolution and conflict management.
3. To establish the procedures for exchanging information via information technology (electronic data transfer) systems through national and international networks (peace research centres and mediator agencies in Europe and North America).

From this work training and educational materials will be assembled in order to provide opportunities for a wide range of groups to learn some of the methods of conflict resolution and to give practitioners of mediation and conflict resolution an opportunity to reflect on their experiences in a workshop setting.

The third part, 'Defence, Disarmament and Peace' examines the military policies of the East–West divide and the apparent unfreezing of the Cold War with its vocabulary and posture of mutually assured destruction, of weapons modernisation and the Strategic Defence Initiative. Malcolm Dando's contribution offers an analysis of the origins and characteristics of Soviet arms control policy under Gorbachev, together with an evaluation of Gorbachev's 'Peace Offensive' on Western Europe. Dando shows how much and in what ways Soviet arms control policy has changed since 1985, how these changes have interesting reflections in theories of conflict management (especially the method of unilateral initiatives for tension reduction outlined by Osgood); and how the impact of perestroika will continue to effect the pace of change in Western Europe. It is important that this complex and now rapid process of change is handled skilfully by politicians and by an informed public opinion.

Paul Rogers reviews the characteristics and nature of British defence policy in the context of a tide of change in Eastern Europe which began in 1989. The political developments which have occurred in Poland, Hungary, East Germany and Czechoslovakia mean that the Western powers in NATO can no longer claim to be facing a monolithic threat from a united Warsaw Pact. The collapse of communist state power in Eastern Europe, combined with the radical initiatives in arms control emanating from Gorbachev and the Soviet Union, means that NATO and all the Western European states must review their defence policies. In many countries this is indeed happening. In the United Kingdom, which is the main concern of Rogers's paper, there appears to be a reluctance to rethink either defence spending commitments or defence policy. Rogers attributes this reluctance in part to a yearning for global status which has been fashioned historically and as a result the UK has paid a high price to retain a global military presence and an independent nuclear force. A radical review of many of the UK's defence commitments is now appropriate, partly because 'the maintenance of extensive global commitments hardly seems consistent with a middle-ranking Western European state', and partly because the improved climate of arms control will bring pressure on the UK government to scale down its nuclear pretensions in particular. For these reasons Rogers identifies two parameters within which a revised defence posture for Britain may be planned:

1. A European Security Alliance crossing the East–West boundaries and entailing defence cuts of up to 50 per cent throughout Europe by the mid-1990s.
2. The need to produce a defensively oriented posture for Britain and for Europe as a whole.

The fourth part, 'Peace and the Resolution of Conflict', explores further the possibilities of applied peace research in the methods of mediation and conflict resolution. The analysis of destructive conflict especially in its extreme manifestation as war, and of ways of constructively managing conflict, lies at the heart of peace research. In universities, research institutes and in schools this understanding is the product of intellectual skill and scholarship. However, the process of the formation of knowledge, in peace research as in all other areas of learning, does not proceed without disagreement and frequently controversy. Chris Mitchell in his chapter 'Recognising Conflict' deals with the issue of the proper comprehension of subjective and objective definitions when applied to conflict analysis. He presents a critical examination of the objectivist approach which holds that a conflict may exist, or at least may be identified, irrespective of the perceptions of the parties involved. A good deal of this approach is associated with Marxist and neo-Marxist interpretations which suggest that certain social structures automatically contain and produce situations of conflict. Not all objectivist approaches are Marxist, however, and both Johan Galtung and Adam Curle have in their work argued objectivist positions. In Galtung's case this is clearest in his concept of structural violence; in Curle's case, in his definition of peace as a set of relationships which enables human potential to be fulfilled (and violence as the opposite to this). Both Galtung and Curle are here applying values to their analyses; they are applying judgements about what human relationships could or should be like and in doing so bring the question of values in peace research to the forefront.

John Pettigrew presents an account of the history of the involvement of Quakers in international conciliation and mediation, including some reference to the work of Curle in this area. Pettigrew's introduction sets the context for an evaluation of the effectiveness of Quaker intervention, applying four categories of measurement of success/failure devised by Bercovitch. Applying these measurements to fifteen major conflict interventions by Quakers between the First World War and the Rhodesia/Zimbabwe situation, Pettigrew claims partial success in ten of them. His paper suggests that Quaker involvement has depended primarily on conviction and concern for suffering rather than on the application of explicit social-science models of conflict resolution, but more recent developments indicate that there is a growing awareness among the Quakers of the need to link with institutions and to develop skills which can be drawn, at least in part, from the theoretical and educational work of academics. Quaker mediation is strongly rooted and will continue to impel Quakers, working either in groups or as individuals, to seek peaceful solutions to conflicts at all social levels as an integral part of their faith.

This chapter is followed by Betts Fetherston's review of the ideas and methods of a group of people including John Burton who have over a period of thirty years or so developed an approach to conflict resolution, the refinement, elaboration and wider application of which holds some hope for addressing the difficulties of people caught up in some of the world's more intractable conflicts. Fetherston provides an account of the work of Burton, who is most closely identified with a relatively new international conflict-resolution technique known as the problem-solving workshop or facilitated problem-solving. At the academic level, the problem-solving workshops provide a means for testing and developing hypotheses about conflict and discovering the elements necessary for its successful resolution. At the applied level, Fetherston points out, Burton's workshop stresses three goals: first creating the conditions necessary for the development of effective communication between the parties to the conflict; secondly re-perceiving conflict as a problem to be solved within a win–win framework; and, finally, the transference of new information and insights gained by the participants directly into the political decision-making process within their respective communities or governments. This kind of systematic and structured approach, more highly organised than the Quaker method, indicates an important avenue of advance for peace research in the immediate future, but for a generalised spread of knowledge and competence in the handling of conflict much more research into its root causes and dynamics is necessary, in conjunction with practical work inspired by a diversity of styles and models of conflict resolution. There is scope at least to learn from cross-fertilisation of ideas from conflict managers across the different levels of conflict experience.

While some progress has been made in the study of conflict resolution at the communal and international levels, relatively little work has been done on another potential area of application, the mediation of disputes over environmental issues. Paul Landais-Stamp's chapter reviews the history of environmental mediation in the USA and explores the potential for environmental mediation in general. He points to the three broad categories in which environmental conflicts can occur: the national and international (conflicts over the use of national resources); the level of regulation (how laws and controls on environmental development are made, interpreted and monitored); and site-specific disputes (conflicts over the development of specific natural resources). The management of the environment has risen high on the international political agenda and will be a central concern in the 1990s. Environmental mediation provides one approach to understanding how the development of resources can be managed so that the claims of the community can be balanced with those of business, although, as Stamp recognises, important general questions related to the ethics of mediation (for example, the question of the neutrality of mediators and the problem of how to work in conflicts where the weak are facing the strong) need to be addressed.

The final part, 'Peaceful Relationships', returns to the core issues with which the book began, explaining the inner and outer connections of peacemaking and the way in which peace should be conceptualised and realised in the ordinary relationships between people.

Elise Boulding's essay is a study of three such people. 'Peacemaking as an Evolutionary Capacity' is an account of the ideas of Teilhard de Chardin, Martin Buber and Jane Addams, in a celebration of prophecy and vision. These three great thinkers shared a tremendous optimism about human potential, an optimism which is characteristic also of the life and work of Curle. De Chardin had a vision of a world developing to ever greater levels of consciousness and freedom. While he wrote little about the maelstrom of violence threatening to engulf the contemporary world, however, Martin Buber said much. Buber's life takes us to the heart of peacemaking in his experience in the Middle East and in his work as teacher, conflict mediator and commune organiser. His demonstration of the I–Thou relationship, discussed by Boulding, explores peacemaking in the same spirit as Curle's essay in this book. Boulding's third visionary, Jane Addams, was a founder-member of the Women's International League for Peace and Freedom and spent her life in the design of practical social inventions to serve the peacemaker's craft. Boulding's conclusion is that an evolutionary capacity does exist within the human species to create the peaceable kingdom. The evolutionary transformation occurring in today's troubled world 'consists of a growing awareness that we live on a tiny planet and that . . . the need to understand the other, the different, is beginning to be acknowledged as a condition for human problem solving'.

Sarah Perrigo's chapter discusses the connections between feminism and peace and explores the nature and extent of the involvement of women in the organisations of the peace movement. She traces these connections from the formation of the Women's International League for Peace and Freedom in 1915, through to the central role of women and women's organisations in the contemporary peace movement of the 1970s and 1980s. The importance of Greenham Common, which became an international symbol of feminist pacifism, is evaluated in a discussion of theories of feminism which raises important questions about the relationship between gender, violence and war.

The chapter by Andrew Rigby is an exploration of the practical dimensions of positive peace. Rigby's study is an observation of the tension between the positive and negative aspects of peacemaking through an account of the life of the Christian pacifist, Wilfred Wellock. Central to his argument is the idea that it is important to balance opposition to armaments with a more positive task of developing a non-violent, non-exploitative social order. In essence peacemaking needs modes of reconstruction as well as of resistance, of knowing what it seeks to achieve as well as what it opposes. Wellock blended the traditions of Christian socialism with the ideas of Gandhi to produce an 'integral pacifism', a political philosophy which has much to say about the problems of living in complex and militarised societies and which was a precursor of many of the issues raised in more recent years by the peace and ecology movements.

As we move into the decade of the 1990s we face as an international community both dangers and opportunities. The polarised structures of the Cold War are breaking down and creating some room for manoeuvre. There is the feeling that the massive resources poured into the military systems of the Warsaw Pact and of the NATO states may now be diverted to tackling problems of poverty, ill health, environmental crisis and maldevelopment. Yet in the process of change it is not entirely clear what kind of new order might emerge and, even as the Cold War recedes, new and potentially more insidious conflicts proliferate. In January 1991, and too late for consideration here, war broke out in the Persian Gulf following the invasion of Kuwait by Iraq. Although the regime of Saddam Hussein suffered a devastating military defeat, peace and stability in the region remain a long way off. It is more important than ever that new thinking is applied globally so that political and social skills may be developed to help cultivate the values of peace in the ordinary relationships between people. Peace studies, as this volume hopes to show, is one key area of knowledge where this new thinking is being generated and is a fruitful source also for acquiring the skills of peacemaking for a troubled world.

PART I

Adam Curle and Peace Studies

1

Peacemaking – Public and Private

Adam Curle

I only began to study peace after having been involved in the practical work of peacemaking. It came about by chance. I had lived and worked, mainly on development problems, in Asia and Africa for several years, but having been trained as a psychologist and anthropologist, I had no experience of politics or diplomacy. However, since I knew the places and some of the main actors, I became sucked in as a mediator in wars in both continents. For several years I was absorbed in the processes of negotiation, bargaining, seeking compromises, face-saving devices, attempts to explain enemies to each other, trade-offs and all the other methods by which a third party attempts to promote a settlement or to reduce the level of hostility. This was how I understood peacemaking – the effort by an outsider to end hostilities between warring parties. This, of course, was public peacemaking, not that most of what we did was not highly confidential, but because the general situation was well-known, as were the procedures of diplomacy and mediation.

Before long, however, I began to see that preoccupation with war could merely distract attention from other situations that were almost as damaging. These were situations in which violence was done to people by injustice, oppression, manipulation, exploitation, by the infliction of terror, by degrading or inhuman practices and all the other countless ways in which we demean and harm each other, physically or psychically. Indeed these forms of violence are just as important as wars, for they are the seed bed out of which wars grow. If we were to analyse the approximately 110 wars of the last thirty years we would find that a very large proportion originated in

This paper was originally delivered as a lecture at Queen's University Ontario, 15 February 1978; and subsequently published as Occasional Paper no. 5, 1978.

such circumstances – in colonialism, the victimisation of a minority (or on occasion a majority) group, or exploitation for economic or strategic purposes. Once the wars begin they develop a terrible momentum and are hard to settle except by military victory, but if the right action is taken early enough the worst violence may be forestalled.

These pre- or non-war situations cannot be tackled by the same methods as wars, at least not those with which I have been involved. When the violence stems essentially from inequality, there is little point in negotiation and bargaining: the strong are not going to give in to the weak, to surrender the advantages they derive from their power because of anyone's persuasive tongue. They may, of course, come to feel that it would be sensible for them to make some concessions, but that is a completely different matter. Essentially the only course open to the weak is to become strong enough to change the structure of inequality. This is what was achieved by Gandhi's struggle for the independence of India and subsequently, peacefully or violently, by many colonial countries. (I should note sadly in passing that independence obtained in this way was not always absolute; often the colonial powers relinquished their political control only to impose an equally harmful, because hidden, economic stranglehold.) Here one role for the peacemaker is to help empower the weak. This may be thought of as a subversive or revolutionary role, for if it is successful there will almost inevitably be a period of turbulence, but this can be justified on the grounds that it is a necessary stage in the establishment of a peaceful society in which justice and harmony eventually prevail. Another important task for the peacemaker is to find ways of making the change as non-violent as possible.

I would not wish to imply that all these peacemaking activities are on a large scale, involving nations or big groups. I have come to feel more and more that anyone who is seriously concerned with peace, by which I mean positive, warm, co-operative and constructive relationships between people, must be attentive to relationships between all human beings, friends, members of a family, teachers and students, doctors and patients, neighbours and so on. Obviously the scale of a relationship to some extent determines its character – there are some elements in an international relationship which do not exist in a relationship between a woman and her husband – on the other hand, there are also some which do. The common factor is, of course, the human one. Although the structure of a relationship may have been built up over centuries, eight of them in the case of Northern Ireland, it is the men and women of today who maintain that structure. They may be born into circumstances which impose certain pressures, but however they may have been moulded it is they who make the decisions, give the orders, throw the bombs, pull the triggers. But it is also they who can talk to each other, help each other, influence each other, break the age-old pattern.

It is the structure of the relationship that is public, objective, capable of analysis in terms of social-scientific concepts. But there is something else, an underside to these more objective peacemaking activities which I call private. It is not very easy to define. I can't even say that it is the personal as opposed to the structural or institutional. It is personal, certainly, but then it has always been acknowledged that individual peculiarities do affect larger issues; prime ministers and presidents are carried along by the momentum of history and have less influence on events than they might like to think, but there is a significant modicum of difference between the reactions of, for example, American presidents Eisenhower, Truman, Kennedy, Johnson, Nixon, Ford and Carter that no statesman can afford to ignore. No, I am referring to something that is more subtle. It has nothing to do with the specific situation, although this must obviously be well understood. It is not even concerned with what we call the personality of individual leaders, meaning their quirks, idiosyncrasies and peculiarities. It is concerned with the extent to which those involved in the situation are liberated from the forces that would make them see both it and themselves inaccurately.

Fairly early in my experience as a mediator I began to be aware that the leaders who have to make momentous political and strategic decisions are not simply icy thinking machines, moved only by a logical evaluation of all factors in the situation, and coming like a chess Grand Master to the best possible conclusion. On the contrary, however able they may be, their judgement is also affected by their fears, anger, resentment, ambition, vanity and by the largely unconscious memory of long-past pains, anxieties and feelings of powerlessness. Often the tenser the situation the more dominant are these feelings, and the more dominant they become the faster the flight from reason. I have sometimes had the impression that if the greatest diplomatic and military minds of history, say Alexander, Napoleon, Machiavelli, Talleyrand, Metternich, with Aristotle thrown in for good measure, were to offer their solutions to the problems of Northern Ireland and the Middle East, they would be rejected. The actors in a conflict perceive the situation unclearly through a haze of violent emotion and only when this is dispersed can they properly assess the situation. To blow away the haze is a very important part of private peacemaking. But of course the peacemaker is in very much the same situation. He carries around with him the legacy of the past and the pressures of the present, both of which interact to impair his judgement, and he cannot help others to be free of this legacy until his own liberation has begun.

It is not enough, moreover, to consider only the leaders. They are very important in taking the first steps towards re-establishing peace, but the consolidation of peace as a peaceful society needs many peaceful people, and peacefulness is a quality of people not driven by violent or desperate feelings. This, it seems to me, is a very important argument for seeking non-violent methods of changing cruel, or corrupt, unjust or unequal social structures. Some dedicated and intelligent people believe that we cannot affect human nature until we have altered the society that flawed it, and that we are unlikely to be able to do this without violence. But the habit of violence and the accompanying insensitivity to suffering tend to persist. Thus all too often in history, and we can think of several contemporary examples, a tyranny is overthrown and those ardent lovers of justice who overthrew it become equally tyrannical. If this were not so, there would be many Utopias in our unhappy world. There are, of course, numerous complex reasons for the difficulty of establishing ideal or even relatively decent societies, but the acceptance of violence as a means of achieving ends is certainly one of them. The ends may at first seem good, but with practice we become less discriminating.

This implies particular responsibilities for peacemakers engaged in working towards the establishment of a peaceful society. I have phrased this positively instead of talking about changing or eliminating an unpeaceful one. Peacemakers may indeed devise strategies of social, economic and political change: this is in the public domain of peacemaking, but it is even more important for them to help their collaborators to work on their problems of personal unpeacefulness. This is the private approach, and it is as indispensable as public negotiation in reaching the final goal, not just the cessation of hostilities or the overthrow of a particular regime, but the establishment of a lasting peace, based on justice and non-violence.

Our tendency to inner unpeacefulness is very pervasive. At the centre of all human conflicts, whatever their cause and whatever the rights and wrongs of any particular case, are our apprehensions, anger, resentment, vanity, hurt pride, insecurity, prejudice, the sense of hopelessness, and above all the blurred understanding and the obscure but potent impact of old pains and fears. Even when we struggle for the most splendid cause, these things render our struggle harder and less effective.

In making this generalisation, I am not suggesting that human nature is in any fundamental sense pathological. Below the confusions that characterise so much of our lives are enormous potentials. Every so often we perceive these, unexpectedly revealed, in each other – great funds of creative ability, powers of concentration, profundity, intellectual clarity and grasp, determination, persistence, courage, love. We have all been taught to believe that to be 'normal' (a synonym for healthy) is a desirable state, but the norm is the average and our average is low – minds fettered by poor concentration, inability to exercise self-control (how many people can keep their minds empty of stray thoughts for more than thirty seconds?), and the compulsions of unconscious motives. If by normal we really mean healthy, or whole, we should not accept the standard of the average; we should aim at the best of which we are capable (perhaps Maslow's peak experiences). The question of intelligence is illustrative. A number of studies have shown that intellectual performance (and test scores) can be vastly improved simply by treating people as though they could do better. But we find it convenient to classify people according to a dubious concept of intelligence, and the more we act upon it the more true does it seem to be; just as people behave 'intelligently' when they are treated as competent human beings so they behave stupidly, and eventually cannot do otherwise, if treated as stupid, thus proving the myth. I have, however, so often found that people are capable of infinitely more than is generally believed that in my view the real normal, what we should be like, is a thing of wonder. We are capable of being, as our experience shows, incredibly strong, diverse, understanding, sensitive, while the average is a pathetic travesty, from which comes most of our miseries, of what we might be.

How is it, then, that most of us, most of the time fall so far below our potential? From a very early age society impinges upon us. First we learn from our parents and then increasingly from relatives, friends, school, which things are acceptable and bring rewards, and which are in some sense punished. We become 'socialised', learning how to respond to social stimuli according to the prevalent social code. We also receive through various media an enormous amount of information about the world and ourselves. Much of this is, of course, factual and accurate, but much is also distorted or untrue giving rise to those habits of mind (a significant phrase) we call racism, sexism, ageism and a limited view of the nature and potential of humankind. We also add to our mental baggage the innumerable fears and hurts which we inevitably sustain in the process of growing up. All these feelings and attitudes are fed into that great computer, the brain, the organ through which we experience the mind. There they remain, some frequently and some infrequently activated, but all ready to be triggered by the right associative stimulus.

The brain is amazingly swift, and highly efficient, except in so far as false information has been fed into the data bank. It responds almost instantaneously to any stimulus by assembling and presenting the appropriate – or what we have been conditioned to consider as appropriate – information. Just consider how much we leave to our computers. Not only do we dress, feed or wash ourselves without consciously thinking out each move, but we greet acquaintances in the street, exchange conventional enquiries and comments in a completely automatic fashion and then pass on almost without memory of the incident. I can even do something as 'intellectually' complex as giving a lecture by computer. It takes over when I am speaking on a familiar theme and in a sense I can then go to sleep, just as if switching on the automatic pilot, but after a while I may awake and not know what point I have reached in my talk. At such times we are what is known as absent-minded. I use the analogy of the computer advisedly because a computer is a machine and there is much that is machine-like and automatic about our behaviour when the 'mind is absent' and there is no real awareness of what we are doing. This is inevitable: we are not fully conscious. While the computer works it dreams, wandering away along a train of associations that we call day-dreams. There is, of course, much about us that is necessarily automatic, not only the autonomic nervous system, but the learned muscular responses enabling us to walk, talk, swim, play games, and so on. It is only when what should be conscious becomes automatic that malfunctioning begins.

Some of the elements in the computer which contribute to the diminution of consciousness are also those which tend to make automatic behaviour damaging or violent. I am speaking of these complexes of fixed ideas about people and society that I would collectively call 'isms', and of memory traces of fear, rejection, loneliness and other painful feelings. Often the isms and the feelings of pain interact: we seek refuge from pain in the false security of an ism that boosts our self-esteem, and so act in a way that pains others – and may thus indirectly contribute to our own hurt. In countless ways our response to pain, especially the pain whose origin and nature are hidden from us, is destructive. We protect ourselves from future hurts, or shield our fragile identity (itself a protective device) by manipulating or dominating others, by pestering them for attention, by assuming artificial or unnatural roles, by trying to demonstrate our superiority, by hurting or humiliating. Like most of what are called neurotic mechanisms these things do nothing to give more than temporary relief from the conditions that evoked them. In general they make things worse.

For most of us the moods come and go, unbidden and often unrecognised, in response to the stimulus. They may not be very important, but also they may determine a whole complex pattern of life. Whenever we find ourselves suddenly and unreasonably (as we realise later, but not at the time) irritated, resentful, alarmed, depressed, it is because something has stirred the dregs of an old hurt which has then taken over and dimmed our consciousness. The anger that we express at that time against a particular person, may well have nothing to do with that person, who in all innocence merely did or said something to stir an association. The pain inflicted upon us is transmuted into anger that we direct against others, who in turn receive it as pain and pass on as pain-giving anger to yet others and so on in an endless spiral of violence – all semi-conscious.

I should mention in passing that it seems unnecessary to debate whether human beings are innately violent, killer apes as we have been termed. I do not believe that we are, and if there are any individuals or societies which are or have been completely non-violent – as I think can easily be demonstrated – we have to find another explanation for the all too prevalent violence. A wise psychiatrist, John Rickman, said that violence was the fruit of unlived life. By this graphic phrase I think he meant that violence stems from the frustration, pain, fear, anguish, desperation, sense of loss and confusion that we have all suffered, though some no doubt more than others. But life *can* be lived and we must learn to do so more fully.

If it is the common predicament of humanity to be less than half awake, to behave – often violently – like machines, to mask our high potential with misinformation, preconceptions and negative emotions, then the would-be peacemakers must work on themselves as much as or more than on those whose violence they would wish to curb, for they are also violent and violent people cannot create lastingly unviolent situations. Only by learning to control their own mal-functioning can they help others to control theirs, and only thus have a fully human relationship with them rather than a largely mechanical interaction.

First it is necessary to recognise how little real autonomy we have; how much we are dominated by the flow of thoughts, memories, ideas, feelings that flicker across the screen of conscious-ness; how little we are capable of attention (this is an activity of the whole self as compared with an absorption that can be as automatic as anything else); how, for all our vaunted free will, we cannot choose our feelings or control our thoughts. At the same time we have to recognise that this is the general human condition and that we must not castigate ourselves or forget that below the surface confusion is a deep source of strength. For all our normal lack of complete consciousness, we are not impotent.

Next, we must seek some means of becoming more and more constantly awake. This is an individual matter for each person. Let me, however, mention a few things which I believe to be of general validity. Our normal state is one of inner noise distracting us from reaching the inner parts of the mind. First, therefore, it is necessary to practice quietness. This is not difficult, if we can only remember to do it. It is only necessary to compose ourselves, sitting comfort-ably but not slouching, for two or three minutes two or three times a day, but preferably between different types of activity. The mind then comes to rest and intruding thoughts ignored or nudged gently aside. During these periods, whatever we are engaged with, we should awake. I mean that we should become conscious of who we are, where we are, what we are doing, what is around us, and particularly what our bodies feel like.

These things are very simple; the only difficulty is in breaking the bad habit of being asleep by the good habit of being awake. If we could be conscious of ourselves the whole time, life would be transformed including, of course, our relationships with others.

It is particularly important to remind ourselves constantly that our essence is flawless, that we are all in that sense perfect. But at the same time we are machines. If we are to prevent the machine taking over what should be the function of mind, of consciousness, we have to understand the machine and so should observe it. Paradoxically we can sometimes get the best insight into its nature from the way in which it impedes consciousness – for example, by the difficulties we have in remembering to be quiet.

It is also very important to trace to their sources those invaders that all too often dominate our minds. These are the paralysing fears, the feelings of impotence, the destructive impulses, the desperate need for reassurance, the miseries, the oft-repeated patterns of behaviour that always lead to the same sort of undesired consequences, the sense of worthlessness that arise unreasonably and unbidden. They not only make us unhappy and distort our relationships with others whom we try to manipulate to assuage our pain, but make us much less effective than we might have been. How can we deal wisely and comprehensively with a complex situation when we are, as we significantly say, 'out of our minds' with worry – or resentment, or hopelessness, or whatever it may be? The best we can do on our own is to try to maintain perspective, understanding that these invaders are unreal, that they have nothing to do with our genuine natures, or the present situation, and to try not to treat them seriously. As we become more self-conscious their origins may become clear to us, and their hold over us weaken. There are, however, certain sorts of help which may be sought. Among more accessible techniques, I am struck by the efficacy of co-counselling which identifies the sources of the dominating pains and fears and enables us to dissolve them by discharging the emotion we originally felt, but for various reasons could not properly express.

The practice of meditation is of great help in our efforts to escape what is inappropriately automatic in our natures. Meditation is, in one sense, a journey inwards. It may be contrasted with consciousness-raising exercises which lead outward and which make us more aware of the body and surroundings. These help to stem the draining of energy in day-dreams and destructive emotions but meditation leads us to the source of that energy. Again I would emphasise that this is a very personal matter, private indeed, and we must seek the help that seems most suitable and most available.

Lastly, I would suggest something very practical. It is not enough

simply to recognise as a general principle that we have great un-
tapped potential, but to demonstrate to ourselves that this is true.
We are dominated by ideas, usually because people have told us,
that we are stupid, no good, inartistic, impractical, lazy, hesitant
and the like. Here are a few hints. Never waste time worrying about
not having time to do something – get on and do it and you will find
you have all the time in the world. If there is something you would
like to do but feel you are unable to – painting, playing an instru-
ment, driving a car, doing household repairs – just do it, and you
will find you can as long as you don't think you can't. If you find
yourself being overcome by the fear of failure don't dignify this
erroneous belief by paying it attention, or it will overcome you.
Have you ever stayed awake all night because you were afraid you
were not going to be able to get to sleep? Just push the idea away
without focussing on it. But beware, also, of another pitfall. When
you find you can draw or play the piano or whatever, don't get
pleased with yourself. To know calmly and objectively that you
have capacities is very different from claiming personal credit for
them. To say 'look at me, how clever I am', is as destructive as
saying 'how stupid I am'. Our success has merely demonstrated one
individual realisation of a universal potential. A wrong concept of
'me' and 'my' is the source of much pain and confusion.

The efforts that we make to liberate ourselves from the invaders
that become a part of the dominant data in our computers must
obviously be connected to our relationships with others. If they are
not, if what we gain is kept hugged to our bosoms as personal
profit, nothing will come of it – even for ourselves. In what I have
suggested as some of the approaches to self-liberation much is
implied for our dealing with others. In this context, I am referring to
our contact with people in the peacemaking relationship, but it would
be almost equally valid for virtually all other human interactions.

First, and most important, we must learn to give people complete
attention. We must make ourselves absolutely available to them, not
interposing our own fears, needs or preconceptions. This means
that we must as far as possible switch off our computers, with their
automatic and built-in needs, and respond to human beings as
human beings rather than as objects who can either hurt or help us.
This type of attention creates an aura of safety in which people can
abandon their prickly defences and, as we say, be themselves. But
even this fully human interaction is always precarious, because we
are not usually very good at it. I recall one counsellor who told me

that if her attention to her client wavered for a minute he or she was aware and resentful – the contact was lost, and the expectation left unfulfilled. In order to give attention we must be constantly conscious of the value and importance of the other person. This means also that we must ignore the possibly bad things we have heard of her or him. I remember visiting a well-known and very dangerous guerrilla leader and attempting to give him attention. After a while he said with some surprise 'no one else has ever come to see me smiling and relaxed'. We became fast friends and were able to explore ways of finding humane rather than violent solutions to the situations he was involved in.

A part of giving attention is listening, not only hearing the words and noting their meaning, but listening to their sound which may convey something different – if you ask me how I am and I answer 'fine' in a depressed tone of voice the sound conveys more than the actual words. And listening involves also sensitivity to unspoken feelings that are conveyed by other means. The native Americans, as I have myself experienced, are very adept at this sort of listening. Attentive listening to another person reaches far below the surface and has a profound influence on the relationship of those involved.

A contact based on attention and listening is far from being a machine-like one. In a machine-like relationship we base our interaction on what is machine-like or automatic in each other. If, at this level, I am asked what I think of a particular man I shall describe him in terms of what we call personality traits. And these traits are simply the quirks, patterns of behaviour, habits of thought, automatic responses derived from his fears and pains that dominate his computer: they are nothing to do with the essential him and I must ignore them. It may not be easy to do this: most of our human evaluations are based on this sort of superficial judgement. I must therefore avoid giving 'character sketches'. I must reach below to what is living and vital. It will help if every time I meet people I consciously avoid the temptation to stereotype them and remain absolutely open to an understanding of their real selves. Moreover, when I meet people I already know well, I must always be as open to them as if I were meeting them for the first time. To say, 'oh, its poor old Joe again; we all know that he is this that and the other' will surely make Joe this that and the other, thus frustrating his capacity to do something quite different. Especially, we must be ready to see great beauty and goodness in the person we thought of as poor old Joe.

Not only must we avoid making judgements about people, we must avoid criticising them – we are all in the same boat, creatures who respond in a way that appears foolish or selfish but which we cannot help until we have learned differently; and if I see something ridiculous in you, you can no doubt see something similar in me. But if we once give in to the impulse to criticise and label people as silly, opinionated, self-centred, or whatever, they tend to live up to our assessment. Tell a child often enough that it is stupid, or can't do mathematics, or draw and he or she wont be able to. I have suffered this myself and to my shame have inflicted it on others.

Instead of criticism, therefore, we must give support, encouragement, validation. Most of us have a poor opinion of ourselves because we have been told we are no good, or feel we have failed. And most of us, I am sad to say, have told someone else, a child, student, or mate, in a fit of irritation, or to get rid of some hurt or anger, that they are in some way deficient – and so contributed to their diminishment. On the contrary, we should do all we can to counteract the miserable sense of incompetence, inadequacy, impotence or folly from which most of us suffer. It is very easy. We simply have to tell people that we see them as wise, brave, good and strong. But we cannot deceive them, we must really feel it because we really perceive it.

This does not mean that we must never tell our friends that they are wrong or behaving badly. There is an Indian legend about a snake that was converted by a guru and swore never to bite another person. But the local villagers took advantage of this and stoned it. The snake, angry and disillusioned complained to the guru who answered: 'but I never told you not to hiss'. We, too, must hiss if we see people doing wrong to themselves and others, but to hiss does not mean to harm. This is part of the obligation to explain and to help others to understand what they are doing. At one level we are able to do this by helping them to identify the fears and pains that dominate their computers, at another by explaining the ways in which they unconsciously manipulate and victimise others.

There are other duties we have towards our fellow human beings. We must refrain from subjecting them to our own fits of depression or anger or other negative emotions; these can only make life harder for them and to make them share our self-centred miseries cannot help us. In general, and at all times, we must be aware of them, conscious of the common ground of our being.

I began to try to apply these principles several years ago when it became clear that the skills of public peacemaking, diplomacy, bargaining and so on, were insufficient. At first I acted more or less intuitively. Later, when I tried to understand the apparent effectiveness of those methods, I had the opportunity to learn more of the principles behind the practice. I am now certain that what is essential to peacemaking is also of the greatest value in all human interaction.

In conclusion, I would like to reintroduce the public dimension of peacemaking. The public and the private, the inner and the outer, the large and the small are merely different facets of the same whole, the same truth. If we consider them as being opposite or irreconcilable principles we won't see that truth. If we concentrate on one to the exclusion of the other the right things will not happen. If I simply work on myself and on my relationship with individuals to whom I am opposed or with whom I am acting as negotiator, I will not take into account the very different principles that govern large-scale events: the large is not just the small magnified; in some ways they differ in kind. Likewise, if I give all my attention to the large, the public, the outer, the right things will not happen because the large, although different from the small, private and inner, is composed of these hidden dimensions. One might say the same of the relationship of a body to the cells of which it is composed. If I simply work on myself and ignore the other how shall I know myself since the other is part of myself, from whom my separation is illusory? If I simply work on the other, ignoring myself, I shall not know him either since I can only see him clearly through eyes lightened by self-knowledge. Peacemaking is the science of perceiving that things which appear to be apart are one. It is the art of restoring love to a relationship from which it has been driven by fear and hatred. And one last definition: public peacemaking is what we do; private peacemaking is what we are, the two being interpenetrating.

2

Making Peace: The Work of Adam Curle

Tom Woodhouse

Early Influences and Career

The nature of Adam Curle's work and the development of his ideas cannot be understood without some acknowledgement of the personal qualities which led him beyond the confines of the academic world to the arenas of conflict where the real skills of the peacemaker are tried and tested. Charles Thomas William Curle was born in July 1916, the son of Cordelia Fisher and Richard Curle. His mother was a member of a large family of seven brothers and four sisters, one of whom married the composer Ralph Vaughan Williams. (His uncles included H. A. L. Fisher, the historian and member of Lloyd George's War Cabinet, Admiral Sir William Fisher, Commander-in-Chief of the Mediterranean and Home Fleets, and Edwin Fisher, who was chairman of Barclays Bank).

From his mother Adam, as he came to be called, developed a self-confidence which was to enable him later to make a series of unconventional moves at critical turning points in his life; it was this willingness to be open to change, which led him gradually and after a rich accumulation of practical field and academic experience to a pioneering role in the advancement of peace research and education. His father's family were from Scotland, but Richard Curle had nothing of the dourness and reserve traditionally associated with the Scots. Richard Curle was a rather larger-than-life character. A close friend of the novelist Joseph Conrad, he was an adventurer with wide-ranging interests. A journalist and a writer (with something of a reputation for womanising!), he abandoned his commitment to family life soon after the birth of his first and only child. He was rarely seen by his son, and he and his wife divorced in 1923. While

30

Adam's confidence and self-assurance came largely from the influence of his mother, the inclination to kick against convention may clearly be seen in the rather eccentric character of his father.

Adam Curle has always had a comfortable belief in his abilities, but this self-assurance has never suggested itself as arrogance. The natural ease and confidence which he has drawn from his upper-middle-class family background, developed via a Charterhouse and Oxford education, has merged with a generous disposition, a warm humour, and an intellect motivated to quarry across a range of academic disciplines and religious traditions in search of understanding. All these qualities combined to make a charismatic teacher, as many who have benefited from discussions with him, inside and outside the classroom, will testify. This writer in particular will always remember the long walks across the Yorkshire moors when the issues of peace or the daily concerns of the young Bradford School were discussed. The Curle household in the Yorkshire Dales, and now in London, has been a welcoming and stimulating refuge for many travellers from near and far, with generous provision of good food and a wonderful selection of home-made wines and beers (always taken, of course, in moderation!)

In 1935 Curle went to Oxford to read history with the idea that the subject was an ideal and conventional preparation for a decent career as a civil servant. Finding the presentation of history rather dull, at the end of his first year he discovered and became fascinated by the study of anthropology. He decided to travel to Lapland for the summer vacation of 1936, where he celebrated his twentieth birthday travelling with a group of Lapps herding reindeer to summer pastures.

Following periods of field research in parts of the Middle East he obtained a Diploma in Anthropology, and then spent six mostly uneventful years in the army, although it was during these years that he began to form an interest in psychology, and particularly in the combination of the psychological and anthropological approaches to social issues. This interest in social psychology was prompted by the influence of a group of people who were involved with the formation of the Tavistock Institute of Human Relations and who were working broadly on the relationship between social structures and psychological conditions in individuals. The approaches of the Tavistock Institute emerged as psychological experiments undertaken during the course of the Second World War were adapted to constitute part of a programme of post-war social reconstruction.

31

The most influential theorist of the new methods of social psychiatry, or psychoanalytic psychiatry, was W. R. Bion, a practitioner of the psychoanalytic methods of Melanie Klein and a man
who had been a tank commander in the First World War and who
became a military psychiatrist in the Second World War. Bion was
associated in particular with the method of group therapy where
'real problems of both individuals and group are made manifest and
the group shows signs, according to the capacity of the individuals
composing it, of mastering an approach to the problems of human
relationships'. Bion and his co-workers believed that through
applying group-work processes they had discovered a method
which would reveal universal truths about the nature of human
relationships which had value not only at the level of the group, but
which would have an impact on the broad social and political fabric:

> Such a development indicates that a creative evolutionary process may
> soon be offered to the community as an alternative to apathy on the one
> hand or revolutionary discontent on the other ... [The method] pro-
> vides a possible link between intimate personality study and political
> attitudes and group dynamics. It ties up childhood patterns with later
> political and social projections, applicable to any group or institutional-
> ised behaviour.[1]

The group process was seen as the location and laboratory for
human regeneration and development, and it was within this exciting climate of new ideas in the application of psychology to social
issues that Curle's early academic career began to take shape.

The experiences of the war brought British psychiatrists out of
the clinics and mental hospitals to deal with the specific social
problems of morale and motivation during the war itself, and with
the problems of demobilisation and rehabilitation after it. This was
heightened in a very particular way when the difficulties of returned
prisoners of war became manifest, and it was decided that the army
should take responsibility for their rehabilitation. During his last
year in the army, Adam Curle served as Research Officer attached
to the Civil Resettlement Headquarters which administered the
work of the twenty Civil Resettlement Units in operation through-

---

1. H. Dicks, *Fifty Years of the Tavistock Clinic*, Routledge, 1970, p. 138 and
   p. 145; quoted in P. Barnham, 'Culture and Psychoanalysis', in B. Richards
   (ed.) *Capitalism and Infancy*, Princeton, N.J., 1984; see also W. R. Bion,
   Experiences in Groups, London, 1961.

out the country by the end of 1945. Curle had the task of evaluating the effectiveness of the civil resettlement project, and the research itself in turn provided the material for both a postgraduate degree in anthropology, awarded in 1947, and a series of articles which were to form the starting point for his subsequent academic career. His first published article was entitled 'Transitional Communities and Social Reconnections', and it appeared in 1947 in the first issue of *Human Relations*. The work described in this article, although it dealt with the special problems of prisoners of war as they adapted to the strains of returning to the home community, was above all about the relationship between the individual and the community and carried an awareness about the importance of the social and cultural health of communities to the well-being of individuals. Here, the quality of personal and social relationships was what mattered and when in later years this approach was linked to conflict analysis, development education and peacemaking in real conflicts, the potent originality of Curle's work became apparent.

The postgraduate degree was followed by an appointment to the staff of the Tavistock Institute in London to carry out research on rural decay in the south west of England. This work led to his appointment to the post of lecturer in social psychology in the Department of Psychology at Oxford in 1950.

At Oxford once again his ideas began to change. While he remained interested in and influenced by the social psychiatry approach of the Tavistock Institute he nevertheless felt that their work was slow and its effect restricted in terms of its impact on community life. He believed that the need for psychiatric or psychoanalytic action could be obviated to a very large extent if education was better organised to give people a more solid foundation from which to cope with life. He regarded educational thinking and provision as very much flawed and felt that it was failing in general to provide people with the psychological stability they needed in order to lead normal, good, constructive lives and to build positive co-operative human relationships. He began to seek an academic approach which would combine interests in social psychology and education, and published a number of articles on educational policy. On the strength of this work, in 1952, and still in his mid-thirties, he was appointed to the Chair in Education and Psychology at Exeter University, where he remained until 1956.

During this time another kind of transition came, one which was to lead him to see issues through an international and global perspective, a critical progression, though as yet unrealised, towards peace education. While at Exeter he was gradually drawn into work, mainly through UNESCO, on development problems with a project which was dealing with underdeveloped parts of Europe. He spent some time travelling around on these short-term projects until 1956 when he was invited to go for a year to Pakistan as adviser on social affairs to the Pakistan government, part of a project which was arranged by Harvard University. He later decided to stay for three years, and consequently resigned the Chair at Exeter. His responsibilities in Pakistan were not confined to education policy and included work on a range of development issues related to housing, health, social welfare, labour relations and the tribal areas. He subsequently returned to Pakistan for two periods of about two months each in 1963 and 1964, as a consultant on education when he contributed to the development of Pakistan's third five-year plan.

When his term in Pakistan came to an end and he was preparing to return to the UK a new opportunity presented itself in Africa, where the newly independent nations were investing in education to lead their development. From 1959 to 1961 he served as Professor of Education at the University of Ghana during which time he was able to travel extensively in Africa as well as to devote some time to more theoretical reflection on the relationship between education and development in a way which was not possible during the period in Pakistan. His inaugural lecture to the University was published in 1961 under the title of *The Role of Education in Developing Societies*.[2]

The book was well received and he was invited to Harvard University to explore the setting up of an institute there to study the way in which education affected development. He travelled to the United States in 1961, and the Harvard Centre for Studies in Education and Development was founded in 1962, as a teaching, research and policy-oriented institute with large field projects in Nigeria, Tunisia, Barbados, and in Latin America, with research students throughout the world (at its height involving up to eighty or ninety people). The practical approach of the Centre was to conduct research into the relationship between education and economic development, and then to provide through field experience for the application of research results to education policy.

---

2. A. Curle, *The Role of Education in Developing Societies*, Oxford, 1961.

Education, Development, Society

Adam Curle's general approach at that stage (during the early 1960s) was conventional enough: if intellectual abilities were improved through a good educational system a new class of people would emerge who would raise the general standard of living, which would in itself be desirable. These issues of education, development and change in Third-World settings were tackled at some length in *Educational Strategy for Developing Societies* published in 1963. The approach in this book is characterised by a general acceptance of Western development models which were largely unchallenged in the 1950s and 1960s – the structuring of a modern labour market, the emergence of a middle class and a competent administration, and of a modern education system. He argues, for example, that economic growth is inhibited by low educational levels and that the influence of the small number of people who are educated is negated by the inequalities and rigidities of the social structure of traditional societies. To overcome these rigidities there needed to be rapid development of education and training programmes 'encouraging, helping, and organising enough people to carry weight in their contribution both to the economy and to the growth of a viable and purposive society'.[3]

It is in essence this concern with a viable and purposive society which constitutes the theme of the book, and in defining it Curle begins to move away from the prevailing Western assumptions based solely or largely on economic measures. While the economy and the administration were the main areas in which development policy was practised, the primary and determining factors lay in the domains of sociology and psychology. Development should be measured not in terms of economic growth but through social and cultural dimensions, in particular, the fulfilling of human potential in social relationships.

Indeed, as he developed this line of thought he anticipated a later definition, as yet unacknowledged, of peace as a set of fulfilling relationships, and his view of development even at this early stage was remarkably sensitive to universal human needs rather than subservient to more questionable Western interests. This openness can best be explained by his real experience over a period of six

---

3. A. Curle, *Educational Strategy for Developing Societies: A Study of Educational and Social Factors in Relation to Economic Growth*, London, 1963.

years in Africa and Asia, living with and among communities affected by the process of development and change. It may also be explained by his ability by this time to look at social issues without the constrictions of a single disciplinary 'mind-set', as a man who already had experience in social and economic planning, in anthropological research, in psychology, education and development theory. So, for example, in *Educational Strategy*, the chapter on definitions of underdevelopment effectively presents an account which denies the validity of a structural functionalist 'stages of growth' approach, finding the models of Parsons, for example, of some general use, but insufficient to explain or elucidate the complexities of particular cases and cultures involved in social change. His experience among the Pathan and Chitrali tribes in Pakistan formed a key part of his awareness of processes of social change.

Part of this work consisted in planning for the tribal areas, where many people lived in 'excessive misery'. Disease, poverty, ignorance and hunger were bad because 'they were conditions of diminished human potentiality'.[4] If it was insufficient to measure development by economic indicators alone, then it was necessary to ask deeper questions about human society and human nature. These would help to guide developing nations to aspire to social and psychological states capable of addressing the stresses which resulted from the weakening of traditional societies undergoing economic and political change.

In general, and in line with his earlier Tavistock training, he regarded most misery as emanating from unsatisfactory relationships, but such misery could be alleviated by the structure of relationships into which people enter, and these in turn could to a large extent be determined by social policy. Here, the principles of social justice and equality, if translated into specific procedures in land reform, taxation, education policy and so on, could do a great deal to establish the viable and purposive society which is the goal of development: 'a community rooted in the concepts of equality and social justice will give no place for . . . frenetic accumulation and must tend to value the type of achievement contributing directly to the community, or to intellectual or artistic creation. Such a society would not destroy the incentive to work, nor would it impair the capacity to love.'[5] Although it is not examined in this

4. Ibid., p. 13.
5. Ibid., p. 20.

early book, the relationships between well-balanced community development and the conditions of peace are hinted at, raising a theme which was to become increasingly dominant in Curle's thinking from the mid and late 1960s: 'a country which constantly tackles development as a human problem first and an economic one second, and which bases its approach on the idea that human beings are themselves of value, may be rather more interested in international obligations, rather less militarily ambitious than one which takes the opposite view'.[6]

A series of publications resulted as the fruits of his time at Harvard, and the progress of Curle's intellectual development towards the distinct field of peace research is best illustrated in *Educational Problems of Developing Societies: With Case Studies of Ghana, Pakistan, and Nigeria*, published in 1973 in a revised and expanded version. This book was first published in 1969 and much of it written some years earlier, when the prospects for development seemed much brighter than they were beginning to appear by the early 1970s. Above all, conflict and violence were beginning to feature in his work as subjects demanding urgent attention and especially so because of his direct experience of the Nigerian Civil War between 1967 and 1970, and the war between India and Pakistan. In Pakistan the events of 1971 'swept away the fruit of development in a tide of death, destruction, and hatred': in Nigeria also 'socio-educational factors could not be separated from the factors which led to violence'.[7]

Curle's academic interest in peace was a product of this kind of demanding front-line experience where he not only witnessed the threats to development from the eruption of violent conflicts, but where in effect he was drawn increasingly into the practice of peacemaking, especially in the form of mediation. Most importantly, during the intensive and searing experiences of the Biafran War he felt a compelling need to understand more about why these conflicts happened.[8]

Violence, conflict, the process of change especially as this affected social attitudes and the goals of development began to be seen as linked themes. Reflecting after some years at Harvard on his own

6. Ibid., p. 169.
7. *Educational Problems of Developing Societies*, London, 1973.
8. Curle's experiences in this war are covered in C. H. Mike Yarrow, *Quaker Experiences in International Conciliation*, New Haven, Conn., 1978, and in Curle's *In The Middle: Non-Official Mediation in Violent Situations*, Oxford, 1987.

experiences on educational planning and development he elaborated more fully the goals of development and the role of education in the process.

In *Educational Problems of Developing Societies* Curle defines development, as he had in *Educational Strategy*, primarily in social psychological terms, as a process which necessitates the achievement of certain qualities for the population at large. He had previously argued that the principles of equality and justice applied to social policy would produce a belonging identity sufficient to hold the developing society together. Nigeria and Pakistan were both devastating examples of the violent divisions which could occur in development, and he sought to understand the primary human satisfactions which the more abstract principles of justice and equality would serve. These he identified as safety (protection from violence from whatever quarter, best achieved by some active part in government); sufficiency (enough food and basic material requirements so that potentialities are not inhibited by material factors); satisfaction (where material progress is not gained at great psychic or cultural cost); and stimulus (where the sense of potentiality – intellectual, emotional and social – is kept in view). This latter aspect, the raising of the sense of potentiality, is one of the primary goals of education.

Educational Problems portrays the potentialities of development illustrated by Curle's accounts of his experience in the tribal areas of Pakistan. These areas comprised, in east Pakistan the Chittagong Hill Tracts abutting Assam and Burma, and in the west a vast zone stretching 1,500 miles from the Arabian Sea through Baluchistan and the north west frontier area up to Tibet and the Sinkiang border. The book describes a set of case studies which consider development in the context of the situation of communities with different histories and cultures (the Chakmas in the Chittagong Hill tracts, the Pathan tribes in the mountain areas between Pakistan and Afghanistan and the people of Chitral in the Hindu Kush).

Experiences in these areas and among these people showed that development was possible given flexibility, understanding and competence. But conditions of change in the later years of the twentieth century were generating underlying conflicts which if not properly understood would jeopardise the prospect of human improvement and progress not only in Third-World areas seeking development, but in the countries of the West as well. In particular, for the peoples of the developing countries themselves, it was more important to consider social, cultural and psychological factors. Purely technical and economic policies for development would result in processes of change which would divide and lead to confusion and conflict, not least because of confusion and conflict in the minds of individuals.

At about the same time that Curle was becoming aware of the potential scale of conflict emerging in Third-World settings, he was beginning to realise that the roots of conflict were embedded nearer home, and that Western countries too would have to consider the problem of their own development. It was true that the wealthier countries had by and large achieved a degree of political modernisation where the state had involved the individual in various ways, but the very fact of this internal stability could more easily bring about a clash of interests with another nation state, resulting in a high potential for organised violence. Life at Harvard in the mid-1960s was inevitably affected by the ferment in which the United States was embroiled as the impact of the Vietnam War built up and the counter-cultural movement based substantially on the students gained coherence. Now an established professor in his early fifties, Curle nevertheless experienced a series of changes in perception about himself, about his own his society and his role as an educator in it. He began to examine these themes in the work which occupied him in the late 1960s and early 1970s, the work which was, in fact, to bring him to Bradford.

Peace and Peacemaking

The three major studies in which Curle's changed perceptions are hardened into substantial analyses are *Education for Liberation* (1973), *Making Peace* (1971) and *Mystics and Militants* (1972). *Making Peace* was written in the course of a sabbatical year spent as a visiting research fellow at the Richardson Institute of Conflict and Peace Research in London. It was an effort to draw together general reflections on conflict and development, but it does not confine development to a Third-World setting. Along with *Mystics and Militants*, it established him as a leading influence within a small, pioneering group of academics in peace studies which included Johan Galtung and Kenneth Boulding. *Making Peace* represents the deliberate application of ideas from peace research (especially those of Johan Galtung), to his own work and experience. In this book he tackles problems of definition, looking at peaceful and unpeaceful relationships and in a general sense at the process of peacemaking. *Mystics and Militants*, written as a sequel to *Making Peace*, looks more closely at the personal beliefs of the peacemakers themselves and at the qualities and skills they would need to develop.

Both books have had a decisive influence on the emergence of peace studies as a coherent area of study. They established Curle as an original and innovative thinker capable of providing a comprehensive view of the academic validity and viability of peace studies and were a significant reason for his move to Bradford when that university decided to add peace studies to its profile of new study areas.

Making Peace presents Curle's definition of peace and conflict as a set of unpeaceful and peaceful relationships, and it is this focus on relationships as the subject of peace which above all distinguishes and characterises his work:

> I prefer to define peace positively. By contrast with the absence of overt strife, a peaceful relationship would, on a personal scale, mean friendship and an understanding sufficiently strong to overcome any differences that might occur. . . . On a larger scale, peaceful relationships would imply active association, planned co-operation, an intelligent effort to forestall or resolve potential conflicts.[9]

Peace was concerned, then, not with the containment of conflict, but pre-eminently with the development of relationships: 'As I define it, the process of peacemaking consists in making changes to relationships so that they may be brought to a point were development can occur.'[10]

Peacemaking consists in moving a wide range of human relationships out of the set of unpeaceful categories identified in the book into peaceful ones. But where other peace researchers have tended to concentrate more on social, political and military systems as subjects for analysis, Curle has generally stressed the importance of the attitudes and values of people within those systems to peace and violence. A good part of *Making Peace*, for example, concentrates on the skills of conciliation and mediation, tasks with which he particularly identified himself. He thought that the skill of resolving conflict by mediation was little understood and developed because:

9. A. Curle, *Making Peace*, London, 1971, p. 15.
10. Ibid.

we do not really understand the roots of conflict, seeing it primarily as an objective state of affairs and not as the states of mind that led to and subsequently sustained or exaggerated that state of affairs. Consequently our approach to conflict resolution is confused and inefficient. We really know very little about it and after hundreds of years of diplomacy . . . have little scientific understanding of it.

Our chief fault is failure to recognise that conflict is often largely in the mind and to that extent must be dealt with on that level; and that even when it is less so, as in the case of political oppression or economic exploitation, emotional factors exacerbate what is already serious.[11]

Despite his own preference for analysis which proceeded by concentrating on human feelings and beliefs, he saw peace studies as a venture which could only succeed by recognising and using a wide range of skills and backgrounds. Having defined the nature of peaceful and unpeaceful relationships Curle presented an account of the basic components of peacemaking and identified six areas of concentration:

1. Research: acquisition of knowledge needed to work effectively in order to reveal the structure of the conflict at whatever level it occurs. Peacemaking is a rigorous and demanding intellectual exercise requiring and benefiting from proper academic formation.
2. Bargaining: in which the two parties to a quarrel try to reach agreement without excessive concessions.
3. Development: in which a formerly unpeaceful relationship is restructured along peaceful lines.
4. Education: the gaining of awareness.
5. Confrontation: through which the weaker party to an unbalanced relationship asserts itself in the hope of gaining a position of parity from which a settlement might be reached. Confrontation may take many forms, from non-violence to revolution.
6. Conciliation: at the stage of conciliation psychological foundations are laid in order to assist changed perception, heightened awareness and a reduction in tension among parties to conflict, a process necessary for rational discussion.

One of the longest sections of *Making Peace* is on conciliation (what Curle subsequently came to call mediation), where he elaborates an approach which is drawn from insights from social and, in

11. Ibid.

particular, humanistic psychology applied to peacemaking in public conflicts. Much of the conflict of which he had direct experience was founded on fear derived from ignorance of oneself. This fear of what self-awareness might reveal frequently leads to the development of a 'public face', a mask; the complement to the mask is the mirage. Through the self-protective mask 'we see a mirage of others':

> If they accept us at what might be called our mask value, thus strengthening our defences, we see them favourably. If they do not, they make us anxious and they become unpopular. At this point, through the psychic trick of projection, we are apt to attribute to them the very flaws we dimly sense in ourselves and are attempting to conceal from ourselves and others by the use of the mask. . . .
>
> . . . Mask and mirage are interconnected to the extent that to alter one almost inevitably involves altering the other. My view of my enemy is related to my view of myself, therefore I cannot change my attitude to him without a corresponding change of attitude towards myself.
>
> The concept of awareness takes these ideas a step further. At the personal level the idea of awareness corresponds exactly to the degree to which the mask is put aside.[12]

So awareness is a key element in peace. Awareness in turn is related to identity, but while loss of identity can lead to insecurity and disintegration it can also lead to rigidity and intolerance. In fact there are two types of identity: first an identity of belonging, an important but limited tool; second an identity of awareness, which refers 'both to the inner life of the individual and to his consciousness of society'.

'It is the task of the conciliator to find ways of stemming the psychological current so that, however briefly, the mask can be dropped, the mirage forgotten, awareness heightened, and the sense of identity broadened beyond the bounds of nationalism.'[13] Given this approach to peace studies, which evolved slowly from Curle's experience and academic formation in anthropology, psychology and development education, it was natural that he should see peace broadly in terms of human development rather than as a set of 'peace-enforcing' rules and organisations. The quest for peace is not solely a quest for appropriate structures and organisations, which are only means to human ends; but there is room, too, in peace

12. Ibid., pp. 209–11.
13. Ibid., pp. 215, 216.

research to identify the kinds of social structures which enhance rather than restrain or even suppress human potential.

By the early 1970s Curle had moved beyond the work which had preoccupied him for most of the 1950s and 1960s. He had become more interested in the causes of conflicts, having experienced the destruction they caused, and had been drawn into the role of mediator, which led him directly to think about the resolution of violent conflict and the cultivation of peaceful relationships.

Curle's own values and beliefs fixed substantially on ways of understanding and realising the potential for good in human nature and human relationships. His intellectual debt to the humanistic psychologists in this search was clear in his published work. His desire to seek within was sustained by his increasing involvement with the Society of Friends (Quakers) and by a broader interest in mystical and spiritual exploration which he followed through the works of Ouspensky, Gurdjieff, and more recently in the teachings and meditational techniques of the Buddhists. The end of all this study and meditation was to find a means of understanding the full range of conditions which led to peace. The fundamental quest, however is rooted in a profound optimism in human potential, despite frequent evidence to the contrary: 'man's nature is richer, his capacity for joy, creativity, intellectual effort, altruistic service, spontaneity, courage, and love far greater than we commonly suppose . . . he is more complete, more consistent, gayer, and stronger'.[14]

These themes of the inner and outer or public and private levels of peacemaking are explored further in *Mystics and Militants*, *True Justice* (1981) and *Peacemaking Public and Private* (1978) where the blend of psycho-spiritual and social-scientific themes are lucidly and concisely presented. The problem for those interested in peaceful social change and the resolution of conflicts is to understand how to move beyond a political and sociological understanding of what causes conflict to a deeper understanding of what moves people to seek or to resist change; and in seeking change to understand how it can be achieved without violence and destruction. It is not enough to demand peace or to proclaim the virtues of pacifism, but it is especially important that peace research should seek to understand the behaviour and reactions of people embroiled in conflicts as a precondition for enabling resolution. In *Mystics and*

14. Ibid., p. 23.

Militants Curle returns to the concepts of awareness and identity in
order to shed light on this problem.

Curle's interest in these concepts was generated from observation
of how people in real and intense conflict situations behaved,
becoming extreme to the point of irrationality, that is, their awareness of themselves and their situation diminished sharply, while
they built up a new sense of identity, based on their own courage,
patriotism, rationality and so on.

> Awareness, meaning essentially self awareness and hence insight into the
> conditions of others, can be higher or lower. Identity can be a sense of
> knowing who one is, based upon awareness (that is, awareness identity),
> or, what is more usual, a sense of belonging (that is, belonging identity),
> and both of these can be stronger or weaker. When the belonging mode
> of identity predominates, we define ourselves in terms of what we belong
> to or what belongs to us, whether it be a civilisation, or cultural tradition,
> family or country, material possessions or social position . . . or any
> combination of these or innumerable other things. . . . Broadly speaking
> the combination of low awareness and a strong belonging identity
> produces the conservative force in society. People in this category find
> their identity in belonging, therefore they tend to want to keep things as
> they are.[15]

By 1970 Adam Curle had developed an imaginative and broad-
ranging vision of peace education and research. He had behind him
involvement in a wide range of unpeaceful situations. He had
mediated in two large-scale armed conflicts, experiencing two
gigantic tragedies in which hundreds of thousands of people had
died. He had experience of racial conflicts in Africa and the USA, of
tribal clashes, and of oppressive tyrannies in remote parts of the
world. His time at Harvard saw him concerned with development
in over twenty countries in the Middle East, North and Sub-
Saharan Africa, Latin America, the Caribbean and Asia. He was also
able to draw on his experience as an early staff member of the
Tavistock Institute and two university appointments in psychology.
He had intellectual influences stretching from the humanistic psychologists, whose ideas he encountered in his early career, and the
psycho-philosophical and spiritual systems of Ouspensky and
Gurdjieff, the Sufis and later the Tibetan Buddhists.

By the end of the 1960s and increasingly during the early 1970s he

15. A. Curle, *Mystics and Militants*, London, 1972, p. 9.

became aware of the work of Johan Galtung and Kenneth Boulding, when he realised that his work and theirs were leading by different pathways to the same general goals of emerging peace research, concerned especially to find new ways of dealing with violent conflicts. Of course in taking this route he was able to draw on a developing base of knowledge about conflict behaviour. Among psychologists the way in which people involved in intergroup competition behave is well understood; and once two groups become involved in a dynamic conflict (whether social groups, organisations, communities or nations) standard behavioural patterns are generally observed:

1. Each group becomes more demanding of internal loyalty; ranks are closed and differences buried; conformity is demanded.
2. Within each group more stress is placed on task accomplishment at the expense of the freedom and needs of the individual members of the group.
3. The group becomes more willing to tolerate autocratic leadership.
4. Each group begins to see the other group as the enemy and begins to experience distortions of perception.

Again the processes of perception distortion are also well known and so common that they can be found at any level of conflict:

1. The mirror image: both parties are firmly convinced that they are right, the other wrong; each party clearly sees all the wicked and vicious actions of the other but completely represses all awareness of the mean things they have done to their opponent.
2. The double standard: even if individuals perceive that they and their side have engaged in identical actions to those of the other side, there is a tendency to see their group's actions as justified, while those of the others are unjustified.
3. Polarised thinking: once the conflict is under way, many members of the conflicting groups have invested so much in it and fear so much from losing it that all the characteristics of negative stereotyping of the other side are maintained, and a self-fulfilling prophecy effect takes hold where each side is fully justified in fearing the enmity and hostility of the other.

There are also a number of general points which can be made

about how these polarised conflict situations can be transformed without one group completely dominating the other, or each group collapsing from exhaustion after a long attrition. First, conflicts are generated and maintained by subjective and objective factors and the former must be dealt with first in the resolution process. Conflict may be seen as a hard core of real issues to be resolved (for example, disputes over territory). This hard core is surrounded and frequently concealed by a layer of subjective factors like misperception, misunderstanding, stereotyping, violent hostility, and so on. Much recent thinking on conflict-resolution theory tends to stress the importance of tackling the subjective dimension; of giving significance not to the 'hardware' of a conflict but to its 'software'. In this sense the discipline of psychology has for some time been of importance in the area of conflict analysis. This point may be illustrated by referring to an observation in Fisher and Ury's study of negotiation:

> Ultimately conflict lies not in objective reality but in people's heads. . . . The difference exists because it exists in their thinking. Fears even if ill founded are real fears and need to be dealt with. . . . Facts even if established may do nothing to solve the problem . . . No study of who developed what nuclear devices will put to rest the conflict between India and Pakistan.[16]

Secondly, conflict becomes more amenable to control as threats become increasingly balanced with trust. In any intense conflict it is difficult, sometimes dangerous, to talk to the other side. One central task of mediation is to help open out communications so that there is some prospect of dialogue and therefore a lessening of distance between the antagonists or combatants. Thirdly, conciliators working in situations of intense international conflict report that a major function is to listen to the views and feelings of those caught up in the argument. What is provided in listening is the opportunity for a sort of venting process allowing people to unburden themselves, to calm themselves down, to sound off and perhaps in the process come to a different view of the nature of the conflict.

16. R. Fisher and W. Ury, *Getting To Yes*, London, 1987, p. 23.

Mediation and Conflict Resolution

In the world as a whole we lack the things we need to maximise the benefits of conflict and to minimise its costs. As a consequence we live in a world where conflicts are rarely understood and often mismanaged so that they easily degenerate to violence.

Can we do any better? Many, of course, would say no. But there are some promising developments which suggest new modes of thinking and action in the way we deal with our conflicts, and before proceeding to look at Curle's approach it is necessary to consider the broader development of the field.

Conflict resolution is not an unproblematic concept, and the methods of application vary according to the styles and values of different practitioners, and according to the conflict setting. Mediation is one of a set of techniques which may be applied by third parties to the peaceful resolution of conflicts, ranging from interpersonal to international levels. Mitchell, in his analysis of third-party consultation in peacemaking, identifies the intellectual traditions and general areas of practice which have contributed to the development of mediatory skills. One tradition comes from Gandhian theories of non-violent action which has developed certain insights into the conflicts process, particularly in its emphasis on redefining conflict so that it is seen not as a fight to be won but rather as an opportunity (through the search for an assumed transcending truth), for the problem to be solved. Unfortunately the usefulness of Gandhian techniques for understanding methods of third-party mediation appear to be limited because most Gandhian non-violent theory suggests that the opponent (while he is respected) must be brought to an awareness and acceptance of its own view of the situation; it relies on the conversion of the adversary based on the assumed existence of a common morality which needs only to be revealed.

Mitchell recognises also the special contribution of pacifist sects and religious groups to mediatory skills. In the case of the Quakers, their peace testimony has provided them with a set of principles to guide their actions in conflicts, while they also have a set of basic principles relating to human relationships which have relevance to conflict management. They believe, for example, in the value of equality (applied to discussions and to the expression of values and ideas). They adopt a position of mutual respect (assuming that people holding different views do so sincerely). They believe in establishing factual accuracy undistorted by emotion as the basis for rational decision-making. Their preference for consensual decision-making implies a belief in the ideal that conflicts of interest are amenable to win–win or non-zero-sum outcomes. Finally the basic religious belief of seeing 'that of God in everyone' provides the fundamental value through which Quakers might seek to reconcile the most violently opposed adversaries.

A third contributory source of mediatory techniques has come from the application of the findings of social psychology to the fields of industrial relations and to human relations generally. In applied terms Mitchell categorises this work as the 'case work method' used by professionals in the fields of marital therapy, social work applied to child care and the old, mental health counselling and the probation service. Experiences in these areas suggest that there are elements present which may have relevance in settings which do not focus on the needs of individual clients and which are relevant to third-party action in social-conflict settings. In particular Mitchell highlights the consultation techniques from casework which are relevant to conflict management and which are essentially (a) supportive (the skills of an outsider sympathetically offered to the client); (b) non-directive (solutions developed according to clients' perceived needs and not imposed by coercion); (c) non-condemnatory (avoiding judgement of the client's behaviour according to moral standards); (d) self-determinate (the key actor in the search for solutions is the client; the role of the caseworker is to assist); (e) analytical (helping the client perceive his actual situation by helping him to perceive more clearly outer reality and his relation to it).

Of course there are distinct differences between client-centred casework in the area of social policy and the application of third-party mediation in social conflicts, yet Mitchell suggests that casework skills and methods can help in the mediation and conflict-resolution process.[17] The alternative (and dominant) form of conflict settlement based on the institution of the legal system is strong in its effects in disputes over material resources where there is an agreed, accepted and enforceable authority structure. But in the more intractable, violent and impassioned conflicts, third-party and

17. Chris Mitchell has contributed greatly to developing an understanding of the relationship between conflict theory and conflict resolution. The discussion of contributory sources to mediation skills relies heavily on Chapter 5 of his *Peacemaking and the Consultant's Role*, London, 1981.

mediatory approaches appear to be more hopeful approaches. This is especially true in world politics, in the conflicts between nation states and in major intercommunal and interethnic conflicts. It is also becoming increasingly true in the case of conflicts within communities where the speed of economic and social change produces stresses and strains, resulting in forms of anti-social behaviour which, in the absence of other mechanisms, too easily results in criminalisation following the heavy-handed application of the law. New forms of alternative conflict management in the community are rapidly developing in the USA and the UK where parties to a conflict are encouraged to resolve their differences jointly under the guidance of a third party.[18]

Curle's most recent study, *In the Middle*, points to the importance of mediation and reconciliation themes in peace research and practice in the conflict-ridden world of the late twentieth century. In this study he identifies three main strands of activity which are relevant to peacemaking: to nurture social and economic systems which engender co-operation rather than conflict; to oppose violent, dangerous and oppressive regimes with non-violence; to bring about reconciliation between those who are in conflict. Mediation is a specific component of this third area of peacemaking, and it is one to which Curle has brought his distinctive style:

Mediators, as the word implies, are in the middle. This is true in two senses. Firstly they are neither on one side nor the other; secondly, they are in the centre of the conflict, deeply involved in it because they are trying to find a satisfactory way out of it. . . . What mediators do is to try to establish, or re-establish, sufficiently good communications between conflicting parties, so that they can talk sensibly to each other without being blinded by such emotions as anger, fear and suspicion. This does not necessarily resolve the conflict; mediation has to be followed up by skilled negotiation, usually directly between the protagonists, supported by a measure of mutual tolerance and by determination to reach agreement. But it is a good start.[19]

The strength of Curle's form of mediation is that even in conflicts which are characterised by a very clear perception of differing interests, for which people are prepared to fight, the fighting creates

18. See T. Marshall and M. E. Walpole, *Bringing People Together; Mediation and Reparation Projects in Great Britain*, London, 1985.
19. The roles or tasks of the mediator are discussed in detail in *In The Middle*. The quotation is from p. 9.

its own dynamic where the contending groups cannot de-escalate from their fixed positions without appearing to be weak. Mediation is appropriate when the parties to a conflict are willing to at least consider, however tentatively, that third-party intervention might have benefits, and at this point skilled mediation may through the removal of misperceptions and the calming of violent emotions provide the window of opportunity for negotiated settlement.

It is interesting to observe that Curle's definition of mediation applied to major political (intercommunal and international) conflicts was one which he claimed had some relevance for all conflict levels: 'When quarrels rise to a certain pitch of violence the difficulty of reaching a peaceful settlement seems to increase sharply. This applies, in my experience, both in war and in family and marital feuds.'[20] Irrational feelings become powerful and dominant, and the explanation for this lies 'beyond the specific exigencies of conflict and into the more general elements of human nature'.[21] His philosophy of mediation is essentially a blend of values and experiences from Quaker practice, with the knowledge of humanistic psychology absorbed in his early professional career; and both of these influences are tempered by his experiences in the field. His understanding of human nature via religious systems is explored further in *True Justice*, with his belief that the negative feelings in the human personality (jealousy, anger, fear, hatred, etc.) are not inherent and fixed characteristics in any human being, but are the result of 'our failure fully to grasp, and so to develop, the amazing potential of our natural endowment'.[22]

The human-potential movement which seeks to explore the positive nature of this natural endowment to which Curle refers has much to contribute to an understanding of conflict sources and conflict behaviour. A basic assumption in this approach is that there exists a set of universal needs which if repressed or frustrated will lead to a variety of forms of social and interpersonal conflict. Maslow, for example, lists these according to importance: physiological needs; safety needs; belongingness and love needs; esteem needs; self-actualisation; cognitive and aesthetic needs.[23] Similar needs can be identified throughout social theory.

The point is that basic needs do exist and are more universal and

20. Ibid., p. 3.
21. Ibid., p. 4.
22. Ibid., p. 5.
23. A. Maslow, *Self-Actualisation*, San Fernando, Calif., 1972.

less culturally specific than is often assumed (of course cultures have different values and the needs can be satisfied in many different ways). The influence of these individual needs is many times stronger than the social (institutional) forces which play upon man in the sense that if social institutions fail over time to satisfy human needs, then these institutions will come under severe (and in many cases violent) pressure to change. It is this fact which makes society dynamic rather than static, and which makes violent conflict an outcome when change is demanded but badly negotiated.

In clarifying the question of how peace research should tackle the problem of violence Johan Galtung has suggested that the best approach is to root violence in the concept of human needs. He identifies four classes of needs which are universal, even if their specific satisfaction varies in time and place: these are for survival, welfare, freedom and identity. Galtung defines violence as the negation of these needs.[24] Human-needs theory then leads to insights about the nature of conflict, and about the possibility of its resolution. Because conflict could be reconceptualised as providing an opportunity to explore ways in which human social needs *which are universal* could be satisfied, and because these needs are held to be universal and related to security, identity and the potential for human development (needs which are not in strictly limited quantity), then it becomes possible to see conflicts as potentially yielding to win–win outcomes.

Of course this is an ideal rather than a real position. Because of the weight of historical experience most people believe that when conflicts happen there must be either winners or losers, and in conflicts most people automatically adopt a position or goal which is either to win or not to lose. Given also this basic assumption about conflict (that it must lead to gain or loss), then people will tend towards the unfavourable misperception of others' motives in order to prepare their personal or group position for the clash. In simple terms one prepares a position where one's own group occupies a place near to the angels, and the enemy is never far from the devil.

It is a commonplace of the psychology of conflict behaviour that distorted perception and the actions which follow from this result in the exacerbation and escalation of the conflict to the point where the

---

24. J. Galtung, 'Twenty-Five Years of Peace Research: Ten Challenges and Some Responses', *Journal of Peace Research*, vol. 22, no. 2, 1985.

original causes may become lost in the mists of time. The positive resolution of conflict, then, depends on creating the knowledge, skills and belief that solutions may be designed to meet the needs of both parties, that is, to define what have been called integrative solutions or win–win outcomes. The starting point for creative and imaginative solutions is an improvement in communication skills so that each side has a better perception of the needs, wants and fears that motivate the position of the other side.[25]

There are different approaches to mediation and to conflict resolution (of which mediation is merely a part). Curle's form is distinct in that it is non-official or independent from political interests. Of course there is a long history of mediation carried out by states intervening as mediators in disputes between other groups and nations, and the United Nations also has a significant role to play. Under its current Secretary General, Javier Perez de Cuellar, it has been active and decisive in the mediation of the Iran–Iraq War and its peacekeeping forces have been awarded the Nobel Peace Prize. Perez de Cuellar has recognised the important role his organisation can play, particularly as a channel of communications between conflicting parties and in helping to prevent the development of crises by the use of early-warning machinery to prevent escalation of the conflict. Recently an Office for Research and Collection of Information has been established in New York to ensure that the Secretary General has the fullest information possible about world developments. While this is encouraging it should be noted that the UN does have political limitations on its potential to act in international conflicts.

The development of the skills and resources for mediation will not be supplied from one source or from one model. An important new approach was developed, beginning in the 1960s and refined since, which has come variously to be called controlled communication, facilitated problem-solving and, more recently, the problem-solving-workshop approach. The approach is most closely associated with the work and ideas of John Burton and his colleagues and dates back to their work at the Centre for the Analysis of Conflict in London. In essence conflicts were to be seen as problems to be solved rather than as contests to be won or cases to be adjudicated.

25. See C. Peck, 'An Integrative Model for Understanding and Managing Conflict', *Interdisciplinary Peace Research*, vol. 1, no. 1, May 1989, pp. 24–33 for the literature on this.

Curle's style of mediation may be summarised in the following manner. He distinguishes four practical aspects of mediation (which mirror the techniques also found in casework practice, noted by Mitchell above): (a) building, maintaining and improving communications; (b) providing information; (c) befriending; (d) active mediation. Although the style of mediation described by Curle differs from the facilitated problem-solving approach developed by Burton, it is important to note some of the common intellectual antecedents in both styles. The development of Curle's thought via humanistic psychology to an elaboration of mediation within peace research has already been noted above. Burton has pointed to the importance of a theory of human behaviour applied to conflict and has identified the significance of the theory of needs building on the work of Maslow and others in the 1950s. When Paul Sites later applied these insights to a theory of power and social control a major conceptual advance in the potential to deal with conflicts occurred. Burton explains this as follows:

> It was he [Sites] who placed power in a realistic perspective by attributing effective power not to governments, but to individuals and groups of individuals who would use all means at their disposal to pursue certain human needs, subject only to constraints they imposed on themselves in their need to maintain valued relationships. . . . There are certain societal needs that will be pursued regardless of consequences.[26]

Both Mitchell and Banks have pointed to the origins of the approach in the application of therapeutic casework methods, developed broadly in the fields of social work, to the field of international conflict. The general method has been concisely defined by A. J. R. Groom as follows:

> Problem-solving has grown rapidly in the last 20 years at many levels: personal, industrial, intercommunal, and, indeed, international. There are many techniques but they all share certain features. They all try to create an unusual nonroutine setting in which consideration of the parties' joint problem is possible rather than a situation in which settlement of the conflict by negotiation and bargaining is the main aim.[27]

26. John W. Burton, *World Encyclopedia of Peace*, Oxford and New York, 1986, vol. 1, p. 177. The work to which Burton is referring is P. Sites, *Control: The Basis of Social Order*, New York, 1973.
27. A. J. R. Groom, 'Problem Solving in International Relations', *World Encyclopedia of Peace*, vol. 2, pp. 298–301. See also M. Banks, 'Mediation', *World*

Burton's exercises in controlled communication began in 1965 at the University of London. At about the same time Doob and Foltz at Yale University were applying the workshop approach to the problem of border disputes in Africa (the Fermeda Workshop in 1969), and later to the Northern Ireland conflict (the Stirling Workshop in 1972). Herbert Kelman added to the work of these two groups by developing an approach at Harvard which was based on a synthesis of Burton's and Doob's methods, a synthesis which was the outcome of a series of workshops held at Harvard involving Kelman and Cohen, both of whom are social psychologists (a workshop involving Israelis and Palestinians in 1971; Indians, Pakistanis, and Bangladeshis in 1972; and Turkish and Greek Cypriots in 1979). Burton has continued to develop and to clarify the theory and methods of third-party facilitated problem-solving, most recently in his book *Resolving Deep Rooted Conflict*.[28] Fetherston's contribution elsewhere in this volume presents an account and evaluation of Burton's ideas, and of the problem-solving workshop as it has been used in international conflicts generally. We have got on to the bottom rungs of the ladder in terms of our ability to understand and to resolve conflict processes. It is clear that problem-solving workshops offer some possibilities, although even within this approach there are different emphases and opinions on the function, methods and operating style of the workshops.

There are a number of remaining difficulties which have been highlighted by Bercovitch, who has argued that there are basically two approaches to conflict resolution:[29] (a) it can be seen merely as subset of negotiation which itself is a process of bargaining over the allocation of power and rewards, or (b) it is distinct in itself and intended as an advance on negotiation. This is the approach taken by Burton.

But essentially the Burton–Curle approach, which we might call new-paradigm thinking (in that it suggests that conflicts can be solved voluntarily on a win–win basis) share many of the following characteristics:

Encyclopedia of Peace, vol. 1, pp. 589–92; Mitchell, *Peacemaking and the Consultant's Role*, p. 78; and E. Azar and J. Burton (eds.), *International Conflict Resolution: Theory and Practice*, Brighton, 1986.

28. J. W. Burton, *Resolving Deep Rooted Conflict: A Handbook*, Lanham, Md, 1987.

29. J. Bercovitch, 'A Case Study of Mediation as a Method of International Conflict Resolution: the Camp David Experience', *Journal of Social Issues*, vol. 12, 1986, pp. 43–65.

1. The role of the mediator is to structure the discussions and to feed in information derived from the third party's general experience and knowledge of conflicts.
2. The conflict is explored and analysed.
3. By using essentially psychological principles, misperceptions and misunderstandings are cleared up and the disputants are enabled to acquire new insights into each others goals, intentions and fears.
4. These new understandings will then feed into the policy-formation process.

There are some very obvious problems with all this. First, increasing communication between disputants may well increase areas of disagreement. If there are real differences of interest, increased or better communication may simply serve to make more stark the different positions of the disputants. A second weakness is the assumption that once a conflict is analysed or understood it can be resolved; people in a conflict may be fully aware of what they are about and in that sense understand the conflict, but they still may have too much invested in things as they are to want to change.

In other words the Curle–Burton approach may be too idealistic in some settings, and it might be better to see conflict resolution and mediation not as dependent on expert and disinterested third-party involvement, but as more likely to succeed when it is regarded as a subset of negotiation, where a third party comes in with power to coerce disputants into an agreement (as, for example, the USA under the Presidency of Carter managed to achieve between Egypt and Israel during the Camp David talks). If this is the case then it is still true that the new paradigm of conflict resolution has applicability, even in the field of conventional big-power negotiation.

Fisher and Ury have offered their principled negotiation methods as a technique which moves conflicts to win–win outcomes through the negotiation process. The principles of their approach can be summarised in the following way: (a) separate the people from the problem; (b) focus on interests not positions; (c) invent options for mutual gain; (d) insist on using objective criteria. While there is not time in this study to provide an account of the important ideas of Fisher and Ury it is relevant to say that they present influential insights into how negotiation skills can be identified so that even conventional power-based conflicts of interest (i.e. conflicts over material resources such as territory, or other sources of power and control) can also be made amenable to win–win outcomes.[30]

It might be suggested that there is a new paradigm of thinking which, given the situation of the world, is at least worth investigating and, while it may not lead us into a conflict-free Utopia, will at least increase our options in the deadly range of conflicts which face us.

It is unwise to dwell too much on the differences of approach; what matters is the development and testing of models and styles which work at different stages, and which are applicable for different types of conflict. Curle concluded *In The Middle* with one such proposal, namely that the feasibility of organising an International Mediation Centre should be investigated, preferably in the form of a non-governmental organisation having voluntary status with the United Nations. The functions of the Centre would be:

1. To develop criteria for the desirability and feasibility of mediation; to carry out research into conflict in general and on mediation and training for mediation in particular.
2. To research global conflicts in order to identify situations where mediation might be offered.
3. To recruit and launch mediation teams when appropriate, and to provide resources and support.
4. To build up the skills and resource base, at present woefully inadequate, for mediators, and in particular to ensure the flow of younger people into the work.

Authorities like Burton, Mitchell, Curle and others have pointed to the need to develop coherent programmes of research into the theory and practice of forms of conflict management and conflict resolution. Common themes include theory development (the effect of different types of mediation initiatives on different categories of conflict), conflict monitoring and conflict mapping, interviewing and codifying the experiences of practitioners and systematising this for future use.

It is possible to identify a model for an international network based on a three-fold structure: at the top level are international organisations like the UN, the Commonwealth and the European Community; at the middle level are 'switchboard' organisations

---

30. Fisher and Ury, *Getting to Yes*; and R. Fisher and S. Brown, *Getting Together: Building a Relationship that Gets To Yes*, London, 1989.

which serve to monitor conflicts and operate referral and information-transmission services; and at the lower level institutions, universities and Non-Governmental Organisations (NGOs) feeding-in research knowledge and practitioner expertise to the upper level groups. In the development of this kind of network model the circulation of information between the levels is of critical importance and is presently deficient. As a minimum there is a requirement to build a bank of resources and expertise so that the void between the key players in the international organisations concerned with conflict resolution can be filled by the identification and development of a deeper resource base of skill than is presently available.

In all the proposals a recurrent theme is the need to identify and gather existing practical expertise in conflict resolution and mediation and to make this available in the training of a new generation of mediators, and for the enhancement of existing skills among current practitioners. There is a need to review and refresh some old ideas about peacemaking, and to develop new resources and approaches capable of addressing the problems of destructive conflicts. In 1990 the Department of Peace Studies initiated a new project with the formation of its Centre for Conflict Resolution. The Centre is working in four areas:

1. Initiating applied research projects. Four are currently under way, covering the role of medical professionals in international mediation; the role of the United Nations in international peace-keeping; the experience of Quaker peacemaking efforts in violently divided societies; and the efficacy of conflict resolution processes in dealing with ethnic tensions in British cities.
2. Training in the methods of mediation and conflict resolution.
3. Organising seminars where people actively involved in conflict resolution may meet and exchange ideas and experiences.
4. Providing a resource and information service.

The world will need such skills and knowledge in the years ahead.

3

From Harvard to Bradford

Robert A. McKinlay

It was a fusion of two concerns which in 1973 brought Adam Curle, a British Quaker, from being Professor of Education and Development at Harvard University to become Professor of Peace Studies at the University of Bradford: the first such Chair in Britain.

Bradford was one of the new technological universities, founded in 1966 both to promote Harold Wilson's 'white heat of technology' and to develop close links with industry, and seemed the most unlikely place for such a novel innovation in the social sciences. But Bradford had always prided itself on its pioneering ventures in the educational field.

It was in 1963 that the government of the day accepted the recommendation of the Robbins' Report on Higher Education and decided that the Bradford Institute of Technology (BIT), one of the Colleges of Advanced Technology, should receive a Royal Charter to raise it to university status. The responsibility for proposing the Charter for royal signature lay primarily with E. G. Edwards, the Principal of the BIT. The model charter, provided for the guidance of emerging universities, contained a clause with the trite and obvious phrase: 'The objects of the University shall be the advancement of learning and knowledge', but this was not specific enough for the Vice-Chancellor designate. After all, every university from Peking to Peru had this as its objective. Edwards required something deeper which would reflect the responsibility of the university to the society which created it. He had what the Society of Friends (Quakers) would describe as a 'concern' to develop the concept of human co-operation for objectives which enrich the human spirit and which produce a more compassionate society.

He devoted much thought as to how his concern might be realised and much midnight oil was burned in considering this and other aspects of the Charter. On one such occasion in discussing this with me, as his deputy, he was inspired to add to the standard objects clause 'and the application of knowledge to human welfare'. This was to be the keystone in the development of the University of Bradford throughout Edwards's regime.

But fine phrases are relatively easy to produce, hence I questioned Edwards as to what he meant by 'human welfare'. As good academics usually do, he responded by posing a further question: 'What do you consider to be the main problems facing society today?' The answer was obvious – 'the bomb' and 'the hungry world'. 'Right,' said Edwards, in his determined way, 'in this, our university, we will do something to tackle these and other human problems.' This was the origin of a university structure which contained a whole range of studies devoted to social advancement.

Inevitably, the initial years of the University saw the establishment and growth of all the Schools of Studies which would be expected in a modern technological university and it was not until 1969 that the first phase of Edwards's aim was achieved by the introduction of the Project Planning Centre for Developing Countries. This venture was, and still is, highly successful in bringing to Bradford students – frequently middle-grade government officials – from all over the world for short courses of instruction by experienced staff in different aspects of development. The reputation of Bradford as a university with an international concern soon grew. This reputation was much enhanced by Bradford – alone among British universities – continuing to resist, at great cost to itself, the government's insistence on charging higher differential fees to overseas students. Edwards publicly denounced the government's policy as 'mean, immoral and dictatorial' and the esteem of Bradford as a 'caring' university grew apace. The ground now seemed to have been prepared for the introduction of the school of studies which would concern itself with the concepts of justice and peace.

And this is where the Quakers came in. There arose within the Cheshire Monthly Meeting of the Society of Friends a 'concern' that we should be devoting more of our national resources to a study of the factors which give rise to co-operation and peace, and less to those which result in confrontation and conflict. This concern was endorsed by the Peace and International Relations Committee of the Society and was accepted by the Meeting for Sufferings – the quaintly named executive committee of the Society of Friends. The 'concern' could, of course, only be realised if taken up by some higher educational institute, hence tentative approaches were made to a few universities but none would even consider the matter unless an assurance could be given that the establishment of a permanent chair would be wholly financed from external sources. Such a long-term commitment could not be accepted by Friends.

However, in the process of the development of the University a Professor of Finance was appointed and it later transpired that he was the Friend who had initially raised the concern in Cheshire. Talks took place between the Peace Committee of the Society and the University, and Friends, impressed by the attitude and aware of the existing concern within the University, readily accepted that the right place to fulfil their complementary concern was Bradford. It was decided that, subject to the agreement of both the University and the Society, each would contribute £75,000 to fund the initial establishment of a Chair of Peace Studies at Bradford. It was thought that some three years might elapse both before the necessary agreements within the University would be obtained and their share of the costs could be raised by members of the Society. There were many obstacles to be overcome but in prospect they seemed slight compared with the formidable task of finding the right person to fill the proposed Chair. Although we seemed to have three years at our disposal, we were not too confident that we would be successful – but how wrong we were!

Normally within any University there is resistance to the introduction of new ventures since they will obviously compete for the limited resources available to the established academics. Bradford had been no exception to this practice. The development of the social sciences was only grudgingly accepted by many of the scientists and technologists. The chances of the acceptance of such an unusual and potentially controversial innovation as a Chair of Peace Studies seemed remote. It seemed that even with persistent effort the process might take even longer than three years.

The proposal was duly considered by the various boards, committees, sub-committees and working parties which constitute the infrastructure of any university, and to everyone's surprise there was no openly expressed opposition within the University. The process of agreement was completed not in three years but in three months. Indeed at the Senate meeting giving formal approval the proposal of a professor of one of the sciences that 'we welcome the establishment of a Chair of Peace Studies' was readily accepted. We were over the first hurdle!

In the meantime the Society of Friends had decided that they would try to raise their £75,000 by launching a public appeal and considered that they would require the expected full term to raise this sum. The Peace Committee in London were astounded when told that the University had been so quick in giving formal approval and were much relieved at the suggestion that the process of conducting the public appeal should be centred in distant Bradford – at The Friends Meeting House and the University.

The Quaker Peace Studies Trust was established and given the task of raising the necessary sum, and planned on the basis of a three years' programme – again, an over-cautious estimate. We were amazed at how well the proposal was received both within and outside the Society of Friends. The appeal brochure which was issued contained a long list of sponsors many of whom seemed almost anxious to be associated with the venture. The list included leading politicians of all parties, heads of all the main religious denominations, captains of industry, heads of trade unions, and the names of well-known figures in the worlds of art and literature. U Thant, then Secretary General of the United Nations, gave a special blessing as he endorsed the appeal.

The official launching took place in March 1972 at a press conference in Friends House, London. The idea must have been right for the time because the impact was instantaneous. There was widespread coverage in the national and international press: the British Broadcasting Corporation announced it in the headlines of their early news bulletins of the day; an interview was recorded for the European Service and there were interviews in Bradford on both BBC and Independent Television. The money poured in. Instead of the anticipated three years the target was reached in less than ten weeks! An average of over £1,000 per day had been received. This was a spectacular success and took everyone by surprise so that within nine months of the original discussions the University and the Society had between them provided the finance necessary to establish the Chair of Peace Studies. But who was going to fill this Chair?

The proposal to establish a Chair of Peace Studies was not, however, as readily accepted in the academic world or even among all members of the Society of Friends. A number of academics from other universities were convinced that no real academic discipline could be founded on such a nebulous and undefinable concept as 'peace'. There was even correspondence in *The Times* on this issue.

Ted Edwards, now Vice-Chancellor at Bradford, forcefully rebutted this view and was always strong in his support for the proposal not only within his University but in top-level academic circles elsewhere. He was stimulated rather than deterred by such opposition since he was convinced that universities must be the spearheads of intellectual and social development. In the past they had led the way in such diverse fields as theology and medicine. Why then should they not take the lead in studying the most significant problem facing society – the attainment of justice and peace and, indeed, survival?

Although there was within the Society general support for the objectives of the Quaker Peace Studies Trust, there was some unease revealed in the correspondence columns of the weekly journal of the Society, *The Friend*. Here it was suggested that the establishment of a Chair of Peace Studies within the cold, calculating academic atmosphere of a university was not the best way to use the resources of the Society to promote their traditional Peace Testimony.

Indeed a number of Quakers occupying senior posts at other universities were quite astringent in their comments because they were convinced that the proposals could not stand up to the rigours of academic criticism and analysis. As the Quaker within Bradford University primarily responsible for pursuing the proposals, I naturally received much of this criticism. It was suggested that I was impelled by emotion and did not appreciate that the project could never be academically viable. Since I remained unconvinced one kindly Quaker academic offered to put me in touch with someone who would 'straighten me out' and suggested that I got in touch with Adam Curle, a British Quaker who was Professor of Education and Development at Harvard University. This I did.

In the correspondence that followed Adam Curle maintained a cautious but sympathetic approach. Eventually, however, he expressed a personal interest in the proposed Chair at Bradford and it was decided to invite him over so that he could assess the situation and learn more of our proposals. When it was made clear that, when appointed, the professor would have complete freedom in how he conducted his School of Studies, Adam became more interested. In the cautious way of Quakers he suggested that he would require some time to consider all the factors involved and he returned to Harvard and his home to do this. In this period he kept in close touch with Bradford and with British Friends.

After much contemplation and long discussions with his wife Anne and his daughter Deborah, Adam felt it right to express a definite personal interest in the Chair. He was therefore formally invited by the University to attend a professorial appointment board in January 1973. The only hesitation among some members of the board was whether Bradford could offer facilities in any way comparable with those to which a professor from such a prestigious university as Harvard might have grown accustomed. The acceptance of the post would involve a considerable reduction in salary and other benefits and would cause all the domestic disruption occasioned by a move from the salubrious surroundings of Cambridge, Massachusetts to Bradford, in the industrial heart of the West Riding of Yorkshire. Adam was offered the post, but always sensitive to the impact of his decisions on others, asked for further time to discuss this matter with his family. It was not long before the University was delighted to learn that he had agreed to accept the offer. He later assured me that he did this with much heart searching and that eventually it was a united family decision which encouraged him to respond to the urge within to help found a School of Peace Studies in Britain.

At Bradford we assumed that with the formal period of notice normally required from a senior professor at one of the world's leading universities we would have at least a year to prepare, amongst our many other developments, for the beginnings of the School of Peace Studies. Adam's colleagues at Harvard were amazed at his decision. To leave the security of the United States for the uncertainties of Britain seemed hazardous enough. A suitable post at Oxford – or even Cambridge – might just be acceptable; London, or perhaps Edinburgh might be considered, but Bradford! – wherever was Bradford? And to crown it all it was a technological university and certainly not in the same league as the neighbouring and world-renowned MIT! Did Adam really know what he was doing? Apparently he did because he persuaded the Harvard authorities to waive the normal period of notice. Whether they did this because of their fear that he had reached the stage of making very strange decisions we shall never know, but Adam and his family arrived in Bradford on 4 July 1973 – Independence Day and his fifty-seventh birthday. When he came to the University he asked what he should do about setting up the School. I told him he could do as he liked. And he did!

Adam had quite a difficult initiation into the strange ways of an emerging British technological university since there could not have been a greater contrast with the accustomed scholarly Harvard approach. He found that as Professor he was, as is normal in most British universities, responsible for the administration of his School of Studies as well as its academic development, but he soon accustomed himself to these strange British ways.

At first he was something of a novelty in Bradford and, coming from Harvard, was treated with great respect by his professorial colleagues, who for the most part were much younger and certainly less experienced in the ways of the academic world. Moreover, he was to develop a School of Peace Studies – something never heard of before and from which nobody had any idea of what might emerge.

He had, of course, the support and encouragement of those in the higher echelons of the University and any proposals he made were well received as they followed the usual processes through academic planning committees, faculty boards and the like. Adam soon realised that it was firmly intended that his School of Peace Studies was to be an integral part of the University and would be financed and supported out of normal university funds. The contribution from the Quakers was seen as but a pump-priming operation and in no way was to be regarded as any attempt at long-term financing. However, the establishment of the Quaker Peace Studies Trust, whose prime purpose was to support Bradford's initiative, indicated that continuing support even if on a comparatively small scale would be coming from the Society of Friends. Since the University was in that happy state of initial expansion the vested interests of those already in post were not in any way threatened. All other professors were being generously treated in the allocation of resources and they saw no need to bother about this new emerging School of Studies.

All seemed plain sailing – encouragement from the top, no opposition from colleagues, adequate finance and plenty of external support, financial and moral, particularly, of course, from his own Society of Friends. But there was inevitably some stress. Adam's services were much in demand both inside and outside the University and he was very fully occupied.

The basis of the academic structure of the University was the School of Studies which consisted of all the teaching and research staff involved in a particular course. The approach was essentially interdisciplinary so that the services of those engaged primarily in, say, one of the usual disciplines in the social sciences, could be called upon for the School of Peace Studies. But it also worked the other way round. Other schools could request the services of the staff in Peace Studies, and since at this time there was still a carry-over from the old College of Advanced Technology insistence on 'liberal studies' within all courses in science and technology, there was considerable demand both from students and staff for the services of the staff of this novel School of Peace Studies. But, apart from Adam, there was no staff.

In the first months of his appointment Adam spent much of his time having discussions with the staff of other schools in the University since it seemed he would require their support and in turn he would be used by them. These discussions helped him to formulate his ideas for the development of his school.

But Adam had many requests to visit the numerous meetings of the Society of Friends. Naturally Friends were anxious to see and hear this new leader in peace studies and he was flooded with invitations to speak from all over the country. Adam felt an obligation to Friends and hence he did his best to fulfil as many of these requests as he possibly could, but the demand was so heavy that I had to suggest to Friends that they resist for a time the temptation to issue more invitations to Adam so that he could concentrate on his immediate purpose of laying the foundations of his new school.

Adam wisely decided to use his first year at Bradford in recruiting his staff and in developing a postgraduate course to begin in October 1974. He realised that the School required something more than his own personal reputation and he set about with great care in seeking staff who had not only the academic qualifications necessary for any university appointment but also had some experience in the vague field of peacemaking or in conflict research.

The emphasis was at first confined to those with direct knowledge in areas of international and other conflict and the spread of experience of those first recruited on a full-time or visiting basis was quite remarkable. Adam persuaded Tom Stonier who had experience of introducing peace studies in Manhattan College, New York, to come for a year as Visiting Professor at Bradford. Later Tom was to become permanent Head of another of the collection of the new and unusual schools of studies, the School of Science and Society, all associated with the School of Peace Studies, which were scathingly referred to by some of the traditional technologists as 'the Bradford Fringe'. With someone from the United States, it seemed only right to preserve the balance with someone from the Soviet Union – a much more difficult task. And yet remarkably there came to our attention one Alexandras Shtromas, an experienced lawyer from Moscow – and a Russian dissident. He offered his services on a part-time basis.

But troubled areas nearer home could not be overlooked. The continuing problems of Northern Ireland were much to the fore and we were fortunate to procure the visiting services of David Bleakely, a Privy Counsellor and until recently Minister of Community Relations in the government of Northern Ireland. Brigadier Michael Harbottle followed. He had been Chief of Staff of the United Nations Peace Keeping Force in Cyprus and had written extensively on his experiences of attempts at reconciliation in this troubled island. The Middle East was yet another area of conflict and Uri Davies, a young philosopher from Tel Aviv who had been active in reconciliation efforts between Jews and Arabs, was appointed as a full-time member of staff. Vithal Rajan, a Ghandian academic who had been involved in troubled areas in India and was much concerned with the problems of developing countries also joined the full-time staff. The British 'peace movement' could hardly be ignored and Nigel Young, a lecturer in politics from the University of Birmingham, with long associations in the field as well as experience in British universities, was a valuable addition to the initial staff. Tom Woodhouse, a young researcher who had recently graduated from Leeds University, was appointed as Adam's research assistant. Adam thus had, when his first one-year full-time postgraduate course started, a remarkably balanced collection of well-qualified staff with first-hand experience in most of the major conflict areas in the world. Was this sufficient?

It was to be expected that those academics interested in pursuing this new and untried 'discipline' of peace studies would have strong motivations and would be likely to be forthright in their own advocacy of the 'way to peace'. Adam was, as would be expected, no autocrat and gave to his staff the freedom which he himself enjoyed. He established no hierarchical structure and saw his role not as a leader but as a co-ordinator. But on occasions he had to adopt the role of peacemaker since conflict was not unknown even in a School of Peace Studies! This was no easy job but he did it remarkably well and soon had an effective team ready to tackle his first group of postgraduate students.

Adam's first academic task had been to devise a postgraduate course to be advertised in time to recruit students for the session beginning in October 1974. Such a course had never been mounted before in a British university and many academics in Bradford and elsewhere refused to accept that peace studies could possibly rank as a university 'discipline' since it was not founded on any recognisable body of knowledge. Adam, however, retorted that he was not concerned with defining disciplines, which were not created by nature but by academics so that they might demarcate their particular areas of intellectual interest. He was primarily interested in problems, both intellectual and practical, and their solutions. Whether or not his fellow academics accepted that this new field of intellectual endeavour qualified as a discipline struck Adam as being relatively unimportant; what mattered to him was that the studies should be carried out with intellectual vigour, offer new and valid insights and generalisations and have some practical significance.

The background of academic doubt was not easy to dispel but that very doubt created much interest in peace studies. This was clearly revealed by the unusually high attendance at Adam's inaugural lecture delivered on 4 February 1975. The attendance at Bradford's professorial inaugural lectures was usually sparse, largely confined to the staff and a few of the discerning and ambitious students of the professor concerned. The normal attendance was about thirty – but in Adam's case well over three hundred came, some to express doubts, and others interest. Many came from other universities as well as from most of the Schools of Studies in Bradford.

Throughout his tenure of the Chair – and indeed since – peace studies rested on these twin pillars of doubt and interest, but Adam exploited both and by his approach created interest and support out of the doubt. Fortunately Adam's ideas co-incided with the inter-disciplinary approach of most of the courses within the Board of Studies in the social sciences and a few of the courses in the newer technologies. He had thus no real difficulty in having his proposed syllabuses accepted by the Academic Committee and the other democratic – some would say bureaucratic – procedures which make up the administrative structure of a British university.

In his inaugural lecture Adam revealed that in his teaching programme he had three aims. First, to engage in a study, made systematic by the analysis of relationships, of important issues, both contemporary and historical; secondly, to attempt to apply analysis in practice; thirdly, to offer a good general education and a useful method of approach to some of the world's most urgent problems.

These same aims were applied to the undergraduate course which, to most people's surprise, Adam decided to start the following year – October 1975. This course did, however, have one special feature, usual in the technological courses within the university but rare in the social sciences. He introduced between the second and fourth years a 'sandwich' element, whereby students spent a year in employment, for example, in community work in Britain or overseas. This was to offer an opportunity for examining ideas in a practical context and to provide a source of information and experience to review and analyse in the final year.

There was no difficulty in recruiting undergraduates and the annual quota of twenty five in each year was easily maintained. The difficulty of financial support prevented many would-be postgraduates from enrolling but there was always a sufficient number of good and mature students who had had interesting and relevant experience in this country and overseas.

There was no support forthcoming from the Social Science Research Council for research in peace studies. Such research, apart from that undertaken by staff, is normally directly related to the availability of finance, hence reliance had to be made on the limited funds available from the University and from support from Quaker and other sources. A number of qualified students, concerned about the increase in violence and the necessity to investigate the causes of this and to make a positive approach to bringing about peaceful relationships, resigned from their jobs in what some described as the 'rat race', to undertake research in the School.

Adam was also concerned that the School should have an influence beyond the confines of the School and University and encouraged the staff and research students to publish as widely as possible and to undertake speaking engagements with organisations of many varied aims. He himself set an example with many articles in the local and national press and in journals of many different kinds.

Adam had obviously established in a remarkably short time a very successful School of Peace Studies, but this was not done without effort or indeed without opposition – and much of this opposition came from within the School itself. Adam was no autocrat and he put the democracy he preached into practice. Except for certain obvious areas such as examination assessment all major issues were discussed at a general meeting of staff and students. Even in such areas as staff appointments, which were jealously guarded by the University, staff and students were consulted. From time to time the whole School retreated to a remote area in Southern Scotland and spent a few days together thrashing out the numerous problems which were inevitable among people highly motivated in their determination to change a world they saw as dominated by injustice and violence. Each seemed convinced that in the search for an elusive peace the only way – political, moral or ethical – was the way he or she advocated. On many occasions in those meetings all Adam's skills in reconciliation had to be brought into play. To pursue the study of peaceful – and unpeaceful – relationships the students did not have to travel very far!

Throughout his period at Bradford Adam had been much involved in practical issues outside the University. It was obvious that there would be a demand for him to use the skills and experience he had acquired in the various reconciliation missions he had undertaken particularly in Africa and India. Inevitably the troubles of nearby Northern Ireland loomed large in his interests and he became increasingly involved in various attempts at reconciliation.

With so many different areas of international tension arising Adam felt impelled to try and make a more direct contribution to international reconciliation. For five years he had lived with the relatively petty problems of a new and experimental department and he had coped with the bureaucratic structures and demands of a university. He needed a wider and freer field and it was no surprise to those who knew him and his aspirations well that when he reached retiring age he decided to leave his full-time post.

In his five years at Bradford Adam had built up a unique academic department whose basic aim had been to establish a concept of peace comprising the coincidence of justice with the lack of violence, and to prepare his students to work for this sort of peace. He urged his students to oppose violence and injustice with skill, and to work constructively for a social and world order which is more harmonious, saner and more equitable. His own life and work was their best example of how this could be done.

In his inaugural lecture Adam defined the scope, nature and problems of peace studies in somewhat intellectual terms. However, and this was the true Adam, he confessed that he had come to this work for reasons which were not primarily intellectual. He had come to it, often with pain and suffering, because he could not resist the obligations imposed by his experiences in this devastating world. Like Martin Luther King he had a dream: 'In this sad age I have a dream which I shall not see come true but which, if we do not seek to realise it, our grandchildren will not see either. I dream of a world in which we are not separated from each other by fear, suspicion, prejudice or hatred; in which we are free and equal, considerate and loving to each other.' By developing the School of Peace Studies on an intellectual and practical level there is little doubt that in some small measure at least Adam's effort might help such a world to be born.

Who could deny that the journey from Harvard to Bradford had been well worthwhile?

PART II

Peace Research and Education

4

Objectives and Methods of Peace Research

Andrew Mack

Approaches to Peace Research

The mid-1980s witnessed a renewed interest in peace research within the OECD countries. This upsurge of support for peace research, and the parallel proliferation of peace studies courses in colleges and universities, was related to increased public concern about nuclear war and scepticism about traditional approaches to national security in the nuclear age. Although there is still a great deal of current interest in peace research, however, knowledge of its history, scope, objectives and research methods remains sketchy at best.

The question of what constitutes peace research is problematic. It is often distinguished from traditional approaches to understanding national and international conflict by its stress on social scientific, rather than historical modes of analysis. But it also differs from much contemporary social science in its rejection of the idea of 'value neutrality'. Peace research is not *simply* the disinterested search for truth and understanding as an end in itself; like cancer research it aims to prescribe solutions for the problems it studies. It seeks to understand the world in a way which will ultimately lead to the avoidance of war and the maintenance of stable peace.

As used here the term 'peace research' generally refers to what might be called 'mainstream' peace research – that is, that which is practised at the major European and United States centres and which is published in the major journals such as the *Journal of Peace Research* and the *Journal of Conflict Resolution*. I do not wish to claim that this usage is more or less 'correct' than any other – simply that it would be acceptable to most individuals who identify themselves as peace researchers.

As an organised and institutionalised endeavour peace and conflict research was a creation of the Cold War, although it has intellectual antecedents in the work of such scholars as Lewis Fry Richardson, Pitirim Sorokin and Quincy Wright, who were writing in the 1930s. In the late 1950s, increasing numbers of social scientists were becoming interested in applying the methods of their rapidly expanding disciplines to the cause of understanding, and ultimately preventing, war. Like the 1980s, this was a period in which fears of nuclear war were pervasive. In Britain, a huge peace movement had taken to the streets and the unilateralist policies of the Campaign for Nuclear Disarmament (CND) had gained considerable public support. In the US a frightened population was flocking to buy nuclear fallout shelters.

In 1957, the editors of the *Journal of Conflict Resolution*, the first peace research journal to be established in the US, outlined in the editorial of their first issue two reasons for their enterprise:

> The first is that by far the most important practical problem facing the human race today is that of international relations – more specifically, the prevention of global war. The second is that if intellectual progress is to be made in this area, the study of international relations must be made an interdisciplinary enterprise, drawing its discourse from all the social sciences, and even further.[1]

Peace researchers, then as now, were divided about how to reduce the risks of war. But there was a broad consensus that the Cold War policies of the superpowers were positively destabilising – that is to say, likely to increase mutual suspicion and hostility, intensify an already escalating arms race and increase the risks of war. A similar consensus regarding current superpower policies exists among peace researchers today.

In sharp contrast to the scholarly practice of established (and Establishment) research institutes, such as the Royal Institute for International Affairs in London, peace research methodology was heavily influenced by the new social sciences. Peace researchers believed that the scientific study of conflict which they were espousing would succeed where the more traditional approaches of the students of *realpolitik* had failed. Political science, sociology, social psychology, economics and rational choice theory took pre-

---

1. *Journal of Conflict Resolution*, vol. 1, no. 1, 1957, p. 3.

cedence in peace research over the older disciplines of diplomatic history, international law and classical strategy.

At this time rapid advances in computer technology were making it much easier for social scientists to process large amounts of data – a necessary condition for correlational analysis – and to run complex simulations of conflict and other societal processes. Much of the quantitative work in peace and conflict research would have been impractical without access to computers.

Economics was held up as a model of what could be achieved when the rigorous methods of the social sciences were applied to pressing societal problems. Keynesian theory had, it was argued, enabled economists – and policymakers – to understand the causes of economic depressions and thus derive scientifically based policies to avoid them. Peace research aspired to create theories which would provide a comparable level of understanding of the causes of war and similarly efficacious policies for avoiding it.

The peace research critique against the traditionalists was mounted at two levels. First, it was claimed that the methodological approach of the traditionalists was unscientific; secondly, that many of the assumptions which traditionalism took to be basic truths were unproven and probably false.

From their social science perspective peace researchers argued that propositions about the causes of war and the conditions for maintaining peace should be subjected to rigorous testing. Arguments had to be *demonstrated*, not simply *exemplified*. The reliance on history which characterised the work of the 'realists' was pre-scientific. To base policy on a pre-scientific analysis of world events made no more sense than basing the practice of medicine on a pre-scientific understanding of human physiology.

This type of criticism together with the intrusion of behavioural social science methods into the traditionalist preserves of international law, power politics, diplomatic history and Clauswitzian strategic analysis, was greeted with incomprehension, suspicion and frequent irritation in the strongholds of traditionalism. Peace research at this stage of its development was very much part of the behavioural revolution.

But if traditionalists were often technically incapable of understanding, let alone evaluating, the methodologies of the social scientists, some of the latter were lamentably ignorant of history and of the philosophical objections which could be raised against the behavioural methods of the social sciences. Traditionalists argued that explanations based on models of causality borrowed from the physical sciences were simply inappropriate to an understanding of human affairs.

Hubris was evident on both sides, and what was to become known as the 'Great Debate' between traditionalism and behaviouralism generated quite as much heat as illumination. Both sides scored valid points in the debate. The traditionalists correctly pointed out that since people learn from history it was impossible to make causal generalisations about conflict behaviour – a goal of many peace researchers – with any confidence. For example, generalisations about US propensities to intervene militarily in the Third World which were based on data collected on pre-Vietnam interventions would have provided a wholly inadequate guide to US policy after the Vietnam War. Moreover, in the realm of politics, many of the key concepts – 'power', 'authority', 'legitimacy', 'will' – are notoriously difficult to measure; some would argue impossible. Economists, psephologists and demographers are more fortunate: *their* key variables – money, votes, and birth and death rates – are far more suited to statistical analysis.

But the debate about methodology was by no means all that divided peace researchers from the traditionalists. Not all the advocates of the 'scientific' approach were peace researchers; many shared traditionalist assumptions about the nature of the world, even though they rejected traditionalist methodology. Peace research challenged not only the methods of the traditionalists but also their 'realist' assumptions.

The Critique of 'Realism'

In the first decade and a half after the Second World War, the study of international relations had been dominated by what had become known as 'realism'. 'Realism' had been a reaction to the Allied failure to deal with the menace of Fascism until it was almost too late. Policies based on the approach known as 'idealism' or 'utopianism' were held in large part responsible for this failure.

'Idealism' emphasised internationalist legal rights and obligations rather than the sovereign exercise of power as a means of ensuring security. It was based on the concept of a 'natural' harmony of national interests – in the antithesis of the Hobbesian view of the international system which the 'realists' tended to embrace. 'Idealism' gained considerable support in the wake of the appalling carnage of the First World War largely as a reaction against the European balance-of-power system which many 'idealists' believed had played a major role in bringing the war about.

'Idealists' called for a system of 'collective security' to replace what they saw as the war-prone system of competing alliances. 'Collective security' required the creation of a world community where the security of individual states was maintained, not by their own individual defence efforts, but through the collective and co-operative actions of the world's nations acting in concert. As Woodrow Wilson, one of the principal exponents of 'idealism', argued in an address to the United States Congress: 'There must be, not a balance of power, but a community of power; not organised rivalries, but an organised common peace.'[2]

The most important institutional manifestation of 'collective security' was the League of Nations, which had been created in the aftermath of the First World War. But the League did nothing to check the threat of Fascism, and the failure of the 'world community' to respond effectively to the acts of aggression perpetrated by Germany, Italy and Japan helped discredit 'collective security' as a viable policy.

The post-war 'realists', like the 'idealists' after the First World War, drew a number of policy lessons from history. But the lessons were very different. For the 'realists' the First World War, and the events which led up to it, demonstrated the absolute necessity of a return to the old verities of the balance of power. 'Idealism', they argued, had been based on naive illusions. Hitler had succeeded initially because Europe and the US had made no attempt to stop him until almost too late. The course of events which had led to the Second World War demonstrated the absolute necessity of confronting the expansionist drive of totalitarian states with resolve, with all necessary force and without delay.

Confronting what they perceived to be a new totalitarian threat from the East, the 'realists' saw the formation of the military alliances, which the 'idealists' had so bitterly opposed, as essential. They believed in the old maxim: 'If you wish for peace, prepare for war.' In the circumstances it is not surprising that the logic of 'realism' should have dominated both policymaking and the study

---

2. Cited in M. Wright, 'The Balance of Power', in H. Butterfield and M. Wright (eds.), *Diplomatic Investigations*, London, 1966, p. 172.

of international relations at the time. A new totalitarian threat had been identified, a new system of military alliances had been constructed to deter and, if necessary, to combat it, and a nuclear-arms race was underway.

Such was the intellectual and political climate within which peace research was conceived and began to grow. Peace researchers challenged not only the methods of traditionalists but also many of their assumptions. They argued that the equation of Soviet Communism with Fascism was misleading. They did not claim that the Soviet system was benign, simply that the 'realists' consistently underestimated the degree to which the Soviets, surrounded by hostile states, and having suffered 20 of the 22 million Allied casualties in the Second World War, had quite genuine security concerns – concerns which had been heightened by the 1950s' US rhetoric of 'rolling back' Communism. Soviet foreign and defence policies, argued the peace researchers, had to be seen, at least in part, as a defensive response to a perceived threat to the USSR from the West.

Seen in this light the Soviet occupation of Eastern Europe and Moscow's brutal repression of any signs of resistance in the 'buffer zone' of its client states constituted examples of 'defensive aggression' – clear aggression against the East European victims, but defensively intended *vis-à-vis* the West. But whatever the reality of Soviet intentions, such actions, plus Moscow's opportunistic post-war attempts to gain influence in Mediterranean states which bordered the USSR, and the inexorable build-up of Soviet military capabilities, were bound to be perceived as aggressively intended by 'worst-case' military analysts in the West. Moscow's actions led, not surprisingly, to Western countermeasures – and vice versa. The effect on East–West relationships of the vicious circle of action and reaction, of escalating mutual suspicion, was predictable. Tensions increased and the nuclear arms race accelerated.

From the perspective of peace research, the gravest, if not the most probable, danger to world peace was that of nuclear war. Peace researchers argued further that in the nuclear age many of the 'lessons' which the Cold War 'realists' had drawn from the Second World War were simply not applicable. Aggressive war might have been a rational, albeit barbarous, act of policy in the pre-nuclear age; it was totally irrational in an era when each side had the means to destroy each other's society no matter who attacked first, and where defence against nuclear attack was impossible. In the 1930s Hitler could hope to gain from launching an aggressive war against other European countries; in the age of the H-bomb no conceivable gain could be worth the costs of waging a war of aggression which would in all probability end in a nuclear holocaust.

Peace researchers argued that the avoidance of a nuclear war which could advantage neither side and risked destroying both, created a common interest between the superpowers which transcended the very real conflict which divided them. In this way they were foreshadowing the arguments of the proponents of *détente* almost a decade later. The conception of *détente* as the 'politics of antagonistic collaboration' captured perfectly the complexity of the relationship in which bitter adversaries were forced to co-operate against a common threat.

In focussing on the conflict as a whole, in taking an international rather than a national perspective, peace research was reasserting one of the central assumptions of the 'idealists' of the 1920s. When competing nations both embraced the logic of 'peace through strength', an increase in security for one side implied a decrease for the other. One nation's absolute security can become its rival's absolute insecurity.

The Cold War 'realists' sought to draw attention to the nature of the threat from the East by invoking the lessons of the 1930s and warning of the dangers of Munich and appeasement. The Soviets inveighed against the threat from the West and worried about 'capitalist encirclement'. Peace research, on the other hand, was less likely to take sides and focussed on the dangers which were inherent *in the system of confrontation itself.* More than two decades later many of these early peace research propositions about security were being reiterated by Olaf Palme's Independent Commission on Disarmament and Security Issues. As Cyrus Vance, US Secretary of State in the Carter Administration and member of the Commission, noted in his introduction to the Commission's report:

There is one overriding truth in this nuclear age – no nation can achieve true security by itself. No matter how many weapons a nation develops, no matter how strong its armed forces become, they can never guarantee its freedom from attack. . . . To guarantee our security in this nuclear age, we must, therefore, face these realities and work together with other nations to achieve common security. For security in the nuclear age *means* common security.

Institutional Development

Much of the early disagreement between peace research and the
Cold War 'realists' was based on a false dichotomy. Few peace
researchers then or now would have argued against the proposition
that armed resistance to Hitler's aggression was necessary. But the
dangers of appeasement and the need to stand up against totalitarian
aggression were not the only lessons that peace research drew from
the rise of Fascism. Many peace researchers would have argued that
a more equitable settlement of the First World War would have
denied Hitler the possibility of exploiting the deeply felt grievances
among the German people which the Treaty of Versailles had
generated.

Where *unambiguous* aggression did not exist, where conflicts
between nations were based on false or distorted images of the
opponent, then 'peace through strength' policies were likely to
exacerbate tensions. Arms competition would become locked into
what was known as the 'reciprocal escalation spiral', with each side
responding defensively (as it saw it) to the 'aggressive' escalations of
the other. Mutual suspicion and hostility would increase.

Peace researchers argued that much of the conflict which
existed between the US and the Soviet Union was of this type. In so far
as this was true, 'peace through strength' policies which generated
escalating arms races actually undermined the security of the states
which pursued them. This was particularly true in the nuclear age
when escalating numbers of nuclear weapons conferred no mean-
ingful military advantage.

Applying the research findings of social psychology, especially
image theory and cognitive dissonance theory, to the study of
international conflict, peace researchers argued that the process of
'stereotyping' – that is, each antagonist depicting the other as the
devil incarnate – reinforced and dangerously exacerbated pre-
existing conflicts. This legitimised and encouraged hardline policies
on both sides – including increased military build-ups.

What psychologists called the 'intolerance of ambiguity' meant
that once the stereotypical images of an opponent had crystallised
they were extraordinarily difficult to change. What one side intended as conciliatory overtures would, in a polarised conflict, be
perceived by the other side as tricks and hence be rebuffed. The
rebuff would humiliate the side that made the overture, signalling
the apparent futility of conciliation. Polarisation would be rein-

forced, subsequent communication made more difficult. Processes which exacerbate fear and suspicion can be particularly destabilising in the context of an arms race.

One of the pioneers of peace research, the Quaker mathematician, Lewis Fry Richardson, had argued that if a country 'A' increased its level of arms expenditure because – rightly or wrongly – it feared another country 'B', then 'B' was likely to respond by increasing *its* arms expenditure. This, argued Richardson, could set in motion a 'self-fulfilling prophecy' further exacerbating and apparently justifying the fear and hostility which 'A' initially felt. The resulting intensive arms race, argued Richardson, was likely to culminate in war. Most peace researchers at this time shared Richardson's belief that arms races increased the risk of war, and later quantitative studies of the history of arms race outcomes appeared to confirm this.[3]

Thus, in its first phase of development, peace research was very much part of the behavioural revolution in the study of international relations. It also offered a thorough-going critique of the core assumptions of the 'realist' approach.

The most important centre of institutional development of peace research in the United States was the Center for Research on Conflict Resolution at the University of Michigan, where the *Journal of Conflict Resolution* began publication in 1957. On the European front Johan Galtung's International Peace Research Institute, Oslo (PRIO) was founded in 1959. In 1964, PRIO started publication of the *Journal of Peace Research*, which was to become the main European peace-research journal. In 1962, the Polemological Institute was established at Groningen in the Netherlands. The Michigan, Oslo and Groningen Institutes have been described by Swedish peace researcher, Hakan Wiberg, as the main 'growth poles' of European and US peace research. In 1945, Gaston Bouthoul established the Institut Français de Polemologie, in Paris, but the French centre never made a great impact on what might be called 'mainstream' peace research.

Other, smaller institutes were being established around the same time – including, in 1961, the Canadian Peace Research Institute at Oakville, Ontario, and the Institute for World Order (now the World Policy Institute) in New York. T. F. Lentz's Peace Research

---

· 3. See, for example, M. D. Wallace, 'Arms Races and Escalation: Some New Evidence', in J. D. Singer *et al.*, *Explaining War*, London, 1979.

Laboratory in St Louis, Missouri, had been established in 1945 and the now defunct Peace Study Institute in New York, in 1957. In 1959, the establishment of the Lancaster Peace Research Centre represented the first step towards institutional peace research in Britain. The Lancaster Centre later transferred to London and became the Richardson Institute for Conflict and Peace Research.

By 1960, an 'invisible college' of mostly academic researchers interested in peace research was growing rapidly in most OECD countries and the growth of peace research was reflected not only in the new institutions, but also in scholarly associations and journals. In 1963, the Peace Research Society (International) (PRS(I)) – now called the Peace Science Society (International) – was established in the US by Walter Isard. In 1964, the International Peace Research Association (IPRA) was set up – initially based at the Polemological Institute in the Netherlands.

Isard's PRS(I) published the *Peace Research Society (International) Papers*, predecessor to *The Journal of Peace Science* and, more recently, *Conflict Management and Peace Science*. IPRA published its own newsletter which was to become the single most important source of information for the widely flung peace-research community. As Charles Chatfield has noted the *Newsletter* 'offers a continuous record of research-in-progress and community-in-development'.[4] *International Studies Quarterly* (*ISQ*) also started publication in 1964. Though embracing a wider research agenda than most peace-research journals, *ISQ*, which is the official journal of the International Studies Association, published works by many of the leading American peace researchers. The Canadian Peace Research Institute started publication of *Peace Research Abstracts Journal* in the same year. Still more journals were to appear later.

Growth, Diversity and Conflict

As the 1960s progressed, peace research became more established – and institutionalised. New institutes were still being established – including the famous publicly funded Stockholm International Peace Research Institute (SIPRI) in 1966 – national and international associations had been created, journals catering exclusively to a

---

4. C. Chatfield, 'International Peace Research: The Field Defined by Dissemination', *Journal of Peace Research*, no. 2, 1979, p. 177.

peace research readership were thriving and peace studies courses were beginning to be taught in colleges and universities. With institutional consolidation came an expansion of the scope of peace research. This change was reflected in a 1973 editorial by the new editors of the *Journal of Conflict Resolution (JCR)*:

> we want to widen JCR's substantive focus somewhat. Although it has always been open to contributions dealing with conflicts within nations, its primary focus has been on international conflict and especially the danger of nuclear war. As a general statement, this still seems appropriate to us, but we want to shift the balance a bit. The threat of nuclear holocaust remains with us and may well continue to do so for centuries, but other problems are competing with deterrence and disarmament studies for our attention. The journal must also attend to international conflicts over justice, equality, and human dignity; problems of conflict resolution for ecological balance and control are within our proper scope and especially suited for interdisciplinary attention.[5]

The expansion of scope arose in large part out of the introduction of a much broader definition of 'peace' than that implied by common usage. Johan Galtung of PRIO argued that 'peace' had to mean more than the absence of war – or other forms of overt violence; it also required the absence of 'structural violence'. Conventional violence resulted in death and injury, but so too did 'structural violence'. In the latter case the deaths arose not from intended acts of direct violence as in war, but the unintended consequences of structured inequalities in social systems. It was in this sense that one could talk about a social system itself being 'violent'.

That 'structural violence' thus described does exist is indisputable. It is evident in the differences between rich and poor, in life-expectancy rates, infant-mortality rates, susceptibility to disease and malnutrition, not just in Third World countries but even in rich nations like the United States and Australia. The suffering which this 'structural violence' generated did not result from any absolute lack of resources but rather from an inequitable distribution of resources – a distribution which was socially and politically determined and which, in principle, could be changed. Peace research claimed that social structures could generate somatic harm as effectively as bombs and bullets.

---

5. 'New Editors for an "Old" Journal', *Journal of Conflict Resolution*, vol. 27, no. 1, 1983, p. 5.

In so far as the attainment and maintenance of peace was part of the *raison d'être* of peace research, then the eradication of 'structural violence' was as necessary as the eradication of war and other forms of direct violence. 'Positive peace' was the term used to describe a state of affairs in which 'structural' as well as 'direct' violence had been eliminated. (The concepts of 'positive peace' and 'structural violence' are both broader and more contentious than this brief review suggests. Further discussion is presented below.)

By the mid-1960s, as popular fears of nuclear war began to recede, the issue of 'structural violence' became more salient, and since the highest levels of 'structural violence' were in the Third World, investigation of its causes meant examining the structure and dynamics of underdevelopment. Third World development and development theory thus became an increasingly important focus of peace research.

Once again the perspective was global and critical of the prevailing conventional wisdom. The idea that the root causes of underdevelopment were to be found in the resistance of indigenous cultures and social structures to the demands of 'modernisation' – which was the prevailing orthodoxy among development sociologists – was rejected.

The central assumptions of neo-classical trade theory were also challenged. According to this theory, countries should specialise in producing for export those goods in which they had a *comparative* advantage over their trading partners. Third World countries were held to have a comparative advantage in the production of raw materials (most obviously tropical products); developed nations in processed goods. The most 'rational' pattern of trade, that is, that which would bring the maximum economic benefit to both parties, would therefore result in a global division of labour in which the developed countries tended to monopolise the production of processed goods while the Third World provided the raw materials.

The most influential peace research critique of this approach was provided by Johan Galtung who argued that it was necessary to look beyond the immediate (and in any case contested) gains of comparative advantage. The problem with such an international division of labour, he argued, was that it concentrated the growth-generating 'spinoffs' involved in processing raw materials in the already rich developed nations and denied them to the poor. Processing imparts *value* to commodities – a kilo of steel is far less valuable than a kilo of razor blades. Since most processing took place in the rich countries they stood to gain most of the added value. But large-scale processing also demanded – *and further stimulated* – transportation, communication, education, training, research and development infrastructures. The production of cash crops or the extraction of minerals for export provided minimal 'spinoffs' by comparison. Processing is growth-generating, argued Galtung, in a way that cutting sugar cane or picking coffee beans can never be.

Galtung's theories and the complementary work of the Latin American *dependencia* theorists provided a central focus for much of the research on underdevelopment within the peace research community. These theories have since been elaborated, tested and subjected to searching critique.

The concern with the Third World during this period was not simply directed towards the question of development. Anti-colonial conflicts, resource diplomacy, ethnic conflicts – including the black/white confrontation in Southern Africa – all figured on the peace-research agenda. But towards the end of the 1960s the issue that caused most controversy within peace research was, without doubt, the Vietnam War.

The initial attack against many of the assumptions of what might be called the first wave of peace research was delivered in 1968 by Herman Schmid, a Swedish sociologist, in the pages of the *Journal of Peace Research*. Peace research, Schmid suggested, had become biased against conflict, it made naive liberal assumptions about common interests where in many cases there were none. 'Liberal' peace research sought constantly to minimise conflict relations, never to sharpen them. Assertions about fundamental common interests which might well have been valid in the context of the nuclear confrontation between the superpowers, were quite invalid in other contexts. What, for example, was the common interest between slaves and slave-owners?

The problem with 'liberal' peace research, according to Schmid, was not simply that its analysis lacked universal applicability, but that the prescriptions that flowed from it could, in some contexts, be positively counterproductive to the cause of promoting peace and justice. It might be wholly appropriate to seek to resolve some types of conflict by mediation, conciliation and compromise and yet wholly inappropriate to apply the same techniques in other contexts. If the cause espoused by one party to a conflict were wholly just and that of the other party wholly unjust – slaves versus slave-owners, for example – then any settlement made on the basis of compromise would be unacceptable since it would compromise justice. Many conflicts between the powerful and the weak, nationally and internationally, Schmid argued, were of this type.

The task of peace research was not to compromise justice but to align itself with the oppressed. This meant taking sides – even in violent conflicts. Thus as Lars Dencik, another of the Swedish radicals, argued:

> in certain situations an open confrontation may be . . . the only way to bring about liberation from structural violence. . . . This is more or less, I think, the reason why so many young peace researchers consider it quite compatible with, and even imperative to, the role of peace research, to actively support, for example, the NLF in Vietnam in its struggle for liberation.[6]

The radicals were arguing, in other words, that it was sometimes more important to win wars than to try and stop them via such techniques as conciliation and mediation. This, of course, was a position that the international relations 'realists' had always held. In the context of the East–West confrontation, notions like 'conciliation' had sounded to some 'realists' too much like appeasement. Indeed the radical critique of the 'illusions' of 'liberal' peace research was in many ways reminiscent of the 'realist' critique of illusions of 'idealism'.

For the radicals the problem was not simply that the prescriptions of 'liberal' peace research were inappropriate in unequal or 'asymmetric' conflicts. From the perspective of 'liberal' peace research polarisation was a problem, serving to obscure underlying common interests in 'symmetric' conflicts like the East–West nuclear confrontation. But in *unequal* conflicts polarisation was not necessarily bad. It increased political consciousness, it intensified group solidarity and the will to resist, and it enhanced resistance to divide and rule tactics by the enemy.

In 1969, the year after Schmid's attack was published, the radical – liberal conflict within peace research flared into an open and bitter confrontation. The occasion was a conference organised by the PRS(I) in Copenhagen, at which two Danish peace researchers launched a polemical attack on the organisers. The particular object

6. L. Dencik, 'Peace Research: Pacification or Revolution?', in G. Pardesi (ed.), *Contemporary Peace Research*, London, 1982, p. 191.

of their attack was a conference on Vietnam which the PRS(I) had hosted in the United States during the previous year. The conference was supposed to present a balance of viewpoints, but in fact was US-centric, addressing itself to US problems. Why, demanded the radicals, at a conference which was supposed to present all points of view, had no representatives from the Vietnamese revolutionary forces been invited?

The fact is that most – not all – of those who had attended the PRS(I)'s Vietnam conference in 1968 would have been opposed to US involvement in the war, but most would also have stopped well short of supporting the National Liberation Front. The 'liberal' peace researchers wanted the war stopped, the radicals wanted the revolutionary side to win.

Debate at the conference grew increasingly acrimonious with some of the participants walking out. Walter Isard subsequently changed the name of his organisation to Peace Science Society (International) (PSSI), in order to distinguish it from peace *research* which he felt had been given a bad name by the controversies in Copenhagen. Since that time the PSSI has eschewed attempts to influence policymakers in favour of 'pure science'. Kenneth Boulding, the distinguished American economist and one of the founders of peace research in the United States, had also attended the Copenhagen conference. Boulding was very disturbed by what happened and years later he was to suggest that the confrontation had had positively Freudian overtones: 'Part of the loutishness of the radicals is an expression of a kind of Oedipus complex against the father figures of the older generation.'[7]

There is however a simpler explanation which owes nothing to Freud. Theories about conflict are not created in a social vacuum. They are conditioned by events. I suggested earlier that the core assumptions about war and peace of both the 'idealists' and the 'realists' had been enormously influenced by the First and Second World Wars respectively. Those whom Kenneth Boulding had described as the 'older generation' of peace researchers were responding to a political climate in which the threat of nuclear war was the central issue. But by the late 1960s there was much less concern about the dangers of nuclear war than there had been a decade earlier. The 1963 Partial Test Ban Treaty (which banned the fallout-producing atmospheric tests) had effectively killed the peace

---

7. K. Boulding, 'Limits or Boundaries of Peace Research', in ibid., p. 84.

movement which had arisen in the late 1950s by removing the source of middle-class concerns about Strontium 90 in babies' milk. For the younger European researchers of the mid and late 1960s, North–South issues – especially Vietnam – were more salient than either totalitarianism or the threat of the Bomb.

There was of course nothing unique about the conflict within the peace research community. This was after all a period in which universities throughout the OECD countries were wracked with controversies far more intense than anything which had taken place within the peace research community.

By the mid-1970s the acrimony had disappeared almost completely. There were a number of reasons for this. First, peace research had by this time grown to such an extent that it could afford to divide into a number of different 'schools' which adopted a *laissez-faire* attitude towards each other. Secondly, many of the radicals simply ceased to have any active involvement in peace research – none of the key activists of the 1969 Copenhagen conference is still involved in peace research. Thirdly, there was a realisation that each side in the debate had exaggerated the failings of the other. Much the same is true about the Great Debate between the traditionalists and behaviourists in the broader community of international-relations scholars. While there are still journals which identify exclusively with one tradition or the other – for example, *Foreign Affairs* and *Conflict Management and Peace Science* – there is now less hubris on both sides and a much greater degree of mutual respect. Historians are increasingly willing to use social science methodologies where appropriate, and the behaviourists are much less likely to be critical of historical approaches. Many of the better journals – for example, *International Organisation*, *Political Science Quarterly*, *World Policy*, *Review of International Studies* – simply cannot be characterised as either 'traditional' or 'behavioural'.

In the 1980s the pendulum swung back towards the original agenda of peace research – an agenda dominated to a large degree by concern about superpower relationships, the arms race and the threat of nuclear war. The issue of 'negative peace' – of avoiding war – was once again more salient than those of 'positive peace' and 'structural violence'. It is primarily because concern about nuclear war is so pervasive and widespread in the Western world – in a way that Third World poverty never was – that there was a resurgence of interest in peace research in the mid-1980s.

Defining the Field

Defining peace research in a way which would command wide consensus is probably impossible. Swedish peace researcher Hakan Wiberg has pointed out that even among peace researchers themselves, 'There is no unanimity on how to define "peace" nor what it means to juxtapose it with "research" . . .'.[8] It might well be asked whether or not this lack of unanimity is of any consequence. For those already involved in peace research the answer is probably not, but if, as is currently the case in Australia, the US, Canada, Denmark and Spain, national governments are in the process of establishing peace research centres then the question is of some importance. The public and their elected representatives have a right to know what it is that tax-payers' funds are to be spent on.

The research orientation of the new Peace Research Centre at the Australian National University (ANU) has already become the subject of speculation and controversy. Similar controversies have attended the decision to establish new centres in the US, Canada and Denmark. In Australia, sceptics and critics as well as supporters have contributed to what is emerging as a lively debate.[9]

Research programmes pursued in peace research centres should obviously differ from those pursued in the departments of international relations or the strategic studies centres – otherwise there would seem to be little point in creating them. That peace research *does* differ from the traditional disciplines is not generally disputed – *how* it differs is. Most attempts to define peace research fail precisely because they do not adequately differentiate it from strategic studies or international relations. Thus the terms of reference of the ANU centre describe its function as involving 'high quality research on topics relating to the conditions for establishing and maintaining peace on national, regional and global scales'. While such a description clearly fits the work most peace researchers undertake, many students of international relations and

8. H. Wiberg, 'The Peace Research Movement', in *Wiener Beitrage zur Geschichte*, Vienna, 1984.
9. See T. B. Millar, 'The Resolution of Conflict and the Study of Peace', working paper no. 73, Canberra, 1983; A. Burns, 'Peace Research at ANU', *Quadrant*, December, 1983; J. L. Richardson, 'Peace Research and the Peace Researcher', *Peace Studies*, March, 1984; H. Freith, 'Where are We Now', *Peace Studies*, July, 1984; G. Foley, 'Technocratic or Humanist Peace Studies: ANU's Peace Research Centre', and M. Bearlin, 'Peace Research for Beginners', both in *Peace Studies*, December, 1984.

strategic studies would wish to argue that it describes their research equally well.

The language of the terms of reference of the Australian peace research centre suggests a research orientation which makes no claim to 'value-freedom' and which, like medical research, is goal-oriented. This is quite correct, but it is not unique to peace research. Seeing the ultimate goal of research as contributing to the attainment of peace rather than simply the acquisition of knowledge and understanding is nothing new. J. L. Richardson of the ANU has pointed out that if this was the *raison d'être* of peace research it amounted to no more than a return to: 'the goal which provided the original impetus for the establishment of the study of international relations in universities after World War I, i.e. to contribute to the prevention of war through the study of its causes and proposed remedies'.[10] One could hardly imagine even the most hawkish strategists or cynical disciples of *realpolitik* arguing that their task was to contribute to the maintenance of war and the prevention of peace. In any case not all peace researchers believe in 'goal-oriented' research; they have remained faithful to a more traditional concept of scholarship arguing that the task of the researcher is to try and explain the world – not to change it.

Yet most peace researchers would affirm that their work *is* different from mainstream strategic studies and from international relations research in its traditionalist guise. What then is the difference? Does it lie, as some claim, in its methodology? Certainly if one were to compare the social science emphasis so prevalent in US peace and conflict research with the fairly traditionalist approach to studying international relations which prevails at the Australian National University or the Royal Institute for International Affairs in London, this claim might seem persuasive. In the first case there is an explicit commitment to the methodology of the behavioural social sciences; in the second, the commitment is primarily to historical analysis. If one were to compare the contents of the *Journal of Conflict Resolution*, *International Studies Quarterly* or the *Journal of Peace Research*, on the one hand, with those of *Foreign Affairs*, *International Affairs* or *International Security*, on the other, the impression of methodological divergence would be strengthened.

There are many scholars who identify themselves as peace re-

---

10. Richardson, 'Peace Research', p. 21.

searchers, however, who are not social scientists. What I describe later as 'investigative research' owes nothing to social scientific methods, nor does the type of work carried out by the Stockholm Institute or the Armament and Disarmament Research Unit at Sussex University. Yet all of these centres would see themselves – and be seen by others – as being involved in peace and conflict research.

Positive and Negative Peace

Many peace researchers – though not all[11] – would argue that it is the concept of peace which they employ which distinguishes their work from strategic studies or traditionalist international relations research. In the latter tradition peace is seen as the absence of war/hostilities/violence, or, as Raymond Aron once put it, 'the more or less lasting suspension of violent modes of rivalry between political units'.[12] But peace research also embraces another, broader, concept of peace – 'positive peace'.

As noted earlier, Johan Galtung, the best known and most influential of the European peace researchers, argued some twenty years ago that the traditional notion of peace – so-called 'negative peace' – was too narrow. Negative peace is what the overwhelming majority of non-specialists understand by peace, that is, the absence of 'direct' violence. 'Positive peace' is the absence of another form of violence – 'structural violence'. The term 'structural' is used because death and injury can result from structured inequalities in social systems – from human *in*action as well as intended acts of violence. In many Third World societies the poor suffer lower life expectancy rates, greater susceptibility to disease, higher rates of malnutrition, and so on, than do the ruling strata. If these differences are a consequence of unequal access to resources such as food, clean water supplies, health care, adequate clothing, and housing, and if the unequal access is *in principle* preventable, then we can speak of 'structural violence' being present.

11. Kenneth Boulding and J. David Singer are among some notable dissenters.
12. Cited in W. Maley, 'Peace, Needs and Utopia' (mimeograph, Royal Military College, Duntroon, 1984). This powerful critique of the concept of 'positive peace' raises questions about the utility of the concept which have never been satisfactorily answered by its peace research advocates. The paper will be published in a future issue of *Political Studies*.

But expanding the domain of peace research by introducing the concept of 'structural violence' failed to resolve any of the problems of defining the field. The new concept of 'structural violence' was in no sense 'a theoretical breakthrough' as some had claimed. 'Structural violence' was simply a novel way of describing what, in the Third World in particular, was a familiar, if depressing reality. The concept had no theoretical implications at all, although, as Galtung pointed out, it raised a number of interesting questions.[13]

It was, of course, possible to hypothesise that 'structural violence' (preventable misery) led to direct violence (insurrection). But research on this question by Ted Gurr and others[14] had already shown that 'structural violence' was neither a necessary nor a sufficient condition for collective 'direct' violence.

The real utility of the concept of 'structural violence' was political. If people could be brought to see Third World poverty and inequality not as accidents of history but as a form of violence this would aid the 'conscientisation' of the oppressed and political mobilisation. 'Structural violence' did after all generate millions of preventable deaths.

To revolutionaries, the 'structural violence' which resulted from oppressive rule provided a utilitarian justification for revolutionary violence. The Cuban Revolution may have cost many lives in the actual fighting, but it may ultimately have saved even more lives by the reduction in 'structural violence' which resulted from resources being shared more equitably in the post-revolutionary society.

For Galtung, and many other peace researchers, however, even this conception of violence was too narrow. 'Structural violence', they argued, also involved 'psychological violence' – a notion which was exemplified but never adequately defined. Galtung complicated the concept still further when he noted in an influential 1969 article that 'We shall sometimes refer to the condition of structural violence as *social injustice*.'[15]

Peace research thinking about this broader concept of 'structural violence' has been inconsistent and, in many cases, confused. The term 'violence' has been employed in ways increasingly remote from common usage and the arguments used to justify the novel

13. J. Galtung, 'Violence, Peace, and Peace Research', in Pardesi (ed.), *Contemporary Peace Research*, pp. 93–125.
14. T. R. Gurr, *Why Men Rebel*, Princeton, 1970.
15. J. Galtung, 'Violence, Peace and Peace Research', *Journal of Peace Research*, vol. 16, no. 3, 1969, p. 171 (emphasis added).

usage have been weak. Far from adding clarity, the new terminology has created confusion. It has never been clear, for example, what is gained by describing all acts of social injustice (which may include relatively trivial incidents) as acts of 'violence'.

Many other examples could be adduced. Some peace educators claim that the highly structured order of a traditional classroom is *in itself* a form of 'violence' directed against pupils. It is easy enough to see why from the perspective of progressive educational philosophy, traditional educational practice might seem to be authoritarian, likely to stifle creativity – indeed thoroughly undesirable – but none of this justifies calling the traditional classroom 'violent'.

Just how far this conception of 'positive peace' and its antithesis 'structural violence' may diverge from common usage can be gleaned from the claim by a West German peace educator that 'helplessness in our private life [and] dependence on expert knowledge' constitute examples of violence.[16] To many people the equation of 'helplessness in our private life' with, say, Hiroshima or the atrocities of the Khmer Rouge is not merely an obfuscatory use of the term 'violence' but also a somewhat tasteless one.

The antithesis of the broad notion of 'structural violence' is 'positive peace'. 'Structural violence' ceases to exist when, and only when, 'positive peace' is achieved. 'Positive peace' is a synonym for a particular conception of 'the good society' – a society which is just and egalitarian and in which human beings can achieve their true potential.

According to Galtung 'positive peace' is achieved when the gap between human potential and what human beings actually realise is bridged – the size of the gap is a measure of the level of 'violence'. Thus *if* humans have a potential to live for seventy or eighty years, but in fact only live for fifty, and *if* the differential is due to unequal access to vital resources, and *if* the inequality of access is avoidable, then violence exists.

But, as Galtung himself has admitted, defining violence as 'the difference between the potential and the actual' is problematic. Human beings have potential for violence, and what if *that* potential is not realised? Still more problems emerge when we move away from questions of somatic health to questions of other, non-somatic human potentials being realised.

16. M. Gronemeyer, 'Present Tasks of Peace Education and Actions', paper presented to International Peace Research Association Conference, Konigstein, FRG, 1979.

This is a point that Christian Bay has taken up.[17] Bay argues that 'violence' is that which denies fulfilment of 'objective' human needs. Bay's typology of needs is borrowed from the psychologist Maslow. The most basic of these alleged needs are physical, and the denial of these is 'structural violence' in the narrow sense; then come safety needs, affection or 'belongingness' needs, self-esteem needs and finally self-actualisation or self-development needs. Positive peace – the 'good society' – requires the satisfaction of all these needs.

The problem with trying to define 'positive peace' in this way is that the further one moves up Maslow's hierarchy of needs, away from the most basic physical 'needs', the more controversial the very existence of the 'needs' in question becomes. This is most apparent when there is a disjuncture between the 'basic needs' identified by Maslow and the subjective *wants* of particular individuals or groups. The problem arises when people don't *want* what the needs theorists say they objectively *need*.

Moreover, with a different conception of the 'good society' it would be possible to posit a different set of 'needs' which have to be satisfied in order for that society to be realised. It is difficult to avoid the feeling that it is the theorists' conception of the 'good society' which determines the 'needs' which they identify. Needs theory appears highly teleological at times.[18]

For John Burton, another researcher in this area, destructive social conflicts arise out of the frustration of basic human needs. These needs are biologically determined: Burton is impressed by the work of sociobiologists such as E. O. Wilson. Needs are not only physical, argues Burton, there are also – and more controversially – 'identity', 'political participation' and 'redistributive justice' needs. Such needs are, it is claimed, 'objective', and this is what makes a truly scientific theory of conflict possible. If human needs are fulfilled we have 'positive peace'; if they are frustrated we have destructive conflict. In other words Burton is claiming that 'structural violence' conceived in terms of frustrated needs can lead to direct violence. Relative deprivation theory, by contrast, explains political violence in terms of frustrated *wants*.

Burton makes much of the fact that the 'needs' that he has

---

17. I am following William Maley's discussion of the concept of positive peace here.
18. See E. D. Watt, 'Human Needs, Human Wants, and Political Consequences', *Political Studies*, no. 4, 1984.

identified are 'objective' – indeed this is a necessary condition for his theory to make sense. In fact his argument assumes what has to be demonstrated. There is no persuasive evidence presented to support the claim that what Burton identifies as psychological 'needs' are biologically rather than socially determined. The needs theorists on whom he relies, such as Paul Sites, are explicit in denying that human needs are directly observable. And Christian Bay admits that 'we cannot even prove, strictly speaking, that particular needs, or needs in general, as distinct from wants, actually exist'.[19] If 'needs' cannot be adequately distinguished from wants, Burton's theory fails.

The most telling evidence against Burton's thesis is found in the existence of societies which have been stable for long periods despite the fact that what Burton claims are 'basic needs' are systematically frustrated. In many traditional societies demands for 'political participation' and 'distributive justice' have either not been made or have been ignored, denied or repressed without generating the instability which Burton's theory predicts.

Notwithstanding the heated debates which have surrounded this issue, there has been little research done on the broad notion of 'positive peace' within peace research – the possible exception being the work associated with the World Order Models Project and the journal *Alternatives*.

In criticising the conception of 'positive peace' I do not wish to argue that peace research should stick solely to the 'negative peace' agenda. But there seems to be no good reason why peace researchers should use language in unnecessarily obfuscatory ways, especially when common usage is perfectly adequate. Social science has enough problems in communicating its ideas and findings to lay persons without compounding them unnecessarily.

Optimism versus Pessimism

I have identified a number of areas where peace research tends to differ from traditionalist approaches to the study of global politics. But, particularly with respect to the 'realist' school, there is another distinguishing feature – one which is difficult to pin down but no less important for that.

19. C. Bay, cited in Watt, 'Human Needs', p. 535.

'Realist' international relations theory shares much of the bleak vision of Hobbes and Machiavelli; the assumptions which underpin much of contemporary peace research are more in the tradition of thinkers such as Kant, Rousseau and Marx. The peace research conception of human nature is more optimistic than that of the traditionalists, while belief in the viability of reform and radical change is much stronger.

Traditionalist approaches to the study of international relations and the art of statecraft have, of course, tended to dominate the actual practice of foreign policy in the age of the modern nation state. So in challenging the core assumptions of traditionalism peace research has also posed a consistent challenge to the assumptions of the status quo. It is in this sense that one can say that peace research is inherently more critical and radical than both the theory and practice of the 'realists'. And it is for this reason that peace research perspectives tend (it is no more than a tendency) to cluster on the dovish end of the security spectrum. Given this and given that 'mainstream' traditionalism tends to be both more hawkish and more conservative it is not difficult to see why some critics charge peace research with being 'political' or 'ideological'. In fact traditional international relations and strategic studies are every bit as 'political' and 'ideological'. *Their* perspectives tend to cluster in the centre and on the hawkish end of the security spectrum and on the centre and right end of the political spectrum. But because the assumptions of the more established approaches are generally closer to mainstream politics they are not usually perceived as being as 'political' or 'ideological' at all.

The optimism about human nature which underpins so much of peace research theory and prescription – from integration theory to unilateral disarmament initiatives – does not imply that peace researchers view the present trend in world politics with any enthusiasm or optimism – quite the contrary. 'Realists' have a much greater confidence in the viability and stability of the status quo than do most peace researchers.

Peace researchers, however, argue that such confidence is unwarranted and that traditionalist prescriptions may be self-defeating. 'Peace through strength' policies, they suggest, too often lead to arms races which exacerbate tensions, generate crisis instability and heighten the risk of war. The task of peace research is to conceive security policies in such a way that the enhancement of one nation's security is not at the expense of the security of others. Such a task is possible because the fundamental barriers to a more peaceful world society lie not in human nature but in social and political institutions which are amenable to reform.

Ultimately, attempts to derive a neat, all-inclusive definition of peace research seem unlikely to succeed – the boundaries dividing peace research from other research fields are too diffuse. So rather than attempt what is probably impossible it may be more fruitful to conceive of peace research as a syndrome. By syndrome I mean a collection of attributes which tend to cluster together. Not all the attributes will necessarily be present in research fields outside peace research.

The peace research 'syndrome' is characterised – though not consistently or uniquely – by a commitment to certain values and to policy-oriented research intended to realise those values; by a preference for the methods of the social sciences; by an enthusiasm for interdisciplinary research; by a conception of human nature which is more optimistic than that of the 'realists'; by conceptions of 'peace' and 'violence' which are broader in scope than those of common usage; also by scepticism about the long-term reliability of the realist approach.

The Controversy over Peace Studies

In many OECD countries the growth of peace studies in schools and universities has generated considerable controversy. Nowhere has this been more evident than in the United Kingdom, where there have been attacks – in Parliament, in *The Times* and in other media outlets – complaining that peace studies lack coherence and rigour, that they are deeply biased and that activist teachers are injecting the ideology of the unilateral nuclear disarmament movement into schools and universities. There are already some signs in Australia that a similar backlash against peace studies (which have been supported by the federal and some state governments) is developing. A recent article in the *Australian* – which itself generated a storm of controversy – charged that: 'No single subject has ever been as fraudulent in its purposes, as shallow in its scholarship, as biased in its politics or as out of place in a worthwhile school as peace studies.'[20] Typically the critics confuse peace studies, a peda-

20. G. Sheridan, 'The Lies They Tell Our Children', *Australian*, February, 1985.

gogic exercise, with peace research, which is very different.

In Britain a pamphlet, published in 1984, entitled, *Peace Studies: A Critical Survey*, by Baroness Caroline Cox and Birkbeck philosopher, Roger Scruton, has become a handbook for the conservative critics of peace education.[21] Many of its arguments are already being used by Australian critics, and it has even been reviewed by the Pentagon's in-house publication, *Friday Review of Defense Literature*.

Caroline Cox is a noted conservative critic of 'progressive' educational reform. Scruton is editor of the *Salisbury Review* and has a regular column in *The Times*. The Cox and Scruton broadside is part of a wider neo-conservative attack on peace studies which was well-received by the Thatcher government.

Cox and Scruton mount their attack on several levels (I deal here primarily with the sections in the pamphlet which cover university-level peace studies). Peace studies are said to exhibit an obsession with trendy 'relevance' – similar to 'women's studies', 'black studies', 'gay studies', and so on. Peace studies do not constitute a 'coherent discipline' and are in any case too complex to be taught at the undergraduate, let alone secondary school level. Finally, peace studies are said to exhibit a pronounced bias towards leftist politics and the 'dogmas' of unilateral nuclear disarmament.

It is worth examining these charges in some detail since they constitute what is rapidly becoming the conventional conservative critique of peace studies, and because any criticism of peace studies is likely to rub off on to peace research. Research and teaching are, of course, quite different endeavours and, as I shall argue later, the narrow focus ('bias') which may be appropriate in research is inappropriate in a teaching environment. It is, however, not surprising that the two endeavours sometimes get confused in the public mind – academics very often choose to teach subjects which embrace their research interests.

Consider first the charge that peace studies exemplify the obsession with 'relevance' – understood as contentious contemporary political issues – which is characteristic of 'progressive' education. The pursuit of these modish subjects is conducted, it is claimed, at the expense of traditional disciplines, and even the acquisition of basic educational skills. But Cox and Scruton provide no evidence to demonstrate that the existence of peace studies in schools and

21. C. Cox and R. Scruton, *Peace Studies: A Critical Survey*, London, 1984.

universities has anything like this consequence. Bradford University's School of Peace Studies is singled out for sustained criticism in this regard. In fact, the School's curriculum embraces a wide range of subject matter which is far from 'relevant' in the sense that Cox and Scruton use the term. Furthermore, since the School of Peace Studies is unique in the tertiary educational sector, its curriculum, whatever its merits or demerits, has no implications for the teaching of peace studies elsewhere.

Bradford is the only academic institution in the UK where it is possible to gain a *degree* in peace studies. Even in the US, where degrees are offered in the most bizarre subjects, there is only a tiny number of private colleges which offer degree courses in peace studies. In most schools and universities, peace studies courses, if they exist at all, form only a very small part of the curriculum.

Cox and Scruton also ignore the argument that the study of contentious issues such as the nuclear confrontation between the superpowers may be an excellent way of stimulating student interest in precisely those subjects which they (Cox and Scruton) believe *are* central to the study of war and peace. Their list – with which few peace researchers would disagree – includes philosophy (especially ethics), logic, probability theory, decision theory, game theory, strategy, theology (especially 'just war' theory), history, economics, sociology and politics.[22] The point that many proponents of peace studies seek to make is that the study of 'relevant' issues may enhance understanding of many of the central issues of philosophy, rational choice theory, and so on – and vice versa. The academically 'traditional' and the politically contentious or 'relevant' are not necessarily antithetical.

Secondly, it is not clear why the authors should object so strongly *in principle* to the 'studies' approach to learning. 'Studies' in this context simply means an interdisciplinary approach to a particular subject area. The number of different disciplines which Cox and Scruton *themselves* see as central to the study of peace suggests that no single discipline could possibly be adequate to the task of studying war and peace. This is a point made by the governmental committee of experts which produced a report for the Danish government on peace and conflict research: 'peace and conflict research . . . defines a problem area to the study of which people from many disciplines devote their energies. Peace and conflict

22. Ibid., p. 12.

research is interdisciplinary in this true sense.'[23] It is difficult to avoid the conclusion that the authors' objections to the particular 'studies' approaches which they list (women's studies, black studies, etc.) owe more to the perceived political *content* of the courses than to the principle of interdisciplinarity itself.

Thirdly, there is the claim that peace studies do not constitute a 'coherent field'. This is true – at least in terms of theory and method. As the Danish committee's report pointed out: 'peace and conflict research is [not] a discipline. There is no body of theory and analytical technique that has been shown to be the correct way of solving problems . . .'[24] Further, since almost everyone agrees that peace research/peace studies are interdisciplinary endeavours, it is obvious that they cannot constitute a 'coherent field' in the same way as the more traditional disciplines might. The lack of 'coherence' is, therefore, hardly a cause for criticism. Moreover, the Cox and Scruton critique completely overlooks the powerful arguments in favour of interdisciplinary research; and geography, medicine and management studies are examples of coherent fields which largely consist of borrowings from a variety of disciplines.

Fourthly, there is the assertion that peace studies deal with a subject matter too complex to be taught at university level. No evidence is presented that this is the case, nor any argument suggesting why it should be. The allegation could equally well be made about sociology or history or international relations.

Finally, there is the claim that peace studies is biased – permeated with unilateralist dogma. Here the evidence is wholly anecdotal. With respect to universities, *all* the evidence on which Cox and Scruton's sweeping assertions are based comes from one department in one university – the Bradford School of Peace Studies. Even if all claims made about Bradford were conceded (they are in fact hotly disputed by the School's staff) nothing at all would have been demonstrated about peace studies in British universities *as a whole*.[25] One wonders how Roger Scruton, as a philosopher, would feel if sweeping generalisations about the totality of British philosophy were based entirely on evidence of its practice at Sussex University.

In generalising from the particular, Cox and Scruton break an

---

23. *Proposals on Promotion of Peace and Conflict Research in Denmark*, Report from the Preparatory Committee of Experts, Copenhagen, 1983.
24. Ibid., p. 6.
25. On this see James O'Connell's essay on peace research in higher education in this volume.

elementary rule of precisely the sort of scholarship they claim to be upholding. There is no evidence in their critique that they either knew of, or had any interest in, research and teaching on conflict resolution at Kent, or conflict theory at the Richardson Institute, or arms control at the Arms Control and Security Studies Centre at the University of Lancaster, or alternative defence strategies at Oxford. Very little of the research or teaching undertaken at these centres fits the distorted picture of peace research/peace studies which the Cox and Scruton pamphlet depicts.

Cox and Scruton seem to believe that advocacy of unilateral nuclear disarmament is almost a defining characteristic of peace research/peace studies. In fact, at least as far as European peace research is concerned, it is extremely uncommon. For example, in the UNESCO publication *Armaments, Arms Control and Disarmament* edited by Marek Thee of PRIO, not one contributor out of a total of forty-six advocated complete unilateral disarmament. The overwhelming majority of the contributors were peace researchers. Where peace researchers in Europe *have* been active is in advocating nuclear disengagement zones, No First Use (of nuclear weapons) postures and so-called 'unilateral disarmament initiatives'.

Unilateral initiatives, it should be emphasised, are quite different from unilateral disarmament. In the context of an arms race, unilateral initiatives are small, unilateral cuts in force levels. The theory is predicated on two perfectly sensible premises. The first of these is that mutual fear and suspicion are major, though by no means unique causes of the arms race. Secondly, it is argued that reductions in nuclear arsenals can be made without any diminution of deterrence – 9,000 nuclear warheads are no less effective a deterrent than 10,000. Unilateral reductions in nuclear arsenals by either side should, it is held, reduce the levels of fear and suspicion between the rival superpowers, thus reducing tensions. If the West made the first reductions the position of Soviet proponents of *détente* and arms control would be strengthened; the influence of the hawks of the Soviet military–industrial complex would be undermined.

The way in which Cox and Scruton conduct their argument is instructive. Ostensibly they are arguing for a 'balanced' treatment of the issues of peace and war and against 'biased' approaches. In reality they seem concerned only with a particular type of 'bias', one which leads to a conclusion with which they disagree. There is no parallel attack on university centres 'biased' towards traditionalist 'balance of power' for 'peace through strength' approaches.

University departments are often 'biased' in the sense that some approaches to the subject tend to be ignored and others emphasised. Given the breadth of most subject areas taught in universities, some degree of selection is inevitable. Some economics departments will be known for their stress on monetarism, others as bastions of neo-Keynesian theory. In some psychology departments behaviourism rules and Freud is ignored; in others the reverse is true. In Scruton's own field twentieth-century continental philosophers are largely ignored in British philosophy courses. At Bradford's School of Peace Studies, the study of conflict is clearly 'biased' in the sense that some ways of examining issues are stressed at the expense of others. But if the School of Peace Studies is 'biased' so too are other university departments. Students studying problems of war and peace at Southampton and Aberystwyth would encounter different emphases. Whatever label we use to describe the differences in emphasis – 'bias' or specialisation – it is clear that the phenomenon is a widespread, indeed commonplace fact of academic life. If it is to be deplored the attack should not be selective.

The Cox and Scruton critique frequently fails to meet the scholarly standards it purports to uphold. It also fails to make a persuasive case against peace studies *in principle*; it does, however, point to a failing of *some* peace studies courses in practice. The narrowness of perspective ('bias') which may be fruitful in a research institute (providing it does not become insulated from searching external criticism) may be educationally counterproductive in a teaching situation. 'Bias' is indeed a problem.

It may be naive to suggest that the problem of 'bias' could be solved if teachers addressed 'both sides of the argument', not least because on many issues there are far more 'sides' than any teacher could hope to do justice to. But there is surely something wrong with peace studies courses, whether in universities, colleges or schools, which systematically ignore conceptions of peace, conflict and defence, which are held, not only by governments, but also large majorities of citizens.

In Australia, for example, large majorities of voters consistently support the ANZUS alliance, increased defence expenditure and a return to conscription. In other words, what may loosely be called the 'peace through strength' perspective has widespread popular as well as elite support. Yet there is no doubt that some peace studies courses do systematically fail to treat the 'peace through strength' perspective either seriously or fairly – if at all.

Conclusion

Since the late 1950s, peace research has evolved, diversified and become institutionalised. Like most other fields of enquiry – including international relations – it was viewed initially with considerable scepticism by the traditionalists into whose domain it intruded. Some of that scepticism still exists.

Within peace research itself the intense controversies which marked the late 1960s and early 1970s have long since dissipated. Lively debates about theory, method and practice remain, but they are no different in kind from those which exist in other areas of academic enquiry. The peace research of today is generally more conservative than that of the 1960s – as is the case with other disciplines like sociology and political science.

For a number of reasons, however, peace research is unlikely to be free of public controversy for the foreseeable future. First, 'peace through strength' assumptions tend to inform both public and official attitudes on security issues. The peace research critique of these assumptions is thus, inevitably, a critique of the status quo. As such it is likely to generate controversy – especially on issues as emotionally charged as that of nuclear war.

Secondly, if past practice is any guide, the new peace research centres which are being established in the United States, Canada, Australia and Denmark can expect to come under attack from sections of the peace movement. They will almost certainly be accused of too narrow a focus, academic elitism, ignoring the concerns of grassroots peace movements, failing to take an unequivocal public stand on such issues as nuclear deterrence and so forth.

Thirdly, within the academic community many traditionalist scholars will continue to view the behavioural social science leanings of peace research with suspicion. Some social scientists, on the other hand, strongly disagree with the peace research rejection of the idea of 'value neutrality' – a rejection which is seen as abandoning the traditional standard of academic objectivity.

Finally, among the general public the confusion which always seems to exist between peace research, peace studies and peace movements means that criticisms of the peace movement and peace studies tend to rub off on peace research.

Given this potential for controversy it is not difficult to see why some governments, research bodies and universities should be wary about embracing – and funding – peace research. But the fact that a research field may be controversial is, in itself, no good reason for refusing to support it. If it were there would have been far less progress in science than there has been.

Even those who disagree with many of the analyses and prescriptions of peace research may nevertheless recognise the value of the role peace research centres may fulfil. In the United States the idea that different research institutes should study the same sort of problems from a variety of different perspectives seems both normal and proper. At one end of the spectrum are the Heritage Foundation, the Hoover Institution and the American Enterprise Institute which are identified with 'peace through strength' assumptions and (especially Heritage) tend to be sceptical about arms control and disarmament. In the centre ground are institutes such as Brookings and the Roosevelt Centre, while at the other end of the spectrum are the Institute for Policy Studies, the World Policy Institute and the Institute for Defense and Disarmament Studies. Here research is generally critical of the 'peace through strength' approach which is seen as flawed in theory and dangerous in practice. There is a strong stress on arms control and disarmament.

The conservative–liberal distinction which is so evident in the case of US research institutes is similar to the differences between 'realism' and peace research discussed earlier. Outside the US the idea that research centres should be associated with particular social and political philosophies is often viewed with great scepticism. But there is a case to be made for such diversity – which is anyway much commoner than the sceptics believe.

The case for encouraging research from a wide variety of different perspectives, is a classic pluralist one. With respect to particular centres, the advantages of working *within* a set of shared assumptions is considerable. They are such as those which accrue from the practice of 'normal science', in Kuhn's sense of that term. In 'normal science' it is precisely because fundamental assumptions are *not* under constant challenge that progress is made. 'Normal science' makes a virtue out of avoiding epistemological introspection. There are dangers as well as advantages inherent in the practice of 'normal science'. The most obvious is the temptation – and ability – to resist critiques from outside. If the 'quasi-paradigm' insulates itself too successfully from external challenge, research will inevitably suffer. But this danger applies equally to traditionalist approaches to the study of international relations and to strategic studies. Here too fundamental assumptions about the nature of the international system, and so on, are not normally challenged. Such assumptions are the implicit axioms from which research proceeds – they are not in themselves normally the *objects* of enquiry.

It might be objected that the US model of a plurality of privately funded research centres has no relevance in countries like Australia which do not have the foundations to permit such a diversity of centres to flourish. Critics who have no objections to private foundations funding whatever research they wish, argue that government-funded research centres have a responsibility to be 'balanced'.

The critics would be correct if, in the absence of privately funded centres, a government were to fund just one centre which dealt with security issues. But this rarely, if ever, happens. In Sweden, for example, while the government certainly gives generous support to the well-known Stockholm International Peace Research Institute (SIPRI), it also funds the more traditionalist Swedish Institute for International Affairs and various strategic studies programmes. In Australia, federal government funding pays for the defence staff colleges, the Royal Military College, Duntroon, the Strategic and Defence Studies Centre and the International Relations Department at the Australian National University. The creation of a small peace research centre, the first of its kind in Australia, would make little difference to the overall 'balance' of research on security issues – no matter how controversial its research programmes might turn out to be. Indeed it may be seen as correcting a degree of *imbalance* which currently exists.

If policies based on the controversial wisdoms of *realpolitik* and 'peace through strength' assumptions had created and sustained a world without war, starvation, injustice and the threat of nuclear Armageddon then the case for the type of alternative perspectives which peace research provides would hardly be compelling. Although it is possible to argue that traditionalist approaches are the least-worst alternatives in a highly imperfect world, their failure to maintain stable peace should, at the very best, raise questions about the assumptions on which they are based.

Peace research evolved precisely as a reaction against the perceived inadequacies of 'realism' and *realpolitik*. It has produced its own analyses and prescriptions as alternatives to the prevailing conventional wisdoms. The pluralist case for peace research is not, however, dependent on peace research analyses and the acceptance of prescriptions but on the legitimacy and utility of alternative research programmes being pursued.

We recognise the value – indeed the vital necessity – of alternative views being expressed in our courts, in the media and in our democratic political institutions. The case for alternative perspectives is no less compelling when vital interests of national security are at stake.

5

Approaches to the Study of Peace in Higher Education: The Tensions of Scholarship

James O'Connell

Introduction

Few would deny the centrality of the issue of peace in our time. Those who differ with one another about peace do so less in terms of peace itself than in terms of values, notably justice and freedom, that are analytically and socially linked with peace. For such reasons the painful paradox continues that everybody favours peace; and yet peace remains a controversial term. It is a controversial term especially for those who believe that many advocates of peace have not properly weighed the claims of justice or would barter freedom for the sake of an empty and fragile peace. For related reasons those who remain uneasy about much advocacy of peace resist also the endeavour to bring in the academic or school study of peace.

If peace has been a central preoccupation in Western Europe, at least since the turn of the century, why has the structured study of peace come so recently into higher education? Three main factors seem to me to explain this lateness. First, the social sciences themselves – amongst which peace studies is best classed – have come late: political science was no better developed by 1900 than when Aristotle left it over 2,000 years before; sociology – and in measure economics – has only slowly built up its house and more slowly again put it in some order. Secondly, political science dealt in good measure with the basic issues of peace, not least the order internal to

A version of this paper was originally published in *Medicine and War*, vol. 2. 1986, pp. 141–7.

the state as well as the order between states. Thirdly, there has been an historic presence in governments and ruling groups of bellicist traditions whose endeavour has been exerted to promote security, and often dominance, through military capacity. Such attitudes made the study of peace as well as the advocacy of peace look marginal: peace was something to be pursued by those outside the main institutions of society and those who held different values from the ruling groups; and often enough those who argued the cause of peace held themselves apart from such institutions and proclaimed values that looked impractical to those with the charge of societies.

As peace studies (irenology or polemology are other terms) now occupies an academic place in higher education in various countries, I want to argue here the benign paradox that peace studies is a proper and needed academic study that has a worth related to the importance of peace, and that none the less the main impact of the study of peace as well as the most pervasive influence of the values of peace come through other academic disciplines, in particular the social sciences of politics, sociology, economics and psychology. One reason for this last argument is that far more persons will study, and research in, the main disciplines than will study peace as such, and the social science disciplines overlap with, and can encompass, the concerns of peace studies. What peace studies does is to take problems of order that are already considered or touched on within the disciplines and to deal with these problems in a coordinated way and with a unified focus. What is also at issue here is the organising of the boundaries of disciplines. There is no perennial orthodoxy in organising a particular study of society. Some may regret, for example, that political economy did not prevail as a discipline but for the sake of a division of labour broke up into politics and economics. Yet in a contrasting approach human geography groups problems that are dealt with in both sociology and economics. The relevance of peace studies is that it has the unifying focus of a concern for peace – as geography has a similar focus in its concern for the uses of the earth – and deals with issues of order where human co-operation is crucial to human development and where violence or disruption is threatened or present. For such reasons peace studies as a subject is best seen as an area study – the same is true of war studies – which deals with social content where other disciplines converge and where their methods are used. It is an area study in the sense of geography and medicine rather than a geographic area study such as European, African or American Studies. It is also an applied study like engineering or medicine (though it is not a professional formation), in so far as it sets out to make its results available for practical action. In short, I am saying that peace studies is an applied area study; and I am arguing its case as a most useful way of organising a study of social order and disorder. What I am not saying – indeed I am arguing the contrary – is that the study of peace is confined to peace studies. In this context it is worth saying also that a concern for peace is clearly not confined to those who group themselves in the peace movement.

Let me finish this section by saying that apart from academics rooted in an unbudging status quo and those upset by the belief that peace studies has fallen into the hands of their political opponents (however disproportionately numerous these groups may be) there is now acceptance of the academic study of peace. The truth is that there is no escaping the problem of peace in our time. Minds have been concentrated on the issue of peace by the technical development of weapons in the nuclear age and a concomitant failure to develop co-operative relations between states. We know now that we will be destroyed if peace breaks down between the superpowers. We know also that within two or three generations the nuclear capacity available to the superpowers at present is likely to become the possession of many more powers. Moreover, there seems little likelihood in the foreseeable future that defence can cope with the potentialities of attack. In these circumstances the nuclear issue and the means needed to resolve it retain for us and our contemporaries an excruciating urgency. For that reason alone there would be an extraordinary failure by academics – an ultimate *trahison des clercs* – were they not to undertake a systematic study of the conditions of contemporary peace. Yet it is also necessary to insist that the study of peace ranges much more broadly than the nuclear issue or international politics. And in the longer run nuclear war may become avoidable only in so far as groups begin to grasp the general worth of non-violent solutions and that the costs of interstate and intergroup violence are higher than has tended to be traditionally received.

Architectonic Ideas in the Study of Peace

The central co-ordinating idea is peace itself. It needs, however, to be flanked by other concepts, notably justice and freedom in whose absence the study of peace is diminished. I have time here to deal in greater length only with the idea of peace. Yet I will begin with a paragraph that acknowledges the links of freedom and justice with peace.

The desire for peace is the correlate of the search for security and survival which is a powerful, perhaps the most powerful, human urge. Yet human survival is not physical only, crucial though the latter is. There is a saying of Socrates: 'My friend, fear evil rather than death because evil runs faster than death.' For such reasons peace is linked to freedom, the absence of which is a great evil and the presence of which enables persons to survive humanly, much as they see and want themselves to be. Finally, peace and freedom remain hollow and fragile without justice. Justice gives everybody their due and if they are not given it, the danger is that they will seek it through violence.

If peace, freedom and justice are intimately linked, peace has a certain practical primacy among them. Peace provides the conditions in which freedom can best flourish and justice best be achieved. It is also the general condition towards which human effort moves. As St Augustine puts it: 'For the good of peace is generally the greatest wish of the world, and the most welcome when it comes . . . the sweetness of peace which all men do love.' All the goods of human endeavour are best held when they can be held in the security of peace. The idea of peace contains two basic elements: willing co-operation among persons for social and personal goals and the absence of violence (in the shape of direct physical, psychological or moral violence). In *City of God*, St Augustine sums up the positive element of peace in saying: 'Peace of all things is a well disposed order' (XIX, 13). Such order in the changing circumstances of human life has to be a dynamic order in which co-operation seeks not only to maintain concord between divergent human efforts but also to perfect it and to adapt it to new situations. This co-operation aims at goals that are ultimately as wide as life, truth, freedom, justice and love. The negative element of peace is the avoidance of discord or inflicted disorder in the shape of violence. It is often the most psychologically salient of the elements of peace. Moreover, it stimulates persons to remove what harms them much as illness stimulates the science of medicine to remove mental or bodily harm and, in practice, conditions the organisation of medicine more than does the preservation of health. While it is easy to point out how inadequate negative peace is, it is worth insisting that such peace is a necessary, though not a sufficient condition of positive peace. Also, the psychological saliency of negative peace reflects the pervasive normality of positive peace in human relations. The danger of concentrating on negative peace, however, is that practitioners and theorists alike may neglect to work on constructing the foundations of peace. Yet in recent Western European history peace between the main contenders in the last two civil wars (1914 and 1939) has been more firmly established by their discovering that their interests converged than by their recoiling from war.

In the previous paragraph the stress has been on the concept of peace. In that sense peace can be understood as a *state* at which people arrive or hope to arrive. At best human peace must stay relative and in measure remain flawed. Yet the state of perfect peace in which the lion will lie down with the lamb is a pervasive human ideal. It is, however, the relative nature of human peace that leads us to see peace as a *process*. Involved in any living concept of peace is a set of attitudes among persons that are dynamic and purposeful, that are ready to carry the costs of the search for peace and elimination of violence and that seek to uphold the values of justice and freedom inherent in stabilising peace. In short, peace is, in St Augustine's words, 'the tranquillity of order' but it is the tranquillity of a dynamic order that seeks to underpin human co-operation and remove not only violence but its causes.

One of the difficulties about peace – it besets both those advocating the study of peace and those opposing it – is that the concept refers to structural situations and operates on a second level of abstraction (in this sense the concept of peace is like the concept of love). But it is concrete relations between individuals and groups – between states not least – that embody peace. It is, in consequence, less peace that has to be sought after than satisfactory relations between groups. Understood in this way peace again is an architectonic idea. Its advantages are that, on the one hand, it faces up to the hard, and sometimes harsh realities of concrete relations, and so avoids turning peace into a mystique and, on the other hand, it takes into account the need to deal with concrete relations in holding to the value of a dynamic and tranquil order that nonetheless has to

111

cope with the presence of tolerable and/or tolerated injustice and less than full freedom.

Against the background that I have been sketching I want next to discuss three teaching approaches to peace studies, and then go on to discuss research. Discussion will in each case be brief because the function of this paper is introductory.

Teaching

Peace Studies as a Degree Major/MA Course

I have argued that peace studies is an applied area study whose content is social behaviour (a) where co-operation is required or where violence is present or threatened; (b) in which the focus of study is a concern for peace, and (c) in which the methods of other sciences, particularly those of the social sciences and disciplines such as philosophy and theology, are used. If, however, there is no peace concern that the study of peace cannot take up, the same does not hold true for organised peace studies in a university or other institution of higher education. Teaching has to accept limitations that stem from combining subjects and curricula within limited time as well as accepting constraints that stem from scarce staffing.

Let me simply mention the topics that peace studies may legitimately take up. It is concerned with concepts of peace and freedom and justice (philosophy and theology); peace between states and between world regions (international politics and economics); peace between races and between ethnic groups (politics and sociology); peace between social classes as well as the social leavening of efforts to remove class divisions (politics, economics and sociology); and peace between labour and management (sociology, economics and industrial relations). Beyond these areas there is a case in certain institutions and places for a study of peace in the family, peace between the sexes, peace between individuals and individual inner peace. It is also more than useful where time and resources permit it to be able to teach and learn about the history of peace thought and action as well as about the main contemporary trends in peace concerns. It is also possible to teach elements of mediating and counselling. It would, however, be a great mistake to overemphasise the importance of these last methods as against, for example, attempts to understand and change political and social structures that militate against peace.

Also, no matter how well organised peace studies may be, it is possible to retain a certain flexibility in its approach. This can be done at any level of study by enabling and encouraging students and teachers to take up research projects that deal with immediate issues as well as by encouraging them to build into their peace studies an experiential element stretching from improvised drama to group dynamics and community work. Finally, if peace studies is an area study where other disciplines meet, it is my personal opinion that its courses should provide a proper training in at least one standard discipline. The most accessible disciplines for this purpose tend to be politics and sociology.

Peace Studies as a Minor Component in a Degree or as an Individual Course

For reasons of strategic allocation of resources in higher education it is unlikely that many new peace studies departments will be founded in the near future. It makes best sense then where one or more academics want to set up a peace studies component in a degree to make use of existing resources. If a single course only is available I would argue for the suitability of a general introduction to the idea of peace and approaches and values in peacemaking. That kind of course can make a reasonable contribution to degrees ranging from those in politics and sociology to philosophy and theology. Moreover, if it is possible to put together as a minor option a set of courses that range from international politics to race relations, I would argue that they are best held together by a paper that works on the conceptualisation and values of peace and peace-making. It is also necessary to establish mechanisms for co-ordinating consultation among those who are assembling the combination of subjects that can be taken by students. Finally, it seems reasonable to suggest that a range of subjects can be knitted together from the broad topics that I have suggested above as belonging to peace studies. In putting together a degree component it is educationally most important to ensure not only that subjects cohere but that they add depth to one another's probings. Spreading students across courses from divergent disciplines thinly held together is a formula for superficiality. Nonetheless room needs to be left for students' own capacities to integrate teaching and to make their own syntheses. In consequence, an excessive insistence on subject/course co-ordination needs to be avoided. The science and art of education have to reach a fine balance in these matters.

Peace as a focus or value in subjects

Teachers choose and deal with the content of their subjects and courses in a multi-focus way; and they do so with a multiple set of values. Three broad peace emphases are possible in a number of subjects. First, in certain subjects ideas connected with peace as well as peace itself can be taken up naturally and relevantly. Secondly, issues can be looked at with a sensitivity to values that include peace and justice and freedom as well as the relationship between those values. Thirdly, values implicit in the traditional treatment of subjects can be reflected on in the light of new sensitivities.

I hesitate to give examples from disciplines in which I do not specialise. Yet it seems worthwhile to venture some tentative ideas that specialists may deepen and extend or, for that matter, replace. I will, however, try to confine my illustrations to disciplines that I have been able to give a little thought to.

1   *English literature*: The war poets and writings of Huxley and Orwell provide direct ideas for reflection on in the teaching of English. They raise the issues of violence and totalitarian control as well as Utopian aspirations and the wreck of hope. Shakespeare provides much thought on national sentiment, especially in a play like *Richard II* where words like 'land' and 'tongue' sound the new Elizabethan sense of national identity. It is also Shakespeare who in *Coriolanus* offers a contrast of personal and social values in the context of war. One way or another the spectre of death peers into the work of the great poets, Donne and Hopkins not least, who meditate on mortality in great language. What reflections on the death of humanity itself work through contemporary poets as they contemplate the possibility of nuclear disaster, and how are previous intimations of mortality taken up?

2   *History*: History taught with a peace concern can point out how often the study of history is organised around wars. Scholars can argue the artificiality of such organisation. There may, however, be less need immediately to seek to change the organisation of data than to sensitise students to the springs of such organisation. Scholars can also elaborate on the profounder approaches to periodisation that organise history around social and economic development, the growth of ideas and the introduction and diffusion of

technology. In dealing with conflict it seems sensible to remove romanticism from wars as well as to suggest that most wars have come too soon. In a direct contribution to the analysis of our own period of history it is useful to examine the stereotypes of one another that opposing peoples have tended to invent before and during wars throughout history.

3 *Physics*: Physics can show how nuclear weapons have come from a long history of scientific discovery and that the bomb arose out of one of the central efforts of modern physics to split the atom. Moreover, the technology now locks in with solid state physics which is currently one of the fastest developing parts of physics. The atomic bomb itself arose out of warfare in an industrial civilisation and was directed against cities. Nuclear bombs as well as nuclear technology are, however, part of scientific developments that are gradually modifying nineteenth-century urban growth. Students may be invited to reflect on these developments; and they may also be invited to examine nuclear technology and nuclear weapons as priorities within the comparative priorities of physical science as well as on the implications for the use of the world's resources. There are no easy answers to questions which take in national security as well as the consumption of non-renewable sources of energy. Students of physics are likely, however, to pursue their discipline in a social and economic vacuum unless they at least know that there are fundamental questions to be raised in the nuclear area of their discipline as well as analogous questions in other parts of the discipline and in other physical and biological sciences.

4 *Christian theology*: Central in religious approaches is a belief that the relations of men and women to God are one side of a coin of which the other side is their relations to one another. Where a concept of creation is accepted the fundamental unity of all persons – Jew and Greek, bond and free, male and female, Russian and American, European and African – is accepted. In other words, there is a common humanity which can be respected only in an ethic of justice and love. This common humanity is harmed by division, and it is warped by stereotypes. Beyond basic forms of justice and love Christian theology reflects on teachings that propound how enemies have to be loved and injuries forgiven, how the face that has been struck on one cheek turns the other cheek, and how with one who obliges one to go a distance one goes voluntarily a greater distance. Theologians are under no obligation to pretend that his-

torically religions, not least Christianity, have lived up to their ideals. But the ideals can be suggested and their doctrinal foundations uncovered. At the same time students may be invited to discuss why churches, for example, at different times have not lived up to their ideals. In this context the social class of churchmen and the nationalism of their congregations may be looked at. Students can be asked to match the weight of class and nation against the strength of religious belonging and to make their judgements on where their own allegiances lie. Similarly, if a religion accepts that all peoples are brothers and neighbours, students may be asked to discuss why problems of just sharing within nations and between nations still remain outstanding. Finally, it can be suggested that where peoples are brothers and neighbours demonisation of leaders or of peoples is inconsistent with an acceptance that they are the children of God and open to the Spirit of God. While I have in our present context used Christianity as my religious example, it is true to say that with certain changes much of what is said could be worked out from the foundations of Hinduism and Islam, while in theologising about the latter two religions it is also possible to add things that are specific to them. Hinduism, in particular, has a long history of concern for peace and a record of having extended peace relations into that part of the world where men and other animals meet.

Research in Peace Issues

There is a close correlation between teaching and research in a discipline or area study. Teaching tends to come out of the balance between the speculative thrust of research, its priorities and its methodology, and the bread-and-butter need to impart basic content in courses. Also, good teaching is rarely maintained where those doing the teaching are not carrying on research.

In this section I want to sketch a series of areas in which research appropriate to peace studies can be carried out. In contrasting this scheme of research with the scheme implicitly set out in the description of teaching courses you may, on the one hand, notice the overlap between the two and on the other hand notice the differences in presentation because there is nothing set in concrete for organising teaching and research in an academic area. The following five sections – overlap though they do – attempt a certain coordination of themes.

1   *Peace history, theory and methods*: There is much research waiting to be done on the history of peace thought as well as on the history of peace groups. There is need to study conscientious objection in the wider sense, including civil disobedience in Nazi Germany, contemporary dissidence in the Soviet Union and disobedience or dissident movements elsewhere. In this area, work needs to be done on the philosophy of just war as well as on the theology of peace and war – the study of the evolution of thinking in the Jewish scriptures is, for example, intimately related to the Israeli–Arab conflict. Peace education is a field of research that is just taking off and provides many opportunities for interdisciplinary work. Finally, a great deal more research needs to be done on negotiating, mediating and counselling.

2   *Nuclear and non-nuclear defence*: The most obvious area of concentration in the nuclear issue is the superpower polarisation. This area is vast and includes politics, technology, economics and ethics as well as the examination of the modern history that has led to the present impasse. It needs to take in the study of the opposing alliances, NATO and the Warsaw Pact. After the policies of the superpowers and their allies comes the issue of proliferation where Pandora's open box seems now more dangerous than in the case of the superpowers, and where regional conflicts may not only wreak havoc regionally but also draw in the superpowers. It is crucial also to cope with national desires for security as part of the effort to seek non-nuclear forms of defence. Finally, much work needs to be done on the politics of arms control negotiations and disarmament.

3   *Relations between economically developed and developing societies*: In a world grown technologically small and where social thinking has not yet come to terms with the new closeness of global neighbours, peace studies needs to do forward research on relations between the world's regions. Peace, justice and development form the strands of such research which needs to include the use and allocation of energy resources, the market for commodities, the export of technology and the sharing and education of skills. Politics, sociology and economics come together in much of this work. Developing societies also need to be studied in their own right as well as in relation to other societies. Issues such as the legitimacy of state authority, the work of government and public administration, the ideologies of development, the role of public and private enterprise, competitive ethnic modernisation, and the reactions of primordial communities to rapid social change – among

117

a host of other topics – provide research opportunities for those concerned about peace.

4   *Industrialised societies*: There are no limits to the research topics in industrially advanced societies. The problem for peace studies is to make an effective choice. Two basic problems are worth researching in many countries. One is the issue of race/ethnic relations – the United States, Soviet Union, Britain, France, Belgium and other European countries face serious tensions of adjustment between groups. The other problem is that of industrial relations/social-class divisions as well as the roots of class/industrial conflict in a country like Britain for example. The most important contribution of peace research may be to develop the positive aspects of peace by looking at worker/management participation policies, the effect of forms of consultation and shared decision-making, and worker collectives, co-operatives or buy-outs.

5   *Regions in conflict*: Unfortunately various regions and countries provide fascinating areas of study: the war between Iraq and Iran in the context of oil revenues and religious and social change; the many facets of conflict in the Indian subcontinent, as well as Afghanistan and Sri Lanka; revolutionary movements in Latin America, the intractable Arab–Israeli conflict, and the Lebanese civil war; communal/ethnic crises in Cyprus and Northern Ireland; civil wars in Angola, Mozambique and Zimbabwe; and, not least, the simmering threat to peace in reactions to the apartheid policies of South Africa. Themes such as social identity, fair access to political power and economic resources, respect for human rights and trauma of social change run as a *Leitmotif* through such research.

I will end this section simply by saying that where peace studies is formally established there is a good case for seeking to correlate research emphases and teaching obligations. Where there is no formal organisation there is a good case for the focus that a well-organised research seminar provides.

Dangers in the Study of Peace

Let me very briefly mention what I believe are the main dangers in the study of peace: lack of focus, marginalisation and Utopianism. First, it is crucial in peace studies to hold on to the negative element of peace – the absence or elimination of violence – because it helps to focus the positive element of co-operation. Without holding both these elements together the danger is that the study of peace will spread and diffuse into a preoccupation with all that is humanly desirable, grow excessively tangled with ideas of social reform and treat of human perfectibility rather than the human search for peace.

Secondly, those who consider peace to be a concern confined to a moral elite, who cannot tolerate political negotiation or compromise without sullying their consciences, set themselves apart from the main decision-making structures of society and render themselves thereby ineffective. Moreover, in carrying on a discussion with like-minded persons only in an intellectual ghetto they risk deepening one another's prejudices rather than testing their ideas against a harsh world of reality and its multi-faceted and multi-group search for truth. Scholars of international politics who do not carry on a dialogue with military personnel and politicians remain insensitive to the mature consideration that comes from a practical concern with security; and they also run the risk of ignoring the information that is available from military, administrative and political sources. Put in another way, occasionally one is tempted to believe that there are too many prophets active in the struggle for peace. Peace is unlikely to be achieved without those who are willing to warn from the fringes of society, without those willing to suffer the odium and hardship of unpopularity and without those imaginatively able to make society-seizing gestures. But together with the prophets we need the priests and the kings, that is, we need the intellectual brokers – academics, teachers, journalists among others – and the politicians – activists in the constituencies, back-bench MPs and ministers of calibre. And we need continuing interaction between the prophets, brokers and politicians.

Thirdly, many hope for too much from peace studies. Those who seek instant recipes for peacemaking can only be disappointed. Also, peace studies will no more create peaceful persons among its teachers and students than will Christian or Buddhist theology among their teachers and their students. Yet if at best peace studies can be no more than a slow intellectual leavening, that humanising development is a precious social contribution. Moreover, reflecting on the logic of modern technology and its organisational structures, on the bitterness of this century's experience with war and on the new edge to human-kind's insecurity it seems fair to say that the time of the idea and process of peace has come. There is a certain strength in working out a timely application of a great human innovation, which is what global peace can be.

Conclusion: Values, Learning and Application

In this final section I want to draw attention to an attitude or conviction that lies at the heart of peace studies, and then move on to look at conditions of scholarship in the area. The conviction referred to is that conflict needs to be – in so far as this is humanly possible – resolved by peaceful or non-violent means. Those who are drawn to peace studies may be fascinated by the intellectual problems of war and peace. But most of them are prompted by a concern for preserving peace. In a similar way I am impressed by how scholars who are concerned with social work are animated by a passion for helping the deprived and how medical scholars are moved by an urge to heal. Yet this moral concern in peace studies has to work in the context of practical operations and needs. An ethical concern is sterile that does not take into account how states, groups and individuals behave and how interests (security not least), sentiments and values other than peace motivate them. For such reasons peace studies needs to take as much interest in the balance of weaponry as does an institute of strategic studies and as much interest in the balance of power as an institute of international politics.

Implicit, however, in my reference to other values is the acceptance that peace is not an absolute value. Peace is a primordial human need which is the condition of meeting many other needs and underpinning other achievements. But I believe that there are evils worse than violence, worse even than the organised violence of war; and I reluctantly agree that a minimal use of force may prevent other or later and greater incidence of violence. This is the logic of a theory of just war. But if a theory of just war is accepted – with the recognition that historically justice has tended to receive one-sided definitions in conflicts and seldom have all other means been used to avoid war before force has been turned to – we have to strive in our time to leaven opinion and convince statesmen that the conditions of just war need to be taken seriously and given proper weight and not be discounted in the hysteria of crisis or the blindness of chauvinist sentiments.

Let me return now to peace studies as an academic discipline. It involves teaching and learning, research and practical application. If its main emphasis is applied, there is in peace studies as in all scholarly study a speculative thrust. For all the importance of application this speculative thrust is essential. Its contribution is to provide a longer-term perspective for peace as well as the detachment and breadth that are sometimes missed out in practical concentration or in ideologically committed orientations. In this sense detachment itself forms part of a broad integrity that puts truth first and in teaching seeks to share truth and not to indoctrinate, and in intellectual contention seeks light in argument and never simply victory in confrontation. Lastly, speculative scholarship thrives in symbiosis with policy-oriented thinking as well as in dialogue with thoughtful action for peace. It is difficult to over-stress that peace studies entails the hard purification of learning. It may contain an experiential component but it is an academic discipline and is not a form of activist enterprise. In order to retain the time and to develop the patience required for learning as well as to maintain the detachment vital to the search for knowledge an academic discipline needs normally to remain distinct from and distanced from activism. This is not to say that persons involved in peace studies should not otherwise be activist in peace issues as are, for example, medical and scientific scholars. In our times, however, it may well be the case that the greatest contribution to activism to be made by the scholars concerned with peace is for them to provide intellectual resources and information for activists.

Obviously studying and teaching about peace is not the only way of building for peace. Moreover, academics should distrust temptations to overvalue their own contributions. They should not forget the observation of Hegel on his own discipline, philosophy: it is the owl that flies in the dark when the light of the day is gone. But it is true that scientific social thinking can inform and sensitise those who influence public decisions and those who make public decisions. Existing peace groups in this country are much better informed now than they were a generation back and have been able powerfully to carry on discussion and argument with governments and other ruling groups. Government and political parties have also begun to work out policies in a more thoughtful and sustained way. At least some credit for this change and its effects on public policy and opinion deserves to go to scholars concerned with peace studies.

Let me end by returning to a central theme of my first section above: there are issues such as peace that our civilisation cannot afford not to study. In the matter of peace what is at stake in our times at certain levels is the intellectual, moral and physical well-being of individuals and groups. What is at stake at an ultimate level is not only physical survival and moral integrity but the whole human condition.

6

Peace Studies in the United States: Challenges and Opportunities

Carol Rank

A National Perspective on Programme Development

During the 1970s and 1980s hundreds of peace studies programmes sprang up at colleges and universities across the United States and, to a lesser extent, in Western Europe and in other countries throughout the world.[1] The first of these programmes was established in 1948 at Manchester College, a small, religious-based college in Indiana.[2] Most peace studies programmes, however, came into existence in the early 1970s in response to the Vietnam War, with a later surge in programme development in the early 1980s due to a growing concern over the escalation of the arms race. The dynamic growth of this new field represents a significant countercurrent to the political and economic conservatism now prevalent in higher education in the United States.

Peace studies in higher education has emerged as a recognised field of study with all the characteristics of established disciplines: a significant body of theory and literature, professional associations and journals, and numerous teaching programmes in the subject. Approaches to peace studies vary, as do the names of the pro-

---

This paper is drawn from chapters of Carol Rank's doctoral dissertation, 'Peace Studies in American Higher Education: The Emergence of a New Field', University of California, Berkeley, 1988.

1. Most peace studies programme development has taken place in North America and Western Europe, with programmes in the US and Canada, England, Ireland and Sweden, and a number of individual courses offered in Norway, Germany, Holland and Yugoslavia. Peace studies programme development is also underway in Australia, the Philippines and India.
2. Manchester College, Manchester, Indiana, sponsored by Church of the Brethren.

122

grammes (Peace and Conflict Studies, Peace and World Order Studies, Program in Non-violent Conflict and Change, etc.) The field is kaleidoscopic, yet underlying the diversity is a unity of assumptions and aims. Minimally it is concerned with the prevention of organised lethal violence (war) and structural violence (systemic oppression), but topics and issues encompassed by the field are wide ranging. Defining the parameters and central distinguishing characteristics of peace studies is an essential and ongoing task.[3]

The administrative structures of peace studies programmes also vary, ranging from clusters of courses, topical concentrations and co-majors (or joint degrees), to full degree-granting programmes and departments or schools of peace studies. Degree-granting undergraduate majors in peace studies are a relative rarity in large part because of obstacles to interdisciplinary innovation and to financial constraints facing higher education today.[4] Because the field is growing rapidly, the exact number of existing courses and programmes is difficult to determine, but is estimated at over 200 in the US alone. As noted by Michael Klare, director of the Five College Program in Peace and Security Studies, Amherst, Massachusetts: 'We have experienced a dramatic expansion of peace studies programs at U.S. colleges and universities. Although precise figures are hard to come by, there are probably three times as many programs as there were just five years ago.'[5]

The following are some of the more well-established peace studies programmes in the United States, listed according to the type of educational setting they represent. These settings include: (1) religious-based colleges, (2) liberal arts colleges, (3) private universities and (4) public universities.

3. For a description of peace studies' central propositions and defining characteristics see 'The Juniata Consultation on the Future of Peace Studies', *COPRED Peace Chronicle*, December 1986, p. 6. For a listing of major theorists who have shaped the peace studies field, see Anita Kemp, 'Image of the Peace Field: An International Survey', *Journal of Peace Research*, vol. 22, no. 2, 1985, pp. 129–40.
4. George Lopez, 'A University Peace Studies Curriculum for the 1990's', *Journal of Peace Research*, vol. 22, no. 2, 1985, p. 122.
5. Michael Klare, 'Choosing Relevance: A New Path for COPRED', *COPRED Peace Chronicle*, August 1986, p. 5. The estimate of 200 peace studies programmes was provided by Clinton Fink, then Chair of the COPRED Executive Committee, at the 1986 COPRED Annual Conference held at the University of Iowa, Iowa City, Iowa.

Religious-Based Colleges

Manchester College, in rural Indiana, was established by one of the historic peace churches, the Church of the Brethren. It has operated its peace studies programme continuously since 1948, with a strong emphasis on international experience and placements in grassroots peace and justice organisations. Some of the required courses include: 'Christian Peace Heritage', 'Religions and War', 'Nonviolence', 'Conflict Resolution' and 'International Law and Organisation'.

Juniata College, in Pennsylvania, also established by the Church of the Brethren, has been offering an undergraduate major in peace studies since 1974. At Juniata, peace studies is considered to be 'applied liberal arts', in which a number of departments, including history, language, political science, sociology and religion, contribute toward the study of war and peace. In addition to courses on war and peace, conflict resolution, international law and the politics of developing areas, courses reflecting Juniata's religious and ethical orientation include: 'War and Conscience in America', 'Religion, Rebellion and Pacifism', and 'Studies in Historic Peace Churches'.

Earlham College, a Quaker school in Indiana, reflects the Quakers' tradition of active pacifist service for peace and justice throughout the world. Peace studies is seen as part of the mandate of the college. Earlham offers an undergraduate degree in 'Peace and Global Studies' and, through the School of Religion, a graduate programme in 'Peace and Justice Studies', with courses on a wide range of topics including 'Methods of Peacemaking', 'Political Violence and World Order', 'Europe in the World Wars', 'The Church and Social Change in Latin America' and others. The Earlham programme has become one of the most well-established and best-known in the US.

Notre Dame, Indiana, one of the leading Catholic universities in the United States, houses the new Institute for International Peace Studies, which offers undergraduate and graduate degree programmes, and an international scholars programme, at the MA level. The programme benefits from faculty with a long history in the development of peace and world-order studies. Topics of study include alternative security, global demilitarisation, conflict resolution and other issues.

Liberal Arts Colleges

The undergraduate peace studies programme at Colgate University, a small liberal arts college in New York state, was instituted in 1970 largely in response to student and faculty concern over the Vietnam War. Having an endowed Chair of Peace Studies has helped the programme become one of the most well-established in the country, with peace studies courses offered in fulfilment of general education requirements for all students at the university. The curriculum incorporates elements of the world-order approach with an emphasis on non-violence and a sociological/historical critique of the nation-state system.

The 'Peace and Social Justice' program at Tufts, a small college in Massachusetts, was initiated in 1982 by faculty and students involved in human-rights work who wanted a programme which would link peace and justice as interrelated goals. The first interdisciplinary course, 'Toward a Just Society', grew into a cluster of courses divided into seven categories: peace, justice, economic development, ecology, human development, popular action and culture. The programme also offers a wide range of internships and field experience in Geneva with human rights and other non-governmental organisations.

The 'Five College Program in Peace and Security Studies' at Amherst has not established a separate peace studies programme, but serves as a catalyst for the development of peace studies courses at five Massachusetts colleges (Amherst College, Hampshire College, Mount Holyoke College, Smith College and the University of Massachusetts at Amherst). The programme also assists in developing new peace studies programmes in the New England region and is important nationally, as it houses archives on existing programmes.

Private Universities

The 'Program in Nonviolent Conflict and Change', established in 1970 in the Maxwell School of Social Research at Syracuse University in New York state, has a national reputation for its courses focussing on conflict management and non-violent social change. Recently, the undergraduate programme has expanded to include diverse global issues such as the arms race, economic development, ecological balance, human rights and international organisation.

The graduate-level 'Program on the Analysis and Resolution of Conflicts' offers MA and PhD degrees and runs workshops for faculty and students, and for local and national organisations, on conflict resolution.

Since 1970, Cornell, in New York, has supported thesis research by graduate students, as well as research by faculty members, postdoctoral fellows and visiting scholars, on problems of peace and war, arms control and disarmament, and foreign policy related to these issues. An ongoing weekly seminar brings in speakers chosen for expert analyses on political, technical and military problems related to arms control and disarmament. Cornell's programme is similar to those offered by Harvard/MIT (Massachusetts Institute of Technology) and Stanford, California, in which arms control, approached from a more traditional international relations or strategic studies perspective, is the central focus of the programme. Cornell has no undergraduate peace studies programme. Doctoral work, while supported by the programme, must be completed within Government, Economics or other departments.

The 'Washington Peace and Conflict Resolution Semester' at American University, with over 200 affiliated colleges, offers students coursework focussing on peace and conflict resolution as well as internships in congressional offices and national offices of disarmament, development and human-rights organisations, including the Centre for Defense Information, Peace Links, Agency for International Development, SANE and others. The programme draws students from political science, international relations, peace studies and related fields. It is supported by a grant from the US Institute of Peace.

Public Universities

The 'Concentration in Social Conflict' in Sociology at the University of Colorado, Boulder, offers BA, MA, and PhD degrees focussing on the analysis, management and resolution of conflict within a framework of sociological theory and method. As with the Syracuse 'Program in Nonviolent Conflict and Change', this programme has established a national reputation for its effective mediation training programmes, applied research in conflict management and internships with peace organisations and dispute resolution centres.

The undergraduate 'Peace and Conflict Studies' programme at the

University of California, Berkeley, founded in 1984 by students and faculty, offers a Bachelor of Arts with courses in five categories: Social Change and World Order, International Conflict, Political Economy, Ethics and Ideology and Ecology. A wide range of electives are available including courses on regional conflict (Central America, South Africa, the Middle East, Philippines, etc.), US–Soviet relations, technology and doctrine of the arms race, non-violence, peace movements, economic planning for peace and other topics.

The Center for Peaceful Change at Kent State University, Ohio, describes itself as a 'living memorial' to the four students who were shot and killed in a Vietnam War protest in May 1970. The undergraduate major in 'Integrative Change' offers courses primarily focussed on non-violence, conflict resolution and theories of social change, with elective courses addressing issues of human rights, economic well-being and ecological balance (i.e., 'world-order values'). Kent State is one of the few peace studies programmes to have its own faculty.

The above listing is not by any means exhaustive but merely represents some of the more well-established programmes. The field is in a dynamic stage of growth and development. State and community colleges, adult-education programmes and teacher-training programmes are other settings in which new peace studies courses are being initiated.

Infrastructure of the Field

In addition to developing a body of theory and establishing teaching programmes in a subject, two other indicators that a recognised field has come into existence are (1) professional associations and (2) academic journals devoted to the subject. Along with administrative support provided by universities, professional associations and journals are essential elements in the field's 'infrastructure', support mechanisms that indicate the acceptance of the field into the academic community.

Peace studies programmes and peace research institutes share a common professional organisation: the International Peace Research Association (IPRA). However, peace studies and peace research have operated in part as separate communities, due to the fact that peace studies programme development often arises on an *ad hoc*

127

basis, according to the concerns of faculty and students. The peace research community, which is active primarily in Western Europe, has little direct contact with teaching programmes. In Western Europe, there are numerous peace institutes, but few peace studies programmes. Conversely, in the US, where most peace studies programmes exist, there are few peace institutes.[6]

The Consortium on Peace Research, Education and Development (COPRED) has evolved into the US–Canada branch of IPRA. Members of COPRED are also active in IPRA. But a difference exists in that COPRED aims at organising colleagues in the US and Canada, while IPRA is an international network. The IPRA Peace Education Commission (PEC), one of the many sub-groups within the organisation, has focussed its work more at the primary and secondary school level than at the university level. On the other hand, COPRED has two networks dedicated to peace education: the Primary/Secondary Peace Education Network and the University Peace Studies Network. Since its inception in 1971, the University Studies Network has functioned as a professional association for peace studies programmes in the US and Canada, offering consultation on programme development and updating lists of new programmes. Over the past few years, due to growth in the peace studies field, this network has taken on a high profile within COPRED.[7]

Like many peace studies programmes, COPRED was created during the turbulent days of the early 1970s. As described by Chad Alger, one of the founders of COPRED, the Vietnam War and 'turmoil on streets and campuses at home' led to the founding of COPRED as an organisation that could 'confront the irrelevance of

6. The International Peace Research Institute, Oslo (PRIO), established in 1959, was the first to identify itself specifically as a 'peace institute' and most of the better-known 'peace-institutes', designated as such, exist in Western Europe. In addition to PRIO, these include the Stockholm International Peace Research Institute (SIPRI); the Richardson Institute at the University of Lancaster, United Kingdom; and other institutes in Sweden, Finland, Denmark, Holland and Germany. Peace institutes also exist in the Soviet Union, and a number of other countries in Eastern Europe, Africa, Asia and Latin America. For a more complete listing see the *World Directory of Peace Research Institutions* (Paris, 1984). In the US, the Institute for Policy Studies and the World Policy Institute could be called peace institutes, but are not identified as such. The US Institute of Peace, established by act of Congress in 1984, is one of the few that identifies itself as a 'peace institute'.
7. For an overview of COPRED's activities see Chadwick Alger and Elise Boulder, 'From Vietnam to El Salvador: Eleven Years of COPRED', *Peace and Change*, vol. 7, no. 1, 1981, pp. 35–43.

peace research to peace activists, and the gap between our educational practice and the competencies required of citizens who would act effectively for peace'.[8] Since its inception, COPRED has thus attempted to provide a link between peace research, peace education and peace action.

The educational networks of COPRED and the Peace Education Commission of IPRA have benefited from the support of the United Nations Educational, Scientific and Cultural Organization (UNESCO). In 1963, UNESCO provided funding for the initiation of the IPRA newsletter, and in 1974 produced a recommendation on 'Education for International Cooperation and Peace', which made reference to university teaching as well as public school education. The Peace and Human Rights Division of UNESCO played an active role in promoting peace research and education during the late 1970s and early 1980s, conducting surveys on disarmament and peace education, sponsoring conferences, and publishing four editions of the *Yearbook on Peace and Conflict Studies* (1981–4). The role of UNESCO in promoting peace studies has waned in recent years due to the criticisms and conflicts it has been weathering, including the withdrawal of US support for its functions. The Peace and Human Rights Division of UNESCO still supports peace research projects at universities, but has no direct role in fostering the teaching of peace studies at universities. Nevertheless, part of UNESCO's *raison d'être* remains the fostering of education for peace throughout the world.[9]

With the assistance of another agency of the United Nations, the UN Institute for Training and Research (UNITAR), COPRED also published a comprehensive international survey of peace research. Other organisations which co-operate with COPRED include the International Studies Association, which established its own Peace Studies Section; the American Sociological Association, which created a section on the Sociology of World Conflict; and the

---

8. Chadwick Alger, 'Peace Studies at the Crossroads: Where Else?', paper presented at the Sixteenth Annual Conference of COPRED, Milwaukee, Wisconsin, November 1987, p. 1.
9. Interview of UNESCO Peace and Human Rights Division staff members by Carol Rank, UNESCO, Paris, September 1985. See also Nigel Young, 'The Contemporary Peace Education Movement', PRIO paper 6/83, Oslo, April 1983, pp. 3–5, and transcripts of a 1985 seminar by Elise Boulding and Nigel Young on 'UNESCO's Contribution to Peacemaking and Conflict Resolution', National Conference on Peacemaking and Conflict Resolution, George Mason University, Fairfax, Virginia.

Conference on Peace Research in History, a group of historians which initiated the journal *Peace and Change*.[10]

In addition to COPRED, another organisation which has played a central role in advancing the field is the World Policy Institute in New York (formerly the Institute for World Order). The WPI has published four editions of *Peace and World Order Studies: A Curriculum Guide* and, through the work of Mendlovitz, Falk, Johansen and others, has articulated the essential elements of 'peace and world order studies'. The WPI now concentrates more on Congressional lobbying than educational work and in 1988 handed on the task of compiling the curriculum guide to the National Curriculum Resources Project of the Five College Program in Peace and Security Studies, Amherst, Massachusetts.[11]

Another component of peace studies' 'infrastructure' is the publication of academic journals devoted to the subject. Major journals include the *Journal of Conflict Resolution* (Yale University), the *Journal of Peace Research* and the *Bulletin of Peace Proposals* (PRIO), *Peace Research Reviews* (Canadian Peace Research Institute), *Peace and Change* (Conference for Peace Research in History), and *Alternatives: A Journal of World Policy* (World Policy Institute). Other regular publications include the IPRA Newsletter and the COPRED Chronicle.[12]

Tensions in the Peace Studies Field

The 'infrastructure' of the peace studies field is becoming increasingly well established, with movement towards greater professionalisation and links with a wide range of organisations and academic disciplines. The field is developing rapidly, but still faces a number of obstacles to its further development. These include the following.

---

10. Alger and Boulding, 'From Vietnam to El Salvador', p. 39. The study sponsored by UNITAR was Juergen Dedring, *Recent Advances in Peace and Conflict Research: A Critical Survey*, Beverly Hills, Calif., 1976.
11. The last of these curriculum guides was Daniel Thomas and Michael Klare (eds.), *Peace and World Order Studies: A Curriculum Guide*, 5th edition, Boulder, Colo. 1989.
12. For a comprehensive overview of peace studies/peace research publications see Charles Chatfield, 'International Peace Research: The Field Defined by Dissemination', *Journal of Peace Research*, vol. 16, no. 2, 1979, pp. 163–79.

Definition of a Substantive Core

A common criticism of peace studies is that 'peace' is too vague a term to form the basis of a field. Some definitions of peace research and peace studies are so broad that this criticism does not seem unjustified. For example, as described by Marek Thee, a peace researcher of long-standing at PRIO:

> Peace research has expanded to encompass the study of armed conflict and conflict resolution, armaments and disarmament, underdevelopment and development, human deprivation and the realization of social justice, repressive violence and the realization of human rights. . . . Indeed, it has taken an aggressive interest in almost everything concerning the human condition and its betterment.[13]

Being concerned with 'almost everything concerning the human condition and its betterment' presents problems in defining a coherent course of study. When the definition of peace is expanded beyond the absence of war to the absence of all forms of direct and structural violence, the scope of enquiry becomes extremely broad and its boundaries unclear. Almost any discipline can be seen to offer relevant insights and, indeed, many peace studies faculty argue that the field should remain open to a variety of perspectives. As described by Alan Geyer, former director of the Colgate Peace Studies programme, for example, peace studies should have a 'wide range of vantage points from which to engage any and all disciplines at the points of their neglect and potential. . . . Every branch of learning has its own contributions to make to the intellectual and practical struggle for peace.'[14]

Should peace studies attempt to limit its scope and consolidate its interests into an integrated body of thought? Or should peace studies aim to 'infuse' a peace perspective into as many disciplines as possible? Ideally it can do both. While involving and contributing to a wide range of disciplines, it also needs to integrate the perspectives it encompasses and to further refine the definition of its theoretical core.

13. Marek Thee, 'The Scope and Priorities of Peace Research', paper prepared for Consultations on Peace Research, United Nations University, Tokyo, December 8–13, 1980, p. 4.
14. Alan Geyer, 'Doing Peace Studies in Universities and Seminaries', *Manchester College Bulletin of the Peace Studies Program*, vol. 7, no. 1, January 1977, p. 6.

Interdisciplinarity and Academic Politics

As described by one peace studies programme director, peace studies is 'at the mercy of existing university departments'.[15] Much of the success of peace studies programmes is dependent on the co-operation of established departments, both in terms of their granting time to faculty to participate in peace studies programme development and in their sponsorship of new, relevant courses.

Peace studies programmes commonly face the criticism that the study of peace is politically biased and therefore inappropriate in institutions dedicated to 'value-free' scholarship. According to the Harvard sociologist David Riesman, who taught in the now defunct Harvard peace studies programme, the programmes meet with opposition 'both because their concern is peace and because they are interdisciplinary – it's the combination that makes the problem so intractable'.[16]

While the strength of the peace studies field lies, in part, in new insights gained through the crossing of disciplinary boundaries, its weakness lies there as well, in terms of its needing a greater degree of curricular coherence and a stronger administrative base. Faculty engaged in interdisciplinary innovation, within universities fragmented along departmental lines, are moving against the mainstream in their attempts to foster co-operation among disciplines. Rewards and advancement in Academia are not meted out to those who attempt to break new ground. On the contrary, faculty who engage in such efforts jeopardise their standing within their home departments.

Despite official rhetoric as to the university's responsibility to foster this kind of education, peace studies programmes rarely are given the resources they need to establish a fully-fledged department with tenured faculty positions and courses of their own. Most programmes run on the voluntary and often unremunerated efforts of faculty members drawn from various departments.

Lack of administrative and financial support holds back the theoretical development of the field. When faculty must draw from

15. Duane Campbell, 'Peace Studies and Civic Responsibility in Higher Education', document on Peace/War Studies at California State University, Sacramento, pp. 2–3.
16. David Riesman, interview by Carol Rank at Harvard University, 30 December 1983. Cited in Carol Rank, 'The Study of Peace at Harvard University', unpublished paper, Harvard Graduate School of Education, March 1984.

existing courses to create a peace studies programme, their new programme may appear eclectic or ill-defined, and may then be criticised for lacking academic rigour. Peace studies programmes are often not given the support they need to establish themselves, yet are faulted for their weaknesses as they struggle to become established.

This lack of administrative support is endemic to the field and is one of the main obstacles to its further development. However, administrative obstacles are merely a reflection of a deeper problem, which is that the study of peace is perceived as ideologically biased.

Ideological Bias and Student Activism

In the words of one critic, peace studies is 'the academic liberal's latest effort to impose his brand of peace on an unwary student population'. According to Herbert London: 'In the 1920's, people who taught such nonsense at least had the courage to define their position as pacifism. Their views didn't masquerade as a new scholarly discipline. Now, however, some scholarship is in retreat before the onslaught of such religious zealots'.[17]

Like peace education in primary and secondary schools, university peace studies has been criticised as being political 'brainwashing'. In the US, Britain, Australia and other countries, where peace education has begun to flourish, governmental opposition has been strong. In the US, for example, peace education in public schools is now widespread, but met with a great deal of opposition in the early 1980s.[18] Likewise in Britain, peace studies at all levels of the educational system has been highly criticised.[19]

In accordance with the United Nations Charter, peace studies questions the right of states to use organised violence to promote national interests. Because of this orientation, peace studies has been called 'biased'. Johan Galtung, one of the founders of the peace research field, says that peace studies *is* 'biased' against war and seeks its abolition: 'There is nothing arcane or inane about that, it's

17. Herbert London, 'Peace Studies: Hardly Academic', *New York Times*, 5 March 1985, p. A27.
18. See *Education and the Threat of Nuclear War*, Harvard Educational Review, Reprint Series no. 18, Cambridge, Mass., 1985, which is a collection of articles on peace education in the US.
19. Caroline Cox and Roger Scruton, *Peace Studies: A Critical Survey*, London, 1982.

the same as the abolition of slavery and colonialism. . . . The abolition of war as a social institution means to deprive the state of its prerogative to wage wars, and the state doesn't like that.'[20]

The 'bias' of other fields towards an acceptance of 'legitimate' violence on the part of the state is usually not criticised or even questioned. For example, strategic studies, a component of international relations, is the study of how to effectively employ military means; violence is simply a given. Peace studies, on the other hand, enquires into the efficacy of non-violent means. According to peace studies proponents, implicit assumptions such as these should be examined and made explicit as a first step in the search for more peaceful alternatives.

Peace studies is no more 'biased' than any of the professional schools. Law schools aim to promote justice, just as schools of public health and social welfare aim to contribute to the public good. Schools of business promote profitable enterprise and schools of engineering are 'biased' toward the building of safe roads and bridges. All of these subject areas assume certain values (health, justice, etc.) and organise their research and teaching accordingly. As Professor John Hurst, former Chairperson of the Peace and Conflict Studies programme at the University of California, Berkeley, says:

> A normative commitment is inherent in all professional school programs, whether at the undergraduate or graduate level, by the very fact that they are professional. . . . Each program draws upon all available knowledge from relevant fields or disciplines to develop and advance professional practices in the direction of the profession's goals and/or values.[21]

Such a value-based orientation, while accepted without question in other fields, is problematic for peace studies. The more that peace studies programmes encourage students to actively work for peace, the more likely they are to be criticised as being 'biased'. The action-orientation of peace studies is seen as a form of advocacy which pollutes the academic purity of detached scholarship. Even

20. Johan Galtung, interview by Carol Rank, Dissertation Fellows Conference of the Institute on Global Conflict and Cooperation, University of California, Los Angeles, March, 1987.
21. John Hurst, 'Supplementary Report on the Peace and Conflict Studies Program', unpublished paper, University of California, Berkeley, 2 December 1986, p. 1.

amongst peace studies practitioners, there is debate as to the extent to which peace studies can or should educate not only 'about' peace, but 'for' peace.

Peacemaking versus Professionalisation

Another tension in the development of the peace studies field is the debate concerning professionalisation and academic 'legitimacy'. The history of COPRED is instructive in this regard. As described above, COPRED works to build co-operative networks between peace researchers, educators and activists, who might not otherwise work with one another. Interactions between people involved in these different aspects of peace work are seen as mutually enriching. Rather than the creation of a professional niche *per se*, COPRED has aimed at the creation of a supportive community of diverse practitioners. In that regard, COPRED has been very successful.

A sign of the dynamism and growth of the peace studies field is that a new Peace Studies Association, independent of COPRED, has now been formed. There is general consensus that this new association can work in co-operation with COPRED to further strengthen the peace studies field.

Some members of COPRED, however, have been wary of the potentially negative aspects of professionalisation: creation of an academic elite, competition, ownership of 'intellectual property', certification of experts, and so on, all of which can work against the maintenance of a supportive, 'peaceful' community of scholars and activists. Some feel that professionalisation of the field could mean that peace studies programmes will cut themselves off from peace activists, primary and secondary school teachers involved in peace education and others working for peace, thereby becoming an increasingly elite community of scholars, spinning theory without putting it into practice.[22]

Others argue that a professional organisation is needed to overcome the significant institutional and attitudinal barriers faced by the field. Although peace studies has begun to emerge as a recognised field, a professional association could help foster faculty and

---

22. For example, in a report on the 1987 COPRED annual meeting, the COPRED Peace Research Network listed as a priority: 'Do not professionalize COPRED, as this will empower some of us at the expense of the rest of us. Non-professionalization empowers us all more equally.' *COPRED Peace Chronicle*, vol. 12, no. 6, December 1987, p. 14.

programme development as well as increase funding and administrative support.

In any case, without institutional roots, the future of the field itself is in question. Ideally, peacemaking and professionalisation are not mutually exclusive. Professionalisation can mean that peace studies graduates are trained in practical skills which can be put to use in a variety of settings, from community dispute-resolution centres to international non-governmental organisations. The challenge in the coming years is, through whatever means, to strengthen and expand existing programmes and thereby further advance the field.

Peace Studies' Unfinished Agenda

Those aspects of peace studies which distinguish it as a field of study (e.g., its interdisciplinarity and its value-based pedagogy) are also the aspects which meet with the most opposition and are in danger of being co-opted. One aspect of peace studies which is particularly difficult to maintain is its global, non-violent perspective. There is a tendency both in peace studies programmes and in peace research to gravitate back to more 'legitimate' areas of enquiry, such as the security interests of states. In a 1972 article on the development of peace research, Elise Boulding points out that although the field was initiated by scholars who were 'consciously separating themselves from the older discipline of international relations' and looking for new ways of thinking, much of the early promise of the peace research revolt 'fizzled out as "the system" took over its new students'.[23]

In a rank ordering of preferred research areas in peace research journals and peace institutes (1972), Boulding notes that what is lacking in the 'top ten' list is 'the concept of transnationalism, integrative processes, and cross-cutting identities in the world community'. Economic, ideological and social injustice issues did not fit the categories very well; issues which failed to appear included attitude change, futures research, international non-governmental organisations (INGOs), and action-research, including the study of non-violence and social 'movements. What was preferred were

23. Elise Boulding, 'Peace Research: Dialectics and Development', *Journal of Conflict Resolution*, vol. 16, no. 4, 1972, pp. 469–75.

studies which pointed 'in one way or another to the issue of adjustment and repair versus radical reconstruction of the international system'.[24]

Nearly ten years later, Boulding and Alger again noted the tendency of the field to gravitate back toward more traditional perspectives. They suggested that peace researcher–teachers found themselves in a 'kind of trap'. Peace and world order studies aimed to be 'globalist', yet in surveying courses represented in the *Peace and World Order Studies Curriculum Guide*, it became clear that while overall the field reflected 'globalism, interdisciplinary problem-solving, futurism and policy-oriented analysis', most of the policy analysis was oriented to nation states, the 'anti-globalist units of the old order'.

Similar overviews of peace research reveal that target audiences for the research are usually national policymakers. In the Parker study of peace research institutes (1978), for example, only one respondent in the entire survey thought that regional and international (or transnational) organisations should be the target audience for peace research.[25]

The gap between 'realism' and 'idealism' remains. Peace studies aims to envision alternative futures, but is still weak in its analysis of how to move 'from here to there', without falling back into old ways of thinking. To become truly global, peace studies should work at identifying policy options for political actors at all levels, from the local community to the international arena. As Johan Galtung points out, peace research (and peace studies, defined as the teaching/learning of the findings of peace research) is research into the conditions of peace with peaceful means, done in a global and holistic manner. Peace studies in the US, he says, is still nationalistic in orientation, rather than global:

> Thus far, I have not found in U.S. peace studies much about peace, as opposed to studies of nuclear arms and 'arms control.' . . . The general peace concept in America is still some kind of pax americana. . . . What is missing almost totally in any teaching I have found in the U.S., be that in (mainstream) international studies or in (countertrend) peace studies, is

24. Ibid., p. 471.
25. Chadwick Alger and Elise Boulding, 'From Vietnam to El Salvador: Eleven Years of COPRED', *Peace and Change*, vol. 7, no. 1, 1981, pp. 35–43. See also Richard J. Parker, 'Peace Research: A Questionnaire-based Assessment', St Louis, Missouri, 1978.

an effort to develop a theory, or at least the concept of a more egalitarian world society, where all nations enter as good world citizens.[26]

The Swedish peace researcher, Hakan Wiberg, has also taken up this theme in relation to peace research. In a retrospective article describing the last twenty-five years of peace research,[27] he concludes that the area of peace research which has been least developed is how to attain 'peace through peaceful means'. Much of peace research has analysed the national security policies of states, criticising theories of deterrence, but not accomplishing much in terms of the analysis of how to eliminate structural violence and bring about peaceful change.

Reviewing the history of peace research, Wiberg notes that only one issue of the *Journal of Peace Research* was devoted to 'peaceful societies and what makes them peaceful', whereas most other issues related to 'non-peace and its causes'. For example, common areas of research included: (1) causes and costs of arms races, (2) causes of wars and other direct violence, and (3) how to end wars (e.g., through negotiation) or to prevent them (e.g., through world law, economic sanctions, etc.). Other areas, which received less attention and which are more oriented toward 'positive peace' include: (1) how to build a 'peace structure' in society (e.g., through economic conversion), (2) how to achieve peace at the micro-level (e.g., conflict resolution, socialisation), and (3) dynamics of peace movements (history, strategies, effects). The key unsolved area, he says, is how to bring about non-violent change and create peaceful societies.[28]

Consequently, part of peace studies' 'unfinished agenda' is to put greater emphasis on social change and alternative visions of a non-violent world order. According to Elise Boulding, areas of peace studies which are in need of further development are: (1) 'strategic nonviolence' and reconciliation, (2) 'global civic literacy', that is, competency in global networks, (3) the United Nations system, including the work of its sixty agencies, (4) competency regarding 'international orders', for example, NIO (New Infor-

26. Johan Galtung, 'Peace Studies in the U.S.: Six Deficits', *COPRED Peace Chronicle*, vol. 13, no. 2, April 1988, pp. 3–4.
27. Hakan Wiberg, 'What Have We Learned About Peace?', *Journal of Peace Research*, vol. 18, no. 2, 1981, pp. 111–48.
28. Ibid.

mation Order), and (5) envisioning the future and 'liberating the imagination'.[29]

These recommendations are again a plea for peace studies to live up to its potential. Peace studies should struggle to 'liberate the imagination' both in terms of political action and in terms of the time-frame under consideration. Most studies of the international system are so grounded in present realities and crises that they fail to develop a long-range vision of the future. Without a positive vision of a better future, we remain trapped in the confines of the present system.

Prospects for the Future

In his studies of higher education David Riesman has described the university as a 'kind of dreamscape for utopian and practical reformers' who project their notions of an ideal community on to the curriculum and who believe that education can change not only the lives of students, but the direction of society.[30] Peace studies is a continual effort to contribute towards a process of societal transformation which goes on over many generations. Faculty and students will come and go, but what they create on their campuses will, they hope, remain for the benefit of others.

Some argue that universities, like all societal institutions, merely replicate the social order and are too much a part of society to be effective in transforming it. Given this fact, what impact can peace studies have? As Paul Wehr and Michael Washburn pointed out in *Peace and World Order Systems: Teaching and Research*, the university, as a 'generator, articulator and transmitter of belief systems' can speed the process of social change: 'Significant portions of the university can be and are being changed. . . . We start from the belief that a self-transforming university is a necessary, though certainly not a sufficient, condition for societal transformation.'[31]

This is the aim of peace studies: to embody and put into practice

29. Elise Boulding, 'Peace Education as Peace Development', speech at COPRED Annual Meeting, November 1987.
30. Gerald Grant and David Riesman, *The Perpetual Dream*, Chicago, Ill., 1978, p. 5.
31. Paul Wehr and Michael Washburn, *Peace and World Order Systems: Teaching and Research*, Beverly Hills, Calif., 1976, pp. 6–7.

ideals of peace, to act as a catalyst for change within institutions of higher learning, and thereby to have an impact on the larger society. Peace studies as a field is still struggling to overcome administrative and ideological obstacles to its further development, but much progress has been made. With increased support, peace studies can continue long into the future, helping to redirect the intellectual resources of colleges and universities toward the challenge of building a more peaceful, just and ecologically sustainable world community.

7

Peace Education in Great Britain

Kevin Green

In the early 1980s peace studies was regarded by many as an extremely sensitive and controversial feature of the curriculum offered by schools. On the one hand there were establishment figures like Rhodes Boyson MP, an education minister, denouncing the subject as appeasement studies, supported by Harry Greenway MP, who declared it to be 'unadulterated unilateralism and pacifism'.[1] Both of their concerns were picked up by the Prime Minister, who used their complaints to carve out a club with which to beat so-called militant left-wing councils. On the other hand were academics like Rick Rogers, who similarly, though for different reasons, sought to emphasise what they saw as the growth of peace education. Rogers wrote that: 'peace education has quietly become a respected and widely taught school and college subject in the UK. . . . Two years ago peace education in Britain was on the periphery of mainstream schooling. The impetus gathered since then is beginning to shift it into the centre of schools' work.'[2]

These assertions were based on a number of high profile developments in the theory of peace education in the curriculum, notably the working party report in Nottinghamshire, and the Avon Peace Education Project which was instrumental in the publication in November 1983 of the Local Education Authority (LEA) document entitled 'Peace Education: Guidelines for Primary and Secondary Schools'.

The actual evidence for the existence of peace education in schools was thin on the ground and basically anecdotal in nature. The first major research in this area was done by Smoker and Rathenow whose work was based on the responses of LEAs to a

1. Hansard, 22 June 1982.
2. R. Rogers, 'Peace Studies', *Where*, no. 181, September 1982.

questionnaire about peace education.[3] They reported that peace studies was included in the curriculum of schools to a very significant level, concluding that: 'if direct and indirect peace studies are lumped together, 63.9% of Labour authorities and 58.8% of Conservative authorities reported including peace studies in their curriculum. This finding is of some interest since it suggests that peace studies in some form is part of the curriculum in the majority of schools.' This report was worked on by Cox and Scruton, who opposed the introduction of peace education and reinterpreted the Smoker and Rathenow findings to argue that politically biased teaching was being practised.[4] The Cox and Scruton critique of peace education was based on very limited and highly anecdotal evidence, and took little or no account of harder evidence offered by the schools' inspectorate, which maintained that the claims made by Cox and Scruton were 'wholly uncharacteristic' of evidence collected by Her Majesty's Inspectors on school visits. In fact, it was doubted by the government inspectorate whether peace studies was prominent as a separate subject.[5]

The views of these academics and politicians seemed rather odd to most practising teachers, whose experience told them that peace studies was not gaining significant ground in their schools. In fact it proved almost impossible to find schools which included peace studies as part of their curriculum. Paradoxically this did not necessarily imply that schools were not developing their curricula along lines appropriate for educating for peace. Rather, it reflected the extent to which the debate about 'peace studies' had been hijacked by politicians and academics, who were defining the subject too narrowly at best, and, at worst, constructing their own version of the subject in order to attack it.

To the extent that non-educationalists were setting the agenda for the debate about peace studies, and to which they asserted that they were discussing the development of a new and separate subject on the curriculum, then peace studies did not, and does not, exist to a discernable degree in British schools. However, it is important to distinguish clearly between 'peace studies' as a subject and 'educating for peace' as a process which is cross-curricular and which

---

3. P. Smoker and F. Rathenow, *Education for Peace: Some Results of a Survey*, Lancaster, 1983, p. 20.
4. C. Cox and R. Scruton, *Peace Studies: A Critical Survey*, London, 1984.
5. Evidence to Wakefield Metropolitan District Council Working Party on Peace Education, 1984.

permeates both the open and the hidden curricula, involving as Haavelsrud pointed out, 'knowing, imagining, deciding and acting'.[6] It is this latter definition of peace education which underpins the progress that has been made in British schools, yet it has been peace studies as defined by non-educationalists which has become the stalking horse for this approach to education. Thus it is important for those interested in this area to sharpen up their understanding of the concept of peace as it is actually being applied, explicitly and implicitly in our schools.

An important contribution to this clarification has been made by O'Connell, who in his inaugural lecture, 'Towards an Understanding of Concepts in the Study of Peace', outlines the differences between the concepts of positive and negative peace, the former consisting of 'willing cooperation between persons for social and personal goals', the latter merely implying the absence of physical, psychological or moral violence. It is towards the former ideal that the aims of peace education are directed. However that does not mean to say that negative peace is not to be desired; it is, in fact, with positive peace, an integral part of the whole concept of peace itself. Positive peace, however, is the dynamic process which is approachable through education, reflecting as it does positive attitudes and values which, celebrating and facilitating freedom and justice, two other states that O'Connell asserts to be fundamental to the fulfilment of human potential, may be striven for within the community of the school.

O'Connell puts great emphasis on this further concept of community in his discussion of peace. This he describes as a sense of belonging to persons, and of sharing objectives with them. It is an essential constituent of peace since it creates co-operation and denies violence as a way of solving the conflicts that necessarily crop up in human society. Thus the task of peace educators is to create a sense of community within schools but also to widen the pupils' sense of that community with which they can identify.[7] Prasad makes a similar point when he asserts the need for individuals to act co-operatively to bring about social harmony.[8]

Thus, to sum up, peace is a concept which involves positive values

6. M. Haavelsrud (ed.), *Education for Peace: Reflection and Action*, Guildford, p. 250.
7. James O'Connell, 'Towards an Understanding of Concepts in the Study of Peace', in J. O'Connell and A. Curle (eds.), *Peace with Work To Do: The Academic Study of Peace*, Leamington Spa, 1985.
8. D. Prasad, 'Peace Education or Education for Peace', unpublished paper held at the Commonweal Library, University of Bradford, 1981, p. 26.

of freedom and justice. It is far more than the absence of violence, and as such cannot be sustained by violence. As Einstein remarked: 'Peace cannot be kept by force. It can only be achieved by understanding.'

Put simply, therefore, peace education is one of the ways in which it is hoped that the understanding referred to by Einstein might be achieved. However, depending as it does on the attainment of values and the desire for and the ability to achieve a sense of community, a successful programme of peace education would involve more than the achievement of understanding, but would need to encompass three major areas of educational practice. These might be summarised as follows:

1. The acquisition of relevant knowledge.
2. The development of values and attitudes appropriate to peace.
3. The development of relevant skills.

These areas would be explored in terms of an examination of the roots of conflict, and the causes of violence: within individuals, in personal relationships and within the societies of home, school, community, nation and globe, together with a search for understanding and harmony also within those relationships, in history, during the present time, and for the future.

Education for peace, therefore, is a very broad and extremely complex matter, which moreover, is not the only perspective of its kind that may inform curricular and classroom practice. It is part of a wide 'family' of subjects which, including multi-cultural education, development education, human rights education, environmental education, world studies and so on, has much to offer. Derek Heater has argued that this spread of activity and interest can be too daunting, and that those who wish to promote what UNESCO has recently described under the portmanteau label 'Education for International Understanding, Cooperation and Peace, and Education Relating to Human Rights and Fundamental Freedoms' are working on too broad a front.[9] Others see this wide spread of superficially different subjects working in the same educational area to be positively beneficial, as they allow a certain flexibility of 'political' approach to the subject, so that in an area where peace education might be frowned on (for example, in Bradford where an

9. D. Heater, *Peace Through Education: The Contribution of the CEWC*, Brighton, 1984.

influential councillor commented about a schools' peace festival that he hoped it was the 'right sort of peace') very much the same sort of activity might continue under the title of 'Education for Citizenship', and so on. Robin Richardson and Dave Hicks have stressed the interelatedness of the family of subjects mentioned above. Hicks, for example, identifies the areas of cohesion between them. He has denoted four basic approaches, each with what he calls a central focussing idea. These four approaches (Development Education, World Studies, Multicultural Education and Peace Studies) raise in turn the organising concepts of development, interdependence, cultural diversity and peace.[10]

Heater gives a list of objectives to which all the members of the family of subjects related to education for peace would subscribe:[11]

1. Knowledge about the world or mankind as a whole. A global dimension to school subjects.
2. Awareness of the inter-relatedness of the modern world. A viewing of problems on a global dimension; an understanding of the systematic nature of the contemporary world and the experiences that mankind have in common.
3. Appreciation that people have rights and duties towards each other and that even the pursuit of self interest necessitates co-operation.
4. Consciousness that one's own perspective on world issues and other peoples is biased by one's own cultural background.
5. Empathy – the ability to view other societies from their own perspectives, and one's own society from the perspectives of others.
6. Appreciation of others; sympathy for the plight of the unfortunate; regard for the achievement of the creative.
7. Skills to understand the rapidly changing world, and to make critical judgements from a mass of information.
8. Ability to communicate with others across cultures both without prejudice in oneself, and to combat prejudice in others.
9. Readiness to act in a responsible way to help resolve world problems.

10. Evidence to Wakefield MDC Working Party, 1984.
11. D. Heater, *World Studies: Education for International Understanding in Britain*, London, 1980, p. 38.

The great breadth of the above curriculum guideline clearly suggests that peacefulness is something which cannot be taught in the traditional sense of the word, a point made by Read, who, in an early study, maintained that moral self-discipline was as important as intellectual virtues.[12] For issues of peace and harmony are not limited to a narrow body of knowledge; they involve process as well as content. Education for peace can only be fully effective when the hidden curriculum is taken equally into account with the open curriculum, and even where this is done schools may only partially tackle the problem, since the school is only a small part of the overall experience of its pupils.

That being said, schools do have a responsibility to assist their pupils to come to an understanding of the world for which they will ultimately assume responsibility; in this respect knowledge is important. However, they must also ensure that the pupils are equipped with the skills to take a part in effecting social change, and they ought to be aware of the advantages of a society which permits peaceful change. In fact, one of the advantages of schools as the places where such education takes place, is that they should be places where difficult issues which will need to be faced in adulthood may be rehearsed by students in a consciously and carefully structured objective manner.

In order to understand how this might be achieved it is necessary to make clear what form peace education takes in schools. The first thing is to make clear the distinction between 'peace studies' and 'education for peace', at least in so far as that distinction is perceived by schools and teachers who are working in this field. Peace studies is usually envisaged as a spot on the curriculum in which knowledge relevant to an understanding of peace and peaceful relationships is imparted. Peace studies, therefore, tends to be about the instruction of a fairly specific body of knowledge which may be dealt with in a fairly formal way. This way of dealing with the subject of peace in schools is, however, very rare. Most of the schools that have decided to attempt an approach to the subject prefer to allow a peace perspective to be a feature of a wide area of the curriculum. They have developed education for peace, which is, in many important ways, much more radical than peace studies, which as a single slot in the timetable runs the risk of being marginalised or

---

12. Sir H. Read, *Education for Peace*, London, 1950.

becoming just another increasingly academically based subject to be absorbed by the pupils.

At its best, education for peace asks the question of what might constitute a peaceful person: one who would be able to contribute towards the development of a peaceful family, society or nation, and ultimately a peaceful world; that is, a person and a world committed to those three elements of peace, freedom and justice which are the hallmarks of positive peace along the lines outlined by O'Connell. Education for peace, therefore, does not look so much at the content of the curriculum in isolation, but considers the roles of the three elements of attitudes, skills and knowledge that I referred to earlier. There is also a need to develop an appropriate methodology to achieve these goals.

In the days when and in those institutions where education was seen merely as the transmission of knowledge, and the role of the learner was merely to memorise facts and opinions long enough to regurgitate them in an examination room, then it was sufficient to have a one-way relationship between teacher and pupil. Education for peace, however, cannot be satisfied with this relationship, because the criterion for success for the peace educator is not merely how much have the pupils learned, but how much have they come to understand what they have learned, and how much are they able to criticise the knowledge that they have made their own. To achieve this the teacher needs to lead the pupils as partners, within the limitations of their respective roles, in the educational task, and thus to run the risk of undermining her or his authority. The peace educator's task is to enable her or his pupils to rely much more on their own opinions (and to do all possible to make those opinions reliable). She or he therefore needs to create an educational environment that stimulates the expression of those opinions in a thoughtful way, and gives them value. The basic mode of education for peace, therefore, is dialogue and discussion. As Wren observes, we cannot talk to our students about justice, equality and peace and then expect them to be the passive recipients of what we say.[13]

Thus educators for peace have to be aware of the hidden messages in their classroom practice: do they ask closed questions; are the statements that they make really open to question and debate; do they allow the expression of opinions opposite to their own merely then to imply that, though acceptable, they are wrong; do they

13. B. Wren, *Education for Justice*, London, 1977.

persist with an organisation of the classroom furniture which emphasises the dominance of their position; do they insist on the right
to decide when a subject is fully discussed and when the class should
move on to something else (usually when the argument is 'getting
out of hand')? Teachers probably all do some of these, either
unwittingly or as part of their survival technique! But these are
practices that the committed peaceful teacher should try to eliminate. I say 'try to' with reason; one of the great stumbling blocks to
the expansion of peace education is not that of political opposition,
nor that of fear of indoctrination, nor that of academic disrepute,
but simply that it is extremely difficult to do!

David Hicks discusses the methodology involved in teaching for
peace in the following way:

> To teach *about* peace, to study it, does not necessarily imply a particular
> way of going about it. To teach *for* peace, however, and this is the sense
> in which the term peace education is generally used, means that the
> teaching/learning situation created must involve cooperation, partici-
> pation, dialogue and self reliance. . . . This stress on teaching method is a
> reminder that the goal of peace cannot be achieved by unpeaceful means.
> The process and the goal must be indistinguishable. This must apply to
> ourselves, our relationships with our colleagues and our students, as well
> as the way we teach.[14]

Thus the ways in which one teaches will be varied. There will be,
for example, the need to teach quite formally on occasion if one is
trying to instruct in a skill or to impart some factual information.
However, all the time one needs to stress the partnership between
teachers and the pupils and to emphasise the importance and validity of their input to the teaching/learning process that both
teacher and pupils are unfolding together. The basis of all of this is
trust, and the sensitivity and commitment of the teacher and the
pupils to establishing a peaceful classroom. However, there are a
number of classroom strategies that it might be useful to mention.

1. *Breaking the Ice* Many of the classroom activities involved in
   peace education involve a positive input from the pupils. It
   makes sense, then, at the start of lessons to involve the students
   in a short game or similar activity in which they all may take

---

14. D. Hicks, 'Education for Peace: What does it Mean?', Occasional Paper no. 1,
    Centre for Peace Studies, St Martin's College, Lancaster, 1982, p. 8.

part. This will relax them and encourage participation and interaction.

2. *Co-operative Games*   These are 'fun' exercises in working
together and can be developed for more 'serious' use as the
pupils become more co-operative through experience. Good
examples of these may be found, for instance, in the excellent
Gamesters Handbook.[15]

3. *Brainstorming*   This is an excellent way to stimulate discussion
as well as a free flow of ideas. Simply, a topic (usually phrased as
a question – e.g., What does PEACE mean to you?) is chosen
and members of the class call out all the ideas that come to mind
in about ten minutes or so. These are written on the blackboard
(or whatever) and can form the basis of later discussion.

4. *Rounds*   The aim of a round is to involve everybody in the class
in an activity. Often a round may follow a brainstorm when each
person in turn is asked to answer the same question: 'The most
important/unusual/funny/ridiculous (etc.) word in the brainstorm is..... because............'

5. *Role Play*   The aim of role play is to enable pupils to clarify
their own views about situations, and to see other points of view.

6. *Simulations*   Simulations are an extended form of role play in
which students play out real or imaginary situations (dealing
with conflict, violence, war, their after-effects, etc.)

7. *Small Group Discussions*   A number of activities will involve the
need for discussion work to go on. This is best achieved in small
groups. The smaller the group the better, but no groups should
exceed five in number if everyone is to be able to play a part.

8. *Self-Directed Individual or Group Projects*   At some time the
pupils should be enabled to work on their own, researching their
own topics and presenting their work in ways that they decide to
the whole group. This requires a high degree of organisation on
the leader's part to ensure that the timetable is flexible enough.

This is by no means an exhaustive list; it is only a guide to the
kinds of things that might be done in the peaceful classroom. Other
things might include an intersubject project, involving team-
teaching perhaps; the introduction of group planning and decision-
making for the class; community action outside the classroom; and
many more initiatives. The important thing, perhaps, is not what

15. D. Brandes and H. Phillips, *Gamesters' Handbook*, London, 1979.

teachers do, but that they engage in activities that place value on the contribution being made by the pupils.

It is, however, important to recognise that many of the methods and skills outlined above are used by teachers who have not been influenced by education for peace. Indeed much is going on in classrooms today which may not be consciously peace-oriented but which is totally consistent with a peaceful approach to education, and this resource of sympathetic expertise needs to be made more of.

The Content of Peace Education

Peace education is in no sense the prerogative of the secondary school system, although since much of the debate about the validity of the subject has been concentrated around its assumed political content it has been associated with the secondary curriculum. In many ways the opposite is the case and the more important work on attitude formation, affirmation, conscientisation and so on is being tackled in the primary and even the nursery sectors of education. Thus it is important to make the case that education for peace may take place at all levels of the education system, but that its content will be designed to be appropriate for the conceptual and emotional development to be expected amongst children of different ages. Nursery and infant children can be introduced to the idea of being friendly and helpful to fellow classmates and should be encouraged to have respect for others. They should also learn about other children's lives in other parts of the world in a respectful manner and be made aware of the problems that are related to peace in the world: poverty, anger, oppression, and so on. Poems, songs, stories, pictures will play an important part in education for peace at this level.

At primary/junior level more practical work can be done, perhaps rooted in the local community, to show the interdependence of peoples, and this area should be expanded as the children's knowledge widens, to include the nation and international co-operation. This development of a cognitive framework for world understanding should go hand-in-hand with a continuing programme of effective teaching.

Instruction in issues of peace and development should continue at the secondary level with emphasis being placed on affirming positive attitudes already possessed by the pupils. At this stage the curriculum should become much more flexible, to allow students to follow up their own interests. At this stage the role of the teacher shifts to that of provider both of information and, crucially, of skills – critical skills, analysis, research, respect for argument based on evidence, and so on.

What emerges from all this is that the curriculum content of peace education goes far beyond a list of areas of knowledge that such a perspective on the curriculum might encompass. Any guide to the suggested curriculum content of peace education should pay as much attention to the skills and attitudes that peace educators try to develop in their students as it does to the areas of knowledge that should be included.

David Hicks and Simon Fisher have looked at the relationship between the different elements which should make up a curriculum in 'world studies'.[16] They identified four major themes – Harmony and Conflict, Welfare, Justice and Equality and Concern for the Environment – as being central issues for education for peace. Each of these themes could be examined with reference to related areas of knowledge, skills and attitudes. Figure 7.1 illustrates this relationship. One of the important things that the figure points up is the quite small extent to which education for peace is limited by a fixed-knowledge element. This area may be related to most easily by teachers of History, Geography, Economics and Religious Studies in varying degrees, but the much wider content areas of skill, attitude and conceptual development are very much open to teachers of all subjects.

The development of positive skills and attitudes is important since, as has been previously indicated, practitioners of education for peace have moved away from the view that the cognitive elements of the subject are of prime importance towards a realisation of the central place of method and structure in peace education. They have also increasingly been interested in the process by which peaceful educational experiences might produce peaceful citizens, parents – peaceful people in the future. Thus the attention of peace educators is now focussed on the attitudes that would typify a peaceful person as well as the skills such a person would need to create and maintain a peaceful world – something that

---

16. D. Hicks and S. Fisher, *Planning and Teaching World Studies – an Interim Guide*, Lancaster, 1981, p. 44.

Figure 7.1 A Checklist for Peace Education

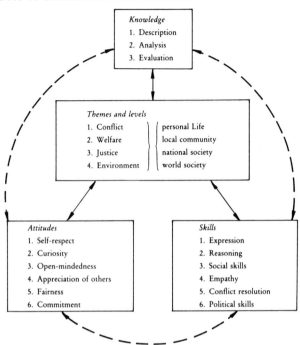

Source: D. Hicks, 'Studying Peace: The Educational Rationale', Occasional Paper no. 4, Centre for Peace Studies, St Martin's College, Lancaster.

would require that person to have the capacity and the willingness not just to think and to react peacefully, but also to act peacefully, and to be empowered to affect the community and ultimately the world in which she or he would live. Pikas puts this very well when describing the two main tasks of peace education in the following way:

1. To teach and learn to live in positive peace when this is present.
2. To teach and learn to manage and resolve crises and conflicts in cases where positive peace is in danger or non-existent.[17]

17. A. Pikas, 'The Concept of Peace Meets Educational Necessities', Occasional Paper no. 11, Uppsala University, 1974, p. 5.

For Pikas, then, the primary role of the peace-oriented teacher is to teach pupils communication skills in response to crises and conflicts, something which also implies the development of attitudes which will ensure that the skills being taught are actually called upon.

Graham Pike also writes about the importance of developing cognitive skills appropriate to peace, arguing that the world citizen's likely increased breadth of experience would demand not so much a greater depth of knowledge as 'a wider range of skills'. He anticipates the need for two overlapping kinds of skills: 'those which are needed to understand and respond to the conflicts and contradictions of everyday life, which might be called the "instructive skills", and secondly the "constructive skills" necessary for making a positive contribution in any area of life'.[18]

To sum up, therefore, the development of relevant skills is central to the task of the peace educator. The skills which should be developed are of three basic kinds:

1. Those which promote harmonious relationships: co-operative skills, empathy, conflict resolution skills, communication skills.
2. Those which enhance undestanding: research skills, critical awareness, analysis, logical reasoning, self-direction.
3. Those which make individuals effective: political skills, negotiating skills, affirmation skills, and so on.

In practice much of the development of these skills would be experiential, depending to some extent on the hidden curriculum. However, it is useful for teachers to be aware of the need to develop these skills so that classroom experiences may be structured towards the goal expressed by Devi Prasad that education should 'liberate the individual from destructive aggression'.[19]

Attitudes, too, are of vital importance to education for peace. Many of the underlying attitudes necessary for this approach are implied by the skills that have already been mentioned. Thus students need to be critically aware, but open-minded in their approach to ideas; they should value truth and honesty; be aware of their own worth, and the worth of other people of other nations,

18. G. Pike, 'Education for Peace: Some Implications and Classroom Proposals', paper presented to Wakefield MDC Working Party, 1984.
19. Prasad, 'Peace Education', p. 19.

cultures or political or religious persuasion; they should value freedom and justice; and should have a proper regard for democratic process at local, national and international levels.

Much of the development of these attitudes will again be experiential. One cannot successfully teach formally about values when the experience of those being taught is inconsistent with what is being imparted. One can't talk seriously of the need for mutual esteem between states when there is precious little similar regard between teachers and pupils. This is not to say that both these groups of individuals have equal roles within schools, but education for peace may only be successful within a teaching structure which avoids dominance. Johan Galtung makes this point forcibly, arguing that: 'Peace education . . . should not just be about peace; it ought to be peace.'[20] Thus, although there should be a necessary role differentiation between teacher and student at all levels of education, a peace education perspective would imply that the relationship between teacher and pupil should not be structured by dominance imposed through physical, mental or moral violence.

As has already been remarked, the main thrust of peace education in recent times has been behind attitude and skill development, with teaching for peace rather than teaching about it. Nevertheless one is obliged to agree with Graham Pike's assertion that knowledge is important for peace education since the root of much that is wrong with the world is ignorance. But what kind of knowledge is appropriate for peace education, and what should we hope to achieve by teaching it?

One source of suggestions as to the possible content of education for peace has been UNESCO. In 1976, at its Paris session, the General Conference of UNESCO issued its Recommendation Concerning Education for International Understanding, Cooperation and Peace which listed the major problems of mankind that all students should have taught to them. These were as follows:

1. Equality of rights of people.
2. Maintenance of peace; types of war; disarmament.
3. Action to ensure the observance of human rights.
4. Economic growth and social development.
5. Conservation of natural resources.

20. J. Galtung, 'Peace Education Problems and Conflicts', in Haavelsrud (ed.), *Education for Peace*, pp. 64–98.

6. Preservation of the cultural heritage of mankind.
7. The role of the UN in solving such problems.

In themselves these suggestions are not particularly remarkable. For example they reflect the tendency, noted by Galtung, for the content of peace education courses to centre on the problems of peace (which Galtung states to be: violence, economic inequality, social injustice, problems of the environment) and to omit reference to conflict formation.[21] They avoid placing the problems within their political contexts, teaching instead about 'problems' in isolation.

What does make the UNESCO recommendations interesting is that they were acceded to by representatives of the UK government and were the subject of an approving Department of Education and Science circular (9.76) to local education authorities expressing the government's confidence that 'the response from this country will be shown to be both sympathetic and constructive', although no fiscal assistance was proposed to help to bring about the positive response about which such conviction existed.

Local Education Authority initiatives also have a bearing on what might be considered as an appropriate knowledge content for peace education. Rathenow and Smoker found that local education authorities in the United Kingdom ranked the topics that should be covered in peace studies courses as follows:

1. Violence and war;
   The nuclear arms race.
2. International understanding;
   International integration and conflict;
   Aggressive tendencies in human nature.
3. Disarmament;
   Discrimination against minorities;
   Group conflicts.
4. Non-violent action.
5. Inequality.
6. Defence policy.
7. Personal freedom;
   Group dynamics.

21. J. Galtung, 'On Peace Education', in C. Wulff (ed.), *Handbook on Peace Education*, Frankfurt/Main and Oslo, 1974, pp. 153–72.

8. Environmental damage;
   Cultural integration.
9. The distribution of social commodities;
   Structural violence.

However, all of the responses to the Rathenow and Smoker survey came from LEAs rather than from practising teachers.[22] Also all of the topics mentioned above were prompted by the questionnaire, so there is room for argument about whether the list is in any way exhaustive, and whether the ranking actually reflects the relative importance given to these issues in the classroom.

In order to explore this idea, I offered to the LEAs a list of aims for peace education which balanced within it three component parts: skills, attitudes and knowledge. What emerged as a possible hypothesis from the results of the ranking of aims for peace education was that the content aspect of peace studies is regarded as of no more significance than the areas of skill and attitude development. Although the sample was small, by a significant margin the teaching of conflict-resolving skills emerged as the most important aim for peace education, something that was especially true for those authorities that identified peace education with the primary as well as the secondary sector of education. Indeed, the interesting thing about the rankings was that the issue which is most identified with peace studies by its critics, that is, Nuclear Arms and Disarmament, was regarded by the respondents as the least important of the aims for peace education. The most important area of content identified was that of learning about other societies and cultures.

The rankings which emerged from the questionnaire, which was responded to by a variety of individuals, including advisers, inspectors and officers of LEAs, are reproduced in table 7.1.

It seems to be the case that a growing number of teachers and schools have educational aims and practise educational methods which are in sympathy with those of peace educators. This latter fact was emphasised by the result of the ranking exercise of aims for peace education, where there had clearly been a movement away from a concentration on the cognitive and towards the affective elements of peace education. This movement was also indicated by the results obtained from LEAs when they responded to a question which asked about their preferred curriculum strategy for peace

22. Rathenow and Smoker, *Education for Peace: Some Results of a Survey*, p. 28.

Table 7.1 What are Peace Studies? Subject Ranking by LEAs

Rank	Peace education aims	Average ranking
1	Teaching conflict-resolving skills	2.4
2	Realisation of human interdependence	3.6
3	Promoting active learning	3.7
4	Learning about other societies and cultures	5.2
5	Explaining roots of conflict	5.5
6	Helping students to be more peaceful	5.7
7	Violence and war	6.1
8	Learning about human nature	6.3
	Racism and other forms of discrimination	6.3
9	Nuclear arms and disarmament	6.8

Source: K. L. Green, 'Education for Peace in the United Kingdom, M. Phil. Thesis, University of Bradford.

Table 7.2 What is the Most Appropriate Curriculum Strategy for Peace Studies?

Curriculum strategy	LEA preference (%)
A separate subject	0
Integrated across the curriculum	4 (12%)
Integrated, and by the 'hidden' curriculum	9 (28%)
In tutorial time by class tutor	5 (16%)
By project work only	1 (3%)
As is appropriate for the school	1 (3%)
No clear answer	12 (38%)
Total:	32 (100%)

Source: K. L. Green, 'Education for Peace in the United Kingdom, M. Phil. Thesis, University of Bradford, 1986, p. 66.

education: should it be a separate subject on the school timetable or handled in some other way? The responses to this question are summarized in Table 7.2

No authority preferred peace education to be a separate subject on the timetable, the great majority preferring a whole school approach involving, logically, the involvement of the great majority of the teaching staffs of schools. Such a strategy would not, of course, be able to rely on the specific expertise of a number of specialist teachers in schools, but would call on the skills, commitment and awareness of the subject of teachers of all disciplines for success.

Other topics of factual content that are certainly part of education for peace teaching include learning about peaceful people in History: for example, Gandhi, Pierre-Marie Theas, Edith Cavell; learning about specific conflict situations: for example, Northern Ireland, the Middle East, South America, South Africa. The potential factual content of education for peace is extremely broad. There is a great strength in the diversity of this potential knowledge content of education for peace since it does provide numerous opportunities for teachers of many disciplines to develop a strong peace perspective in their teaching. History, geography and social science teachers have, as Connell suggests,[23] an important role to play in peace education, but to concentrate too strongly on these areas of the curriculum which tend to deal with substantive issues is to run the risk of allowing peace to become just another area of knowledge to be acquired and not necessarily acted upon. Promoting a peace perspective on the whole of the curriculum helps to emphasise the idea that such a perspective is appropriate for all areas of life, and is not merely about dealing with substantive problems, however real. Connell does make this clear when he lists areas of study appropriate to the secondary level, and when he argues that these studies are appropriate to the achievement of lasting peace:

1. **Human relations**, e.g. co-operation and competition, group dynamics, nature of negotiation, community participation, moral and social obligation;
2. Analysis of social institutions, **structures**, and structural change, e.g. structures of governments of different kinds, social class, social and economic institutions within communities and across communities, nationality and nation states, news media, international organisations;
3. Analysis of **ideas** and social policies, e.g. social justice, peace, power, development, the making of public policy, international law;
4. Analysis of **conflict** and conflict mediation, e.g. history of modern war, class struggle, revolution, character of aggression, nature of present conflicts, methods of mediation;

23. W. Connell, 'Curriculum for Peace Education', *The New Era*, vol. 64, no. 1, 1983.

5. The planning of **non-violent social change**, e.g. equality of opportunity, mass participation, creative role of education, possible outcomes of social change.[24]

To sum up, therefore, the content of education for peace is potentially huge, but it does not necessarily mean the inclusion on the school curriculum of what might be seen as an increasing number of new 'educations'. Rather, it offers new perspectives on traditional areas of the existing school curriculum. It can also form a natural part of the National Curriculum, not as a separate subject on the timetable, but in the way in which teachers prefer to deal with it at the present time: as a cross-curricular issue. The Report of the Records of Achievement, National Steering Committee, which was published in January 1989 identifies a number of skills and themes which should be developed across the curriculum. This preliminary list includes such issues as working with others, personal qualities, economic awareness, environmental issues, media studies and health education, all of which could be related to peace issues.

24. Ibid.

8

Peace Research, Peace Studies and Peace as a Profession: Three Phases in the Emergence of a New Discipline

Johan Galtung

My thesis is very simple: after research comes studies in the sense of education; after education comes professionalisation. Occasionally this sequence is run backwards, usually with less than fortunate consequences. Often the process is stopped, curtailed or castrated, after phase 1 or phase 2. This is not necessarily with bad consequences, but what a waste! If research serves to accumulate a lot of knowledge then it should definitely be communicated to others; that is, if it is of any value or solidity. And this is very much a two-way traffic, as any academic person knows. It takes much research to build up a body of knowledge sufficiently coherent to be taught. One simple reason for this is buried in the word coherent: researchers place lights in the desert; education requires some light also in the dark places. Education may set agendas for research in order to fill in the gaps. Students will ask: 'but what if ——' and the answer 'Nobody has looked into that yet' will not satisfy anybody.

The same can be said for professionalisation. If researchers are writers who also turn into talkers as teachers, and like students who presumably also listen, then professionals are doers. Of course all three should be all four: but there is a difference in emphasis. We would not necessarily expect a peace researcher to go out into the field and really try to do peace, however much he or she may want a contract to write about how to do it. Nor would we necessarily expect a peace professional to write a first-rate research piece, however much he or she might love to be invited to a think-tank 'to write up their experiences', although UNITAR often serves this function, and countless US think-tanks and universities use professionals this way. Very useful, but not always very deep.

Professionalisation is the logical consequence of research with a clear value focus, such as health research (medicine) and peace research. In the day-to-day workings of research, pursuing themes into the darkest corners and beyond, not to mention below, the purpose of the whole exercise is easily lost. And the purpose of peace research is, of course, not only to understand better the conditions for peace, but to do something about it. In high-flown terms, which can stand repetition: the purpose of peace research is exactly the same as the purpose of the peace movement, that is, *the abolition of war as a social institution*. And, beyond this: peace research should contribute to more conviviality on this planet.

At this point something might be said about the nature of social science knowledge. It differs from natural science knowledge, at least the way that the latter is currently conceived, in a very significant way. Schematically the difference can be put like this. The natural scientist discovers his or her laws and then verifies them; the social scientist chooses his or her laws and then, in praxis, searches for the conditions under which they become true. A good example is 'modern' (i.e., neo-classical) economics. Example of a law chosen: 'Human beings act always in their own self-interest.' One condition under which this law becomes true is very frequent propagation of the law; another is through structuring the economy in such a way that individuals can operate in the economic system, as producers, distributors and consumers. The natural scientist assumes a rigid reality and tests singular hypotheses; the social scientist assumes a very flexible reality and searches for coherence in a web of interrelated propositions – a 'peace system', for instance, or 'conflict-solving capacity'.

As a consequence, the borderline between research, study and praxis becomes less clear. There is so much to study, everything is interrelated and hangs together; all experiences are somehow relevant. Peace research and peace study go sideways rather than in depth at a single point; they who think that is the way will soon be disappointed. More is gained by knowing the conditions that favour research and development of, for example, destructive technologies than by knowing the details of these technologies. Correspondingly, more is gained by knowing the broad circumstances of successful negotiations than by knowing in detail what happened on the way from the first draft to the final and adopted text. It all calls for a synergy between the atomistic knowledge possessed by the researcher, the superficial but broad knowledge acquired by the student and the holistic knowledge (called 'experience') developed in praxis by the professional.

Concretely, what I am saying is this: the time has come really to move on. We have done enormous amounts of research in these years. Peace research, however defined, has served to unleash productive research in quite a lot of people. I do not think it is so difficult to identify two clear sources of that productivity: the international and the interdisciplinary character of peace studies. Peace researchers travel frequently and have such networks abroad – far beyond what other social scientists use for their 'comparative studies'. The reason is obvious: we are studying the system as a whole. And that also calls for extensive intellectual travel across disciplinary borders. A great deal of this has also been disseminated. In a number of places the significant step from research to education has been taken. However, I am sceptical when that step is taken without a solid research base. The saddest way of doing peace studies is to make an inventory of the courses given at University X 'that have something to do with peace and conflict', putting together a roster hoping that out of some *bric-a-brac* a solid *objet d'art* will eventually emerge. Peace research is more than the sum of the parts, however useful those parts may be in the longer run in building solid peace research and studies.

So, let us move one step forward and start the first training courses for peace professionals. I am not thinking of the college level; that is insufficient in maturity, however important it is for peace studies. Nor am I thinking of the PhD level; that is and remains a level particularly suited for peace research. I am thinking of the level in-between, the Master's level. But this should not be confused with a Master of Arts specialising in peace studies; this is fine for peace studies and in the case of the exceptional students or universities also for peace research. I am thinking of a Master of Peace Studies exactly in the sense of training doers: in conflict analysis, conflict negotiation, mediation, non-violence, alternative security, peace economics, peace with the environment, human rights, peace education in the sense of knowing how to help set it up, peace culture, knowing where it is.

Such a course would involve one year's training in existing theories and numerous case studies (much like in a business school), and at least one year's practical experience with peace specialists

162

from a variety of professional arenas (the United Nations and its agencies; other International Governmental Organisations; international peoples' organisations; governmental ministries, particularly the foreign office, defence, trade, development assistance; voluntary organisations such as trade unions and religious bodies; municipalities; school districts; the media). There is so much to be done! Let us have at least 1,000 graduates per year by the year 2000!

It goes without saying that this has to be undertaken in a spirit of international and interdisciplinary co-operation, to the point of achieving global and holistic identification. At the same time the graduates' dedication to peace has to be more clear than for the more conventional concerns of peace research and peace studies. A Hippocratic oath at the end of a Master of Peace Studies course might serve this purpose, and would also communicate to the prospective employer what kind of person he or she is hiring. When hiring a doctor the hospital has a right to assume that drugs will be used to cure, not kill patients. Similarly, the peace professionals should, in principle, not be available for purposes that are not covered by the 'peace by peaceful means' short formula (the shortest I know for what the whole thing is about, also an effort to capture Gandhi's ethical intuition about the unity of means and ends).

Global, holistic: but this raises the question of whether peace studies cannot also be undertaken in a different way. Thus, are we really to believe that peace studies in a superpower like the United States – where most universities have tremendous difficulties arriving at a critical, yet sympathetic understanding of their own country – can lead to adequate education for peace and professionalisation? And if the answer is negative, would that not also hold, to a lesser degree, for less 'super' powers? In short, would not a multidisciplinary, travelling university around the world be a more adequate way of studying the world politics of peace and conflict, precisely if unity of means and ends is so important? I think the answer lies in the question. In short, get going!

PART III

Defence, Disarmament and Peace

9

The Impact of Gorbachev's Perestroika Programme on Western Europe

Malcolm Dando

Introduction

During the last part of the 1980s we witnessed an accelerating change in many aspects of the East–West confrontation. The fundamental reasons for these developments are clearly internal to the Soviet Union. Yet perestroika has, from the beginning, had an external aspect, and no one can now doubt that what is happening in the East has profound implications for the West.

Understanding these implications is not easy for us, not only because of the startling rate of change in Eastern Europe and the Soviet Union but also because there are major changes taking place in the West; for example, in conventional military technology and declining finance for the military weapon systems. This paper is an attempt to investigate some of the mechanisms that are producing the events now unfolding in the West. It is hoped that this will allow a better understanding of some of the possible future scenarios that we could face.

In the first part of the paper an investigation of events in the Soviet Union leads to the proposition that Gorbachev's foreign policy towards the West could be a sophisticated exercise in building trust. The position taken here is that the conventional military balance in Europe has always been much more favourable to NATO than is commonly supposed in the West. With this in mind the following sections review the impact of external perestroika in

The author wishes to thank Mr. S. Freckleton for helpful discussions on the material for this paper.

the Western context. Particular attention is paid to the modernisation of conventional forces, the difficulty of negotiation, and the potential for disarray in NATO.

These sections form the basis for a more detailed analysis of some of the mechanisms that might be involved in generating future scenarios: the effects of Soviet policy in the West European context. The viewpoint is generally pessimistic. It is suggested that preventing a further escalation in dangerous military technology (applied to conventional weapons, in particular) will be difficult, that policy paralysis over arms control is possible in NATO, and that a Franco-German centred alliance could be growing.

Finally, in contrast, the paper returns to its original theme and suggests a possible success for a trust-building process which could help to transform Europe in a significant and benign manner. Whilst the present circumstances are hopeful, the outcome of perestroika is still uncertain and, therefore, the need to try to grasp the underlying features seems particularly important.

The New Soviet Foreign Policy

That there has been a change in Soviet foreign policy under Gorbachev is undeniable. I take no position on the question of whether the change is largely a matter of manner or of real substance: indeed, I will argue that different parties in Western Europe perceive the policy in different ways. What is important is that there *has* been a change of potentially fundamental significance.

The People and Organisations Involved in Moscow

Sweeping changes in the Ministry of Foreign Affairs began in March 1986, at the time of the 27th Party Congress, after Andrei Gromyko's long period as foreign minister had ended and Gorbachev's chosen colleague, Eduard Shevardnadze, had taken over. In May 1986 a foreign policy conference in Moscow was addressed by Gorbachev. Attended by all the senior figures involved in foreign policy, the conference could have been left in no doubt that a major shake-up was under way.[1]

---

1. M. Light, 'New Thinking in Soviet Foreign Policy?', *Coexistence*, vol. 24, 1987, pp. 233–43.

The two first deputy ministers were replaced and four new deputy foreign ministers (including V. Petrovskii, to whom we will return later) were appointed. Five new units required to deal with the new policy were set up in the ministry. These included: Viktor Karpov's Arms Reduction and Disarmament Unit and G. Gerasimov's Information Department. Additionally, by October 1986, a third of Soviet ambassadors had been replaced.

More importantly, though, and perhaps partly as a result of Gromyko's departure, the Central Committee began to regain power in foreign policy decision-making and an arms control sector under Major-General Starodubov was established in the International Department.

Anatoly Dobryuin, ex-Ambassador to the United States, became the International Department Secretary of the Central Committee. He, together with Vadim Medvedev, the secretary of the department which looked after bloc relations, reported to Alexandr Yakovlev, a full member of the Politburo and Secretary with responsibility for domestic ideological affairs and foreign relations.[2]

Yakovlev previously had a long period of service on the Central Committee, but had been in 'exile' for a decade as Ambassador to Canada when Gorbachev met him there. Yakovlev was quickly brought back to head the Moscow Institute of World Economy and International Relations (IMEMO) in 1983, prior to his rapid rise to power when Gorbachev took over. Many observers believe that Yakovlev became Gorbachev's main adviser on both internal and external affairs.

IMEMO is a large social science research institute which then had three departments that are of particular interest: Oleg Bykov's Department of International Relations, Grigorii Morozov's Department of International Organisations and Aleksei Arbatov's Department of Arms Control and International Security. Aleksei Arbatov is the dynamic son of Georgii Arbatov, Director of the Institute of the USA and Canada (ISKAN), but more importantly, by the summer of 1986 Oleg Bykov, Deputy Director of IMEMO, was in *de facto* control of all three departments.[3] Bykov also held a dual

2. J. F. Hough, 'Gorbachev Consolidating Power', *Problems of Communism*, vol. 36, no. 4, 1987, pp. 21–44.
3. J. P. Litherland, 'Soviet Views of the Arms Race and Disarmament: Arms Control and Foreign Policy Research and the Development of Gorbachev's "New Thinking" on Nuclear Weapons', PhD Thesis, University of Bradford, 1987 (unless stated otherwise, data in this section are taken from this source).

post in Dobrynin's International Department of the Central Committee.

At the smaller USA and Canada Institute two departments are of interest: Genrikh Trofimenko's Department of US Foreign Policy and A. A. Vasilev's Politico-Military Department. All of the institutes interested in arms control and disarmament were linked in the Scientific Council on Peace and Disarmament, which was set up in 1979.

It has been a matter of substantial debate in the West as to whether these institutes were, in the past, merely propaganda outfits or whether they had real influence. The answer is probably that they played both roles. What is clear now is that some people from the institutes became members of Gorbachev's top foreign policy team. The major example is clearly Alexandr Yakovlev, but another was the Deputy Foreign Minister who had responsibility for arms control – Vladimir Petrovskii. At the time of his appointment in 1986 Petrovskii was a senior research worker at ISKAN, a member of the controlling Bureau of the Scientific Council on Peace and Disarmament, and a frequent contributor to the academic literature on arms control. However, since 1957 he had also had a career in the Foreign Ministry and had been in charge of the Department of International Organisations there since 1979.

In such circumstances, it is not surprising that many of the ideas regarding foreign policy and arms control in perestroika can be found in the writings of these academics. One very important theme is that of *mutual responsibility* for the arms race. As Dobrynin has put it:

> The creation of new weapons by one side prods the other to take counter measures on the assumption that events will take the worst possible turn. And this reaction is then fed back to the side that started the current round of the arms race. The vicious circle is thus completed. The arms race acquires its own momentum.

Given this new interpretation, which rejected the idea that the West was solely responsible for the arms race and that the Soviet Union only responded when forced to do so, a new policy was clearly needed.

It is interesting for our analysis that Oleg Bykov chose to address this issue in a paper at the time of the 27th Party Congress. After roundly criticising the previous record of arms control, he argued strongly for the use of unilateral initiatives by the USSR.[4] He appeared to believe that restraint by the USSR would influence Western domestic politics in favour of arms control. As we shall see later unilateral initiatives have been a core feature of Soviet policy since 1985. We will, therefore, need to examine the theory behind the use of this technique.

The Theory of Unilateral Initiatives

By far the best-known open presentation of the theory of unilateral initiatives is by the American psychologist, Charles Osgood,[5] and the best-known analysis of their operation is by the American sociologist Amitai Etzioni.[6]

Before turning to these studies, it will be helpful to note two points from Geoffrey Vickers' classic analysis of 'The Management of Conflict'.[7] Vickers argues that the management of conflict between two parties is largely concerned with preventing the interaction passing beyond a threshold where it becomes self-exciting and destructive of the parties' resources for resolving the conflict. He argues, further, that this threshold is set by the constraints and assurances the parties feel in their membership of a common system. In a significant passage he notes: 'But constraints based on *self*-expectations and assurances based on trust in the *self*-expectations of others . . . alone create those bonds of responsibility, loyalty and mutual trust without which human societies neither function nor cohere'. In short, mutual trust is crucial to containing and resolving conflict. Although some, such as Herbert Scoville, former CIA analyst and President of the US Arms Control Association, have argued for the use of unilateral initiatives directly to de-escalate the arms race through significant hardware reductions,[8] Osgood's proposals are clearly concerned with the use of limited initiatives, in

4. M. Ahmad, *et al.* 'Unilateral Disarmament Measures', Report of the Secretary-General of the United Nations, A/39/516, 1984.
5. C. E. Osgood, *An Alternative to War or Surrender*, Chicago, 1962. Chapter 5 is reprinted in *Peace Research Reviews*, vol. 8, no. 1, 1979, pp. 1–50.
6. A. Etzioni, 'The Kennedy Experiment', *The Western Political Quarterly*, vol. 20, no. 2, 1967, pp. 361–80. Also reprinted with a selection of other relevant articles based on Osgood's work in *Peace Research Reviews*, vol. 8, no. 1, 1979.
7. G. Vickers, 'The Management of Conflict', *Futures*, June, 1972, pp. 126–41.
8. H. Scoville, 'Reciprocal National Restraint: An Alternative Path', *Arms Control Today*, vol. 15, no. 5, 1985, pp. 1–6.

order to increase trust and to develop a context in which multilateral negotiations can successfully proceed.

Osgood put forward a proposal he calls GRIT: Graduated and Reciprocated Initiatives in Tension Reduction. He argued that, as an arms race involves a series of reciprocated escalations in tensions, it should be possible to go in the other direction by the use of reciprocated concessions. The strategy, suggests Osgood, should be based on the following criteria for selecting initiatives:

1. They must not affect the West's minimum nuclear retaliatory capability or its basic conventional military capability.
2. They must be graduated in risk according to Soviet reciprocation.
3. They must be diverse and somewhat unpredictable.
4. They must represent a sincere attempt to reduce tensions.

The intent, Osgood argues, is to convince the opponent of the US's good-will without taking risks with its national security.

Mounting what he calls a 'Peace Offensive' also requires attention to tactics. Osgood therefore suggests that the initiatives also: be announced prior to implementation; be implemented if announced; explicitly invite reciprocation; be continued over a protracted period of time; take advantage of mutual interests if possible; be as unambiguous as possible; and be as verifiable as possible. Osgood also discusses the problem of timing of different initiatives, overlap of initiatives, fall-back positions and so on. It is important to note that he also lays great stress on the fact that the use of his method allows a state to take the initiative in foreign policy rather than having to go through the long process of negotiation before any results can be announced. In summary, he suggests that, in present conditions, 'the variable most under our control is perceived external threat, and therefore this must be the focus of our strategy. We can behave . . . so as to lower it'. It is worth bearing this theoretical contribution in mind when analysing Soviet strategy towards the West since 1985.

Etzioni's contribution was to examine the sequence of events, between June and October 1963, which began with President Kennedy's American University speech and which resulted in the conclusion of three major arms control agreements: the Partial Test Ban, the Hot Line and the Outer Space Treaty. He suggested that Kennedy could have been following something like the set of rules produced by Osgood and therefore looked at the initiatives, re-ciprocations, negotiations, and so on in an attempt to judge how effective Kennedy's 'experiment' had been.

He demonstrated, for example, that Kennedy's speech took a very conciliatory tone towards the Soviet Union and argued that stopping atmospheric tests was a significant gesture. He suggested that the publication of the speech in *Izvestia* and *Pravda*, the unjamming of the 'Voice of America' radio broadcasts, Krushchev's speech of 15 June and the halting of Soviet strategic bomber production were adequate reciprocation. Following further similar moves by both sides, the Partial Test Ban was quickly negotiated.

Whilst carefully setting out his reservations as to Kennedy's precise intent, and as to the possibility of using history as an experiment (no 'control' run being possible), Etzioni did conclude that a sequence of GRIT-type initiatives took place and that they did affect public perceptions – particularly of the Soviet Union in the West! Other examples have been examined by well-respected specialists in the study of conflict with similar conclusions as to the effectiveness of the method as a means of facilitating the achieve-ment of agreements between East and West once the political decisions to move in that direction have been taken.[9] In line with Bykov's analysis, the effect is to increase public support for arms control and disarmament measures.

Soviet Arms Control Policy Since 1985

The arrival of Gorbachev, Shevardnadze and Gerasimov at the top has radically altered the presentation – and therefore the potential effect on Western public opinion – of Soviet arms control policy. Whilst opinions may differ, it is also my belief that, in line with Osgood's theory, no great risks have been taken with the basis of Soviet national security. I view the events at the Reykjavik Summit in 1986 as more important in showing how far the Soviets would be willing to proceed rather than as an indication that they are pre-pared to take extreme risks. Similarly, in my view, the unilateral Soviet test moratorium did not involve significant risk. Although the US conducted twenty-six tests during the moratorium,[10] these

9. L. Kreisberg, 'Noncoercive Inducements in US–Soviet Conflicts: Ending the Occupation of Austria and Nuclear Weapons Tests', *Journal of Political and Military Sociology*, vol. 9, 1981, pp. 1–16.
10. Maj. Gen. G. Batenin, 'The USSR announced a test of less than 20 kilotons at

would not have been sufficient to make any appreciable military difference, given the amount of testing both sides had carried out in previous years.

On the other hand, I would argue that Soviet efforts to extract themselves from Afghanistan, though no doubt having diverse motivations, did fit in with Osgood's ideas for initiatives to take place across a wide range of policy issues. Undoubtedly, as the Soviets were able to withdraw from Afghanistan in reasonable order, one of the major remaining reasons for distrust of their basic intentions was reduced in significance in the West.

In regard to the central issue of arms control, what is noticeable is the wide range of initiatives undertaken within this field of policy. Just as examples, we may cite the Soviets' invitation to US scientists to carry out test measurements at their nuclear explosion test site, in order to assist development of verification procedures, and their acceptance of the bomber-counting rule for the Strategic Arms Reduction Treaty (START) which clearly – given US predominance in this section of the triad – is a major concession.

Osgood-type programmes, however, have to be judged in regard to the obtaining of signed, multilateral treaties. Clearly, in the negotiations for a chemical weapons treaty we have seen a series of concessions by the Soviets. In August of 1987 they accepted a hard-line Western view on mandatory challenge inspections of suspected violations, in October representatives of forty-five states visited their chemical weapons research station and in December they announced the level of their stocks of chemical weapons.[11] Undoubtedly though, there are still many difficulties of a technical nature to be overcome before a chemical weapons treaty will be signed. The one nuclear arms control treaty that has been achieved to date, on Intermediate Nuclear Forces (INF), quite clearly involved a series of Soviet concessions,[12] for example, the exclusion of British and French forces, the de-linking of INF from START/ Space talks, and the inclusions of the second SRINF (short range) set of forces. In the long term, perhaps more importantly in the public's mind, is the Soviet Union's altered position on verification. Who, just a few years ago, could have anticipated the type of

Semipalatinsk', *Arms Control Reporter*, 608. B.130, Institute for Defense and Disarmament Studies, Boston, Mass., 26 February 1987.
11. *Arms Control Reporter*, 704. B. 234–55, IDDS, Boston, Mass., 1987.
12. *Arms Control Reporter*, 403. A. 4, IDDS, Boston, Mass., 1987.

intrusive verification scheme in INF agreed by the Soviet Union?[13]

Osgood would probably have strongly approved of the following comments by A. G. Savelyev of Aleksei Arbatov's group at IMEMO:

> The verification problem was seen as a particularly acute one in the atmosphere of suspicion that has existed and, basically, has not completely disappeared in relations between our countries . . . one can draw the conclusion that the verification measures elaborated in the sixties and seventies and the national means of implementing them were evidently not enough . . . if we intend to disarm, if we want to proceed along the path of trust that kind of secrecy (former Soviet practice) can only do harm, in my view. The Soviet leadership is fully aware of this.[14]

We cannot conclude that the Soviet Union *is* following the programme set out by Osgood. But I think that we *can* conclude that it has a rather similar programme in mind. It follows that we can reasonably expect more of the same – a series of well-presented, clear, wide-ranging verifiable initiatives – over a protracted period of time. That, I believe, has profound consequences for the possible effects of the policy in Western Europe.

Statements on European Disarmament

The negotiations on European disarmament will be reviewed below. The intention here is to get a grasp of the kind of proposals that the Soviet Union is likely to press from the official declarations they made following the 1985 leadership change. President Gorbachev's speech of 15 January 1986 is chiefly remembered for its call for a three-stage de-nuclearisation by the year 2000.[15] However, after dealing with the issues of nuclear weapons and chemical weapons, the speech did make some brief reference to European disarmament in noting the need for progress on reduction of forces, for the development of confidence-building measures and for adequate verification.

These proposals were substantially developed in the 'Address', in

---

13. Treaty details in *Arms Control Reporter*, 403. A. 2–8, IDDS, Boston, Mass., 1988.
14. A. G. Savelyev, 'The ABM treaty might not have had enough verification', *Arms Control Reporter*, 603. B. 149–150, IDDS, Boston, Mass., 20–22 December 1987.
15. *Soviet News*, 22 January 1986.

June 1986, by the Warsaw Pact to NATO on reducing armed forces in Europe,[16] and then again in the Communiqué of 3 June 1987 of the Warsaw Pact Political Consultative Committee.[17] The Communiqué, of course, dealt with the major nuclear negotiations between the superpowers but, in regard to Europe, it expressed the hope that a deal on medium-range missiles could be followed by a solution to the problem of tactical nuclear weapons.

With regard to conventional forces it was suggested that, concurrently with discussions of tactical nuclear systems, there could be negotiations for a 25 per cent cut in armed forces and conventional arms. This would be followed by more substantial cuts in forces, arms and military spending by the year 2000. It was clearly stated that the problem of asymmetries in the forces could be addressed by the side which is ahead in a particular system making larger cuts.

The Communiqué stated that a top priority should be measures to reduce the threat of sudden attack. Ideas put forward included reciprocal withdrawal of the most dangerous offensive conventional weapons from the zones of direct contact between the opposing forces: so-called depletion zones. The 1986 'Address' had given more details on the need for further control of and information about military exercises for similar reasons of confidence building.

The Communiqué stresses the need for proper, thoroughgoing measures of verification and the 'Address' amplified in some detail the need for data exchanges and for the setting up of an International Consultative Commission to regulate the complex observation, control and verification measures envisaged. Another set of ideas concerned nuclear and chemical-free zones in the Balkans, on the Central Front and in the north. These ideas, of course, are well-known from the work of the Palme commission.

In all of these documents, the specific proposals were set in the context of an analysis of the danger of nuclear war, and hopes for economic co-operation and development following major disarmament agreements were outlined. The East's ideas were, perhaps, most concisely set out in the Jaruzelski plan of 8 May 1987.[18]

It is not difficult to see the problems in what was being proposed. For example, the Warsaw Pact might call for extensive discussions

---

16. *Soviet News*, 18 June 1986.
17. *Soviet News*, 3 June 1987.
18. *Memorandum of the Government of the Polish People's Republic on Decreasing Armaments and Increasing Confidence in Europe*, Mimeograph, June, 1987.

of military doctrine between the blocs, but would these address the offensive structure, training and exercising of Pact forces? Again, how are differences over the inclusion of air and naval forces in Confidence-Building Measures to be resolved? Nevertheless the West must expect a continuing flow of such initiatives from the East.

Trends in Western Europe and NATO

Ongoing Modernisations of Weapons and Strategies

To suggest that there is a rough balance of forces, at the conventional and nuclear levels, between the Warsaw Pact and NATO in Europe does not imply that there is any kind of stability. Clearly, if both sides believe that 'deterrence' is best achieved by giving every impression of being strong and ready to fight, there are some situations which could be very unstable. In particular, if both sides were to have very offensive strategies and appropriate new, precise, long-range weaponry, there would be strong temptations, and fears, about first-strike attacks in crises. The general problem of surprise attacks, and the particular problems of nuclear weapons and fragile command and control systems in Europe have been extensively analysed in the open literature.[19]

It is generally argued that the Soviet Union has been moving towards a strong preference for avoiding use of nuclear weapons should war break out in Europe.[20] Their conventional strategy was seen in the West to be based on the idea of a rapid, overwhelming offensive. Concerns over the development of Operational Manoeuvre Groups merely added to the basic concern over their whole strategy. What were really significant, however, were Ogarkov's very influential views on the significance of the scientific–technical revolution on military affairs. Writing in 1987, Dale Herspring noted that despite Ogarkov's demotion: 'Ogarkov should not be taken lightly. His ideas have been carefully thought out and widely publicized in the USSR.'[21] The military press in the West continued

19. D. Frei, *Risks of Unintentional Nuclear War*, Geneva, 1982; P. Bracken, *The Command and Control of Nuclear Forces*, New Haven, Conn., 1983.
20. M. MccGwire, 'Soviet Military Objectives', *World Policy Journal*, vol. 3, no. 4, 1986, pp. 667–95.
21. D. R. Herspring, 'Nikolay Ogarkov and the Scientific–Technical revolution in Soviet Military Affairs', *Comparative Strategy*, vol. 6, no. 1, 1987, pp. 29–61.

to stress the significance of his ideas and disciples.[22]

In essence, Ogarkov has consistently argued that: nuclear weapons are becoming more and more unuseable; improvements in conventional weapons make such weapons more and more significant; the important qualitative characteristics of conventional weapons are changing very rapidly; and that these developments are altering the characteristics of modern warfare. Therefore, in Ogarkov's view, in order to defend the country, more and more effort had to be put into developing modern military technology. The Soviet military, in short, had to move apace into the missile and computer age. Whilst Ogarkov has certainly stressed the impossibility of fighting a strategic nuclear war to any purpose, it is easy to see how the continuing development of conventional military technology, in line with his arguments as listed above, could cause disquiet in the West.

In considering NATO strategy, it has to be stressed, as General Sir John Hackett has pointed out, that rational military planners in the Kremlin might not have seen NATO's plans in the defensive way in which they are standardly presented. They might well have seen NATO attempting to solve its problem of lack of operational depth by defending very far forward – into Eastern Europe.[23] Undoubtedly, NATO has been affected by the same scientific–technical revolution as the Soviet Union and the Warsaw Pact. The evolution of new plans for warfare, such as AirLand Battle and Follow-on-Forces-Attack (FOFA), was clearly predicated on the development of new, longer-range precision munitions. With the stress on the offensive in AirLand Battle, and FOFA involving attacks 400 km beyond the forward edge of battle, it is not difficult to see how such developments could be seen as threatening by the other side.[24]

To the analyst attempting to assess the possible outcomes of this process there is one obvious potential result. We appear to have a positive feedback process under way which may well lead to increasing crisis instability between the forces of the two blocs in Europe. It can be noted that this process is under way in Naval

22. M. C. FitzGerald, 'Marshal Ogarkov and the New Revolution in Soviet Military Affairs', *Defence Analysis*, vol. 3, no. 1, 1987, pp. 3–19.
23. General Sir John Hackett, 'The Real Danger to World Security is Nuclear Proliferation', *International Defence Review*, no. 2, 1984, pp. 123–4.
24. A. P. Kelly, 'The Conventional Balance of Forces', M. Phil. Thesis, University of Bradford, 1986.

Forces as well as on land and in the air.

We will return to this issue below. For the moment, it is necessary to address the argument that problems with defence budgets will provide negative feedback which will greatly slow the development of this arms race. Whilst it is true that even in the US and UK there has been a slowing – indeed a reversal – in the growth of defence budgets, the question remains as to whether this will really affect what are seen to be crucial military developments. The defence industries are so large and powerful that really significant expenditure cuts are unlikely in the short term, and there is so much potential for the elimination of inefficiency and waste that core production is likely to continue unabated and unhindered by any foreseeable cuts.

Finally, whilst it is true that there have been extensive discussions of 'alternative defence' strategies outside of military establishments in Western Europe,[25] and that these have been noted in the Soviet Union, there is little sign that the professional military find ideas such as 'Non-Provocative Defensive Deterrence' very persuasive. Whilst it is correct to argue that two defensively organised military blocs might produce conditions of much greater stability in crises, the military reasonably ask, for example, if it is plausible to have forces without offensive power – or even how one should go about defining offensive and defensive systems. A reasonable view must be that much more work is needed on the more far-reaching of such ideas they are likely to be implemented.

Disarmament Negotiations

Four sets of negotiations are of some interest in a European context: Mutual and Balanced Force Reductions (MBFR), Chemical Weapons, INF and the Conference on Disarmament in Europe (CDE). Whilst the dismal history of MBFR eventually reached a non-productive end and the talks on Chemical Weapons have some way to go, INF and CDE are more important from our perspective.

The INF Agreement is of interest in part because of the concessions made by the Soviets, but also because of what it reveals about NATO's dilemmas. As Cruise and Pershing II were deployed to help bolster European belief in 'coupling' to the US strategic

25. Alternative Defence Commission, *Defence Without the Bomb: The Report of the Alternative Defence Commission*, London, 1983.

nuclear umbrella, not as a response to SS 20s, the Soviets were not expected to accept the 'Zero Option'. When they had the good sense to do so, they did indeed cause 'gas pains' for many besides General Rogers. There will certainly be more problems for Western European establishments as modernisations and circumventions are attempted against the background of differing views – particularly in West Germany – and continued Soviet pressure for more denuclearisation.

The general issue, however, concerns the dependency relationship in military matters which persists between the Western Europeans and the United States. Jane Sharp has described an eight-stage 'NATO Arms Control Dilemma' as follows:

1. US–Soviet negotiations begin;
2. Western European fears of abandonment are triggered;
3. Western Europeans seek reassurance from the US;
4. The US responds with more armaments;
5. US–Soviet tension rises and negotiations stall;
6. Western European fears of entrapment (in nuclear war) are triggered;
7. West Europeans urge conciliation on the US;
8. US–Soviet *détente* develops;
   and (1) US–Soviet negotiations begin the cycle again.[26]

This cycle is traced by Sharp, in some detail, for INF from the mid-1970s. It is not necessary to follow the analysis through here. The crucial point is that Soviet diplomacy, if the analysis is correct, *necessarily* exposes such problems, and against a background of declining US economic power.

Whilst attempts at structural conventional disarmament in MBFR – if they were ever serious – have been a failure, the Stockholm Conference of the CDE, with the more modest goal of operational arms control, is generally considered to have been a great success. Following on from the limited Confidence-Building Measures agreed in the 1975 Helsinki Final Act of the Conference on Security and Cooperation in Europe (CSCE), the Stockholm agreement has improved on measures to reduce the risk of confrontation in Europe. These measures can be summarised as follows:

---

26. J. M. O. Sharp, 'After Reykjavik: Arms Control and the Allies', *International Affairs*, vol. 63, no. 2, 1987, pp. 239–59.

1. Prior notice has to be given of certain types of military activity.
2. Observers from other CDE states are to be invited to defined exercises.
3. Annual calendars of intended military activities have to be exchanged.
4. Certain large-scale military activities not forecast in advance are prohibited.
5. Inspection to allow compliance to be verified, in case of doubt, is agreed.

Whilst critical observers have voiced concerns, for example over exception for 'alerts' and mobilisation activities,[27] it is certainly to be expected that this type of arms control will proceed further. It does seem to offer hope of increasing stability in crisis conditions.

It is clear that the scope of the new negotiations on reductions of conventional forces in Europe will be most significant, including reductions, limitations and redeployments, particularly of offensive forces that could be used for surprise, large-scale attacks.[28] Not surprisingly, there are major differences, for example, over how dual-capable systems and air and naval systems should be included. Again it is reasonable to conclude that, if we are correct in assuming that the Soviet Union will continue to press ahead with its present policies, there could be considerable disarray within NATO and difficulty in holding on to common positions.

The State of the NATO Alliance

It has been argued so far that the new Soviet foreign policy is being put forward in the context of a conventional arms race (and, of course, of the ongoing nuclear arms race). It has also been suggested that this conjunction has caused considerable confusion and difficulty within NATO. At this stage, however, we have to bring in a new factor which will cause further difficulty for the Western Europeans: the US bid for a defence in the nuclear age – the Strategic Defense Initiative (SDI).

Whilst it may be agreed that a perfect defence is unlikely to be achieved, that does not mean that it will not be attempted. Indeed,

27. J. Borowski, *et al.*, 'The Stockholm Agreement of September 1986', *Orbis*, vol. 30, no. 4, 1987, pp. 643–63.
28. 'Positions of the Governments', *Arms Control Reporter*, 407.A.3, IDDS, Boston, Mass., 30 January 1988.

when the US defence industry has dealt with the Strategic Modernisation Programme, what else had it to turn to if not SDI? A key issue is whether the US can afford to buy SDI. Calculations have appeared in the open literature which suggest that SDI might not be impossible for the US economy.

A detailed review of the macroeconomics of strategic defences by Blechman and Utgoff was published in the Harvard-based journal, *International Security*. The paper set out four schemes for strategic defences from near-term, kinetic-energy, land-based kill systems through to directed-energy, space-based kill systems. The assumptions and costings for each of the schemes was then examined in some detail. The paper concluded that: 'In aggregate economic terms, it is feasible for the United States to build comprehensive strategic defenses'.[29] Moreover, the paper was dealing with systems deployed, at the latest, in thirty years' time. Such calculations are presumably also available to the Europeans from more sensitive sources.

In the context of the INF agreement and Reykjavik, the Western European establishments might well be asking themselves how much the US really does care about them. But SDI signifies something infinitely worse – and quite openly – the end of US belief in deterrence itself. Together with the Soviet 'Peace Offensive', this could well appear a quite lethal combination in the eyes of the old faithful Atlanticists.

The problem in NATO is, as always, the question of whether the United States would willingly sacrifice Washington for Bonn. The strategy of Flexible Response was designed to disguise this dilemma and, therefore, the removal of Cruise and Pershing II after all the public difficulties of bringing them in, and the private drive to alter NATO's plans for nuclear use, is an undoubted blow. The near-agreement – without consultation – at Reykjavik was certainly also an unwelcome reminder of dependency; but SDI and Mutual Assured Survival between the superpowers signals irrelevance. Even the British Government has not been reticent in signalling its desire for the Anti-Ballistic Missile (ABM) Treaty to be strongly maintained.

Perhaps, however, the real politicking has been taking place in France and West Germany. Over the past twenty years France has

---

29. B. M. Blechman, and V. A. Utgoff, 'The Macroeconomics of Strategic Defenses', *International Security*, vol. 11, no. 3, 1987, pp. 33–70.

steadily modified its military strategy in order to be able to support West Germany in conventional operations, should war come to Europe, and to put plans for use of its nuclear weapons further away from rapid tactical employment.[30] Recently there has been the creation of joint West German–French Economic and Defence Councils.[31]

The Defence Council is based in Paris. It deals with joint strategy, weapon developments and the use of mixed units. The first joint brigade was established in October 1988. Command of the brigade rotates between French and German officers. The idea that the two countries are 'one space' for the purposes of defence has been stressed.

Finally, we should note here the strange rebirth of the Western European Union over the last few years, following its decade-long deep sleep.[32] This is quite openly aimed at developing a common European security identity and involves new, regular, high-level meetings of politicians and officials. It has also been used to develop and express joint positions, for example, in regard to the Reykjavik meeting. We will return to these issues below. The overall impression, however, is of an alliance not exactly well-prepared for a disarmament onslaught from the East.

Possible Consequences of Soviet Policy

Attempting to predict the future is fraught with difficulties.[33] In particular, trying to develop scenarios combining different elements over a variety of timescales is a task that must be approached with great care. For our purposes here, a more useful approach is to try to analyse some of the elements which would certainly have to be considered in discussing possible futures in Western Europe under the impact of perestroika. I have chosen to concentrate on three

30. D. A. Ruiz Palmer, 'Between the Rhine and the Elbe: France and the Conventional Defense of Central Europe', *Comparative Strategy*, vol. 6, no. 4, 1987, pp. 471–512.
31. 'The FRG and France set up Joint Defence and Economic Councils', *Arms Control Reporter*, 407.B.6, IDDS, Boston, Mass., 22 January 1988.
32. A. Cohen, 'The Emergence and Role of the Western European Union', Anglo-American colloquium on European Defence Co-operation and the Anglo-American Special Relationship, University of Newcastle, 9 December 1987.
33. C. Morgan, *The Shape of Futures Past: The Story of Prediction*, Exeter, 1980.

which appear to be strong possibilities as sources of instability: (a) the scientific–technical revolution in military affairs, (b) the difficulty of a well-managed demilitarisation of Europe, and (c) Franco-German co-operation in a disintegrating NATO. In each case we will be searching for a view of the mechanisms which are likely to operate in regard to these factors, rather than specific predictions of what is, or is not, likely to happen.

The Scientific–Technical Revolution in Military Affairs

As they have devoted considerable analytical attention to this topic, it is convenient to begin the discussion with the Soviets. MccGwire has argued convincingly that when they achieved strategic nuclear parity with the US the Soviets began to make substantial changes to their military doctrine and force structure – in the direction of emphasising the role of conventional forces. As he puts it:

> Several factors combined to bring about this shift. NATO's switch from a strategy of 'massive retaliation' to one of 'flexible response' indicated that, if NATO had its choice, the early stages of a war in Europe would be conventional; it could also be read as US reluctance to make good its nuclear guarantee of Europe, now that the growing Soviet Intercontinental capability made America itself vulnerable.

Yet if the superpowers' homelands were to be safe, given the United States' economic power, 'it was essential that the United States be denied any advanced position . . . that would allow it to build up the military capacity for a ground offensive against the Soviet Union. Thus the defeat of NATO in Europe and the eviction of US forces from the continent became a strategic imperative.'[34] The offensive, clearly, was to be kept conventional and nuclear forces held in reserve to deter nuclear use by NATO. (MccGwire carefully stressed that the Soviets do not wish to invade; his argument is about what they would try to do if compelled).

In this context we can better understand the concerns set out by Marshal Ogarkov[35] and apparently shared by Marshal Akhromeyev[36]

---

34. M. MccGwire, 'Soviet Military Objectives'.
35. M. C. FitzGerald, 'Marshal Ogarkov on the Modern Theatre Operation', *Naval War College Review*, vol. 39, no. 4, 1986, pp. 6–25; FitzGerald, 'Marshal Ogarkov and the New Revolution'; Herspring, 'Nikolay Ogarkov'.
36. D. R. Herspring, 'Marshal Akhromeyev and the Future of the Soviet Armed Forces', *Survival*, vol. 28, no. 6, 1986, pp. 524–38.

and many other officers.[37] Essentially, under the cover of nuclear deterrence, they see modern, precise, conventional weaponry opening up a new form of warfare because: (a) it can approximate the *effectiveness* of nuclear weaponry without the collateral damage, (b) it can have *ranges* of up to 2,500 km, (c) it can have a *strategic* effect, and (d) it can be used in surprise attacks on decisive targets in the *initial* stages of a war.

Moreover, as we have discussed previously, changes in technology – and demands on the military to change their operations accordingly – are proceeding at an increasingly rapid rate. The technologies involved were fully described by Michael Klare in the early 1980s:

> The revolution in conventional weapons is being driven by a variety of interrelated technological advances: the introduction of 'smart' weapons, or precision-guided munitions (PGMs), capable of sensing their intended targets and making in-flight course corrections so as to ensure direct hits; the 'clustering' of many 'bomblets' into dispensing systems that can explode them over a wide area; the use of new explosives and warhead technologies that can endow conventional arms with near-nuclear blast capabilities; and the introduction of new 'target-acquisition' systems that enable planes and helicopters to pinpoint enemy forces far behind the front lines for attack by PGMs and cluster munitions.[38]

These technologies clearly also involve the increasingly widespread use of modern computers for command and control on the battlefield.

The problem for the Soviets is that they cannot produce and absorb the new technology as quickly as the West. Therefore, whilst they certainly see new Western strategies such as FOFA and Air-Land Battle as developments dependent on the new technologies, they cannot proceed as fast as they would like in that direction. In order to glimpse the future, we must therefore turn to the West.

The origins and characteristics of FOFA and AirLand Battle are well known and need not be detailed here.[39] Both clearly involve

37. P. Weiss, 'Ogarkov's Men Move Up', *International Defence Review*, no. 2, 1988, p. 116.
38. M. R. Klare, 'The Conventional Weapons Fallacy', in the series 'The New Arms Technology and What It Means', *The Nation*, 9 April, 1983, pp. 420–58.
39. F. Hussain, 'Emerging Technology: Economic and Military Implications for the Alliance', *Brassey's Defence Yearbook*, London, 1985; J. L. Romjue, 'The Evolution of the AirLand Battle Concept', *Air University Review*, vol. 35, no. 4, 1984, pp. 4–15.

the use of new conventional technologies for 'striking deep' into enemy territory.[40] It is also fair to say that the key concept of 'Deep Strike' has been subject to virulent and thoroughgoing criticism. For example, in Steven Canby's view:

> The concept has yet to be demonstrated in a benign environment, much less in a realistic or dynamically hostile one. The Deep Attack system will be vulnerable to attack and jamming, and its many diverse functions have yet to be stitched together. While some of its deficiencies can with time and money be corrected, others remain beyond the pale of correction.

On such matters Canby speaks with long experience and authority.[41]

Yet in regard to the same technology, the US Office of Technology Assessment reported in 1986 that, for FOFA: 'The technologies of primary interest are now relatively mature, and could result in fielded systems over the next decade.'[42] Indeed, a year earlier the US official responsible for Conventional Initiatives had summarised the technical situation as follows:

— The sensors and sensor platforms required to detect, identify, and track echeloned manoeuvre units at short and long range are either in production or under development.
— Battlefield correlation and fusion of multi-sensor information is being demonstrated in Europe.
— Air-launched and ground-launched missiles for delivery of weapons to targets in any echelon have been demonstrated and are under development for production in five years or less.
— Unguided submunitions for large area engagement and destruction of unarmoured and lightly armoured targets are in production in Europe and in the US.
— Smart submunitions of various kinds have been demonstrated

---

40. B. W. Rogers, 'ACE Attack of Warsaw Pact Follow-On Forces. Part 1 of "Strike Deep": A New Concept for NATO', *Military Technology*, vol. 7, no. 5, 1983, pp. 38–60.
41. S. L. Canby, 'The Conventional Defense of Europe: The Operational Limits of Emerging Technology', working paper 55, The Wilson Centre, Smithsonian Institute, Washington, 1984.
42. A. Shaw, *et al.*, 'Technologies for NATO's Follow-On Forces Attack Concept', Office of Technology Assessment, Congress of the United States, Washington, 1986.

and are either in engineering development or ready for engineering development.
— Technology for submunition lethality is sufficient for the near-term threat, and can be improved to match the evolution of the threat.[43]

Therefore, whatever the military reality, there is a strong probability that the technology will prevail. The new systems will be deployed and then counter-systems will be deployed by the other side.

The kind of world we are moving into can be pictured from the development of Sea-Launched Cruise Missiles (SLCMs) in the US Navy, with a wide variety of different platforms carrying a mixture of nuclear and non-nuclear, accurate, long-range cruise missiles. One can, of course, add to that the developments in stealth technology and electronic warfare[44] and it is not difficult to see very great concerns arising in the military over crisis stability in Europe. How could one feel secure in an environment in which a large-scale strategic attack with precision munitions might suddenly appear out of an electronic fog?

A Well-Managed Demilitarisation of Europe?

So one theme in the development of Europe's future is the familiar story of a fast-developing, high-technology arms race. What, then, are we to make of the possibilities of effective arms control and disarmament?

In his major book on the East–West problem in Europe, the former US Ambassador at the MBFR talks, Jonathan Dean, argued in 1987 that the military confrontation was essentially over.[45] The problem is how to manage the removal of the forces and allow political relationships to develop. In some ways his analysis was less pessimistic than many. For example, his views on the military balance in Europe do not differ greatly from those held here. However, when looking at current hopes for significant agreements

43. J. A. Tegnelia, 'Emerging Technology for Conventional Deterrence', *International Defence Review*, no. 5, 1985, pp. 643–52.
44. P. J. Klass, *et al.*, 'Electronic Warfare: Special Report - Part 2', *Aviation Week and Space Technology*, 16 February 1987, pp. 48–113.
45. J. Dean, *Watershed in Europe: Dismantling the East-West Military Confrontation*, Lexington, Mass., 1987.

on arms control in Europe, Dean is, unmistakeably, not hopeful of rapid progress. In his view:

> We know what we want arms control in Europe to achieve: to make real progress towards dismantling the military confrontation. But we have to look dispassionately at the actual prospects. These hopes were premature . . . Today, with good luck, we may be on the verge of first results . . . But these results will be limited and modest . . . it will take a long time before decisive progress can be made.[46]

With analyses which suggest that only cuts in force ratio levels of 1:5 in NATO's favour are acceptable apparently being well received in the West at the present time,[47] it is not hard to see the force of Dean's argument.

Indeed, it is not hard to find analyses which basically dismiss Gorbachev's new foreign policy as a fraud,[48] and more balanced accounts naturally take that in as a possibility.[49] In a paper aimed at discussing what the American response should be, Milam Svec suggested the following range of reasons for Gorbachev's actions:

— The possibility of getting some dramatic results from external perestroika whilst the internal reforms are given time to develop.
— To increase the Soviet's access to Western technology.
— To keep the United States 'off-balance' and at a disadvantage in foreign affairs.
— To prevent or delay development and deployment of the West's new technologically advanced weapon systems.
— To put the West in a double-bind where they either help the Eastern Europeans with their economies (and reduce Gorbachev's problem) or throw these countries back to the Soviet Union.[50]

46. Ibid.
47. 'The US Administration was influenced by a Rand Study Pessimistic About Conventional Reductions' *Arms Control Reporter* 401.B.188, IDDS, Boston, Mass., 11 November 1987.
48. G. Wettig, 'Dimensions of Soviet Arms Control Policy', *Comparative Strategy*, vol. 7, 1988, pp. 1–15.
49. Borowski, 'The Stockholm Agreement'; D. B. Rivkin, 'The Soviet Approach to Nuclear Arms Control: Continuity and Change', *Survival*, vol. 29, 1987, pp. 483–510.
50. M. Svec, 'Removing Gorbachev's Edge', *Foreign Policy*, vol. 69, 1987, pp. 148–65.

A further reason, Svec believes, for the priority given to arms control is that the Soviet Union is so deficient in aspects of super-power status other than the military. In short, arms control is his main field of possible action.

Svec notes that Gorbachev has changed the statements about what resources are going to be available to the military to suggest that only ruling out superiority for the other side will be funded. We might also remember that Ogarkov may have been dismissed because he was likely to argue too strongly for funds. Yet Svec feels that Gorbachev probably does not have a grand design, rather, he presents the US with a dilemma.

> On one hand, if the United States accepts possible far-reaching Soviet proposals, especially if political and military fractures in NATO cannot be shored up, a a variety of dangers could ensue: Soviet political gambits in Europe, the Soviet economy's eventual modernisation – with Western help, a gradual decoupling of the US and West European defenses, and encouragement to pacifist and leftist movements.

But:

> On the other hand, if the United States chose to reject Soviet offers for radical, supposedly balanced, and verifiable cuts in nuclear and conventional forces . . . it would be vulnerable to withering Soviet criticism and political polarisation and disaffection at home.[51]

Svec's fears that the most likely outcome will be *policy paralysis* in NATO – and under the pressure of increasingly strong Soviet initiatives such as major troops withdrawals or the removal of the Berlin Wall! His conclusion is that NATO needs to rethink its structure and strategy and then attempt to combine an imaginative arms control regime with use of its superior technology to guard its security and manoeuvre the Soviets into acceptable deals.

The short-term prospects would appear to be that Gorbachev – whatever his real motivations – will press on with his initiatives and that this will cause disarray in NATO. Arms control is therefore unlikely significantly to tame the arms race in Europe during that time. How things will develop in the medium to longer-term will depend on how the politics within NATO develop. It is to that issue which we now must turn.

51. Ibid.

Defence, Disarmament and Peace

Franco-German Co-operation in a Disintegrating NATO

If Gorbachev's aim, as some believe, is to pursue an anti-coalition strategy under the guise of a peace offensive,[52] he could hardly have been displeased with the NATO summit meeting of March 1988 in Brussels. The meeting began with a ringing reaffirmation of the United States' commitment to Western Europe from President Reagan, but in a context in which everyone knew that cuts were being made in the US defence budget. Moreover, it was clear that such cuts were likely to fall on the US Army and could easily involve reductions in its forces in Europe.[53] Even the director of the International Institute for Strategic Studies (IISS) had openly speculated about such cuts in the previous year.[54] And no amount of fudging of the issues[55] could hide the burden-sharing disputes on the horizon, or the influential voices in the United States seeking a new foreign policy.[56]

At the meeting the British Prime Minister Mrs Thatcher loudly proclaimed the necessity of urgent modernisation of European nuclear systems and the need for agreements on conventional and chemical arms control before any consideration of further nuclear disarmament in Europe. However, the West German Chancellor Mr Kohl had gone to Washington prior to the summit and agreed a deal with Mr Reagan in which further modernisation could be considered a long-term goal. Additionally, the final communiqué made it clear that further nuclear arms control in Europe would be pursued *in conjunction* with conventional and chemical arms control. The predictable result was a great deal of argument about the meaning of different languages and words in the communiqué.

I shall omit a detailed discussion of the situation in West Germany. Suffice it to note here that, given West Germany's economic and military strength, and its people's pronounced opposition to

52. R. F. Laird, 'The Soviet Union and the Western Alliance: Elements of an Anticoalition Strategy', in the series 'Soviet Foreign Policy', *Proceedings of the Academy of Political Science*, vol. 36, no. 4, 1987, pp. 106–18.
53. A. H. Cordesman, 'US Defence in 1988: The Morning After', *Royal United Services Institute Journal*, vol. 133, no. 1, 1988, pp. 27–35.
54. F. Heisbourg, 'Can the Atlantic Alliance Last Out the Century?', *International Affairs*, vol. 63, no. 3, 1987, pp. 413–25.
55. J. B. Steinberg, 'Rethinking the Debate on Burden-Sharing', *Survival*, vol. 29, no. 1, 1987, pp. 56–79.
56. I. Kristol, 'US Foreign Policy has Outlived its Time', *The Wall Street Journal*, 21 January 1988.

further modernisation of nuclear weapons on its soil, the problems that arose at the Brussels summit are unlikely to go away. The focus here is on the position of France. It was, of course, remarkable that France attended the summit but notable also that President Mitterrand sided with the West Germans in opposing further nuclear modernisation by NATO.

France is crucial in any consideration of the potential impact of external perestroika because it epitomises the possibility of the 'Balkanisation' of Western Europe. President De Gaulle left the NATO military structure in the 1960s because he saw the introduction of Flexible Response as an indication of the *unreliability* of the United States' nuclear guarantee. France has subsequently invested heavily in building up a miniature strategic triad and tactical nuclear forces, and all of these systems are being modernised at the present time.[57] Whilst it is clear that there has been an evolution of French strategy since the 1960s which has made French conventional forces more available for use in Germany, these forces are extremely weak because of the need for finance in the nuclear systems.

However, De Gaulle's position was not just military. He wanted to show that there was an alternative political position to the 'Atlanticist' reliance on the United States which had been necessary when Europe was devastated after the Second World War. According to Jolyon Howorth, the main elements of this 'Atlantic to the Urals' European alternative were:[58] (a) phasing out of the military confrontation between the superpowers; (b) neutralising the strength of a reunified Germany in a larger setting; and (c) giving Europeans across the whole Continent greater control of their future. In this way De Gaulle was offering a much more enlightened and broad alternative than the narrow nationalism for which he is often mistakenly known. In Howorth's view, the structural changes which have taken place in Europe since the 1960s have made De Gaulle's alternative even more relevant. The emerging ideas of a culturally reunited Soviet Union serve to reinforce this process.

It is in this context of the gradual evolution of French foreign policy in a developing Europe over the forty years since the last war that we can best understand 'Das Bündnis im Bündnis' – the Alliance within the Alliance.[59] The idea of seeking security *with*

---

57. P. Rogers, *Guide to Nuclear Weapons*, 3rd edition, London, 1988.
58. J. Howorth, 'The Third Way', *Foreign Policy*, vol. 65, no. 1, 1987, pp. 114–35.
59. R. Fritsch-Bournazel, 'The French View', in E. Moreton (ed.) *Germany Between East and West*, London, 1987.

rather than *from* Germany surfaced in France surprisingly soon after the Second World War and there is a long record of military co-operation.[60] But it is also clear that fear was always an ingredient in French policy:

> It was long a Gaullist trauma that the Federal Republic, the main ally of the United States in Europe, might emerge as the hegemonic power of the continent and reduce France to a peripheral role. This worry led to the 1963 Franco-German treaty, which was conceived as a counterweight to the political, economic and military ties between Bonn and Washington.[61]

But of course, if the power of the United States in Europe declines, France has an equal worry over German–Soviet rapprochement without French involvement:

> in France the fear was that Bonn might turn its interest towards Eastern Europe in a new version of earlier nineteenth- and twentieth-century *Schaukelpolitik* that kept Germany swinging back and forth in alliance between East and West. A free-wheeling powerful Germany trying to manoeuvre between the two blocs, seeking to exploit the country's unique geographical position in the heart of Europe for its national goals, and reversing Adenauer's postwar policy of alliance with the West clearly would pose a challenge to the European balance of power.[62]

Added to all these fears the French cannot have been sanguine at the growth of the Greens, anti-nuclearism and anti-Americanism in Germany. Too receptive an audience for Gorbachev in the Federal Republic could cause many difficulties for France, which now more openly recognises the need to keep the United States in Europe as the basis of a continuing security system. Or, to put it more bluntly: 'On the quiet, many French people feel the Federal Republic might betray and destroy the European edifice built after World War 2, and do so for a Soviet mess of pottage that gives it deceptive hope of reunification.'[63]

It is clear surely that growth of the European pillar in NATO will involve French attempts to forge closer links with the Federal

---

60. L. Benecke, *et al.*,'Franco-West German Technological Cooperation', *Survival*, vol. 28, no. 2, 1986, pp. 234–46.
61. Fritsch-Bournazel, 'The French View'.
62. Ibid.
63. Ibid.

Republic. And in the background lie the French nuclear weapons, and the possibility of a Franco-German-centred European nuclear superpower as one eventual outcome.

Conclusion: Instabilities and Opportunities

In his classic paper on the post-war stability in Europe, 'The Long Peace: Elements of Stability in the Postwar International System', John Lewis Gaddis deliberately calls upon the applications of Systems Theories to International Relations.[64] He notes that:

> An 'international system' exists, political scientists tell us, when two conditions are met: first, interconnections exist between units within the system, so that changes in some parts of it produce changes in other parts as well; and, second, the collective behaviour of the system as a whole differs from the expectations and priorities of the individual units that make it up.[65]

It seems reasonable to suggest that we are dealing with an International System in that sense at the present time. Perestroika in the Soviet Union has produced changes in other parts of the world and these have not all been as intended by the originators – whatever their real motives.

Gaddis goes on to point out that Systems Theory is valuable because it helps to distinguish between stable and unstable political configurations. He notes that two famous political scientists, Karl Deutsch and J. David Singer, have defined stability as the probability that:

— the system retains all of its essential characteristics;
— that no single nation becomes dominant;
— that most of its members continue to survive; and
— that large-scale war does not occur.[66]

Moreover, Gaddis points out that Deutsch and Singer stress two very different types of process and potential outcome for a system:

64. J. L. Gaddis, 'The Long Peace: Elements of Stability in the Postwar International System', *International Security*, vol. 10, no. 4, 1986, pp. 99–142.
65. Ibid., p. 102.
66. Ibid., p. 103.

the capacity for self-regulation: the ability to counteract stimuli that would otherwise threaten its survival, much as the automatic pilot on an airplane or the governor on a steam engine would do. 'Self-regulating' systems are very different from. . . . 'self-aggravating' systems, situations that get out of control, like forest fires, drug addiction, runaway inflation, nuclear fission, and . . . all-out war.[67]

These processes refer, of course, to dominant negative and positive feedback loops respectively.

It is clear that the three issues that have been investigated here in detail contain strong potentialities for instability. In regard to the scientific–technical revolution in military affairs under the nuclear stalemate there is a strong positive feedback system in which the perceived importance of conventional weapons leads to more research and thus more improvements in lethality, accuracy, range and penetrability. The development of such weaponry seems unlikely to do anything to improve crisis stability in Europe. It therefore increases the threat of warfare.

In regard to the European Pillar in NATO, the increasing difficulties with the US budget seem increasingly likely to lead to US withdrawals from Europe. This will only feed the perception of West German power and influence and Franco-German cooperation. Thus it appears possible that one of the essential characteristics of the post-war West European system – US domination – could be lost.

The external aspect of the perestroika programme could similarly lead to disintegration with some parts of NATO responding to Soviet initiatives whilst others grow increasingly concerned over a possible Soviet tactic of causing divisions and dissension. Again it is not difficult to see how such a process could accelerate the growth of divisions once it started.

In contrast to such malign possibilities, however, we should keep in mind a fourth mechanism and potential outcome. It could be that Gorbachev actually means what he says, and he might be able to convince us in the West of his trustworthiness. Consequences could then flow from a self-reinforcing build-up of trust as described by Osgood's theory. In Europe we could then see arms reductions and less dangerous strategies, but also the removal of superpower forces that would increase the freedom of all Europeans. A new Europe

67. Ibid., p. 103.

could be in the making, but there are dangers as well as possibilities as the post-war structures of East–West relation change. Peace research has much to do in elucidating processes which will enhance the prospects of a benign outcome.

10

British Defence Policy in a Changed Europe

Paul Rogers

Introduction

During the course of 1989, political developments in Eastern
Europe combined to alter the security map of the entire continent.
Following the changes in Soviet foreign policy in the mid-1980s
under President Gorbachev, and especially his progressive stance on
many arms control issues, it was already clear that relations between
NATO and the Warsaw Pact were becoming more cordial. The
improvements had commenced while Ronald Reagan was still in the
White House, but the first year of the Bush administration seemed
to confirm that his presidency would not block further improvements.

Bush's first summit meeting with Gorbachev, on-board ship off
the coast of Malta in December 1989, did not produce any historic
new agreements, but the liberalisation of East–West trade and the
tentative timetable set for the first stage of the Strategic Arms
Reduction Treaty (START 1) and the Conventional Forces in
Europe agreement (CFE 1) showed that the trend of improving
relations was set to continue.[1]

The Malta summit coincided with further stages in the political
liberalisation of two key East European states, East Germany and
Czechoslovakia. These states followed two others, Poland and
Hungary, where changes were already far advanced. In Poland, a
government with a strong Solidarity presence was in power by the

---

1. For an assessment of the state of arms control negotiations at the end of 1989,
see Paul Rogers and Malcolm Dando, *Directory of Nuclear, Biological and
Chemical Weapons, 1990*, London, 1990.

middle of the year under a non-communist prime minister, and in Hungary, the existing liberal tendencies were being further encouraged. Even in Bulgaria, a change in the leadership was likely to be just the first step down a similar road. Finally, in the closing days of the year, the momentous events in Romania overturned a seemingly secure totalitarian state. Only Albania seemed shielded from change.

Apart from Romania, the two most dramatic events during the year were the collapse of communist rule in East Germany following the breaking down of the Berlin Wall, and the remarkable advent of a non-communist-led coalition government in Czechoslovakia.

The many changes in Eastern Europe appeared to have the tacit if not always open approval of the Soviet leadership and amounted to a radical change in the nature of European security. From a bloc structure in which NATO saw itself as threatened by the massive military machine of the Warsaw Pact countries, there was emerging in Eastern Europe a new, less formal, security alliance, still overshadowed by the Soviet Union, but likely to be concerned as much with a potentially unified Germany as with a threat from the West as a whole.

Certainly, the result of this would be that NATO could no longer claim to be facing a monolithic and singularly aggressive military force. The political changes were quite profound, in that any idea of a co-ordinated Warsaw Pact capability to invade Western Europe now appeared frankly far-fetched. It was no longer possible to envisage, if indeed it had ever been the case, that the Soviets could rely on Poles, Czechs, Hungarians and others to form part of a united invading force. Furthermore, the unilateral force cuts announced by President Gorbachev in his speech to the United Nations in December 1988, and followed by other cuts during 1989, suggested that the priority for the Soviet Union really was to cut military spending and concentrate on restoring the Soviet economy. A number of studies from Western government agencies and strategic studies centres undertaken during 1989 all conclude that the Warsaw Pact threat has diminished substantially.

Although at the time of writing (December 1989) it is too early to be sure that the changes are entirely irreversible, it is now clear that they *have* been quite fundamental. There may yet be strong counteraction in one or two East European states, but the collapse of Communist state power in most countries has been so considerable that it will not be fully restored. It is certainly possible that President Gorbachev could be forced from power in some way, but the state of the Soviet economic crisis is so severe that any successor would be faced with similar priorities and would certainly be unable to rebuild a re-united Warsaw Pact threat to the West in less than several years.

We thus face the progressive diminishing of the security threat from the East, a threat which has been the justification for NATO and its military organisation. The changes in Eastern Europe require NATO to rethink its whole strategy and, possibly, its whole existence. They require, furthermore, that all the Western European states review their individual defence policies.

Even before the end of 1989, it was apparent that this was already happening in some countries, if not within the upper echelons of the NATO bureaucracy. At that level one sensed, if anything, only a deep wish to return to the *status quo ante* – a system of two vigorously competing blocs was so much easier to handle! West Germany, though, was clearly preparing for substantial defence cuts, had announced withdrawal of some naval units in the Baltic and was moving determinedly against NATO nuclear modernisation. France was expected to trim its defence budget and a variety of plans to reduce the US armed forces were being prepared, and leaked to the press, in Washington.

Even so, none of this amounted to the fundamental rethinking which the new circumstances in Eastern Europe required, and an even more remarkable feature of Western European security politics was that one NATO member state seemed determined to carry on as though nothing had happened.[2] In Britain, talk of defence cuts was regarded by the government as entirely premature and, indeed, the autumn financial statement, which traditionally indicates the levels of government spending in forthcoming years, actually gave notice of a modest rise in defence spending.

Britain thus seemed least willing or able to respond to the changes in Eastern Europe, yet, from a position of high defence expenditure, had the potential to make far-reaching cuts. It is, therefore, worthwhile exploring the context of Britain's current attitude to defence and to suggest the kind of defence review that is necessary and desirable for the 1990s. Britain is a country in which defence is

2. An analysis of future options for NATO is included in Alternative Defence Commission, *The Politics of Alternative Defence*, London, 1987.

much more a matter of status than security, and defence spending has consistently been amongst the highest of any NATO country. In a rapidly changing Europe it may finally be possible to come to terms with our economic circumstances and produce a defence posture which aids security and stability in Europe at a very much reduced level of spending.

The British Defence Context

Britain developed as a naval power over several centuries and used its power extensively in pursuit of colonial gain. Although it was capable of raising a massive army during the First World War, much of its global military power derived from the wealth of its overseas territories, especially India and its financing of the Indian Army. Following the crippling economic effect of the Second World War and the retreat from Empire in the two decades afterwards, Britain's economic status and the desperate need for industrial investment in the domestic sector should have dictated a defence budget lower than its principal competitors such as West Germany, France and, increasingly, Japan.

In practice, British politics in the 1950s were dictated by a yearning for global status. Indeed, a common belief among much of the population was that Britain was one of three world super-powers. Much of this belief focussed on the need to maintain a global military presence and to develop and maintain an independent nuclear force. More generally it resulted in consistently high levels of spending on military research and development.

This reached the height of economic folly in the middle 1950s. At that time, Britain had around 800,000 people in its armed forces and was maintaining 80,000 troops in the Suez Canal Zone alone, with many thousands more 'East of Suez'. It had tested and begun to deploy nuclear bombs, was developing a thermonuclear bomb, and was developing, simultaneously, three different medium-range nuclear-capable jet bombers. Furthermore it was investing in several other advanced military projects including the Black Night rocket and TSR2 supersonic bomber, which were ultimately cancelled.

Some small sense of reality intervened after the Suez débâcle of 1956, with an end to conscription, a scaling down of Britain's global role and a partial redirection of defence commitments to NATO, but Britain persisted with high levels of *per capita* defence spending

into the 1960s. It can be argued that right through until the end of
the 1970s Britain consistently failed to match defence spending to
the realities of its reduced economic power. Typically, defence
spending at any one time tended to be in tune with Britain's actual
global status perhaps twenty or thirty years before.

Britain was particularly adept at maintaining a very substantial
defence research and development sector, with up to half of all
spending on science and technology R & D going into the defence
sector, contrasting with countries such as Japan, West Germany and
Italy, where the figures ranged from 5 to 20 per cent.

Britain's commitment to high spending on defence was maintained and indeed enhanced in the first six years of the Thatcher
administration from 1979. Substantial increases in defence budgets,
of around 28 per cent in constant figures between 1979 and 1983,
were partially a response to new Cold War tensions but partly a
reflection of the priorities of Thatcher-style Conservatism. Even the
attempt to curb the size of the surface navy from 1981 onwards was
thwarted by its conspicuous role in the Falklands/Malvinas conflict
in 1982. By 1986–7, defence spending topped out at figures substantially higher than those typical of the 1970s, but modest increases were planned for 1990 and 1991.

In the late 1980s, Britain's armed forces were maintaining six
distinct roles, just four of them directly related to NATO:

1. The maintenance of the British Army of the Rhine (BAOR) and
   RAF Germany, with around 80,000 personnel and a large infrastructure, including tactical nuclear forces.
2. A major commitment to the security of the North Sea, Channel
   and North East Atlantic, mainly comprising surface combatants
   and submarines but with some maritime patrol and strike aircraft
   as well, including tactical nuclear forces.
3. The defence of air space around the UK, especially in the
   northern part of the North Sea and towards Iceland.
4. The maintenance of an independent nuclear force, normally
   committed to NATO but available, like the tactical nuclear
   weapons, for independent use.
5. The defence of UK territory itself, a function partly overlapping
   with the first three roles although including the major security
   commitment in Northern Ireland.
6. 'Out of area' activities including the Falklands garrison, the Gulf
   Patrol, the West Indies naval presence, garrisons in Gibraltar,

Cyprus, and Hong Kong, and numerous training and advisory roles in more than twenty countries.

Restructuring Britain's Defence Forces

The radically changed circumstances in Eastern Europe by the end of 1989 suggest that a fundamental review of many of Britain's defence commitments is appropriate. This could involve a considerable scaling down of commitments to BAOR and RAF Germany, if not their eventual elimination, and a scaling down of the naval commitments in the North East Atlantic and the long-range air-defence commitments in the same broad area. It may separately be argued that the improved climate for arms control will bring heavy pressure on the British government to scale down if not abandon its nuclear pretensions, and the maintenance of extensive global commitments hardly seems consistent with a middle-ranking Western European state.

The changes relating to NATO might best be undertaken in the context of the establishment of some kind of alliance which replaces NATO and the Warsaw Pact and concerns pan-European security, albeit with a role for the United States and the Soviet Union. The pace of events from 1985 to 1989 suggests that a European Common Security Alliance (ECSA) is feasible by the very early 1990s, overseeing progressive withdrawal of foreign troops from the territories of European states and the progressive demilitarisation of those states, together with the US and the Soviet Union, down to, at the very most, half of the levels typical of the 1980s.

If such deep cuts are to be achieved within five or so years, then they should be undertaken with a view to increasing stability by concentrating on the elimination of the more offensive forces currently deployed. These include most tactical nuclear forces, deep-strike air forces, many types of ground-launched area-impact munitions and some classes of naval forces. Emphasis should be placed on defensive systems including air defences, anti-armour weapons and highly mobile lightly-armoured ground forces.

Little or no work has been done on such radical force restructuring within the strategic studies community, but the research into alternative defence strategies which was carried out in the early 1980s in Britain and other Western European countries is certainly relevant. This work broadly started from a different stand-point compared with the present position. Concerned over the dangers of Cold War tensions, peace researchers sought to develop defence strategies which were non-nuclear and defence-orientated. They applied some of the force postures adopted by countries such as Sweden and Switzerland to the circumstances of NATO member states such as Britain, adapting them to the different circumstances. Some studies went further still, investigating the possibilities for non-military defence.

In Britain, the largest study was that undertaken by the Alternative Defence Commission from 1980 to 1983.[3] This study proposed that Britain adopt a non-nuclear defensive posture, with membership of NATO being conditional on changes in NATO's own strategy, and further suggested that if the climate of East–West relations were to improve Britain could go still further towards radically scaled-down military forces. It then went on to suggest a number of force postures involving financial savings of up to 60 per cent.

Such proposals seemed beyond the bounds of the possible at that time of tension, yet are not dissimilar, at least in the extent of the cuts, to those being actively contemplated in the Soviet Union and the United States, admittedly over a timescale of at least a decade. They cannot be applied precisely now, not least because of changes in force structures and in political circumstances, but they do provide many useful guidelines, especially in relation to the possible make-up of specifically defensive forces.

We can thus observe two parameters in considering a revised defence posture for Britain:

1. A European Common Security Alliance crossing the East–West boundaries and involving deep cuts in defence budgets and force postures, certainly to the extent of 50 per cent by the mid-1990s.
2. The need to produce a defence-orientated posture for Britain and, indeed, within Europe as a whole.

On this basis, we can indicate some possible developments within the three services which would involve financial savings of the extent now possible over five years and also move the force postures towards a more defensive orientation.

---

3. Alternative Defence Commission, *Defence Without the Bomb*, London, 1983.

The Army   Withdraw all but one division of BAOR (i.e., more than two-thirds) within three years, with possible complete withdrawal, depending on European security context, by mid-1990s. The regular army as a whole to be cut by around 50 per cent but with reserves maintained at 75 per cent of current levels. New Challenger 2 main battle tank to be cancelled. Emphasis on mobility and anti-armour capability but without providing for long-range offensive operations.

The Royal Air Force   Reduce personnel progressively by about 50 per cent, maintaining interceptor and reconnaissance squadrons but cutting back severely on longer-range strike aircraft. Ten Tornado strike squadrons to be reduced to three, with just one (plus reconnaissance squadron) in West Germany. Harrier squadrons to be retained but transport and tanker squadrons severely curtailed. Reserves to be retained at near present levels.

The Royal Navy   All pre-1980 frigates and destroyers to be scrapped or placed in reserve (i.e., Type 21, Leander, Type 82 and some Type 42). Production of Type 23 frigate to be halted and replaced by new shorter-range and lighter Type 24, with aim being to have an escort fleet of twenty-five to thirty, down from the present fleet of forty-five to fifty, within five years. Only one carrier to remain operational, two in reserve. Amphibious forces to be halved. Nuclear-powered attack submarine production to be halted in favour of low production rate of diesel-powered boats, with pre-1980 submarines to be put in reserve. More emphasis to be placed on patrol craft.

   In addition to these changes, it should be possible to ensure that Britain's nuclear forces and infrastructure are eventually eliminated, within the context of arms control negotiations if not unilaterally, although the costs of dismantling these forces will ensure that financial savings are relatively low, at least in the short term.
   In response to the changed Europe of the 1990s, we are therefore considering military forces of around half of the current levels, but with relatively more emphasis on reserves, allowing for a partial rebuilding of forces if the recent political developments in Eastern Europe were, in a worst-case scenario, to be reversed.
   It should be possible to cut defence spending by about half within five years, rather faster than is likely in much of Europe, but from a

current spending level which is well above average. Provided that the developments in Eastern Europe continue through the 1990s, this level of cuts could be regarded as a first step. By the end of the decade it should be possible, in a largely demilitarised Europe, to maintain a defence budget of around 30 per cent of current levels, involving armed forces which are configured in a primarily defensive posture. Given that current spending is around £20 billion per year, the average annual savings over the 1990s would be around £10 billion, giving a total of £100 billion, available for redirection into other sectors of the economy.

There are two significant contexts to these changes. The first is that there would have to be substantial attention paid to industrial restructuring and conversion in the armaments industries. While some research has been done on this in the UK, the extent and quality of the work in the United States and Scandinavia is much higher, and may aid the process in Britain.

The second, and much more important context, is that of future political developments in Europe. We are considering radical changes in Britain's forces as part of similar changes throughout most of Europe, East and West. These would be codified, at least in part, in verifiable treaties and agreements, perhaps under the aegis of a possible European Common Security Alliance which would be developed as a matter of priority and which might, by the mid to late 1990s, replace NATO and the Warsaw Pact completely.

Furthermore, this excessive concern with European security should not obscure the many problems in other regions of the world, and at least part of the massive financial savings likely to accrue from the defence cuts could be redirected towards global problems of the environment and human development. The greatest danger is that the recent decades of East–West tension could be replaced by a northern power bloc intent on maintaining control of the global economy and, in a world of increasing environmental problems, retreating into a siege mentality and seeking to maintain its wealth in the face of deep global inequalities.

Within Britain, the financial resources made available by substantially reduced defence budgets would provide the means for substantial industrial regeneration, investment in social and economic infrastructure including housing, transport, health and education, and a greater commitment to action on global environment and development.

As on a global scale, so too domestically, the new opportunities open to us as a result of the changes in Eastern Europe in the late 1980s provide a remarkable and possibly unique opportunity to beat swords into ploughshares.

PART IV

Peace and the Resolution of Conflict

11

Recognising Conflict

Chris Mitchell

The Concept of Conflict in Peace Research

It would be pleasant to be able to record that, after a preliminary era of uncertainty and discord, the conflict and peace research movement was fundamentally agreed about the basic phenomena it was attempting to study and evaluate, as well as about some tried and tested procedures for moving from situations deemed undesirable to others regarded as more satisfactory. Unfortunately, anyone who has followed the growth of the movement since its inception in the early 1950s will realise that this is far from the case. The movement as a whole is still divided into many approaches, many schools of thought and many competing views about the nature (and proper functions) of conflict and peace research. The split in the middle years of the movement between the basically American-dominated, international-conflict orientated wing, and the Scandinavian and West German radicals, with their emphasis on structural violence, 'positive' peace and the long-term benefits of conflict creation, is only the most noticeable of the many cleavages within an overall movement that currently resembles a set of diverse and isolated research groups rather than a unified intellectual tradition.

These, possibly very healthy, divergences might well be typified by the failure of academic conflict and peace researchers even to be able to agree whether or not a conflict actually exists in a particular social system. Outsiders might well imagine that the problem of recognising or identifying a conflict should be one on which conflict researchers ought to unite, but this is far from true. The divergence of view in our field takes the form of a fierce debate about whether human conflict can be defined *objectively*, in the sense that a conflict exists, irrespective of the beliefs and perceptions of those involved;

209

or *subjectively*, in the sense that the parties themselves must identify whether, in fact, their goals are mutually exclusive, so that some conflict exists.

This particular division within academic conflict research is an unexpected but important one. On the one hand there is a strong tradition that argues that it is more realistic, and analytically more useful, to hold that a conflict situation only exists when it is perceived to exist by those people involved, who are convinced (possibly incorrectly) of the existence of some goal incompatibility. A conflict situation, the 'subjectivist' argument runs, must be perceived as such by the participants themselves in order for conflict behaviour to develop. Opposed to this approach is an 'objectivist' view, which is based upon the argument that the parties may actually be in a conflict situation, yet themselves remain unaware of this fact (possibly because of ignorance, or mistaken perceptions of circumstances). Hence, no conflict behaviour occurs, and no conflict attitudes, such as fear or mistrust, arise.

It may seem at first as though such a debate about the 'genuine' nature of human conflict is yet another example of academic trivialisation, in the same vein as the number of conflict researchers that can be placed on a silicon chip. However, the question of whether conflicts are, indeed, objective phenomena is of crucial importance, not merely for theoretical conflict analysis, but also for the practical problems of ending conflicts by a compromise settlement or by a thorough resolution. The achievement of a successful resolution of any conflict, whereby the conflict disappears once and for all, depends upon the conflict being basically a subjective phenomenon. If conflicts of interest exist in any objective sense (irrespective of their being perceived as conflict situations by the people involved) then a split-the-difference compromise (or the defeat of one party) becomes the only logical outcome.

A further important factor in the debate, which significantly affects arguments about the validity of different approaches to ending conflicts, is the objectivist criticism of the very concept of conflict resolution itself. It is frequently argued by Marxist sociologists, Scandinavian conflict researchers and those who argue that social structure produces fundamental and inevitable conflicts of interest, that those seeking to resolve conflicts are actually in the business of 'pacification' (when they ought to be in the business of revolution). The essence of this argument is that one of the practical dangers of arguing that conflicts are subjective phenomena is that such an argument might create a tendency to play down actual, if submerged and unrecognised, conflicts of interest. In other words, a subjectivist approach to human conflict might lead to the acceptance of highly unequal and inequitable relationships because no conflict situation is recognised by the parties, or because no conflict behaviour has taken place. A genuine, existing conflict is 'pacified' rather than resolved, and pacification normally benefits only one of the parties involved (or, at least, benefits are distributed with significant inequality). Thus, peasant uprisings are 'bought off' with minimal land reforms, and industrial workers pacified by minor concessions such as representation on management committees. In both cases, the 'fundamental issues' – a radical restructuring of the economy or the complete change of power relations within a firm or industry – are ignored. The fundamentally unequal situation remains unchanged, and the dominant position of one party is confirmed at the expense of the other.

Although there may be some practical justification for such accusations, I do not agree that there is any reason why, in principle, the adoption of a subjectivist approach to human conflict should necessarily imply anything about one's view of appropriate action in any given situation or an appropriate outcome for a conflict. The fact that a subjectivist approach to *recognising* conflict might, in a particular case, lead to the conclusion that, currently, no overt goal incompatibility exists does not mean that it will also lead to the conclusion that no inequality, injustice or outright tyranny exists (or does, and should not exist). However, while admitting that some of the criticisms of a subjectivist approach to conflict research do demand to be taken seriously (both by researchers and activists) the objectivist position requires closer scrutiny than it is sometimes afforded, and an examination of some of the claims and assumptions of this school of thought in conflict and peace research is the main focus of this chapter.

Incipient Conflict: Low Awareness of Goal Incompatibility

An 'objectivist' position on the definition of social and international conflict is taken up by a wide variety of conflict researchers, ranging from American operations researchers to neo-Marxist sociologists. There are two basic versions of this objectivist approach. The milder form argues that it is possible to state that two parties are in a relationship of conflict when a situation of conflict arises from the goals or acts of one party harming the goals or interests of another, even though both may be unaware of this fact. Conflict is any situation in which 'the behavior of Party A imposes unacceptable costs on Party B (even though A may do this unwittingly, and as a result of behavior which was not intended to affect B in any manner at all)'.[1] These circumstances represent a situation of potential conflict, which does not become overt until: (a) B identifies the source of the costs he is being forced to pay; and (b) B makes his objections regarding A's cost-imposing behaviour known to the latter. At this point both are aware of the cost-imposition, and some form of conflict behaviour, either persuasive or coercive, is likely to begin.

Two important features of both these definitions of conflict situations need to be stressed:

1. It is perfectly possible for a situation of genuine goal incompatibility to exist quite independently of the perceptions of both parties, in the sense that both might recognise that their goal-seeking behaviour is not achieving its objectives, but that both are unable to identify the existence of mutually exclusive goals as the source of failure.
2. The existence of a conflict depends, in such a case, on the recognition by both parties that they are (somehow) failing to attain goals that they are conscious of possessing and pursuing (even though the actual goal incompatibility may only be obvious to an outside observer).

In one sense, then, even this kind of definition of conflict takes on 'subjectivist' elements, as it is the parties themselves who decide which goals and outcomes they value, and which they wish to pursue, in spite (possibly) of their continued failure. The implication of such definitions is that if both parties could be educated or 'enlightened' into realising why the pursuit of their objectives is failing then they (as well as some omniscient observer) would be able to recognise that their interests – *defined by themselves, in their own terms* – were in conflict, and thereupon act accordingly by

1. A. V. S. De Reuck, 'The Resolution of Conflict', mimeograph, Centre for the Analysis of Conflict, University College, London, 1970.

indulging in some conflict behaviour *vis-à-vis* the now recognisable opposing party.

This point may seem rather obvious but it is a necessary preliminary in order to distinguish this first argument from another, radically different objectivist position concerning situations of social conflict. It should be emphasised, then, with respect to this first objectivist view of human conflict, that:

1. The existence of an 'objective' conflict situation can become apparent to an observer in spite of a lack of observable conflict behaviour (or even awareness of incompatibility by the involved parties) through the existence of identifiable incompatible goals (or conflicting values) of the parties concerned.
2. Awareness by the parties that their goals and values conflict with those of other groupings may not exist, but nonetheless each party is *conscious* of possessing definite goals and valuing certain outcomes, even if they are not (yet) aware that others possess goals which, if achieved or even sought, would make it impossible for them to achieve their own goals.
3. An observer could make parties aware of the inconsistency of their positions and aims by pointing out the *objective* fact that, given the parties' own subjectively determined goals, a conflict situation (although no conflict behaviour and, presumably, no conflict attitudes) exists. In this case, the observer makes no attempt to impose his own values on to the situation, but merely accepts those of the parties as being relevant.

The distinguishing features of such 'objective' conflict situations are, therefore, that there exists a significant lack of awareness on the part of the parties that their conscious goals are mutually incompatible, or that their behaviour is adversely affecting the achievements of others' aspirations or goals. This lack of awareness leads to an absence of hostility, antagonism and other conflict attitudes, and to a lack of conflict behaviour *vis-à-vis* another party. In plain language, the parties don't (yet) know that others possess competing goals which are frustrating achievement of their own, even if they do know precisely what they want for themselves.

It may be helpful to label the kind of situation described above as *incipient* conflict, defining it as a condition where, given the values and goals of particular groups and individuals, goal incompatibilities (i.e., conflict situations) actually exist, but the parties are not consciously aware of this fact. It might be suggested that complex social processes frequently involve various entities (categories, collectivities or existing organised groups) passing from an environment in which no goal incompatibilities exist (isolation or co-operation) into one where such incompatibilities develop but the entities remain unaware of them, possibly because of lack of information, deliberate misinformation by one of the parties, or straightforward lags in recognising that change has occurred. The stage of *incipient* conflict, where goals are incompatible or pursuit of them imposes unrecognised costs on others, ends with the recognition of the goal incompatibilities and the source of the costs. At this point, the conflict can be said to enter a *latent* stage, where the clashing goals are recognised as such, yet no actual conflict behaviour is directed against the other party. Ultimately, the conflict becomes *manifest* (unless behaviour is suppressed or deterred), and recognisable conflict behaviour becomes a feature of the relationship between parties. Hence, this particular version of an objectivist view of conflict can be accommodated in an ideal type of a 'developmental sequence' for human conflicts as illustrated in Figure 11.1.

Figure 11.1 A Developmental Sequence for Human Conflicts

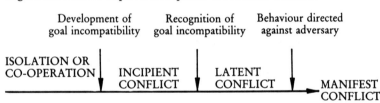

Social Structure and the Inevitability of Conflict

The second version of the 'objectivist' approach to defining situations of conflict is far more radical than that outlined above. The group of conflict researchers espousing this version rejects completely any approach that holds conflict situations to be subjectively defined phenomena in any way. They argue that there are certain fundamental objective standards that exist, independent of any single situation or relationship, which can be applied to reveal clearly whether a conflict situation exists. (In this case, 'objective' is defined as according to externally applied criteria.) This school argues that a conflict situation stemming from a goal incompatibility can exist not merely when parties remain unaware that, given their current values and objectives, their goals are in conflict with others, but also when one party possesses values giving rise to goals which are wholly complementary with another's, so that no perceived goal incompatibility exists nor will exist until the underlying values and related goals themselves change.

Many of this group of objectivist conflict researchers could be called 'structuralists', in that much of their analysis follows ideas originally proposed by Marx to the effect that, first, social structures contain within themselves certain inherent 'contradictions' which lead inevitably to social groups or classes developing mutually incompatible goals and (eventually) indulging in conflict behaviour. Secondly, at times, individuals and social groups may be unable to recognise the contradictions and resultant clashing goals, or be deluded into believing that their interests and aims *are* compatible with opposing groups. Hence, while suffering from 'false consciousness' or being 'mystified' by their (often dominant) opponents, some social groups or categories (usually the 'exploited') will be unable to identify their 'true' interests and goals. They may not even see themselves as being in conflict with others as their subjectively defined (but 'false') goals do not clash. Only by applying externally derived objective standards to such circumstances, and ignoring the subjective definitions of those actually involved, will the true situation of conflict be revealed.

This version of the objectivist approach has many adherents among Scandinavian and German conflict researchers. One of the clearest expositions of the position is put forward by Herman Schmid, who argues that conflict 'is incompatible interests built into the structure of the system where the conflict is located'.[2] Schmid positively rejects the position that a *situation* of conflict is best viewed as a clash of party-defined goals:

In an objectivist model of conflict . . . conflict is seen as built into a structure and as determined by this structure. Behavior and attitudes are but symptoms of the conflict which is independent of what the actors think or do. A class conflict is located in the structure of the capitalist mode of production, is determined by this structure and not the actors. This conflict between labour and capital is there, quite irrespective of whether there is open struggle or not, hostile feelings or not. Conflict is

2. H. Schmid, 'Peace Research and Politics', *Journal of Peace Research*, vol. 5, no. 3, 1968, p. 217.

never solved by behavioral/attitudinal integration, only disguised and turned into a latent state. The class conflict would be solved only by eliminating the contradiction between labour and capital.[3]

The line of argument of this school of objectivists is, thus, that out of certain (identifiable) social structures, situations of conflict automatically arise, whether or not they are recognised as such by the individuals, groups or collectivities involved in those social structures. (In passing, it should be noted that most structuralists refer to 'class' conflicts over resources or power distribution within a national society or between international rich and poor, when they give examples of objective conflict.) Conflict may be identified by outside observers, even when mutually incompatible goals are not recognised as such by the involved actors. Lars Dencik, for example, differentiates *conflict behaviour* from *conflict* (defined as incompatible interests) noting that such interests 'are here defined *objectively* i.e. by the observing scientist according to his theory and it is independent of the actual subjective consciousness of the actors involved. This means that incompatible interests are conceived of as structural (actor independent), the structure defined according to the theory of the scientist.[4] He then presents four possible sets of circumstances involving conflict situations and conflict behaviour to indicate how, according to an objectivist viewpoint, the two interact (see figure 11.2).

This classification scheme raises problems for an objectivist, as Dencik admits. Situation A is easy to explain (conflict perceived by both observer and actor, implying that the goals of one and the 'theory' of the other coincide). Similarly, D is fairly straightforward. Situation C is one in which, 'according to the theory of the observer', there should be a recognition of incompatible interests by the actors and conflict behaviour to pursue those interests. (Dencik refers to this as 'peaceful co-existence between the oppressor and oppressed'.) However, the people or groups involved might consider their goals to be compatible and no conflict behaviour occurs. This case is frequently exemplified by the classic situation of the contented serf; or as an accepted (even if unequal) differentiation of

3. H. Schmid, 'Peace Research as a Technology for Pacification', *Proceedings of the Third International Peace Research Association Conference*, vol. 3, 1970, p. 23.
4. L. Dencik, 'Peace Research: Pacification or Revolution?', *Proceedings of the Third International Peace Research Association Conference*, vol. 3, 1970, p. 79.

Figure 11.2 Subjective and Objective Views of Conflict

Basic incompatible interests
(defined 'objectively' by an observer)

		Yes	No
Overt conflict behaviour (by the actors involved)	Yes	A	B
	No	C	D

Source: L. Dencik, 'Peace Research: Pacification or Revolution?', *Proc. Third International Peace Research Assoc. Conference*, vol. 3, 1970.

roles, or distribution of social rewards.

Situation B presents some awkward problems for structuralists, since this is a situation where parties indulge in conflict behaviour, presumably over what seem to them salient and mutually incompatible goals, while the observer, according to his theory, can see no objective conflict situation involving incompatible interests (stemming from the nature of the social structure). It is here that arguments about false consciousness or mystification come into play which, crudely expressed, state that the actors do not really know what their true interests are (given their social situation), and if they did they would be indulging in some conflict other than the one with which they are currently preoccupied.

This criticism is probably being unfair to the structuralists. Dencik does try to explain B with reference to two possibilities:

1. 'Inertial' conflict, whereby conflict behaviour continues after the basic, real conflict has been resolved. (Dencik's example is of former slaves continuing their conflict behaviour *vis-à-vis* the owners after the abolition of slavery.)
2. 'Displaced' conflict, or conflict behaviour over issues which 'are not relevant to the solutions of the basic conflict'.[5]

In connection with this latter type of conflict, Dencik gives the example of conflict between black and white workers over scarce jobs, and comments that this issue (security of work) is something

5. Ibid.

separate from 'the basic conflict . . . being one between capital and labor'. Another illustration might be the dispute in the United Kingdom container industry (and also within the Transport and General Workers Union) in the early 1970s over which a group of workers packed and unloaded large containers. The dispute between the dockers and container workers over scarce jobs in the container depots may have had 'objectively' nothing to do with the 'fundamental' conflict between capital and labour. Nonetheless, it was very real to the participants; both sides were well aware that they possessed mutually incompatible goals; hostility and other conflict attitudes abounded; and behaviour ranged from unofficial picketing to an attempt by one group of workers to use the Industrial Relations Court against its rivals. If this is an unreal conflict to objectivists, to subjectivist analysts it has all the marks of a conflict, and a highly developed, self-conscious one at that.

In such situations, structuralists seem to put themselves in a position of saying that conflict behaviour, over what are to the involved parties very salient and real goals, is somehow unrealistic and that only the observing structuralists know what the 'real' objective conflict is about. Some have echoed Bernadette Devlin's remark about the Northern Ireland conflict not 'really' being about religious or communal differences, but instead being about 'class', while others have attacked any subjective approach as being one which has led to a concentration on unreal elements in situations of social conflict (those defined by the participant), thus helping further to mystify the actual state of affairs:

> Subjective theory . . . leads to concentration upon purely ideological conflicts that have no objective basis – like the religious conflict in Northern Ireland, the language conflict in Belgium or the race conflict in the U.S.A., all of which cut across the objective conflicts which are defined by the distribution of wealth in these three societies.[6]

Not all objectivists are neo-Marxists, however. Johan Galtung has explicitly denied indulging in any kind of a Marxist analysis, but some of his ideas on social conflict contain objectivist elements.[7]

---

6. R. S. Jenkins, 'Some Notes on the Social Functions of Conflict Theory', Danish Institute for Peace and Conflict Research, Copenhagen, Studies in Progress, 1 July 1969, p. 47.
7. See, for example, J. Galtung, 'Violence, Peace, and Peace Research', *Journal of Peace Research*, in G. Pardesi (ed.), *Contemporary Peace Research*, Brighton, 1982, pp. 93–125.

Taking his concept of structural violence as an example, it is plausible to interpret this view of social relationships as falling well within the orbit of those who argue that conflict exists independent of the perceptions, or subjectively determined goals, of the parties involved in any social relationship. For Galtung, 'structural', as opposed to physical violence results from the arrangements in any social system which deprive individuals and social groups of values or goals which they would otherwise attain. Note that in the case of structural violence, no actual physical harm need palpably be carried out by some person or group against another person or group; it is enough that one party's existence, behaviour or attributes prevent another from realising their values, that is, the long-range beliefs they hold about how things ought to be. As Dencik interprets the concept:

> Violence may be built into the very relationship between two parties so that, for instance, one's possibilities for development may be limited by the other's . . . 'peaceful' presence. Violence – *in the sense of value-deprivation of one party by the other* – is said to be based on *structural conditions*. This kind of structural, 'silent' violence may then have much more destructive and disastrous consequences than the open palpable violence. The . . . existence of most people in the slums of Latin America and the black ghettoes of the U.S. are not harmed by bullets or napalm, but by exploitation.[8]

If we take an obvious example, such as the black ghettoes in US cities, it is immediately obvious that, by their own and most observers' standards, the inhabitants are suffering an extreme form of value-deprivation and are, in Galtung's terminology, the victims of structural violence (a position they have attempted to rectify by the occasional use of physical violence). However, in less obvious cases, the problem emerges of who is to say when a group of people is suffering from value-deprivation, and whose criteria (the people involved or some external observer) can be used to measure the existence and degree of structural violence. Galtung is very little help here, for he merely claims that structural violence exists when human beings are so influenced that their potentials are not realised. The problem remains; who is to say which 'realisations' are being denied? How does an observer define a person's or group's potential? Should a third party impose his own values on what potential

8. Dencik, 'Peace Research', p. 81.

and opportunity ought to exist, or should this be left to the people involved? Galtung is imprecise about this point, but a reader cannot escape the impression that he adopts a basically objectivist approach, whereby some observing third party, by the application of that party's own (external) criteria, is also to determine the existence or non-existence of structural violence and hence of (objectively) incompatible interests.

If this is the basis of the structuralists' argument then it becomes important for them to be explicit about which criteria (according to Dencik, which theory) they use to evaluate whether an 'objective' goal incompatibility exists in any specific social situation; and also about the bases upon which such criteria are established. Is it, as is sometimes claimed, a theory (and if so, is the term theory used in the positive, analytic sense) which has considerable empirical backing for its acceptance, or is it merely a set of values used in some normative sense, which states that this is how a conflict-free social situation *ought* to be, and anything that does not conform to these values must, by definition, be a situation involving some conflict of interests?

'Objective' or 'Normative' Approaches to Identifying Conflict

Undoubtedly the clearest (and in many senses the most honest) exposition of the objectivist position comes from Adam Curle in his stimulating book, *Making Peace*.[9] This is not the place to review all of Curle's ideas, most of which are highly relevant to third-party efforts to settle or resolve a conflict, nor to go too deeply into his distinction between *peaceful* and *non-peaceful* (though perhaps also non-violent) *relationships*. However, Curle does state his position on objective conflict very clearly, and his arguments are worth following for the additional light they throw on the structuralist position. His initial definition of conflict is conventional, involving situations in which 'one individual, community, nation or even supranatural bloc desires something that can be obtained only at the expense of what another individual or group also desires'.[10] He then goes on, however, to modify this definition considerably by arguing

9. A. Curle, *Making Peace*, London, 1971.
10. Ibid., p. 4.

that a conflict may exist independently of the conscious desires of
the participants, and this will depend on whether or not the existing
relationships are 'unpeaceful' or exploitive and limiting according to
the observer's (Curle's) own values. Curle states quite openly that
his position constitutes a 'value' (not a theory, as some structuralists
have argued) and that if 'one holds that relationships that impede
human development are unpeaceful, it follows that one holds an
objectivist view of conflict . . . conflict is a question not of perception but of fact. Thus, if in a particular social system, one group
gains what another loses, there is – even if the loser does not
understand what is happening – a structural conflict.'[11] This is a
clear point of view, but what happens if both parties *understand*
their respective gains and losses, and *accept* them? (After all, social
relationships are complex, and parties often *both* gain and lose from
them.) And again, what of an observer who accepts a (possibly
unequal) relationship because of a value system differing from the
observer's?

The main point, which Curle freely admits, is that it is an
observer's *values* which indicate whether a situation of conflict
exists in the observed situation or not; and this really only amounts
to another *subjective* assessment of the situation and its relationships by some third party rather than by the participants. Curle
states his own values and conclusions fairly explicitly – those of
Western, liberal egalitarianism – and holds that 'it is reasonable to
treat the master-slave relationship . . . as one of conflict, which
should be changed'. We might accuse Curle of loading the evidence
by his selection of examples here. (Most people would agree that
slaves are usually in conflict with their masters and, anyway, Curle
himself agrees that there would almost inevitably be a subjective
conflict in such a situation: happy slaves tend to be a myth, and
slaves' attitudes towards their masters are nothing if not unpeaceful.) However, he does clearly state that any assessment of any
observed situation and 'our judgment of what ought to be done [is]
based on . . . very subjective values'.[12]

The whole problem may best be summarised as one involving the
coincidence of observer and participant *values*. If these do not
coincide, then differing conclusions about the existence of a conflict
situation may arise (see figure 11.3).

11. Ibid.
12. Ibid., p. 5.

Figure 11.3 Values and Goals of Observers and Actors in Recognising Conflict

A subjective conflict situation
(according to the values and goals of the actors)

		Yes	No
An objective conflict situation (according to the values and goals of the observer)	Yes	A. 'Real' conflict [Conflict behaviour plus antagonistic attitudes.]	B. 'Mystification' [No overt conflict behaviour.]
	No	C. 'Unreal' conflict [Conflict behaviour plus antagonistic attitudes]	D. 'Real' peace [No overt conflict behaviour]

For the objectivist, one major problem exists when actor values legitimise a situation which, according to observer values, is fraught with conflict (situation B). This may occur in situations involving individuals, small groups, classes or even complete societies. In each case the participants' values may legitimise a social structure which to an observer with quite different values may seem unjust and riddled with contradictions and conflicts. Chalmers Johnson, in his analysis of revolutionary social change has suggested that widespread violent behaviour does not occur within what he terms an 'equilibrated social system', which he defines as one in which the structural factors (division of labour, differentiation of roles, and distribution of social rewards such as status and goods) are generally legitimised in the eyes of the groups and individuals that make up that society.[13] In stable circumstances, the values and structure of a social system are congruent with the existing environment, the values helping to explain and justify the manner in which the social structure is adapted to coping with that environment. The situation changes either when the environment alters radically, so that the existing values no longer justify a given social structure, or when the

13. C. Johnson, *Revolutionary Change*, Boston, Mass., 1967.

value system itself alters, and postulates desirable alternative structural arrangements for coping with a given environment. (In both cases, perceptions of incompatible goals will grow up between separate social groups and classes.) The main point that emerges from Johnson's argument is that as long as the values held by actors explain and justify an existing social structure satisfactorily no perception of major incompatible interests are likely to exist, no hostile attitudes will develop among social groups and no conflict behaviour will occur: the Hindu untouchable will continue to occupy his position in Indian society because the accepted values of the caste system both explain and justify this position within that system. Only when the untouchable becomes aware of other interpretations of society, or other value systems, and accepts their premises, will he begin to perceive a conflict of interests between himself and the higher castes; although to any external observer, who possesses Western, liberal or Marxist values based upon egalitarianism and materialism, the traditional Hindu social structure may appear a mass of conflicting goals, issues and parties.

This example highlights the one major problem with the objectivist's normative view of conflict. Using this approach, a conflict exists (although no clash of goals is perceived by the actors in the situation) because the structural situation is *interpreted* by an observer according to certain values. A further difficulty with this objectivist approach can be seen by pushing its major argument to a logical conclusion, and recognising that two observers holding different sets of values will interpret the same circumstances in radically different ways. For example, the most egalitarian, non-class-ridden society, with rewards and status distributed absolutely evenly, would present an 'objective' conflict of interests to an observer possessing a set of values based upon the principle that some elite (racial, temporal, intellectual, responsible or sexual) actually deserved a favourable distribution of rewards. A second observer, sharing the egalitarian values of the members of the society, is unlikely to perceive any 'objective' conflict arising from that social structure.

It is useful to underline this argument by considering the values of people living in social systems that anthropologists have termed 'limited goods societies'. In such societies, the key characteristic is the propensity for conflict situations to arise from the assumption that everything is in limited (i.e., finite) supply, so that any individual's gain on *any* dimension automatically means a diminution of

223

that good for another individual, or for the whole community. All, and any, 'goods' are perceived within this finite supply framework ('not merely food, but friendship, not merely land but love'); hence gains are seen as threats to others, and as an inevitable source of conflict (thus giving rise to a need for structural mechanisms to remove such conflicts). In G. M. Foster's words:

> peasants view their social, economic and natural universe . . . as one in which all the desired things in life, such as land, wealth, health, friendship and love, manliness and honor, respect and status, power and influence, security and safety, *exist in finite quantity, and are always in that supply* as far as the peasant is concerned . . . in addition, there is no way directly with peasant power to increase the available quantities.[14]

Now, within such societies it would be possible for observers with widely differing value systems to identify the existence of objective conflicts of interests, or – given an egalitarian division of goods within the society – no objective conflicts yet large numbers of strangely irrelevant disputes over children or friendship or safety. Similarly, a member of such a limited goods society might well, in the role of outside observer, perceive numerous objective conflicts (objective according to his value system) in societies where land and wealth were equally shared (but all groups were increasing their attainments for the latter) and honour, friendship and status were maldistributed and changing. In fact, to our limited goods observer, any change in a dynamic society would automatically mean that 'objectively' a new conflict had arisen!

Conclusion

The essential point is that different views of any social system and the presence or absence of objective conflict therein, must depend upon two sets of factors: (a) the structure of the society (or set of relationships) under observation, but, more particularly, (b) the values (or ideology) of the observer. Hence, it might be more accurate to label those who subscribe to this version of the objectivist position as constituting a normative school of conflict research, in that they are not afraid to make judgements about the

14. G.M. Forster, *Tzintzuntzan: Mexican Peasants in a Changing World*, Boston, Mass., 1967.

existence or non-existence of conflicts according to their own value criteria. The major contribution of this normative approach to conflict research is that it helps to underline a sometimes neglected moral dimension in the field, particularly for those who are committed to playing some active part in a particular conflict (often with a view to attempting to end it). Is one justified, for example, in attempting to terminate a conflict by altering the values and goals of the participants, so that their objectives no longer appear to be mutually incompatible? Alternatively, should one accept the situation, and allow them to 'fight it out'? Again, when is one justified in approaching an ostensible conflict-free but inequitable situation (one in which even *incipient* conflict does not exist) and pointing out that one party is deluded in its values, hence in its perception of non-clashing goals, and (given an alternative set of values and goals) ought to be in a situation of conflict, where satisfaction can only be gained by a coerced restructuring of existing circumstances? All of these questions arise to confront any conflict researcher concerned with the analysis and exposition of human conflict, or with the search for solutions to conflicts. First recognise your conflict, then determine whether one should help to resolve it, and how.

12

Quaker Mediation

John Pettigrew

Introduction

There is a history of Quaker mediation stretching back to the very origins of Quakerism in the seventeenth century, because their fundamental commitment to non-violence and conflict resolution arises out of their beliefs, testimonies and witness. This first took the form of appeals to political and religious leaders in times of war to examine themselves and their political conduct. These appeals were couched in religious language. Robert Barclay (1648–90),[1] William Penn (1644–1718) and John Bellars (1654–1725) wrote such appeals, though none actually offered Quaker mediation. William Penn[2] and John Bellars[3] did however propose machinery for the settlement of disputes. William Penn, founder and an early governor of Pennsylvania, put his proposals, which were intended for Europe, into practice in his treaties with the Indians and the jurisdiction which they contained to deal with complaints on both sides.

Because of their refusal to participate directly in conflict or to countenance the resort to warfare as a way of settling disputes, there gradually arose in the Society of Friends (Quakers) an awareness of the need, not only to exhort those in power to find an alternative to war and to suggest a machinery for the settling of disputes, but to become involved directly in the resolution of conflicts. In some

---

1. Robert Barclay, *Epistle of Love and Friendly Advice to the Ambassadors of the Several Princes of Europe met a Nimeguen, 1677*. Copy on reference in Friends House Library, Friends House, Euston Road, London, NW1 2BJ.
2. William Penn, *An Essay Towards the Present and Future Peace of Europe*, Zurich and New York, 1983.
3. John Bellers, *His Life, Time and Writings*, ed. George Clarke, London, 1987.

instances, for example in America, they were already unavoidably politically involved. They were in positions of power in which they were required to take political action and to create conditions for peaceful relations between themselves and the Indians, and between themselves and other political factions, amongst them the British Crown. In other instances they were drawn into the resolution of conflicts by others.

Another important contributory strand to mediation has been previous Quaker presence in the area of conflict either by resident Quakers or by Quakers working on the relief of suffering and other service projects. Consequently there has been an 'on the spot' understanding of the social and political background and of the leading figures in the disputes, who frequently have been known to the Quaker mediators.

Experiences in all these fields have enabled Quakers to make their contributions to international conciliation in the twentieth century. A description of these examples of mediation can be found in Quaker literature: many are summarised in 'Quaker International Conciliation – an Evaluation of its Roots, Character and Development',[4] and three of the major ones are examined in depth by Mike Yarrow in *Experiences in Quaker International Concilation.*[5] Some others of more recent date, notably in Rhodesia/Zimbabwe and Sri Lanka, are yet to be the subject of detailed description and evaluation. To both, however, Quaker mediators including Adam Curle have brought their expertise and traditions.

The first of Yarrow's three major examples of Quaker conciliation is that between the two Germanies 1961–73. The construction of the Wall between them meant for the socialist government of East Germany security to develop their economically egalitarian system, to the West it was the concrete expression of a permanent division and a denial of the human right to freedom of movement. The urgent need for reconciliation was seen by a German Quaker, and in 1963 Roland Warren, an American Quaker, was the first to become involved in a long process of mediation, in which Quakers proved to be the message carriers trusted and accepted by both sides, and in which they gave support and encouragement to leaders

4. John A. Pettigrew, 'Quaker International Conciliation – an Evaluation of its Roots, Character and Development', M. Phil. thesis, University of Bradford, 1989.
5. C. H. Mike Yarrow, *Quaker Experiences in International Conciliation*, New Haven, Conn., 1978.

in the painful process of guiding public opinion to an acceptance of the reality of the two Germanies at that time. Both sides in the dispute have recorded their appreciation of the efforts of the mediators. Yarrow quotes Heinrich Albertz, the deputy mayor of West Berlin as saying: 'The Quaker representatives provided moral support of immense value, since we stood alone.'[6]

The second of Yarrow's choices was the dispute between India and Pakistan over Kashmir in 1965. Quakers in Britain and later in the United States reacted with concern when open warfare erupted, because of their century-long interest in Indian affairs and their sympathy with the movement for independence. There had been work on humanitarian relief and programmes of conferences and seminars.

Adam Curle, at that time director of the Centre for Studies in Education at Harvard University, was a member of the Quaker mediation team. He had wide experience in Pakistan having served as adviser on social affairs to the Pakistan Government from 1956 to 1959. Joseph W. Elder, an American Quaker, associate professor in the Departments of Sociology and Indian Studies at the University of Wisconsin, was another member. He spoke Urdu and Hindi and had had five years' experience in India. Although Quakers were not successful in achieving a major breakthrough, they did, according to Yarrow, nevertheless play an important role.[7]

Yarrow's third choice for detailed analysis was the Nigerian Civil War in 1967–70. During this civil war, the Quakers felt that the best contribution they could make to relieve the terrible suffering on both sides was to seek an end to the war by negotiated settlement. During the conflict, therefore, a team of three Quakers – John Volkmar, Adam Curle and Walter Martin – stood ready to undertake conciliation measures. They became well known in top governmental circles in Lagos and the capitals of the secessionists in Biafra, and were able to act as an unofficial third party. Official bodies like the Organisation of African Unity (OAU), United Nations, Commonwealth Secretariat, and governments like those of the UK and US could not make initial contacts with either side for fear that communication with a recognised authority would constitute a concession and a preliminary victory for an unrecognised body. Quakers were able to meet the leaders, carry messages and become

6. Ibid., p. 140.
7. Ibid.

facilitators in a process of conciliation.

There was little general knowledge of Quakers in West Africa, like there was in the Germanies and in India and Pakistan, but influential leaders had come to know individual Quakers through participation in Quaker programmes for diplomats. Adam Curle also had contacts in academic circles. There were few indigenous Quakers and only small indigenous Quaker meetings. It was important too that the personalities of the team enabled them to adopt a friendly low-key approach and to understand the African resentment of white domination. The Quakers were also able to keep their conciliation efforts out of the limelight, albeit with some difficulty.

Since one of the objectives of Quaker conciliation is to effect change in the perceptions of the parties in conflict, it is worth noting that although a settlement was not achieved, military victory was followed by a change of perceptions and by what Yarrow referred to as magnanimity towards the defeated rebels.[8] General Gowon, in accepting the surrender, ordered that all measures be taken to effect a peaceful transfer without any vindictiveness and he welcomed all people back as brothers.

In attempting an assessment, Yarrow concludes 'that the Quakers were drawn into a conciliatory role which they sustained with sensitivity, flexibility and imagination and without making mistakes serious enough to detract from the whole effort'.[9] The policy of Gowon and the federal government in favouring negotiation from the beginning, a view supported by the Quakers, had prevented extreme vindictiveness and insured a better future for the Nigerian people. In this respect the Quaker effort can be said to have been successful.

In addition to these major initiatives described by Yarrow, there have been others. Quakers have over the years taken major initiatives in mediation in the Middle East. The interest and concern of Friends dates from the early days of the Friends Syrian Mission in the 1830s. Swiss, British and American Friends set up hospitals and schools like Brumanna High School and those in Ramallah. These schools drew students from many areas of the Arab Middle East and many of their graduates became leaders in the countries from which they came. Quakers became known also from this humanitarian work including the administration of the Palestinian refugee relief

8. Ibid.
9. Ibid., p. 245.

229

programme in the Gaza Strip in 1949–50. Amongst those who came into contact with Quakers in the Middle East was Gamal Abdel Nasser, then a colonel in the Egyptian army, and encircled by Israeli troops at Faluga near Gaza. Quakers negotiated agreements with the Israelis and with the Egyptian army that permitted food supplies to be taken through Israeli and Egyptian lines to the local civilian population. Colonel Nasser handled their negotiations and carried out the distribution to the complete satisfaction of the Quaker group. This encounter between Nasser and Quakers, their reputation for fair-mindedness and their administration of the Palestinian relief programme in the Gaza Strip set the stage for the Egyptian approach to Quakers in the spring of 1955, which culminated in a dramatic, and until 1983, secret bid for peace in the Middle East confrontation between Egypt and Israel. The story of the secret Egyptian–Israeli peace initiative is told by Elmore Jackson, the lone Quaker conciliator, in his book *Middle East Mission* published in 1983, when the need for confidentiality agreed upon at the time was no longer necessary.[10]

The next major effort at conciliation in the Middle East was of a contrasting nature and grew out of an informal search by the US Friends Service Committee to see if anything constructive could be done after the 1967 war. An effort was mounted to fill the communication gap following this conflict and a working party was set up with the status of a committee of observers – informed and concerned amateurs attached to no government.

By 1970 this working party of Quakers and associates produced a significant study, 'Search for Peace in the Middle East'. The study was an approach to conciliation of a different order. It was neither a 'speak-truth-to-power' approach, nor active mediation between two sides. It was, in effect, an approach to the conflict between Arabs and Jews which did not entail actual mediation between any two governments or entities. The approach consisted in producing a study paper prepared by a working party; it went through nineteen drafts, each version being discussed with the parties involved, with the purpose of exploring peaceful solutions to the Middle East conflict.[11]

10. Elmore Jackson, *Middle East Mission*, New York, 1983.
11. *Search for Peace in the Middle East*, ed. L. R. Bolling, Report, Friends Peace and International Relations Committee and Friends Service Council, London, 1970.

Mediation in such a complex situation, where so many countries are involved, and where the United States and the USSR and even the United Nations are also concerned, was proving difficult, but Quaker interest in conflict resolution led them to prepare this objective and candid description of the political scene, as interpreted by all sides, and the attitudes of Jews and Arabs to their problems. It was produced out of concern for both peoples (it is 'both pro-Jew and pro-Arab') and was based on the conviction that the rights and interests of both sides must be recognised and reconciled on some just and peaceful basis.

This report was followed by another in 1982 – *A Compassionate Peace – A Future for the Middle East.*[12] Again it did not in itself constitute a mediation process, but it bore some of the hallmarks of such a process – communication and proposals for the resolution of the conflict.

The report takes an informed and detailed look at the political situation and spells out options, proposals and recommendations on issues as varied as the creation of a nuclear-free zone and terrorism. It extends its scope to include Iran and Afganistan. It concludes by suggesting that despite the important current political problems the real issues that emerge from the conflicts and crises are employment, hunger, political liberty, human rights and the less tangible question of national self-identity and economic development. The final paragraph of the report returns to the consistent theme of all Quaker conciliation, the primacy of faithfulness to their religious tradition of seeking peace through justice. It suggests in its conclusion that this tradition is common to Judaism, Christianity and Islam and that peace and security will be achieved if the peoples and their leaders in the Middle East courageously pursue their prophetic traditions.

Evaluations

So far this paper has outlined some of the major cases of Quaker mediation and the variety in Quaker response during their history to the need for the resolution of conflict. If by evaluation one means careful scrutiny and analysis of the processes of mediation as a guide

12. *A Compassionate Peace – A Future for the Middle East*, ed. E. Mendelsohn, New York, Harmondsworth, 1982.

to future developments, this has been attempted in the literature referred to. If by evaluation one means objective estimation of the success or failure, that is another matter. Such evaluation should at least be possible, but there are difficulties to be faced. In the first place, historical judgements are notoriously difficult to make and interpretations are subject to bias. Where confidentiality and discretion, if not sometimes secrecy, are also an important ingredient of the process, assessment becomes even more difficult. Mediation may even become undesirable, unnecessary or even counterproductive. Perhaps the only assessment to which any importance can be attached is unsolicited comments by the disputants, where these are available. In some circumstances the honest but subjective views of the conciliator might be used.

Objectivity may be possible and one such objective index of effectiveness could be the length of time that conciliators retain continuing access to the parties in the conflict. Further objectivity is possible by using the analytical methods of the social scientist. Quakers have in the past tended to avoid the issue of objectivity and measurement, by holding that external success is irrelevant and that what is important is the intention of the conciliator. The Quaker mission to the Czar in 1854 for example, though it did not stop the war, was not considered to be without value. Stephen Hobhouse says of it in his biography of Joseph Sturge, who was one of the Friends who went on the mission: 'Humanity does not progress to greater perfection merely or chiefly by achieved success, but rather by moral effort put forth and repeated again and again in the midst of apparent failure.'[13] Hobhouse is suggesting that apparent failure in the long run is 'success' if judged by the moral effort expended. This attitude cuts little ice with the social scientist and the student of conflict analysis who require objectivity. How can you hope to measure moral effort, they will ask.

It cannot be denied that such an attitude on the part of Quakers could lead to woolly thinking, inadequate planning, flaws in performance, wasted efforts and resources, but there have been signs recently that more objectivity has been sought and achieved by Quakers. Mike Yarrow, whilst aware of the inherent difficulties of evaluation, has throughout applied more tangible methods of evaluation of the three Quaker case studies he describes in detail. He sums up his views on evaluation with the following words:

13. Stephen Hobhouse, *Joseph Sturge: His Life and Work*, London, 1919, p. 146.

The three cases studied show a serious attempt to play a useful role in three highly complex situations, using a mixture of resources and techniques. In looking back one can see flaws and inadequacies but, on the whole, a valuable effort. In general, a greater in-put from the intellectual disciplines of conflict analysis would have helped. There is no basic incompatibility between expressing Quaker faith through conciliation and using scientific procedure and methods to do the job better, but there are practical problems and a difference of emphasis.

At the end of each case study we have tried to evaluate the methods used and ask the question of results obtained. In the case of the two Germanies, an emerging detente was influenced by a host of factors. The process would have gone on without any Quaker intervention. All one can say is that the Quakers assisted at certain key points. In the case of India and Pakistan just after the war over Kashmir, the heads of each government used the Quakers to communicate with each other opinions and intentions that could not be publicly stated, particularly with a view to testing the strength of moderate forces working to continue the truce. In the Nigerian war, the Quaker aim of a negotiated peace was not achieved, but peace by military victory resulted in an amazing degree of magnanimity toward the defeated side. The Quakers may have had a small part in this result, because their efforts were welcomed by certain Nigerian leaders.

The one objective index of effectiveness available was the fact that the persons involved retained continuing access to top leadership over a considerable period of time rather than being sent away as importunate meddlers. It is perhaps safe to conclude from this that the Quakers were carrying on an operation which others found useful and not just fooling themselves. Heinrich Albertz, former deputy mayor of Berlin, testified to this. Continued usefulness to the parties in conflict is still not an adequate gauge of influence and a long way from any measurement of 'success'.[14]

Yarrow, to paraphrase the above quotation, is saying that his methods of evaluation may not be adequate to enable success to be gauged with any assurance, but that there is no incompatibility between expressing Quaker faith through concilation processes – the 'conviction approach' – and using scientific procedures and the intellectual discipline of conflict analysis to understand and improve the methods used. Yarrow's evaluation takes us along the road to objectivity, yet doesn't, and isn't intended fully to achieve it. Anatol Rapaport, the distinguished social scientist and peace and conflict

14. Yarrow, *Quaker Experiences*, p. 299.

researcher, applauds Yarrow's views in the preface to Yarrow's book:

> The account of the three peace actions presented in this book contains ample evidence that these undertakings certainly deserve to be regarded as research as well as efforts in the cause of peace. Experiments are not reported here but a rich treasury of experience. The results are not evaluated by statistical significance tests, but they are evaluated by profound analysis drawing on the experience, generated by action. . . .
> . . . Not being a scientific hypothesis, this religiously inspired conviction of the Quakers is not subject to criticism on scientific grounds. But the specific methods and techniques of the Quakers can be subjected to careful scrutiny, and this is certainly done in this book. Moreover, this scrutiny is seen to be not far removed from the self-critical scrutiny of the scientist, once the vital role of the sensitized human being as an indispensable instrument of observation is recognized.[15]

Rapaport may believe that Quaker conviction is not subject to criticism on scientific grounds, yet although Quakers may seem to have what a critic has described as 'an almost mystical faith in the healing powers of communication between contending groups'[16] and base their interpretation of third party intermediary efforts on biblical, and religious premises, their interpretation has found favour with those engaged in the socio-psychological study of conflict. Yarrow also quotes the social scientist Roger Fisher as saying 'Improved communication is perhaps the most pervasive third party function, since it is required to clear up initial misunderstanding, to make accurate diagnosis possible, to explore alternative means, goals and areas of commonality.'[17] This could well be a Quaker statement.

For greater objectivity, however, more scientific and statistical studies of a greater number of cases would be necessary. There are of course not enough Quaker cases to make this possible. There is such a study, not of Quaker cases, but of seventy-two international disputes in which mediation has been attempted since 1945 by the UN, Organization of American States (OAS), the Arab League, OAU, NATO, the World Council of Churches, the Council of Europe and the Warsaw Treaty Organisation. In his paper Jacob

15. Ibid., p. xix.
16. Quoted in ibid., p. 283.
17. Ibid., p. 284.

Table 12.1 Effectiveness of Quaker Mediation in Selected Twentieth-Century Conflicts

	No success	Ceasefire	Partial Success	Settlement
First World War	*			
Manchuria	*			
Second World War	*			
Korea	*			
Quakers visit Russia			*	
Quakers visit China			*	
Vietnam	*			
E–W Germany			*	
India/Pakistan			*	
Nigerian Civil War			*	
Middle East				
(i) Jerusalem 1948			*	
(ii) Nasser/Ben Gurion 1955			*	
(iii) Working Party 1, 1970[a]			*	
(iv) Working Party 2, 1982[b]			*	
Rhodesia/Zimbabwe			*	

(a) Middle East Working Party 1 produced *Search for Peace in the Middle East*.
(b) Middle East Working Party 2 produced *A Compassionate Peace*.

Source: J. A. Pettigrew, 'Quaker International Conciliation – An Evaluation of its Roots, Character and Development', M. Phil. thesis, University of Bradford, 1989, p. 126.

Bercovitch uses four categories as a measure for failure/success: no success, ceasefire, partial success and settlement. He applies them to each mediation attempt and uses them as diagnostic tools to explore the conditions likely to affect a successful outcome of mediation.[18]

Table 12.1 is an attempt at assessment of twentieth-century Quaker conciliation using Jacob Bercovitch's categories of failure/success, as a basic guide. If we use these four measures in relation to Quaker mediation, some of them would have to be dismissed as having 'no success'. In none was there a 'ceasefire' due exclusively to Quaker efforts. In most there was a 'final settlement' of some kind, but in none was the settlement attributable entirely to Quaker

18. Jacob Bercovitch, 'International Mediation. A Study of the Incidence, Strategies and Conditions of Successful Outcome', *Co-operation and Conflict*, vol 21, 1986, pp. 155–68.

mediation, though Quaker involvement did no doubt contribute to it. The only measure, therefore, which could apply would be 'partial success' and here I have used more accurate, but still sometimes subjective criteria which enable a decision to be made in applying 'partial success' to the process. These criteria are:

1. Subjective assessments of mediators from their own descriptions.
2. More objective assessment by the parties in conflict from their published comments and unsolicited judgements.
3. Evidence of change of attitude of the parties to each other.
4. The part played by mediators in contributing to a final settlement and the effect of mediation upon the provisions of the final settlement.
5. The length of time mediators had access to, and retained the confidence of the parties.

Some of these criteria are obviously more reliable than others, some more amenable to accurate assessment. All could be used for a more objective assessment, but are still open to criticism. Taken as a whole, it would be possible to say that most Quaker mediation falls within the category of 'partial success'. In using Bercovitch's criteria this appears to be but a moderate achievement. However, if one adds to this assessment what Rapaport has said about 'the religiously inspired conviction of the Quakers' and bears in mind the complexities of each conciliation process, a distinct justification for Quaker involvement in each attempt can nonetheless be recognised.

Bercovitch uses his assessments as a diagnostic tool to examine the conditions likely to affect a successful outcome for mediation. Perhaps it is possible to do this for those Quaker conciliation processes cited above, though it must be said, that helpful as this may be for analysis, the findings would not deter Quakers from attempting any conciliation, however unpromising it might appear to be, if a way opened. This examination will be undertaken under the headings Bercovitch uses.

Identity and Characteristics of the Disputing Parties

Conflict management by third parties can only occur between adversaries with well-defined identities, Bercovitch maintains. Moreover, if possible, it needs to be two united parties, which recognise each other.

In this connection it is interesting to observe that though Biafra was in rebellion and not recognised by Nigeria, Quakers were able to make contact between the two parties when official bodies were unable to do so. It is also interesting to note that settlement in the Middle East defies most efforts because of the many conflicting identities and the non-recognition of some.

Bercovitch further maintains that where the differences between the power of the disputants is small international mediation is more effective. Quaker conciliation has included attempts between disputants of all power ratings, but has been manifestly more successful where the power ratings have been smaller and more evenly matched. The difficulties presented by disparity of power rating would be a factor in Quaker peacemaking in South Africa should this have become a possibility. Hitherto, the powerlessness of the African National Congress (ANC) would have been a far more intractable problem, though the release of Nelson Mandela in February 1990 has resulted in the use of the language of conciliation.

The nature of the dispute has an influence on the outcome. Bercovitch holds that issues of sovereignty and security are more amenable than ones of ideology to resolution. Quaker conciliators have, however, never feared to embrace ideological discussions and indeed have sometimes as in the East–West Germany, Nasser–Ben Gurion disputes and in their missions to Russia[19] and China[20] encouraged the parties to engage in discussions of ideological differences. This attempt to understand each other's position has furthered the possibilities for mediation and conciliation.

Identity and Characteristics of a Mediator

It is here that Bercovitch draws perhaps the most significant conclusions for Quaker mediation. The first conclusion is that since mediation is a voluntary process mediators cannot function without the trust and co-operation of the adversaries. He adds significantly, however, that effective mediation depends upon the prestige and authority of the mediator and his access to resources, as well as upon his originality and ability to act unobtrusively.

19. Kathleen Lonsdale, *Quakers visit Russia*, Peace Committee of the Society of Friends, London, 1952.
20. Pettigrew, 'Quaker International Conciliation', p. 92.

This is where on two counts there is a marked divergence between official mediation and Quaker mediation. Originality of ideas and ability to act unobtrusively are certainly requisites for the Quaker mediator, but he or she does not possess and cannot use prestige or authority, other than that arising from their own individual strengths and skills. They have no resources of power to use as leverage in order to influence the outcome.

Bercovitch gives percentage figures which appear to support his view, and shows success rates by rank of mediator.[21] The highest success rate is with mediators who are leaders of governments and the lowest success rate is for leaders of international organisations. It is significant for the Quaker conciliator that *representatives* of international organisations (rather than leaders) have also a reasonably successful record, indeed seem to be numerically the second largest groups.

Bercovitch's figures are small and inconclusive, but he maintains that the success of government leaders (and foreign ministers) is attributable to their prestige and institutional assistance (resources). There appear to be, however, large areas where representatives of international organisations and Quakers have enjoyed success.

Bercovitch also uses three levels of mediator involvement which he describes as Communicator, Formulator and Manipulator.[22] The most successful mediation method is that of the Manipulator, who brings to bear resources such as power, influence and persuasion to obtain success.

Few would be the Quaker mediators who would claim to be Manipulators; most, if not all, would describe themselves as Communicators and perhaps Formulators. Does this mean that Quakers perhaps have to accept that their role in international conciliation is one with predictably lower success rates if judged by objective standards?

Perhaps Quakers have another role, one with longer-term effects and based on individual and corporate conviction that attempts in apparently intractable circumstances must be made in and out of season in the interests of ultimate success. The criteria for such success are undefinable and the secrets of success will be found to lie within the individual Friends and their supporting Society of Friends. The success is possibly brought to life in those who are the

---

21. Bercovitch, 'International Mediation', p. 164.
22. Ibid.

disputants in the mediation processes, by the undefinable 'conviction' that success is always possible if expectations of a solution can be maintained.

Evaluation and Development of Quaker Conciliation and Mediation

What can be learned from this analysis which may have constructive import for the future? It is that despite the difficulties in accurate assessment of such a heterogeneous mixture of processes conducted over a wider spectrum of issues, some ideological, some concerning sovereignty, others concerning independence and security, partial success can be said to have been achieved in a not inconsiderable number of cases.

There have been a succession of successful conciliators drawn mostly from the ranks of Quakers in business, Quakers employed by the Society in a service capacity, academics and other professionals, all of them committed and fitted by experience but rarely by training to conciliation. Resources to support them have been forthcoming and usually adequate.

The Quaker conciliators without exception, have possessed the characteristics deemed to be necessary for the task, whether they were self-selected or selected by others for the work. In effect their role was an unenviable one and needed courage and dedication beyond the normal course of duty; there are in addition no tangible rewards. It would appear that there has been no dearth of conciliators to match the opportunities which have arisen.

Their methods, though similar to those of professionally employed mediators, have been uniquely Quaker. They have often become involved where the chance of success seemed minimal but have nonetheless effected changes of attitudes, which have enabled apparently insoluble conflicts to move towards a solution and importantly to magnanimity in the post-conflict situation.

Opportunities for conciliation have usually arisen from previous long-term concern and have often had effects only observable in the long term. In any case Quakers have always come forward regardless of the prospects of a successful conclusion.

This means that there is a future for Quaker international conciliation. What are the opportunities and what form will it take? The opportunities, both within and outside the Society of Friends, for Quakers to make a study of conflict resolution and to begin its practice have increased enormously since the Second World War. It would be impossible in this study to enumerate all the opportunities, but some important ones will now be considered.

As has been seen, Quakers as a body have always been interested in promoting peaceful solutions to conflicts, and in the relief of suffering by service projects in the field; it is integral to their faith. They have perhaps been more concerned with Quaker programmes in the field and with the resolution of conflicts in the field, than with theoretical conflict analysis and peace research. There has been the usual gap between practitioner and theoretician. Mike Yarrow, in the concluding chapter of his book, attempts an evaluation of Quaker experiences in conciliation: 'In general a greater input from the intellectual disciplines of conflict analysis would have helped'; and again as he looks to the future, he writes: 'A Quaker conciliator could benefit from a training programme, such as that pioneered by the International Peace Academy with its seminars on conflict analysis and peace-making or the peace training advocated by Paul Wehr, former executive director of the Consortium for Peace Research Education and Development (COPRED).'[23]

Individual Quakers have nonetheless been in the forefront of new approaches to theoretical peace research. The English Quaker Lewis Fry Richardson pioneered the application of statistical method to arms races and the causes of war from the end of the First World War to his death in 1953. It is interesting to note that his first tentative ideas began to develop during his active service with the Friends Ambulance Unit in France during 1914–18. He gives his name to the Richardson Institute for Peace and Conflict Research at Lancaster University, renamed the Richardson Institute for Peace Studies in 1988.

Many research institutes and organisations now available to Quaker students were initiated by Quakers and some still have important Quaker connections and leadership, such as the Canadian Peace Research Association, the British Conflict Research Society, the Conference for Peace Research in History and the forementioned COPRED. The impetus too for the foundation of the International Peace Research Association came from a conference of peace researchers at Clarens in Switzerland in 1963, arranged by the Geneva Office of the Friends Service Council and the American

23. Yarrow, *Quaker Experiences*, pp. 299, 281–2.

Friends Service Committee. The Chair of Peace Studies at the University of Bradford resulted from the concern of a single Quaker and the support and concerted effort of the wider Society of Friends and the University. It is certainly significant, in the context of the gap between theoretician and practitioner, that the first professor to occupy the chair was Adam Curle, then Professor of Education and Development at Harvard University, a veteran field conciliator, who had played a prominent part in the Quaker conciliation efforts in two of the disputes mentioned here and in many others.

The interest of Quakers individually and corporately in the theory and practice of conflict resolution has been extended. The reasons for this no doubt arise from the perceived urgency of the political situation with the proliferation of conventional and nuclear weapons and the increase of terrorism, conflict and violence in our world. It has also arisen from the increasing awareness of and knowledge about the numerous official and unofficial international mediation efforts now increasingly available for those who seek them out (they tend to be neglected by the media). There is now also a vast literature of research into conflict management and resolution coming from the many research bodies, institutes and university departments which now exist world-wide.

Since the Second World War (and even before it) there have been a number of Quakers with special expertise and experience who have engaged, as we have seen, in specific conciliation processes. These Quakers have written about their experiences and through conferences and seminars have been willing to share them more widely in the Society of Friends.

As well as this interest in international conciliation, there has been a wider interest within the Society of Friends in conflict resolution at practical and local levels. Conflicts occur in families, in groups, in schools and in local communities. In the UK, Europe, Australia, New Zealand and particularly in the USA there are programmes aimed at teaching creative solutions to conflict at a personal and community level. There has also in some instances been administrative machinery and formal Quaker support for such programmes. The Friends Mediation Service of Philadelphia Yearly Meeting is one example.[24]

In the UK there has been a growing number of local schemes, which in response to a need for settling disputes in local communi-

24. Friends Mediation Service, 1515 Cherry Street, Philadelphia PA, 19102, USA.

ties have pioneered projects to explore constructive ways of overcoming conflicts without violence and without residual bitterness. Some of these have had a Quaker origin.

In Britain, one such notable example is that of Kingston Friends Workshop Group. It originated in 1981 when two members of Kingston Meeting, with the help of Quaker Peace and Service, met to prepare a Sixth Forms' Workshop on problem-solving in personal relationships. Subsequently, though progress was slow, the local education authority asked for a course at their teachers' centre and this led to the publication of a handbook. The Workshop Group has now extended its activities to include working with business executives, care staff, truanting youngsters, peace and church groups, and Quakers' own Elders and Overseers. A class teacher involved in an early workshop in school moved to a polytechnic and launched a programme into teacher training.

A further example is the Reading Mediation Centre, a neighbourhood dispute centre stated by Reading Preparative Meeting in 1986. The centre is funded by Quaker Peace and Service Peace Committees' Local Peacework budget. The centre currently has ten trained mediators who have been selected for their ability to listen carefully and impartially.

Quaker interest in neighbourhood dispute centres and in problem solving in personal relationships in schools as a way of tackling the violence which afflicts schools and neighbourhoods has not been restricted to the UK and the US alone. The Quaker Council for European Affairs (QCEA)[25] has promoted relevant studies in these areas. One of these is a study paper on 'The Teaching of Non-violent Behaviour and Co-operation in Schools among the Member States of the Council of Europe'. The idea arose in the context of a Council of Europe hearing on 'A Cultural and Educational Approach to the Problem of Violence'. Two representatives from QCEA, which has NGO status with the Council of Europe were present and introduced the idea that as a way of coping with interpersonal relationships children might be taught non-violent problem solving at school in order to reduce aggressive behaviour. Adam Curle, Nicholas McGeorge and Brian Stapleton subsequently made suggestions about ways of reducing current levels of violence and made a proposal that a project be undertaken to assess the current situation on the teaching of conflict resolution in schools.

25. QCEA, Quaker House, 50 Square Ambiosin, B 1040, Brussels, Belgium.

This proposal became the subject of a resolution adopted by the Parliamentary Assembly of the Council of Europe in 1983 which hoped to ensure that the systematic teaching of non-violent behaviour became an integral part of all compulsory education. This study is now completed.[26]

In Australia Quakers and others have trodden a similar path. David Purnell, an Australian Quaker, has run courses on conflict in secondary schools and devised a radio programme on conflict for community radio stations. He has conducted many workshops on the subject and works as a consultant on conflict resolution and peace education. In a James Backhouse lecture for 1988, entitled 'Creative Conflict', he includes an impressive list of channels being used to assist in resolving conflicts. These he calls Models and Structures. He gives details of thirty such channels ranging from Family Conciliation Centres and Community Mediation to Commercial Dispute Agencies and a Supranational Independent Thinking Organisation, which he compares with Adam Curle's projected Mediation Centre.

An expanding field has been in peace education and already there have been appointments made for professionals to develop this work. Quaker Peace and Service (QPS) has a peace education organiser, and Warwickshire and Staffordshire Monthly Meetings have appointed an organiser for their peace education project. Of those who have held such appointments all have been involved in the study of conflict, some have become mediators and at least one has been drawn into the field of international conciliation.

In the preparation of Quaker workers for the field, increasing attention is being paid to seminars on conflict resolution in order to equip workers with mediation skills necessitated by the very nature of their assignments which are almost always in areas of tension. Quaker United Nations Offices in Geneva and New York and Quaker Centres in London, Brussels and Vienna have not only done sterling work in the field of international mediation but provide in-service training for young interns, which introduce them to the mediation process, where theory and practice marry.

---

26. Jamie Walker, *Violence and Conflict Resolution in Schools*, Council for Cultural Co-operation, Strasburg, 1989. Available from Quaker Council for European Affairs, Brussels.

Prospects

Regardless of whether or not international conciliation can be evaluated or said to be successful, or of how Quaker mediators equip themselves, the whole of Quaker literature on the subject of international conciliation and the experience of Quakers, whether or not they are directly involved in conciliation, would seem to say that the object of Quaker thinking and action is reconciliation arising from the conviction that there is 'that of God' deeply rooted in everyone. This makes the resolution of conflicts not only desirable, even obligatory, but also possible. The object of service, in whatever capacity, is not to be successful or to convert others to the Quaker way, but to enable all men to live peaceably together as far as that is possible.

To abandon their objectives would be impossible for Quakers. There is, therefore, no doubt that mediation and the pursuit of reconciliation will continue to be an important ingredient of Quaker activity and central to their life and service.

In summary, it would appear that Quakers have always, throughout their history, been ready to give practical expression to their deep-seated commitment to reconciliation and to engage therefore in international mediation. Quakers have always been found who were ready to respond to this challenge to serve in areas of the world where there is tension, to mediate and to reconcile. As far as one can predict Quakers always will be found wherever the dispute, whatever the social and political implications, and however they may be recruited, trained or supported. This is again not surprising. Quakers acting under concern have perceived a need and hoped to meet it in each generation, and the on-going work of practical service in the field has inevitably and perhaps increasingly employed Quakers in a mediation capacity.

In the seventeenth century a deep concern over the conflicts of that time and the devastation caused by war led to Quaker Epistles to those in authority, counselling conciliation. It led also to concrete suggestions for political structures to prevent wars and facilitate negotiation. There was little call or opportunity for actual mediation.

In the eighteenth century Quakers were caught up both in America and in England unavoidably in the political field in the processes of negotiation and conciliation. Quakers were found to engage in these processes and continued to carry messages to those in power.

The nineteenth century saw the development of Quaker programmes of relief work in war-torn areas and of Quaker service in
mission fields throughout the world, both programmes establishing
Quaker centres of interest and a growing understanding of Quaker
commitment to peace and reconciliation. They laid the foundations
for subsequent opportunities for international conciliation.

The twentieth century has seen the fruits of earlier centuries and
opportunities for the more specifically 'intentional' and classic
Quaker international conciliation of the type described by Mike
Yarrow. Again Quakers under concern have emerged to meet these
opportunities. Conscription in two world wars resulted in a number
of Quakers adopting by design a change in their circumstances, and
their experiences in wartime as conscientious objectors led some to
take careers reflecting an interest in peaceful change, in international
affairs and mediation. The aftermath of two world wars and in
particular of the Second World War, and the nuclear threat which
followed it, has meant that many Quakers have become interested
in the peace movements and a few in the process of mediation. In
parallel with this, social changes in British society have thrown up a
need for mediation in our own communities too. The process of
mediation in small communities and in international affairs has a
common core so that transfer of interest and experience from one to
the other is seen as increasingly possible.

The growth of violence in our societies has prompted Quakers, as
individuals and corporately, to examine the roots of violence and
conflict and to consider how schools and our other institutions can
meet the problem of violence with conflict resolution. The core of
peace education and peace studies lies here and Quakers are also
coming forward from this background to become involved in
mediation.

What will happen in the twenty-first century can only be guessed
at. The indications from past history are that Quaker conciliators,
prompted still by their fundamental beliefs, will continue to emerge.
Whatever structured changes may be necessary to recruit, train and
support individual Quakers, their international conciliation will
continue from its roots in Quaker traditions with no doubt new
emphases. There will be developing links with institutions outside
the Quaker community and reliance on them for professional
training, research and theoretical input and perhaps project selection. There will be Quaker involvement in the establishment of
non-Quaker mediation centres, whether they offer mediation ser-

vices in communities or in international political conflicts. Adam Curle gives us his views on the functions of such a mediation centre in his study *In the Middle*.[27] The unique contribution individual Quakers and Quakers as a group have made to international mediation shows every sign that it will continue.

27. See Adam Curle, *In the Middle*, Oxford, 1986.

13

The Problem-Solving Workshop in Conflict Resolution

A. Betts Fetherston

Introduction

This chapter sets out to describe a relatively new international
conflict resolution technique known as the problem-solving workshop or facilitated problem-solving. John Burton was the first to
reformulate and then apply the workshop technique to international
conflict. The problem-solving workshop had previously been utilised at other systems levels ranging from industrial disputes to
group therapy for the mentally ill. In this chapter the technique as
designed by Burton will be described followed by a brief explanation of the theory behind it. Other attempts have been made to
apply Burton's ideas to international conflict and several of these
will be highlighted. The emphasis here is on applications of facilitated problem-solving in an international context; other areas where
the method has been exercised more frequently will not be described and evaluative and theoretical aspects of the workshop will
only be touched upon.

Burton's Problem-Solving Workshop

General Aims

The overall goals of Burton's workshop technique can be assigned to
three categories: academic goals, short-term applied goals, and
long-term applied goals. At the academic level, problem-solving workshops provide a means for testing and developing hypotheses about
conflict, and discovering the elements necessary for its successful

resolution. All this is done, according to Burton, in order to 'provide a clinical framework, and a means by which an applied science of International Relations can develop'.[1]

At the short-term applied level, Burton's workshop stresses three goals. Initially, emphasis is on creating the conditions necessary for the development of effective communication. The establishment of effective communication must coincide with changes in what may be rigid stereotyped attitudes of the participants towards each other – that is, enabling them to view each other and deal with each other as individual human beings. Secondly, resolution as opposed to settlement becomes the sought-after outcome. The accomplishment of this second goal requires that the participants change their view of the conflict as a win–lose phenomenon and re-perceive it as a problem to be solved within a win–win framework. Finally, Burton emphasises the transfer of new information and insights gained by the participants directly into the political decision-making process within their respective communities or governments.

In the long term, Burton views problem-solving as making two major contributions. First, it will eventually replace conventional settlement techniques. Burton envisions a future in which Track II diplomacy (a much expanded, researched, and, most importantly, institutionalised version of facilitated problem-solving) is the accepted, agreed-upon norm for resolving disputes at any level. A second and related goal is that of conflict avoidance. The success of conflict avoidance rests on the early prediction of conflict. For this to become a reality, much more research into the root causes and dynamics of conflict is necessary in conjunction with practical work aimed at reducing the number and destructiveness of disputes world-wide.

Influences

The problem-solving workshop has gained inspiration from a number of sources. Mitchell describes four main influences: (1) concepts of non-violence, (2) reconciliation work, (3) social casework, and (4) therapeutic group dynamics.[2]

From work in non-violence, especially from the Gandhian tradi-

---

1. John Burton, *Conflict and Communication*, London, 1969, p. xiii.
2. Chris Mitchell, *Peacemaking and the Consultant's Role*, Westmead, 1981, pp. 71–86.

tion, come three important strands of thought. These include non-coercive behaviour, respect for the adversary and mutually satisfactory outcomes, that is, win–win outcomes. From reconciliation work, particularly the work of the Society of Friends, comes emphasis on the importance of creating good-will between disputants, adopting a non-threatening stance and giving special attention to the internal dynamics of self-improvement, growth and evaluation. The Society of Friends and other Christian organisations involved in reconciliation work base their efforts and thinking on the assumption of the basic goodness of all human beings. This underlying assumption is an integral part of the theory and methodology of facilitated problem-solving.

The field of social psychology continues to be an excellent resource for problem-solving through its work on the dynamics of group behaviour, and, in particular, conflict behaviour. For Burton this is useful in two respects: (1) the workshop itself constitutes a small group to which theories from social psychology can be directly applied, and (2) through analogous reasoning Burton applies small-group conflict dynamics, with some adjustment, to the larger, more complex context of international conflict. Burton takes from social casework the principles of supportive, non-directive, non-condemnatory, self-determinate and analytical interaction. From therapeutic group methods Burton utilises such fundamentals as participatory learning, self-learning and growth, immediate feedback and personal evaluation.

The Problem-Solving Workshop

Pre-Workshop Phase   As the title suggests, this phase of Burton's problem-solving workshop consists of all the preliminary work necessary to ensure that the actual proceedings run smoothly. It entails initiating conditions which will be amenable to achieving the three basic goals of change, transfer and resolution. Some of the more crucial elements of this phase are discussed below.

Before a workshop can take place, the parties to the dispute must be identified. This is a complex, delicate process as most international conflicts support many parties each with different needs and different levels of involvement. Once it has been decided which parties to the dispute will be involved in the workshop, intraparty divisions must be examined. This is the case for two reasons: (1) it is important that representatives selected to take part in the workshop reflect as wide as possible a spectrum of intraparty views, and (2) if severe factioning has occurred so that communication within the party has become ineffective, this dispute will have to be dealt with as a preliminary to holding a workshop focussed on the larger conflict.

Just as the parties to a dispute must be identified, so too must the issues. It is important to note that issues vary greatly depending upon which systems level is being viewed. Recognition of underlying issues enables the third party (in this case the social scientists running the workshop) to suggest pertinent topics to the participants. While the participants themselves determine much of the content of discussions, Burton has used functional issues, such as tourism or economic development, to initiate dialogue because these are easier to consider in an analytic framework, whereas actual conflict issues are more likely to be highly emotive thus inhibiting the analytic approach. Once dialogue has commenced, the social scientists (also called 'the panel') attempt to move emphasis to more salient areas, although this can happen without such impetus. In general, Burton's position is that it is crucial for the parties themselves to decide which issues are important to them. He maintains that conflict will not be resolved unless it is the parties to the dispute who choose the issues and then create and implement solutions.

The number of participants appropriate for the workshop's interactive format can be a difficult problem, since it is important that within each delegation there exist representative views including the extremes of opinion. Burton suggests that the optimum number of participants is two to three per party and the optimum number of panel members is four to six. Requirements for the participants themselves are fairly open-ended. The most important qualification is that the participants be able to effectively communicate what they have learned to decision-makers. According to Burton, the key to the success of a workshop and ultimately to the resolution of the conflict is this transference of insight and knowledge directly into the policy process.

Finally, the setting for a workshop should be novel, neutral, confidential and should convey an academic atmosphere. An academic atmosphere is adopted for several reasons. First, it confirms and supports the analytic approach which will be pursued. Second, it provides a set of norms different from the participant's usual 'conflict norms' which serve to set limits and rules for appropriate behaviour.

Workshop Phase   This phase includes all those interactions which take place within the actual workshop. The workshop is basically a small isolated group of people who, over a set period of time, try to learn to communicate more effectively and to view their conflict in an analytic framework, as a precursor to engaging in the process of conflict resolution. It is during this period that the role of the third party – the panel of social scientists – comes to the fore. Panel members must be neutral, but they must also be able to identify with all parties in the sense that they judge neither side as right or wrong. Rather they must see each party as acting in response to their environment based on available knowledge and in such a way that benefits for themselves and their identity group are maximised. The panel, according to Burton, *does not* propose solutions but instead tries 'to establish a condition in which all the parties join with it [the panel] in defining, identifying and solving the problem'.[3]

While, in general, proceedings are based on a relatively unstructured agenda, the workshop does go through three basic stages. The negative stage is an initial period characterised by high tension. It opens with prepared presentations given by each party expressing their view of the conflict. Typically, the parties offer official positions which are confrontational and accusatory in nature and address the panel – as if the panel are judges – as opposed to addressing the entire group. After the initial presentations the parties are invited to engage in a more productive analytic discussion of their conflict. This is the positive stage. Substantive issues raised by the parties in their initial presentations are discussed and the panel members attempt to facilitate changes in the parties' perceptions of one another and move the discussion into an analytic framework which focusses on the conflict as a problem to be solved. In the final functional stage, the panel directs the parties' attention to substantive issues with possible functional solutions. These are then discussed and a provisional agreement may be drawn up.

Post-Workshop Phase   Ideally, the outcome of a problem-solving workshop would be the cessation of hostilities and the establishment of institutionalised functional co-operation at all levels through face-to-face, non-facilitated negotiations. However, because of the complexity and magnitude of international conflicts this is not a realistic short-term prospect – although it may be a

3. Burton, *Conflict and Communication*, p. 62.

realistic long-term one. More probable in the immediate future would be a series of workshops focussing on a particular conflict combined with follow-up investigations by researchers in order to assess effects and to adjust emphasis for successive workshops. This type of procedure would also aid in the collection and analysis of data which in turn might become the basis for new theory and methodology.

The Development of Theory: Problem-Solving to Generic Theory

The problem-solving workshop is the practical outcome of Burton's theoretical positions. There are three ideas which together constitute the most significant part of Burton's theorising . These are (1) problem-solving, (2) human needs theory, and (3) generic theory. It is important to keep in mind the connections between these ideas which, together, are an attempt to build a coherent approach to conflict as a universal concept.

Problem-Solving versus Puzzle-Solving

One important distinction Burton makes is the difference between puzzle-solving and problem-solving as approaches to resolving conflict and creating more positive global conditions generally. Burton defines puzzle-solving as containing three elements: 'First, there is a known answer. . . . Second, puzzles assume the application of known theories or a known set of techniques and these are adequate for the purpose. Third, puzzles deal with closed systems, i.e., there is no reaction to an environment that could be changing during the investigation.'[4] Most science is done within a puzzle-solving framework, utilising a particular paradigm. This scientific approach is the inductive or descriptive method. It is based on a methodology which requires that theories be formed from observation of events. Use of induction arises out of the employment of the puzzle-solving method. Burton considers this approach to be a limitation to scientific advance and to be a threat to global survival because it is resistant to change, has difficulty accommodating innovation and operates within a closed system. In Burton's view

4. John Burton, *Deviance, Terrorism and War*, Oxford, 1979, pp. 3–4.

the use of coercive techniques by states to control conflict is an attempt to impose a puzzle-solving solution on to a situation which requires a problem-solving one.[5]

Problem-solving is defined as the opposite of puzzle-solving. Burton asserts that:

> first, the solution is not the final end-product. It is in itself another set of relationships that contains its own sets of problems.... Second, problem-solving frequently requires a new synthesis of knowledge or techniques and a change in theoretical structure. Third, the system of interactions is an open one, i.e., the parts are subject not merely to interaction among themselves, as is the case with a mental puzzle, but to interaction with a wider environment over which there can be no control.[6]

The methodology suggested by a problem-solving approach is based on deductive thinking and analogous reasoning. There is a dialectical process between theory and observations tempered by the insistence that theory must not be derived solely from those observations. Instead, it must be created through thinking about a relevant body of knowledge and its assumptions and methodologies and placing that within a framework of events and a wider environment. Once theorising becomes a closed system based only on one discipline and one observer, it has ceased to be a problem-solving approach and become a puzzle-solving one.

A Generic Theory Based on Human Needs

A generic theory attempts to provide a set of assumptions from which all other theories can be deduced. Such a theory might be described as a paradigm, or a specific way of seeing and trying to solve any problem. All human beings are familiar with paradigms. Without the benefit of a basic set of assumptions through which we can categorise and filter information, our brains would become overloaded and we would spend much of our time 're-inventing the wheel'. The function of a generic theory is similar to the brain's filtering system in that it locates and organises basic categories or causes. Once established, a generic theory can be taken for granted, thus enabling its adherents to avoid the time-consuming work of

5. Ibid., pp. 5–6.
6. Ibid., p. 5.

re-proving basic theory (or re-inventing the wheel) and allowing time for more specific research. Without such a system scientific progression would be a painstakingly slow, monotonous endeavour.

An example of a generic theory is Burton's theory of human needs. This is founded on the idea that there are universal, ontologically derived human needs, which human beings strive to fulfil or maintain. According to this theory human needs are a basic cause of human behaviour. Although Burton's particular interest in needs theory is in discovering the origins of conflict – Burton asserts that conflict is caused by the frustrated attempts of individuals to meet their needs – he considers his theory generic because it posits a basic set of assumptions purporting to explain the origins of *all* human behaviour.

Burton suggests that there are nine universal needs which are more basic than cultural values, become operational only within the social context and are, at least partially, based on ontology. Eight of these needs Burton takes directly from the work of sociologist Paul Sites and one he adds himself.[7] These needs are: (1) a need for consistency in response, (2) a need for stimulation, (3) a need for security, (4) a need for recognition, (5) a need for distributive justice, (6) a need to appear rational, (7) a need for meaning in response, (8) a need for a sense of control, and finally, Burton's addition, (9) a need for role defence.[8] Burton conceptualises the first eight needs as forming an individual's *role* and so defines 'role defence' as an individual's attempt 'to secure a role and to preserve a role by which he acquires and maintains his recognition, security, and stimulation'.[9]

Burton's generic theory of conflict is an attempt to universalise a specific approach to human behaviour, thus making it the basis for the deduction of other theory and methodology. In one sense Burton's generic theory represents an important advance since it suggests a systematic, adisciplinary approach to conflict. In addition, if it can be determined that conflict is indeed a manifestation of the frustration of certain human needs, not only would the claims of Burton's generic theory be significantly strengthened, but the explanatory power of widely accepted theory and methodology arising from a puzzle-solving paradigm would be weakened.

7. Paul Sites, *Control: The Basis of Social Order*, New York, 1973.
8. Burton, *Deviance*, p. 73.
9. Ibid.

The idea of human needs as theory of human behaviour is in direct contention with the traditional assumption that societal needs are superordinate to human needs. This conventional approach is derived from an inductive puzzle-solving method which is continually reaffirmed based upon observations made from within its own paradigm. These observations tend to be self-fulfilling prophesies instead of the objective fact they are meant to represent. Burton and others, most notably Paul Sites, suggest, rather than this traditional approach to behaviour, an alternative that asserts the primacy of human needs set within a problem-solving paradigm.

Not surprisingly, Burton's ideas are controversial and have engendered debate within the field of conflict studies and elsewhere. The problem-solving workshop is conceived within a paradigm which assumes the primacy of human needs. It is, therefore, not only contrary to traditional practices, but a threat to the status quo. This is a critical dynamic. If a theory of needs becomes the dominant paradigm, it follows that coercive policies used to maintain social order would be changed in favour of policies aimed at fulfilling the needs of the individual. Such an approach would inevitably involve reducing concentrations of power and wealth. In this sense it may be labelled revolutionary. If needs theory has some basis in reality, and evidence exists that this is so (albeit normative evidence), then problem-solving workshops and other approaches which are founded upon Burton's generic theory of conflict are eminently pragmatic and realistic in view of the long-term goal of conflict avoidance.

Alternative Applications of the Problem-Solving Method

Burton is not the only scholar to appreciate the possibilities of applying psychological group techniques to conflicts at the international level. Others have developed very similar methods and have conducted workshops utilising them. Three different models of the problem-solving workshop will be explored here. They are (1) the Fermeda and Stirling Workshops run by Leonard Doob and associates from Yale University in the United States, (2) several workshops run by Herbert Kelman and associates from Harvard University in the United States, and (3) a number of workshops run by A. M. Levi and A. Benjamin, two Israeli academics.

The Yale Group

Leonard Doob, Professor of Psychology, William Foltz, Professor of Political Science, and Robert Stevens, Professor of Law, all based at Yale University, formed the nucleus of social scientists working on the Fermeda and Stirling projects. They decided, after long discussions and numerous consultations, that the laboratory method (or sensitivity training) would be employed in an attempt to ascertain whether or not such a technique might aid in the resolution of international and intercommunal conflicts.

The goal of a sensitivity-training workshop is to facilitate participatory learning and the transfer of that learning into the real world. In this sense the workshop is identical to Burton's. Where they differ, and this is a crucial diversion, is in the emphasis placed on individual training in Doob's workshops versus the emphasis placed on the political process and research in Burton's.

Within the larger structure of Doob's workshop, small group sessions or T-groups (T for training) form the basic learning unit. These groups are characterised by intense interaction and self-revelation. They are guided by a Trainer or Consultant (a person trained in the laboratory method) who intervenes to comment on group process. The critical dynamic in such an intense group situation is the development of group trust. The participants not only learn about group process in an analytical framework but they learn about their own behaviour within that group process. By following such a format, the workshop focusses almost exclusively on individual change and the transfer of that change into the individual's life. The transfer of learning into the policy process of the particular conflict is not given priority, since it is felt that initiating permanent change within each participant is the most effective and appropriate means of affecting the course of the conflict in the long term.

The Fermeda Workshop   The Fermeda Workshop took place in August 1979, at the Fermeda Hotel in South Tyrol, Italy. It brought together six scholars from each of three countries, Kenya, Somalia, and Ethiopia, for a two-week period, to discuss what might be done about their on-going border disputes. The workshop format was based on a relatively unstructured agenda. Although each day was divided up into five basic activities – (1) two T-groups of nine participants each, (2) simulations and theory presentations, (3) planning committee, (4) general assembly, and (5) free time – within the meetings (especially the T-groups) there were no rigid schedules. The first week of the workshop was spent teaching the participants about group process and how to communicate more effectively. During the second week, the group focussed specifically on the border disputes and attempted to apply the first week's insights and knowledge to finding a solution. Toward the end of the second week some time was spent discussing the re-entry problems which might be encountered by the participants once they returned to their home countries.

It was generally agreed that the T-group discussions were valuable because they provided new knowledge about the dispute and about the participants themselves. The participants gained insight into the problems faced by the other countries involved and in this way might be said to have re-perceived the conflict. The criticisms made by the participants included such difficulties as the unreality of the T-groups, the excessive permissiveness of the atmosphere, the feeling of being guinea pigs and the non-applicability of the games. Doob and his colleagues mention the possibility that learning can be impeded, not helped, by the workshop, and that perceptions of the other side can worsen due to such close contact.

The Stirling Workshop The Stirling Workshop centred around the Northern Ireland conflict. It took place in Scotland for nine days in August 1972. Fifty-six Catholic and Protestant community leaders and organisers from Belfast took part. The aims were similar to those of the Fermeda project, although Stirling adhered more strictly to the training goal, emphasising the application of specific skills to the development of projects – not solutions – within the workshop which would then be transferred back to Belfast (the Fermeda Workshop spent the second week focussing on creating solutions utilising the training received during the first week).

The first half of the workshop utilised the Tavistock model. The goal of this model is 'to stimulate learning about the ways in which people function in organized groups'.[10] During this initial phase the Trainers remained aloof and reticent in order to prevent the group from adopting easy comforting answers or otherwise avoiding core

10. L. Doob and J. W. Foltz, 'The Belfast Workshop: An Application of Group Techniques to a Conflict', *The Journal of Conflict Resolution*, vol. 17, no. 3, 1973, p. 496.

conflict issues. The second half of the workshop followed the National Training Laboratories model which aims to 'give participants an opportunity to plan back-home activities in some detail and to both develop and practice specific skills which might aid in the realization of those plans'.[11] In all other respects, the structure, in terms of the T-groups, general assemblies and the use of alternative teaching techniques, was similar to the Fermeda Workshop.

The Stirling Workshop has since become a controversial subject. The results of the efforts of Doob and his colleagues are all but impossible to assess. In addition, both the results (partial as they are) and Doob and his colleagues have received heavy criticism for alleged unethical practices. Several members of Doob's team found that some participants suffered psychological distress as a result of the techniques employed within the workshop and claimed that the workshop made the situation in Belfast worse.[12]

The Harvard Group

Herbert Kelman, a social psychologist at Harvard University, and his associates have been involved in a variety of workshops focussing on international and intercommunal conflict.[13] Kelman has tried to combine elements of Burton's research-oriented workshop and Doob's training-oriented one. Although the format of Kelman's workshops are almost identical to Burton's, elements of Doob's training approach have been integrated into the role of the facilitator (the panel of social scientists are sometimes referred to as facilitators). In Kelman's workshop, while many interventions are set within a general conflict analysis framework (Burton's approach), some focus on the group process as it is happening and as it affects each participant (Doob's approach).

Kelman's experience and research have led him to conclude that workshops need to be developed according to the needs and circumstances of each conflict. Problem-solving workshops, in Kelman's view, exist along a continuum between Burton's research

11. Ibid., p. 497.
12. G. H. Boehringer, *et al*, 'Stirling: The Destructive Application of Group Techniques to a Conflict', *The Journal of Conflict Resolution*, vol. 18, no. 2, 1974, pp. 257–75.
13. B. J. Hill, 'An Analysis of Conflict Resolution Techniques: From Problem-Solving Workshops to Theory', *The Journal of Conflict Resolution*, vol. 26, no. 1, 1982, p. 126.

workshop and Doob's training workshop. Kelman isolates six critical elements which must be re-analysed and re-fitted to each dispute. They are: goals, participants, setting, interaction focus, tone and facilitator interventions. His significant contribution has been to demonstrate the wide applicability and flexibility of the problem-solving method through a systematic analysis of its various critical elements.

Levi and Benjamin: A Model of Conflict Resolution

Levi and Benjamin, academics at the University of Haifa in Israel, have both had extensive experience with problem-solving workshops. They have developed their own method which is more structured, task-oriented and amenable to empirical testing than the models of Burton, Doob or Kelman. Levi and Benjamin's main criticism of these other workshops gives insight into their own method: 'Dealing solely with process treats symptoms, not the disease itself. Not enough attention has been paid to the central task problem of conflict resolution.'[14] Consequently, the main goal of their workshop is:

> to attempt to construct procedures facilitative of conflict resolution problem-solving – procedures involving both task and process considerations – and then to test them empirically in a real yet relatively safe situation (where failure will not harm the participants). The learning obtained will, it is hoped, result in improved procedures for future tests.[15]

Levi and Benjamin offer a highly structured workshop based almost entirely on the process of resolving conflict. They utilise a very specific model which attempts to find a balance between focussing on a specific problem while, at the same time, incorporating enough flexibility to allow for creative innovation and selection of different options. Levi and Benjamin stress that 'focus pin-points the crucial elements of conflict as flexibility opens the way for new solutions'.[16] The workshop is constructed around the idea that if

14. A. M. Levi and A. Benjamin, 'Focus and Flexibility in a Model of Conflict Resolution', *The Journal of Conflict Resolution*, vol. 21, no. 3, 1977, p. 407.
15. A. M. Levi and A. Benjamin, 'Jews and Arabs Rehearse Geneva: A Model of Conflict Resolution', *Human Relations*, vol. 29, no. 11, 1976, p. 1037.
16. Levi and Benjamin, 'Focus and Flexibility', p. 408.

balance is found between focus and flexibility, given an appropriate framework, conflicts can be resolved.

The most impressive aspect of Levi and Benjamin's model is its testability. The model incorporates a scale of ratings from -10 to $+10$. The participants decide where on the scale they would place a particular option or solution in terms of their satisfaction with it, that is, if a solution were totally unacceptable it would rate -10. This process of rating is followed by redefining the conflict, gathering more information, and so on, and eventually rerating another solution. Because the rating system quantifies the 'amount of satisfaction' variable, information regarding progress is not only immediately available to the workshop participants, but also is available, later, to the researchers, enabling them to compare the relative effectiveness of alternative techniques.

Levi and Benjamin's model of conflict resolution differs significantly from Burton's. Levi and Benjamin have emphasised the importance of reaching resolution with high levels of satisfaction from all sides within the workshop context itself. They do not, as yet, suggest how this might be transferred into a policy process.

Conclusion

The different models of facilitated problem-solving presented here are not an exhaustive list. They are representative of the type of work that has been and is currently being done (see Tables 13.1 and 13.2).[17] Although the problem-solving workshop has limitations, it is important to credit the wealth of methodological innovation apparent in the work of Burton, Doob, Kelman, and Levi and Benjamin. And, indeed, the exciting prospects embodied in their efforts, as it is the future, rather than the present state of the art, which seems to hold the most promise. The potential for significant improvement in the capacity to resolve major conflicts on a global scale inherent in the theory first espoused by Burton and applied through his problem-solving workshop, rekindles hope in the ability of human beings to change and thus survive what continues to be an extraordinarily volatile era. This is not to say that Burton is right,

17. R. J. Fisher, 'Third Party Consultation as a Method of Intergroup Conflict Resolution', *The Journal of Conflict Resolution*, vol. 27, no. 1, 1983, pp. 309–10.

Table 13.1 International Conflict Resolution

Setting and Study	Parties	Third Party	Major Approaches
Burton, 1969	Conflicting nations	British and American social scientists	Problem-solving discussions
Doob, 1970	Ethiopia/Somalia/Kenya	American social scientists/human relations trainers	Laboratory learning
Cohen et al., 1977	Palestinians/Israelis	American and Canadian social psychologists	Problem-solving discussions
Cohen and Azar, 1981	Israelis/Egyptians	American and Canadian social scientists	Problem-solving discussions
Fisher, 1980	India/Pakistan	Canadian social psychologist	Problem-solving discussions
Kelman and Cohen, 1979	India/Pakistan/Bangladesh	American and Canadian social psychologists	Problem-solving discussions
Wedge, 1970	Dominican Republic (University)/United States (Embassy)	American psychiatrist	Problem-solving discussions

continued on page 262

Table 13.1 *continued*

Duration	Method of Assessment	Reported Outcomes
1 week	Case-study analysis	Increased understanding
2 weeks	Case-study analysis, post questionnaires	Improved attitudes
2 days	Case-study analysis	Increased understanding
2 days	Case-study analysis	Increased understanding
15 hours	Pre/post interviews	Improved attitudes
2 days	Case-study analysis	Increased understanding
on-going for about 1 year	Case-study analysis	Improved images, improved relationships

Source: R. Fisher, 'Third Party Consultation as a Method of Intergroup Conflict Resolution', *The Journal of Conflict Resolution*, vol. 27, no. 1, 1983, p. 310.

Table 13.2 Group Conflict Resolution (Community; Racial and Religious Groups)

Setting and Study	Parties	Third Party	Major Approaches
Benjamin and Levi, 1979	Jews/Arabs in Israel	Applied behavioural scientists	Problem-solving discussions
Carkhuff and Banks, 1972	Blacks/whites	Clinical psychologists	Interpersonal skills
Cobbs, 1972	Blacks/whites	Group leaders	Sensitivity training
Doob and Foltz, 1973, 1974	Catholics/Protestants in Northern Ireland	Social scientists, human-relations trainers	Laboratory learning
Lakin et al., 1969	Jews/Arabs in Israel	Human-relations trainers	Laboratory learning
Levinson, 1954	Blacks/whites, Catholics/Jews/Protestants	Social scientists	Lectures, discussions, extracurricular activities
Lippitt, 1949	Blacks/whites/Jews	Social scientists	Problem-solving discussions and exercises

continued on page 264

Table 13.2 *continued*

Duration	Method of Assessment	Reported Outcomes
2 days	Case-study analysis ratings of solutions	Mutually satisfactory peace plan
20 hours	Pre/post skill ratings	Improved inter-racial communication skills
2 days	Case-study analysis	Improved attitudes
10 days	Case-study analysis, post-interviews	Increased understanding
1 week	Pre-questionnaires, post-interviews	Increased understanding
6 weeks	Personality and attitude scales control group	Reduced prejudice
2 weeks	Pre/post interviews, observations	Improved attitudes

Source: R. Fisher, 'Third Party Consultation as a Method of Intergroup Conflict Resolution', *The Journal of Conflict Resolution*, vol. 27, no. 1, 1983, p. 309.

but rather that he has provided a method and theory to explore and develop which may also serve as a catalyst for change and growth.

Because facilitated problem-solving and consultative methods in general are a relatively new approach to dealing with international conflict, they are in the midst of a period of heightened development, expansion and change. The state of the art, as it is now, represents the seeds out of which more effective, predictive and concrete method and theory will grow. The beginnings of the process can be descried in the workshops of Doob, Kelman, and Levi and Benjamin and in a generic theory of human behaviour based on human needs put forward by Burton. However, without a more concerted effort to move from a normative to a more predictive theory utilising quantifiable research methods, further growth will be limited. There is a great deal of work to be done at all social levels and across all cultural, racial and national lines. The work of Burton and others involved in the problem-solving workshop approach indicates a promising line of advance.

14

The Mediation of Environmental Conflicts

Paul Landais-Stamp

Whilst initiatives with victim–offender, interpersonal, community and even international mediatory attempts have a long history, no comparative history exists of environmental mediation, with the exception of the United States where it was first used in the 1970s.

This chapter explains the concept of environmental mediation and explores its history in the United States. As we enter the 1990s, with environmental and 'green' issues high on the political agenda – and likely to remain there – the chapter looks, too, at the general potential for environmental mediation, as well as highlighting a few of the problems that the mediation process must address.

Defining the Area: What is 'Environmental Mediation'?

Environmental disputes can be characterised as conflicts over the use and allocation of environmental resources. Such a broad definition is necessary simply because the term 'environmental' covers such a large area: from the landscaping of an area of land, the siting of a new road, airport noise control, the disposal of hazardous waste, pollution control, public access to the countryside, the management of green-belt land, the preservation of listed buildings and many more besides. We can all give examples of environmental issues that have at some time concerned or directly affected us. Increasingly, environmental disputes are crossing international boundaries. The environmental problems of acid rain and global warming of the earth, for example, are not confined to specific countries or even continents, but are literally of global significance. This globalisation of environmental concerns and conflicts is a phenomenon that calls for co-operative efforts to find common solutions across international boundaries. Environmental mediation, perhaps under the auspices of the United Nations, may offer some hope in this direction.

A concern with environmental issues is not a new phenomenon but there has been since the 1960s a considerable increase in environmental disputes. In the United States, the interest in environmental mediation since the mid-1970s was part of the wider interest in seeking alternative processes to the courts for resolving community disputes, but it can also be traced to Congressional federal legislation on environmental issues at the time. Acts such as the National Environmental Policy Act of 1969, the Clean Air Act Amendments of 1970 and the Clean Waters Act Amendments of 1977 created the framework through which an increase in the number of challenges through the courts became possible. It was both a growing awareness of environmental problems and a new framework within which to take action that led to an increase in the frequency of confrontations between environmental interest groups and government, industrial and development agencies.

Few would disagree that the litigation process tends to be lengthy, expensive and often embittered, so the promise of an alternative that would resolve rather than simply settle environmental conflicts, and which was (it was claimed) both faster and cheaper than the courts was always likely to arouse considerable interest.

However, environmental conflicts between different interest groups are marked by their ritualistic, and some would argue irrational character: 'The debate on a whole spectrum of environmental issues abounds with charges of irrationality, sentiment and emotion on both sides. Too often, the protagonists face each other in a spirit of exasperation talking past each other with mutual incomprehension. It is a dialogue of the blind talking to the deaf.'[1] At the core of the ritualisation of much environmental debate lies the fact that many environmental disputes reflect ideological as well as substantive conflicts. That so many environmental debates are couched in the language and terms of factual, scientific and technical debate may in fact obscure the underlying conflict which is concerned with beliefs and values. According to Cotgrove there are two

---

1. Alan Miller and Wilf Cuff, 'The Delphi Approach to the Mediation of Environmental Disputes', *Environmental Management*, vol. 10, no. 3, 1986, pp. 321.

Table 14.1 Environmental Ideologies

	Technocratic	Humanistic
Core Values	Material (economic growth); natural environment valued as a resource; Domination over nature	Non-material (self-actualisation); natural environment intrinsically valued; harmony with nature
Economy	Risk and reward; rewards for achievement	Safety; incomes related to need
Policy	Authoritative structures (experts influential); hierarchical; law and order	Participative structures (citizen/worker involvement); non-hierarchical; liberation
Society	Centralised; large-scale; associational	Decentralised; small-scale; communal
Nature	Ample reserves Nature hostile/neutral; environment controllable	Earth's resources limited; nature benign; nature delicately balanced
Knowledge	Confidence in science and technology; separation of fact/value, thought/feeling	Limits to science Integration of fact/value, thought/feeling

Source: A. Miller and W. Cuff, 'The Delphi Approach to Mediation of Environment Disputes', Environmental Management, vol. 10, no. 3, 1986, p. 322.

main ideologies which come into conflict in the realm of environmental debates. These he describes as *technocratic* and *humanistic*.[2] Alan Miller and Wilf Cuff have modified Cotgrove's two ideologies in Table 14.1.

In essence, the technocratic ideology believes that only material growth and human domination of the environment can result in human well-being and advancement. The management of the environment should be centralised and large-scale, and decisions affecting the environment should be based primarily on scientific and technical information. The humanistic ideology believes the

2. S. Cotgrove, *Catastrophe or Cornucopia: The Environment, Politics and the Future*, New York, 1982.

opposite. Non-material goals, harmony with ecosystems and a decentralised approach to environmental planning is at the core, together with non-elitist participation in decision-making. Conflicts which are based on such fundamental ideological differences are extremely difficult to resolve since there is no (or at best very little) common ground on which to build a dialogue. It has become common that almost any effort to protect or enhance environmental quality is seen by some interest groups as a threat to their economic livelihood or technical advancement. Similarly, attempts to develop land-use, introduce new technology and promote economic development are invariably criticised by some groups as a threat to the natural environment or the ecological balance. As Susskind and Weinstein have noted; 'environmental and developmental interests . . . are locked in a fierce and widening battle'.[3] This problem of environmental conflicts often being based on value or ideological judgements certainly poses considerable difficulties for mediation, but the problems are not necessarily insurmountable.

Before moving on to look at the US experience of environmental mediation in more detail and at its possible application to environmental disputes in Britain, it will be useful to highlight the three main issues over which environmental conflicts take place.

First, there are conflicts over wide-ranging national policy issues. These disputes are concerned with the broadest definition of the 'national interest'. In generalised terms they are disputes which refer to the desire of development interests to see government or local authority money used to encourage economic growth through the building of roads, housing, schools and other facilities which stimulate private investment. On the other hand, environmental interests in the policy arena would generally rather see public revenues used to enhance environmental quality and to protect endangered species or areas of natural beauty from the effects of continued economic growth.

Increasingly, there are also environmental conflicts that have an international or global dimension, and which require international action towards their resolution. In this respect, the distinction between national and international environmental conflicts is becoming blurred. The national policy of Japan to continue its whaling operations, for example, has an international significance.

---

3. Lawrence Susskind and Alan Weinstein, 'Towards a Theory of Environmental Dispute Resolution', *Boston College Environmental Affairs Law Review*, vol. 9, 1980, p. 311.

Similarly, the destruction of rainforests, the development of Antarctica and the international trade in endangered species are all examples of ostensibly national environmental concerns having international ramifications. In an increasingly 'environment conscious' world it is less and less possible to isolate national environmental policies from international responsibilities.

A second area of environmental conflicts are those concerned with environmental quality standards. These conflicts usually centre around the application of particular laws, statutes or regulations.

The third major area of environmental conflicts involves site-specific disputes. These disputes, whilst often sharing similar traits, are unique to a particular area and refer to those cases of conflict that concern a specific natural resource defined by its proposed use; for example, whether the mining of a particular parcel of land should be permitted.

The Growth of Environmental Mediation in the United States

The 1980 Conference of the National Association of Environmental Professionals in the US was entitled 'The First Environmental Decade and Beyond: From Regulatory Confrontation to Conflict Resolution'. The conference title reflected the phenomenal growth of interest in the environment of the past decade, which had resulted in a hitherto unprecedented range of environmental regulatory laws being introduced by the US Congress. In total, approximately eighty major laws, and amendments to existing legislation covering almost every aspect of environmental management were adopted during the 1970s. The passing of so many acts meant that 'environmentalism' became both firmly entrenched in public consciousness and a source of considerable financial lobbying. In the words of US Senator Edmund Muskie: 'Those laws set standards of protection, cleanliness and safety whether we have an energy shortage or an energy surplus; whether we have high inflation, or a low inflation rate; whether the polls are up or down. Our laws codify a way of life, not a decade of cleanliness and conservation flanked by eras of profligate waste.'[4]

4. Edmund S. Muskie, 'Earth Day 1980 – Toward a "New Conservation"; Remarks of Senator Edmund S. Muskie', *The Environmental Professional*, 1980, p. 5.

Inevitably, the passing of so much legislation and the high profile for environmental issues led also to an increase in the number of environmental disputes. These disputes shared with community, labour and international conflicts an adversarial approach to their management and settlement. The 'us against them' attitude of disputants led to 'winning' environmental cases being seen not simply as the most important thing, but the *only* thing. This adversarial attitude, whilst in no way unique to environmental disputes, has perhaps been a particularly noticeable trait of them because of their tendency, as mentioned earlier, to be based on fundamental values and ideologies.

During the past two decades, however, there has been a growing interest in the United States concerning the role that mediation may play in the resolution of environmental disputes. It was during the early 1970s that significant changes took place in the way that some environmental disputes were settled. Instead of lengthy and expensive fights in the courtroom, environmental groups and their industrial opponents sought to reach agreements through mediation whereby some environmental damage was accepted in return for greater environmental safeguards than the industrial groups had originally planned.

It is generally agreed that the first explicit attempt to mediate an environmental dispute began in late 1973, with the involvement of Gerald Cormick and Jane McCarthy in discussions with parties to a flood-control/land-use planning conflict in Washington State.[5] Cormick and McCarthy were based at the Community Crisis Intervention Center in St Louis and during discussions with environmentalists, lawyers, industry representatives and government officials they became aware of an increasing frustration with the confrontational approaches to settling environmental disputes. The idea of extending the conflict resolution and mediation skills which were already being practised at the community level of disputes encouraged Cormick and McCarthy to seek funding and a suitable test-case for environmental mediation. The funding came initially from the Ford and Rockefeller Foundations, and the test-case from a conflict concerning the damming of the Snoqualmie

5. See, for example, Douglas J. Amy, *The Politics of Environmental Mediation*, New York, 1987; Scott Mernitz, *Mediation of Environmental Disputes; A Sourcebook*, New York, 1980; Gerald Cormick, 'Mediating Environmental Controversies: Perspectives and First Experience', *Earth Law Journal*, vol. 12, 1976, pp. 215–24.

River in Washington State.

Following a devastating flood in 1959 the US Corp of Engineers proposed building a flood-control dam across the River Snoqualmie to prevent similar disasters in the future. The proposal was welcomed by homeowners, businesspeople and farmers in the affected areas, but opposed by a coalition of citizen and environmental groups who claimed that the dam would open the flood plain to urban sprawl, interrupt a free-flowing river and could not be justified on a cost-benefit basis. The State Governor, Daniel J. Evans, agreed with the environmental/citizen lobby and refused permission to build the dam, but this only led to more lobbying and demonstrating from the dam's proponents. It was at this point – nearly fourteen years after the initial controversy – that Cormick and McCarthy were invited to attempt to mediate in the dispute, and after seven months of negotiations with the interested parties, a mediated agreement signed by them all was presented to the State Governor. According to Amy, the agreement 'illustrated what proponents of mediation claim to be its main asset – its ability to generate creative solutions that satisfy the interests of all the various parties involved'.[6] The agreement reached provided for a smaller dam at a different site on the river to prevent a repeat flooding, and the establishment of a river-basin planning council to co-ordinate planning for the entire area. With this agreement, and the widespread media coverage that it received, mediation as a viable alternative to litigation in environmental disputes became a reality. Interestingly, the central issue in the dispute, the building of a dam, has never been resolved. Despite the agreement to build a smaller dam it has not been built. Nevertheless, many of the land-use recommendations have been implemented and the river-basin planning council, although disbanded in 1986, lasted for almost ten years.[7]

It was perhaps fortuitous that Cormick and McCarthy chose to mediate a dispute which they clearly believed was mediable from the outset, and in which they were at least nominally successful, for it served as a launch-pad for other mediation efforts, and the establishment of institutes with environmental mediation as their main focus. Cormick founded the Office of Environmental Media-

6. Amy, *Environmental Mediation*, p. 5.
7. Gail Bingham, *Resolving Environmental Disputes; A Decade of Experience*, Washington, DC, 1986, p. 15.

tion in Seattle, and by the late 1970s other institutes included the Institute for Environmental Negotiation at the University of Virginia, the New England Environmental Mediation Center in Boston, ACCORD Associates, and the Centre for Environmental Problem Solving (ROMCOE) in Boulder, Colorado, and the Public Disputes Program of the Harvard Law School. Other mediation efforts in the United States included in 1978–9 a successfully mediated agreement between environmental groups, politicians and water-users in Colorado over the construction of a water-treatment plant south-west of Denver.

In 1978, the RESOLVE-Center for Environmental Conflict Resolution, the Aspen Institute for Humanistic Studies and the Sierra Club Foundation (an environmental lobby group) co-sponsored a conference entitled 'Environmental Mediation: An Effective Alternative?' which further pushed the concept of environmental mediation and its successes to the forefront of environmental politics. Participants at the conference included Susan Carpenter of ROMCOE who emphasised the importance of 'conflict anticipation' and 'conflict assessment'[8] and Malcolm Rivkin who had founded a private consultancy, Rivkin Associates, which had been hired by a developer to negotiate with a local community group over the construction of a large shopping centre. The number of private consultants in the field of environmental negotiations/mediation has grown considerably in the US since this time. By the early 1980s, the concept of environmental mediation had permeated a number of the bureaucratic legislative and administrative agencies in the United States. This was illustrated in 1982 when the Administrative Conference of the United States recommended policy guidelines for what is now known as negotiated rule-making. Five Federal agencies, the Department of Transportation, the Environmental Protection Agency, the Occupational and Safety Health Administration, the Federal Trade Commission and the Department of the Interior all adopted procedures that provided for the negotiated agreement on the language of any regulation between the interested parties.[9]

There has been a steady increase in the number of environmental disputes which have been mediated in the United States during the past fifteen years. Accompanying this increase has been the gradual

8. Mernitz, *Mediation of Environmental Disputes*, p. 71.
9. Frank P. Grad, 'Alternative Dispute Resolution in Environmental Law', *Columbia Journal of Environmental Law*, vol. 14, 1986, p. 160.

professionalisation of environmental mediation, as witnessed by the establishment of a number of centres in the US concerned specifically with the teaching and analysis of dispute-resolution procedures. This professionalisation perhaps suggests that environmental mediation has moved forward from being something of an interesting and novel concept to being an accepted part of environmental decision-making. In part this may be due to the fact that: '[T]he successful efforts to resolve long-standing disputes makes "good copy"; the notion of solving problems to everyone's relative satisfaction is an appealing one.'[10] Appealing as it undoubtedly is, it may, however, obscure the serious limitations of the research so far conducted on the process and efficacy of environmental mediation. It has been said, for example, that its successes to date have been due not least to the careful selection of the disputes to be mediated, rather than any inherent advantage of mediation over traditional (adversarial) attempts to settle environmental conflicts.

Features of the US Experience

It is clear even to the lay-person that in environmental decision-making there are an enormous number of interrelated variables which need to be considered before a good decision can be reached. As Donald Strauss has said:

> You can't construct a new building without affecting land utilisation, population concentrations in the area, demand for water, the need for sewage and solid waste disposal facilities, schools, churches, stores, road requirements . . . employment opportunities, the quality of the air, and so many others. Larger and more technologically sophisticated facilities such as an atomic energy plant, offshore oil development, dams or other industrial establishments multiply the complicated chain of interrelated considerations.[11]

Many of the decisions reached may also be the subject of highly technical judgements which are only understood by a group of 'experts' and which even then may also prove inadequate because of

---

10. Gerald Cormick, 'The Myth, the Reality, and the Future of Environmental Mediation', *Environment*, vol. 24, no. 7, 1982, p. 15.
11. Donald B. Strauss, 'Mediating Environmental, Energy and Economic Trade-Offs', *Arbitration Journal*, vol. 32, pt 2, 1977, p. 98.

an incomplete understanding of their longer-term impacts. Decisions such as these will frequently require the careful analysis of current and clearly perceived benefits as opposed to the less clearly understood future costs. It is common, for example, for a pro-industrial lobby to promise future jobs with a building or factory development. But although this may be seen as a short-term benefit it cannot take account of longer-term uncertainties regarding employment loss after construction, economic difficulties, changing demographic and social patterns and so on. Clearly, the area of environmental planning and management is fraught with complexities and risks perhaps greater than those found in many other areas of conflict such as labour–management relations and community disputes.

There are perhaps three salient features that come across from the US experience of environmental disputes:

1. They are costly (not only financially, but also in terms of time and social cost).
2. They involve a large number of interested parties, with a mix of public interest, community and business organisations.
3. They frequently involve great disparities in power between the interest groups. 'David versus Goliath' conflicts are common, with the business developer (for example) having huge resources compared with the small interest group, but where the latter can still 'spoil' and delay decisions.

With environmental issues having had such a prominent profile in the late 1980s, developers tended to become increasingly sensitised to the risk of costly delays to their projects through environmental protests, and began to employ their own environmental teams both to anticipate and to avoid environmental conflicts which tarnish their public image. But however true it might be that environmental issues (and so *de facto* environmental groups) are listened to more intently now than perhaps ever before, this does not in itself deal with the issue of considerable power differentials between groups in an environmental dispute, and more significantly with what the role of a mediator should be in such a case. It is an area of considerable importance in determining both the desirability of environmental mediation and with its potential for success.

The Role of the Mediator in Environmental Disputes

The roles that a third party may adopt in a dispute may be initially determined by the status of the intermediary. Official interveners (often acting on behalf of a government), for example, will generally have more 'clout' than unofficial mediators who lack the institutional political, economic and even military leverage of their official counterparts. Furthermore, a mediator's role may range from a simple servicing function among the conflicting parties to a more directive role in the supervision and advancement of complex agreements. However, before the issue of mediator roles becomes of particular significance, the mediator must first find a way in which to gain entry to a dispute.

Gaining Entry to a Conflict

The two obvious ways in which a third party may become involved in an attempt to mediate a conflict are by the invitation of one or more of the parties in the conflict, or by self-invitation. Citing his experience at the Institute for Environmental Negotiation in the United States, Dotson comments that although the Institute sometimes initiates the first contact with the disputing parties, it is more common for the initiative to come from one of the parties themselves or from government officials.[12]

Having gained entry to a conflict by whatever means, what should the role of the mediator be? In general, most writers on the subject agree that the initial role of the mediator is to examine each of the parties, their relationships and the history of the conflict. Folberg and Taylor view mediation as a seven-stage conflict resolution process involving:

1. Introduction – creating trust and structure.
2. Fact finding and isolation of issues.
3. Creation of options and alternatives.
4. Negotiation and decision-making.
5. Clarification and writing a plan.

---

12. Bruce Dotson, 'Issues from the Practice of Environmental Mediation', in Dennis J. D. Sandole and Ingrid Sandole-Staroste (eds.), *Conflict Management and Problem Solving: Interpersonal to International Applications*, London, 1987, pp. 159–60.

6. Legal review and processing.
7. Implementation, review and revision.[13]

Although other writers place different emphases on particular stages, most cover the same ground. One particularly thorough guide to the process of mediation in environmental disputes is provided by Susskind and Weinstein who list ' "nine steps" to resolving environmental disputes'.[14] These 'nine steps' form a comprehensive overview of the issues to be raised and roles followed by a mediator in environmental disputes and are paraphrased below.

Step 1: Identifying the Parties that have a Stake in the Outcome of a Dispute This first step is arguably one of the most important for the mediator and may be a source of controversy and debate. It is not only a procedural problem that must be solved before mediation may begin, but also a substantive problem in some conflicts. As Susskind and Weinstein comment: 'Conflict may arise . . . because one group feels it should be involved but a second group insists that the first group be excluded.'[15] In general, the first task of the mediator should be to identify *all* the parties that want to take part in the mediation process; it being better to include too many people or groups than too few. The risk that a large number of participants may make dialogue a lengthy and difficult process is unavoidable, but may be alleviated to some extent by shifting the focus away from the sheer *numbers* of parties involved to the categories of *interests* that want representation. If this is done, then every person in each category need not take part in the negotiations but may be represented by delegates.

Step 2: Ensuring that Groups or Interests that have a Stake in the Outcome are Appropriately Represented Following on from the idea that there should be interest-group representation, it is essential that the spokespersons for each interest group really do accurately represent their group. It is important, however, that there should remain some fluidity regarding the delegates chosen. For example, as the mediation process develops it might be expedient to introduce

13. Jay Folberg and Alison Taylor, *Mediation: A Comprehensive Guide to Resolving Conflicts Without Litigation*, London, 1984, p. 32.
14. Susskind and Weinstein, 'Environmental Dispute Resolution', pp. 336–45.
15. Ibid., p. 337.

different representatives who are specialised in a particular area of the dispute being discussed. In any event some sort of revolving membership is preferable to figurehead leaders.

Step 3: Narrowing the Agenda and Confronting Fundamentally Different Values and Assumptions   It has already been mentioned that one of the characteristics of environmental disputes is that they tend to be based on differing ideologies and values. According to Susskind and Weinstein this should not mask the fact that very often contending parties, who appear to be dialectically opposed to each other, have only a vague idea about why they are for or against a particular environmental project. In short, it is suggested that beyond the rhetorical stand-offs the issues are not so clear-cut. Using the example of a proposal to build a dam, Susskind and Weinstein show that often the issues at stake are difficult to specify: 'Involved are such considerations as the protection of endangered species, the use of water by nearby as well as distant consumers, power generation, farming, sport fishing, and real estate development.'[16]

The task of the mediator is to narrow the issues down to their fundamentals, which may mean to their value and ideological components. This is necessary for two reasons. First, it allows the issues at the heart of a dispute to be understood, and secondly the process of confrontation may lead to changes in the positions of disputants. This second reason is perhaps the most important in terms of achieving a sustainable mediated agreement. Sometimes adversaries are selective in citing evidence to support their particular claims, so any challenges to these selective perceptions (so long as they are based on objective evidence and handled carefully) can be instrumental in achieving changes in position.

Step 4: Generating a Sufficient Number of Alternatives or Options   A fundamental role of the mediator is to ensure that in addition to an adequate representation of all interested parties, and a recognition of deeply held value differences, there exists a sufficient number of policy or project alternatives. This is to say that every group involved in the mediation must be able to find an option on the mediation agenda with which it agrees. Two extremes, using the example of a proposal to build a new factory, would be to build all

16. Ibid., p. 340.

of the factory or none of it. Within these extremes, of course, there lie any number of options.

Because not all the appropriate alternatives may be known during the early stages of mediation, it is also necessary for the structure of mediation to be such that new options or alternatives may fruitfully be added at any time.

Step 5: Agreeing on the Boundaries and Time Horizon for Analysis The need to specify the boundaries of a dispute and to establish a time zone for analysis is of great importance. If the boundaries used to assess the impact of a proposed policy or action are too broad, it is possible that the overall cost–benefit analysis will be such that the costs outweigh the benefits. Similarly, an open-ended time framework for mediation may not aid the prospects for a successful outcome. It is necessary to view each of these considerations as negotiable in any environmental dispute. The conflict of boundaries and time horizons may fall into the category of being either procedural or substantive issues. As a procedural issue, it is difficult to make mediation work unless there is some tentative agreement by the parties as to boundaries and time frameworks. As a substantive issue, a conflict about them may well lie at the very heart of dispute.

Step 6: Weighting, Scaling and Amalgamating Judgements about Costs and Benefits All the parties involved in a mediation effort must ultimately accept financial and time constraints and have faith in the appropriateness of forecasts about, for example, the environmental impacts of particular courses of action. The resolution of environmental disputes can be hampered – sometimes irrevocably – by disagreements over the facts used by opposing parties in support of their particular case.

Some of the differences may be easy to verify. Disputes over precise boundary lines between properties, for example, can usually be resolved fairly quickly and conclusively. The real problems begin to arise over questions for which no precise answers exist, but for which there may be any number of scientific predictions. Examples here would include the probability of earthquakes or hurricanes. Similarly 'factual' disputes can arise when there are several different means of collecting data. There are, for example, different measures to determine the quality of air or water, or to assess the extent of a flood plain. Furthermore, there are also questions which cannot be resolved given the current state of scientific knowledge. Even when the parties agree on the methods of data collection and the facts it produces, they may still disagree over the way these facts are used and the weight that is given to them in making predictions or constructing models. One possible solution to these problems may be the use of data mediation.

Data mediation may take several forms. One approach is for the contending parties to share the information they intend to use to support their arguments. As the data is gathered each party is able to comment and lodge objections regarding the validity of sources and so on. Another approach is to secure agreement from the contending parties that all modelling and predictions carried out will be based on a common data pool. In this case there would be a jointly constructed computer model by all the parties involved in an environmental conflict.

Step 7: Determining Fair Compensation and Possible Compensatory Actions Another important role of the mediator in environmental disputes is to make explicit the elements of an environmental project that can be bartered or traded. Furthermore, it is important for the mediator to discover what compensatory or mitigation measures are acceptable to each party. This is a difficult task and it has been shown that financial compensation is often inappropriate to certain circumstances and to particular groups. More likely to succeed are trades, be they swops of land or preferential action on other matters that arise at a later date.[17]

Step 8: Implementing the Bargains that are Made It is possible that the groups involved in a mediation process will reach an agreement that is impossible to implement. This may be because the agreement is outside of the law or because outside parties are able to refuse to co-operate and effectively sabotage the agreement. It is therefore crucial that all the parties to mediation understand fully the obstacles to implementation that may exist when they attempt to reach an agreement. This is not only because the implementation of an agreement may be hindered, but also because, in the words of Susskind and Weinstein: 'Disputes that occur subsequent to a failure to implement a previous bargain are much harder to reconcile; all the parties to the bargaining have good reason to doubt the

17. Ibid., p. 344.

prospects of fulfilling the agreements that are being proposed.'[18] The role of the mediator is thus to ensure that agreements are not made which would be impossible to uphold.

Step 9: Holding the Parties to their Commitments   Following on from the above, it is important when agreements are reached that there also exists a mechanism for ensuring that the parties will be bound to them. All the parties to an agreement must be sure that the agreements reached are capable of objective measurement. This means that agreements must be self-enforcing or subject to legal enforcement through a binding contract.

An agreement between parties on environmental matters may require some form of monitoring activity. This monitoring may involve measuring predicted or prescribed impacts and outcomes of an agreement. Here again, the parties' acceptance of the reliability of the monitoring data is important, as is the ongoing funding of any such monitoring.

It is clear from these 'nine steps' towards resolving environmental disputes that the roles of the mediator are wide and varied. The precise roles adopted will inevitably vary from one dispute to another, and indeed from one mediator to another. Flexibility in approach should be seen as a plus for mediation. However, the larger question is whether these roles should always be underpinned by what might be described as an ethical code of intervention. That is to say, whether there are certain codes of conduct (or less formally basic principles) in mediation that are, or should be, inviolable. The debate which surrounds the wider issues of mediator roles is fundamental to the whole question of both the desirability and efficacy of mediation. Furthermore, it is a debate which is applicable to all levels of mediation, from the interpersonal to the international. The issues raised may be summarised as the ethics of third party intervention.

The Ethics of Intervention

In the concluding section of this chapter some of the ethical questions raised by environmental mediation will be discussed. Briefly, these comprise: the problem of power, mediator neutrality, the

18. Ibid.

confidentiality of the mediation process and the accountability of mediators, the 'voluntary' nature of mediation and the motivation to mediate. Although each of these questions is addressed separately, there is, of course, a considerable overlap between them.

The Problem of Power

It has already been mentioned that a common characteristic of environmental conflicts is the wide disparity of power that exists between the disputants. For James Laue and Gerald Cormick, the single ethical question that must be asked of all mediation and by all mediators is: 'Does the intervention contribute to the ability of relatively powerless individuals and groups in the situation to determine their own destinies to the greatest extent consistent with the common good?'[19] Their reasoning is simple; if only certain people or groups are empowered, then other people and groups will be unable to protect themselves and speak for themselves. In this context, the mere *settlement* of environmental conflicts should not be the foremost aim of the mediator, since the settlement of a conflict in which there is a considerable imbalance of power between the parties tends merely to strengthen the status quo by reflecting the relative strength of the parties. Unless mediation allows all the parties in a conflict to have some form of negotiable power, then joint and fair determination of the outcome becomes impossible. In such a situation, the powerful groups (which in the context of environmental disputes invariably means the development interests) will simply be able to use the process of mediation as the most efficient means to achieve their ends.

In a similar vein, Douglas Amy argues forcefully that mediation can easily become seduction.[20] The informality of settings and meetings can 'seduce' environmentalists into compromising their ideals and granting overly generous concessions to their opponents. The solution to this is that the mediator, through training or other approaches, should empower weak or powerless groups to negotiate their own interests and rights.

19. James Laue and Gerald Cormick, 'The Ethics of Intervention in Community Disputes', in Gordon Bermant, Herbert Kelman and Donald Warwick (eds.), *The Ethics of Social Intervention*, Washington, DC, 1978, p. 218.
20. Amy, *Environmental Mediation*, pp. 97–127.

How Voluntary is Mediation?

The supposed voluntary nature of participation in mediation is often cited as one of its most positive aspects. Indeed, often the 'fairness' of mediation is illustrated by the fact that participation and any subsequent agreement is voluntary. But it is worth asking just how 'voluntary' the process is for powerless groups. A local environmental group, for example, may have no hope of sustaining a prolonged court battle, and have little influence with bureaucratic local council structures. In such cases, the 'choice' of mediation may not amount to much of a choice at all, if choice means choosing one option among several. As Amy comments: 'The illusion of voluntariness that surrounds mediation not only obscures subtle forms of coercion, but also grants an air of reasonableness and legitimacy to mediated agreements.'[21]

Mediator Neutrality

The concept of a mediator empowering a weaker party is a difficult one for many writers to accept. After all, the 'neutrality' of the mediator is often seen as being central to the whole mediation process, but, in reality, simply by advocating mediation as a way of dealing with a conflict, the mediator has already adopted a non-neutral position: advocating positive change rather than continued conflict. It is often argued that the mediator is or should be neutral as to the outcome of a dispute, but there continues to be debate concerning whether the mediator also has a responsibility to oversee a just outcome and therefore cannot be strictly neutral. If a mediator accepts the need for the empowerment of weak parties then she or he cannot also claim to be neutral, since such neutrality has the effect of maintaining the status quo.

Confidentiality and Accountability

One of the most difficult ethical questions for mediation at any level concerns the confidentiality of the mediation process. General agreement exists that 'successful' mediation depends in large part on the expectation of privacy and confidentiality. A principal task of

21. Douglas J. Amy, 'The Politics of Environmental Mediation', *Ecology Law Quarterly*, vol. 11, no. 1, 1983, p. 10.

the mediator is to allow the disputants to alter their positions without any loss of face. To this end, they must have confidence that any 'sounding out' of possible agreements undertaken with the mediator will be dealt with in strict confidence. However, the issue is not simply whether the mediator treats communications in confidence during the mediation sessions, but whether these communications are protected from compulsory disclosure in any subsequent litigation. If no testimonial privilege exists for mediators, it is impossible for them to uphold the much vaunted and valued promise of confidentiality.

Although there may be strong arguments for granting environmental mediators testimonial privilege, there are, however, also problems with this. Testimonial privilege can encourage both the mediator and the disputants to shield themselves from public scrutiny. This is of great importance in environmental conflicts where the outcome of an agreement is likely to significantly and permanently affect large numbers of people and the natural environment. Furthermore, it has been argued that in the absence of any licensing or accreditation of mediators there needs to be an open scrutiny of their work in order to deter dishonest practices.

If the suggestion then becomes that mediators should be accountable, the question remains to whom. There is much debate on the merits of accreditation or licensing, since this can imply professionalisation, elitism and bureaucratisation just as much as high standards of fairness, responsibility and codes of conduct. Similarly, would 'accountable' mediators find themselves liable for prosecution if their mediation efforts failed? Not surprisingly several US writers warn against environmental mediators making implicit or expressed promises about the results of mediation.[22]

The Motivation to Mediate

Most of the focus on ethical questions concerning mediation tend to be on the issues discussed above, but another area of considerable importance is the motivation of the mediator. What factors induce a third party to intervene in an environmental (or other) conflict? Payment may be one benefit for the mediator but this has ethical

22. Karen L. Liepmann, 'Confidentiality in Environmental Mediation: Should Third Parties Have Access to the Process?', *Boston College Environmental Affairs Law Review*, vol. 14, 1986, p. 108.

considerations attached to it as well. Who pays the mediator, and how much? An hourly rate would perhaps ensure a lengthy dispute; a lump sum might suggest a shorter mediation session with the mediator reluctant to spend more time on a problem even if the parties' interests warranted it. Salaried mediators may be the answer, but finding sources of funding that can be shown to be from a 'neutral' source poses some difficulties, particularly in the long term. It may be that mediators are attracted by the prestige attached to a successful mediation. This has value in itself, but also for advancement in other fields of work (the problem here is how this fits in with the issues of low-key approach and confidentiality). A third incentive to mediate is through a feeling of social responsibility, although one should of course be cautious of mediator claims to be neutral or disinterested.[23]

Conclusions

A decision on whether or not to enter into the mediation of an environmental conflict is complex and difficult. Certainly it should not be taken lightly, and the foregoing comments perhaps suggest that it should not be taken at all. But the intention here has been to highlight some of the problems and dilemmas faced by environmental mediation in the United States during the past fifteen years. The US experience suggests that there is much to learn, and that some of the ethical questions concerning mediation and mediator roles need careful consideration. In particular, one must question whether environmental conflicts which so frequently display considerable disparities of power and influence can be mediated without there first being the empowerment of the powerless.

With the 1990s looking set to be a decade of heightened environmental concern and awareness, the potential for environmental mediation in Britain is great. Obstacles undoubtedly exist, but there have been indications that both industrialists and environmentalists are keen to develop new approaches to jointly solving environmental problems. With an understanding of the ethics of third-party intervention, environmental mediation in Britain may be able to avoid some of the problems experienced in the United States. The

23. Laurence S. Bacow and Michael Wheeler, *Environmental Dispute Resolution*, New York, 1984, pp. 248–78.

development of mediation techniques in the resolution of environmental disputes is an exciting and overdue development, so long as it is underpinned by a firm commitment to the empowerment of weaker parties 'to the point where they can advocate their own needs and rights, [and] where they are capable of negotiating their way with other empowered groups on the sure footing of respect rather than charity'.[24]

24. James Laue and Gerald Cormick, 'Ethics of Intervention', p. 219.

PART V

Peaceful Relationships

15

Peacemaking as an Evolutionary Capacity: Reflections on the Work of Teilhard de Chardin, Martin Buber and Jane Addams

Elise Boulding

Celebrations are the stuff of life. We celebrate the changing seasons of the solar year, the changing seasons of our individual lives and the changing seasons of history. It seems fitting to celebrate the extraordinarily creative life of Adam Curle, peacemaker and peace researcher, by dedicating to him a study of three great peacemakers of this century whose centennials have been celebrated within the past two decades: Teilhard de Chardin, Martin Buber and Jane Addams. The optimism of the analysis is like the optimism of Adam Curle himself. It is congenital, and cannot be stifled by the threat of nuclear doom.

In centennials we capture the dynamics of a century in an experiential moment. Thus centennials anchor us more securely in the social and spiritual developments of our time, developments which cannot at all be understood by examining only our own decade or even by looking back several decades. Social process happens in bigger chunks than our present-focussed minds can easily digest.

We will begin by looking at the most recent centennialist, Teilhard de Chardin, whose centennial was celebrated in 1981. Teilhard was a man who dealt with evolutionary sweeps of time in ways that leapfrog many of our present problems. I want to focus on one aspect of the evolutionary process he lays before us in his works: the evolution of the human capacity for peacemaking.[1] This seems

---

1. By peacemaking I mean the creation of a new reality in situations of conflict which allows for future growth for all parties to the conflict.

all the more appropriate because if anything could bring to a halt the evolutionary process as Teilhard describes it, it would be the involvement of the superpowers in a major nuclear war, whether accidentally or intentionally. Never has the human capacity for violence been clearer to us, as we witness rising levels of street violence, terrorist violence, police violence, family violence, media violence, violence in sports, in art and in our occupational arenas. Internationally we have witnessed colonial violence and its legacy, large numbers of what are euphemistically called border wars in the Middle East, Africa, Asia and Latin America.

Is there any possibility of a further development of the somewhat fragile human capacity for peacemaking? To answer this, I will draw not only on Teilhard, but on two other major centennial figures of world significance who have lived and worked through the same past 100 years, experiencing in their own persons the full impact of human capacity for violence. One, Martin Buber, stood at the very centre of the implacable Arab–Israeli struggle. The other, Jane Addams, lived in the midst of ethnic violence and the ugliness of nationalistic fervour in the mid-western heartland of the United States itself. Each witnessed in the midst of violence to a world-in-the-making which would be a concrete embodiment of Isaiah's vision of the peaceable kingdom. Teilhard was born in 1881, Buber three years before and Addams two decades before. I believe we see reflected in the lives of these three individuals the emergence of fresh peacemaking potentials over the past century in spite of our experience of increasing domestic violence, two world wars and the threat of a third in that same period.

Teilhard, Buber and Addams were all born in a time of unbridled optimism in the West about the future of humankind. They entered early adulthood at a time when the West had experienced a relatively long period of freedom from wars. There was widespread hope that science was going to bring an end to the major forms of suffering – violence, poverty and disease. French-born Teilhard was fed that optimism with his mother's milk. For Austrian-born Buber, the Western heritage of optimism was tempered by the somberness of anti-semitism. American-born Jane Addams was forced to reconcile that Western optimism with the realities of ethnic violence repeatedly witnessed in the Chicago of her day. All three were nevertheless profoundly affected by the belief that the world could be reshaped – a belief particularly nurtured in the West. All three had a European education, and each drew on that education and blended it with their own experience in their own way.

Teilhard and Buber, being men, found platforms provided for them by the society in which they lived, platforms from which they could speak of their visions and be heard by millions, unpopular though their views might be with authorities. Jane Addams, being a woman, had no platforms provided for her. She built her own, using the ingenuity of hands, heart and mind. During the First World War a passionate nationalistic fervour pulled much of the platform right out from under her feet, even in the local neighbourhoods of Chicago to which she had given her life – but she held to her vision even when all support was gone. Only toward the end of her life, as clouds of economic depression gathered in 1930, was there again any acknowledgement that she had given something important to the world in which she lived. Since women have never been able to count on platforms, they have never been able to count on a support network for unpopular views. They have always had to be their own carpenters. The energy it takes to be your own carpenter means less time and creativity left over for the visioning and broader work of reconstruction. There have been many potential Jane Addamses around the world in this past century, but few who could muster the incredible energies needed to make their visions an acknowledged and visible part of the social order. In celebrating prophecy and vision we must never forget this powerful biasing process which makes the work of opening new pathways to the future appear to be primarily the work of men. Only by looking at the totality of human action, both the visible and the invisible, the action of women and the action of men, can we really know what we have to work with to make planetary society peaceable.

Teilhard's Perspective

We begin with Teilhard de Chardin. To a humanity mistrustful of itself and fearful of its own capacity for evil, Teilhard brings a wonderful vision of undreamed-of flowering of human goodness aided by science and the action of God incarnate. We are all starving for vision, and we love Teilhard for the hope he sets before us. It is important to remember that his great vision of the divinisation of the world came to him as a stretcher-bearer in the muddy blood-soaked trenches of France in 1916. The vision evolved in complexity and depth over the years as Teilhard the scientist forged the concepts he needed to further elucidate the vision, but the core of the vision remained the same to the very end of his life. To put it simply, Teilhard, fell in love with the planet and its Creator in the trenches and remained faithful to his passion all his life. As he himself put it in 1916 when he began writing:

> What follows springs from an exuberance of life and a yearning to live: it is written to express an impassioned vision of the earth, and in an attempt to find a solution for the doubts that beset my action – because I love the universe, its energies, its secrets, and its hopes, and because at the same time I am dedicated to God, the only origin, the only issues and the only term. I want these pages to be instinct with my love of matter and life.[2]

With men dying around him, Teilhard was nevertheless able to see the earth as taking on new life as the body of Christ. His essays entitled *Cosmic Life* are a love song about the new body of earth. He looks over aeons and sees 'the disordered anthill of living beings' arranging itself in long files that creep toward greater consciousness, in a vast cosmic movement from alpha to omega. He feels his own body as a multitude of atoms, molecules, cells in turmoil inside its casing, and feels the whole cosmos emerging in him. Over a period of two years in the *Cosmic Life* essays he develops the concept that it is the task of the human race to master the universe through science.

> we men [*sic*] represent that past of the world that has won through, that in which all the life-sap of a recognizable evolution flows, in which all its efforts are concentrated, towards the break-through that has finally been effected. It is we, without any doubt, that constitute the active part of the universe; we are the bud in which life is concentrated and is at work, and in which the flower of every hope is enclosed. If, then, a man who has heard the summons of the cosmos is to remain faithful to it, he must overcome his repugnance for contact with the mob, for the promiscuity and constraints of cities and the smoke of factories, and, with all his soul, turn back to mankind: for mankind is the object in which rather than in his own being, he must re-discover himself and to which his love for his own self must be given.[3]

Humankind's work is seen as a cosmic work with nature. The earth is raw material for divinisation, and we must spend ourselves

---

2. P. Teilhard de Chardin, 'The Prayer of the Universe', in *Writings in Time of War*, translated by R. Hague, New York, 1968, p. 41.
3. *Ibid.*, p. 65.

to the utmost to make divinisation possible. The suffering we experience is necessary to the process. Teilhard is fired with enthusiasm for the war, grateful for the chance to die that an ideal civilisation might be born: 'The more I serve the earth, the more I belong to God.' The incarnated Christ at work in the world stands at the heart of this paradox.

The dark thread in Teilhard's thought is his concept of the cleavage that runs to the end of time: a cleavage between the redeemed parts of the earth and cosmos, and the unredeemed monads, the forces for evil, which continue to the end and are then sloughed off into outer darkness. (Teilhard does in fact pray that this may after all not happen.) His attitude toward war is complex. On the one hand, the concepts of complexification and involution in human development which produce the noosphere, the web of thought which envelops the planet, imply more and more co-operation and unity in diversity among humans. He places great faith in scientific mastery of planetary problems, and speaks of the world brotherhood of scientists as if it already existed. He debunks the 'bourgeois millennium', that golden age automatically-to-come, longed for by the simpleminded. He emphasises the necessity of works of charity for the well-being of society. On the other hand, there is the implication that divinisation comes about in a predetermined transformation process, apart from human effort. This is certainly what people read into Teilhard's writing, because it is what they want to hear.

Teilhard felt that his task was to delineate the vision so people would know what they had to work for. He skipped over the intermediate process between biological evolution and the development of the planet-wrapping noosphere that binds humanity into one. Unfortunately, it is precisely that intermediate process, the necessary intervening evolution of the *sociosphere*, which holds us back through its enormous difficulties. The sociosphere is the planetary web of social interaction. To date it is represented by intergovernmental relations between the 165 nation states; by the non-governmental transnational interactions among the members of the 4,000 or so non-governmental organisations formed to further human interests in all fields from culture, science and religion to labour and sports; by the United Nations and the world-wide networks of its thirty agencies, by the multinational business corporations, and by students, volunteers and travellers, all moving about the planet and interacting in a multitude of ways.

The web of the sociosphere is full of big dangerous holes, rent by the actions of nation states in the interest of national security. Teilhard never visualised the situation in which we find ourselves today, when half of all the world's expenditures on research and development are devoted to military purposes. He never pictured that the majority of the best and brightest graduates of schools of science and technology in the most 'developed' nations would head for the weapons development laboratories of their respective countries, making the borders of the nation state coterminous with the boundaries of their allegiance to science and truth. When we do manage to bring a halt to further military research and development, we will have a very large group of Western-trained scientists in every country between the ages of twenty-five and seventy whose adult working life has been spent at the service of the Nuclear Elite, the military weapons planners. How will these scientists be helped to shift their work in the Teilhardian direction of the divinisation of the planet?

It is humbling to realise how Teilhard, great lover of humankind and the planet, rejoiced over the first test explosion of the atom bomb in the Arizona desert; to know that he saw a new humankind emerging, on a new plane of consciousness, from that explosion. Humbling to know that he was able to write off the subsequent deaths in Hiroshima and Nagasaki as part of the 'necessary pain' of evolution. Humbling because we too may be making judgements about human progress before which later generations will stand aghast. One wonders if Teilhard would have continued to write off as necessary pain the mounting deaths decades later from exposure to these early desert tests and from exposure to chemical warfare on the country-wide battlefields of Vietnam.

After his stretcher-bearer days Teilhard saw very little of the turbulent seething interactions of the sociosphere, moving as he did between school, laboratory and oratory. He knew very little of the great intercivilisational dialogues about the human path to development which were to emerge by the 1960s. His concept of cephalisation, of an increasingly developed intellect or head leading the body social, was based on the idea that the West was the head, the leading shoot of further evolution. He thought of other cultures and civilisations as fossils. He had no problems with the phenomena of centralisation, hierarchy, authority.

And yet for all that Teilhard skipped over much of our present agony, he remains a profoundly inspiring singer of the future. He was not indifferent to the sufferings of war, but he was so convinced that the 'signs were changing' that he refused to take the signals of violence at face value. We are experiencing, says Teilhard, '*not an irresistible increase in tide of war, but simply a clash of currents:* the old disruptive surface forces driving against a merging in the depths which is already taking place'.[4] What is emerging is a sublimation of war, a new way of dealing with conflict. Conflict itself is the very stuff of evolution. Teilhard sees humankind straining shoulder-to-shoulder in a universal resolve to raise ourselves upwards towards ever greater heights of consciousness and freedom, with a new speciation emerging from the human phylum in a gradually divinised world.

Martin Buber's Perspective

But how to deal with the maelstrom of violence right now? Teilhard doesn't tell us, but Martin Buber does. The Vienna-born Jewish philosopher, social scientist, teacher and saint lived through an age of pogroms in Europe which culminated in the Holocaust; and he lived in very practical everyday ways for his vision of Zion, Isaiah's holy mountain where none shall hurt nor destroy. He was one of the early leaders of the non-nationalist, turn-of-the-century zionist movement, a founder of some of the earliest Palestinian communes and an advocate of a Near East Federation of Arabs and Jews, which might have avoided a half century of Middle Eastern bloodshed had it been tried. Buber saw the cosmic vision, the gradual making holy of the planet in a movement from creation to kingdom – his word for Teilhard's alpha and omega. But something happened to Buber in the same decade that Teilhard worked in the trenches, to make him retreat from his own inclination to become absorbed in the cosmic vision, in the experience of mystic union with the Creator. He became instead a craftsman, crafting the relationships between person and person, firming up that very network of human connectedness we call the sociosphere, the intermediate stage which Teilhard skipped over.

What happened to Buber? Little incidents that changed the look of the world. After a morning of religious exaltation during his

---

4. P. Teilhard de Chardin, *The Future of Man*, translated by N. Denny, New York, 1968, pp. 156–7.

mystic period, Buber was visited by a young man with whom he conversed kindly enough as he came down from his clouds of glory. Subsequently, however, he learned that the young man had died soon after, having come to Buber with great burning questions he found no chance to bring up and which would now remain forever unasked. Buber realised that his own exaltation had kept him from being fully present to the young man. The stuff of suffering had remained unseen, untouched. Buber recounts other small incidents as he meets with European peace leaders to try to prevent the gathering war clouds from erupting into full-scale violence. These coincidences show him gradually learning how to be present to others through encounter after encounter. He was to break through both the heady mystical rhetoric and the utilitarian, task-oriented, technique-focussed peace strategising to an understanding that the real work of peacemaking lies in the act of relationship, in coming face-to-face with the other in the I–Thou meeting. The vision of the peaceable kingdom at the omega point remained as clear to him as to Teilhard, but he saw that it could come in no other way than through the crafting of human relationships on the pattern of the human–divine relationship.

His whole life was spent in demonstrating the I–Thou relationship in his work as a teacher, political adviser, conflict mediator and commune organiser. He worked under heavy pressures to produce more immediate political products, but remained faithful to his spiritual calling. What is the I–Thou relationship? In the I–Thou relationship we stand over against the Other (any other with whom we have to do) and let that Other be in all their wholeness and uniqueness. We may not measure, define, utilise or even experience the other person. We may only relate. We *meet* the other person. The event of meeting lies in the betweenness, in the space that must reverently be left there, between one being and another. This is how we meet God. All meeting, all relationship must partake of that character in the process of making the world holy. The act of meeting happens also to be the act of making peace with another. To see Buber address an audience on a university campus as I did in the 1950s, and to feel that each of us sitting in that audience was a Thou, to see him bring post-lecture questioners up to face him on the stage and put their question to him under that steady penetrating regard, to feel answered by the very expectancy of his own expression, was an unforgettable experience. That same quality of meeting the Other he brought to the tensest political discussions and community conflicts. He carried it to Germany after the war ended in 1945 when in an ultimate act of meeting God in the Other he accepted a peace prize from the German Association of Book Publishers, speaking frankly but lovingly of how hard it was to do this, and how necessary.

Buber's hard-won discovery of the I–Thou relationship enabled him to state for our century the central dilemma for those who would rebuild the social order. As a social scientist and an adviser to policymakers, Buber knew that humans must learn to analyse, identify, measure, map, organise and utilise the resources within a society including its people, its institutions and its physical environs, in order to improve human welfare. This is what science is all about, this is what progress means. This is certainly what my own field of peace research does, whether mapping the conflict resolution resources of a social system, testing mediation strategies and non-violence techniques in a simulated or actual conflict or studying how altruism develops in children. It is also what peace activists do when planning symbolic public events, demonstrations, sit-ins and so on. But where Teilhard sees the analytic mode – at its purest in science – as part of the divinisation process, Buber sees it as destructive of divinisation, as creating an I–It world of objects to be exploited. Buber sees it as creating in us a mode of meeting things and people which continuously if unobstrusively draws us towards the pole of violence in our dealings with the world. Only the intervention of the I–Thou relationship can save us from using science to destroy ourselves.

Buber often speaks of the narrow rocky ridge that humans have to walk in order to balance the I–It and the I–Thou. His view of the evolutionary process is of a continuous inward spiralling as humankind ascends from the creation to the holy kingdom, swerving outward and away from The Good in bursts of I–It activities of conquest and exploitation, then returning towards The Good in a repentant rediscovery of the meeting with Thou, the Other. The lode-star for Buber is the Covenant, the autonomously arrived-at agreement between the Creator and peoples of the new species, humankind, by which humans agree to take up God's handicraft and *build* the holy kingdom in partnership with the Creator.[5] The spiral has a direction, the swings are not meaningless, and we come

---

5. M. Buber, *Israel and the World: Essays in a Time of Crises*, New York, 1948, pp. 76–7.

closer to the goal as we learn to be better craftworkers. However, the craftworker may never simply shape a tool and use it. Developing the tool for redistributive justice, the institutions of conflict resolution and the skills of mediation, will do us no good unless we continually remember to stand back and affirm the Other in that with which we work, in those with whom we work. Buber has given us a way of evaluating everything we do as parents, workers, activists, educators and researchers. We are all craftworkers who must continually step back to affirm and meet the Other. There is no place for simply getting by, simply 'doing the job'.

This is a hard path to follow, but it is possible because we are loved, and can love in return. The act of meeting is the act of loving; the I–Thou relationship is a love-relationship. In the end, nothing, no one, will be left out of that love relationship. *All* is to be made holy. Love becomes the great dynamic out of which all meeting, all peacemaking, all rebuilding of the social order, all social transformation towards the omega, the peaceable kingdom, takes place. Teilhard's and Buber's visions meet.

Jane Addams's Perspective

A third visionary who has been at work in this violent century is Jane Addams of Hull House, Chicago, and Geneva, the World. Jane Addams never had to come down from the clouds of mysticism because her earliest childhood visions of a peaceable world came while watching women working in the wheat fields of her grandfather's farm, women grinding flour in the farm courtyard with hand mills, women carrying water from well to kitchen, women kneeding bread in that kitchen. Jane the child saw past the Illinois farm, saw women as breadmakers and breadgivers, feeding hungry mouths all over the world. Jane the teenager, aware of social injustice, saw the work of the breadgivers destroyed by violence and war. She saw the breadgivers transformed into Cassandra, the Everywoman from Greek legend, continually foreseeing the evil consequences of the deeds of men in a world ruled by the sword. She saw Cassandra continually disbelieved and rejected by sword-bearing Everyman. Her high-school graduation essays depicted this vision of the breadgiver-turned Cassandra, warning of evil while pointing to the good. The adult Jane Addams spent the rest of her life working out the visions of childhood and adolescence.

Hers was the prophetic voice connecting the covert violence of the comfortable middle classes against the immigrant working poor, with the overt violence of nation against nation. Hers was also the prophetic voice connecting the sharing of bread with peace between nation and nation. Jane Addams refused to let her visions hang in the air. She came on foot to wherever there was suffering, and painstakingly taught the connections between a millhand's daily life of toil in Chicago and Councils of State in Washington and Geneva. She taught millhands, factory inspectors, congressmen and presidents. She was able to teach human connectedness because she walked its paths with her own feet. She was able to speak of that connectedness in ways that were understood because she listened wherever she walked, and learned from what she heard.

Addams identified in the confused ramblings of aged work-worn immigrant women the remnants of youthful dreams, 'containing within themselves the inchoate substance from which the tough fibered forces of coming social struggle are composed'.[6] In every bitter or hostile act of a human being, rich or poor, young or old, she could identify the nascent distorted groping towards goodness. She evoked forgotten yearnings, not through preaching, but through an extraordinary series of practical social inventions at the neighbourhood level. Many of these inventions stemmed from the basic invention of the settlement house itself as a strongly local social institution. By showing people new means to aid themselves and one another she helped people rediscover the moral community, the larger we, that they had forgotten.

Addams walked Martin Buber's razor edge every day. She drew neighbourhood maps, collected neighbourhood data and forged neighbourhood action instruments, on the one hand, with finely tuned I–It crafting skills. On the other hand she listed and looked reverently with the inward ear and eye for the hidden Other in each person she met.

The severest test of her visions came during the First World War when as a pacifist she was almost universally vilified as a traitor to her country. Yet even then she went on with her work of social invention, drafting arbitration mechanisms for use by the yet-to-be-born League of Nations, developing practical models of world food-sharing based on wartime government food production and distribution systems. While she saw the war as continually forcing

6. J. Addams, *The Long Road of Women's Memory*, New York, 1916, p. xii.

humans into what she called an 'earlier and coarser mold', and foresaw that all human becoming could be irretrievably lost in a holocaust of violence, she fixed an unwavering eye on the gentlest, quietest movements of the human heart and what they could lead to. Her sense of evolutionary possibilities was very strong. In her own words:

> It took the human race thousands of years to rid itself of human sacrifices; during many centuries it relapsed again and again. . . . So have we fallen back into warfare, and perhaps will fall back again and again, until in self-pity, in self-defense, in self-assertion of the right of life, not as hitherto a few, but the whole people of the world will brook this thing no longer.
>
> It is possible that the appeals for the organization of the world upon peaceful lines have been made too exclusively to man's reason and sense of justice. . . . Reason is only part of the human endowment; emotion and deep-set racial impulses must be utilized as well, those primitive human urgings to foster life and protect the helpless of which women were the earliest custodians.
>
> We [the Women's International League for Peace and Freedom] wish . . . to loosen within our own members and in all people . . . those natural and ethical human impulses which, once having their way in the world, will make war impossible.[7]

Only the grandmothers, and that steady band of younger women who carry on the work of the organisation she helped found, the Women's International League for Peace and Freedom, remember Jane Addams today. Even her centennial is now more than two decades old. Her life and teaching, however, remain fresh in her writings, offering to the despairing the possibility of the recovery of humanity's peacemaking potential.

Teilhard, Buber and Addams are children of the West. Had there been space, the lives of Gandhi, Tagore, Madame Pandit, Sarojini Naidu, Kagawa, Luthuli and many other centennial bearers of the signs of evolutionary potentials for peace from Asia and Africa could have been included. This essay should be considered an invitation to others to explore them all more fully.

What can we conclude from the three centennial figures chosen here? Teilhard's teachings about the human role in the divinisation process, and the place of a world brotherhood of science in it, have

7. L. S. Kenworthy, 'Jane Addams Speaks', unpublished paper, New York, Brooklyn College, 1945.

not saved us from unprecedented world militarisation of an increasingly sophisticated technological order. Buber's crafting of I–Thou relationships in a troubled Middle East has not saved that part of the world from escalating terrorism and the threat of an all-engulfing war. Jane Addams's social inventions did not create a world wide system of bread-sharing to replace war.

Yet if all three were alive today, not one of them would give up or say that their insights had been disproved, their work destroyed. There is such a thing as an international sisterhood of science with outstanding men and women of the physical and social sciences providing its voices. While many scientists still work on bombs, the voices of science for peace become daily more vocal, more co-ordinated. The old medieval *universitas* rooted in the more ancient universities of India, Egypt and China is developing into new academic networks assisted by the United Nations' University based in Japan, and the United Nations' Peace University in Costa Rica. Growing separately, but with links to the *universitas* are the grass-roots learning networks of new–old world-wide localist groups that practice under other names the wisdom and underdeveloped skills that Teilhard, Buber and Addams sought to strengthen. The Islamic tauhid, the Tanzanian ujama, the Sri Lankan shramadana, the Indian sarvodaya, the Israeli commune, the Protestant intentional community, the de-cloistered Catholic religious order and the secular Western New Society Commune all point in the direction of the development of human capacities in supportive and sharing local communities. There is more attention to the linking of knowledge and competence with spiritual maturity. There is a livelier sense of wholes, whole individuals, whole households, whole communities, a whole world. The new linkage skills are both local and global.

Non-violent action is a slow-growing plant, but its roots are everywhere. The localist groups mentioned above support a variety of training networks for non-violence on each continent. Since every cultural and religious tradition has its own history of non-violent response, it is not a question of grafting new techniques on old cultures, but of sharing strengths across cultures.

In Poland we have seen a badly strained non-violent movement rooted in centuries of experience with oppression addressing its superpower neighbour, the Soviet Union. In El Salvador and elsewhere, unarmed monks and nuns confronted ruthless military governments buttressed by another superpower neighbour, the

United States. In the Middle East, desert-dwelling Moslems and Jews are building cities and planting gardens and all the while living in fear, not daring to trust in age-old traditions of peacemaking taught by the prophet Mohammed, yet weary of trusting only in the sword. The existence of the ancient vision found in all civilised traditions of the human species at peace suggest the possibility that the species may indeed still be in its childhood.

If there is an evolutionary transformation going on in this time of troubles, it consists of a growing awareness that we live on a tiny planet, and that technology and power alone cannot ensure peace or justice on that planet, nor control or eliminate violence and war. The dimension of human caring has entered the public domain, and the need to understand the Other, the different, is beginning to be acknowledged as a condition for human problem-solving.

We could not have seen the planetary whole so well without Teilhard's vision. We could not have understood the difficult task of partnering our intellectual capacities for skill and mastery with our spiritual capacity for affirming the Other so well without Buber, nor seen as clearly the link between peace and bread without Jane Addams. None of these three, or of the host of unmentioned teachers of peacemaking, ever promised a peaceable planet without human effort. Not one would ever confuse *feeling* loving with doing what love calls for. Not one would ever confuse knowledge with wisdom, or skill with caring. The evidence is strong that the evolutionary capacity for creating the peaceable kingdom lies in our species, but only with great effort will human beings actually develop it.

16

Feminism and Peace

Sarah Perrigo

Feminism and Peace in Historical Perspective

It is not uncommon for feminists researching aspects of women's lives to discover a rich history which has been ignored or systematically distorted by a predominantly male historiography. Feminists exploring the issue of rape and domestic violence in the 1970s, for example, discovered an impressive record of women's involvement in political struggles to expose and remedy the violent abuse of women in the nineteenth century. The same is true of women's involvement in the movement for peace and disarmament. Feminist historians and women in the peace movement are beginning to reveal a long and sustained history of women's participation which has been hitherto neglected in most histories of peace.

Concern over war is as long as recorded history, but it has only been in the twentieth century that such a concern has become manifest in large-scale organised resistance, as modern warfare has directly begun to involve wholesale populations and in consequence has obliterated the distinction between combatants and civilians. From the very beginning women have made a contribution to that movement. What is striking about the history of women's involvement in the peace movement is that then, as now, the issue brought together women from widely different social backgrounds, with disparate religious and political views, some of whom identified themselves as feminist and others who clearly did not.

It is difficult to access the part that feminism played in the development of the various organisations that made up the women's peace movement in the early years of the twentieth century. At a minimum, the very existence of an organised women's movement in Europe and the USA before 1914 clearly gave many women the confidence and the courage to speak out openly on an issue which touched them so deeply and over which, as voteless 'non-citizens', they appeared to have no control. At the same time there was clearly no consensus amongst feminists in their attitudes towards the war, or whether 'peace' had any connection with feminism at all. In fact, the First World War actually split the feminist movement down the middle. In Britain, a significant number followed the lead of militant suffragettes like Mrs Pankhurst and her daughter Christabel in abandoning the feminist struggle for the duration of the war. For them there was clearly no connection between war and the feminist cause. For others, however, opposing the war followed directly from their understanding of feminism. This division amongst feminists in 1914 is interesting in that it foreshadows some of the debates within the contemporary women's movement on feminism and peace.

Before 1914 the major goal of the women's movement was the removal of legal barriers which prevented women participating in the public world on equal terms with men. For some, this demand was seen as a matter of justice and an end in itself. Drawing upon the liberal theory of universal human rights they argued that women, as human beings, should be free to compete equally with men for positions of power and prestige in the public realm. Women, they argued, had the same talents and abilities as men and there were no rational reasons for confining them legally to the private sphere of home and family life. The argument for equal rights tended to ignore, or deny any important or significant difference between the sexes. For others, however, the struggle to open up the public sphere to women was not seen as a question of abstract equal rights, but was based upon the conviction that women as women had a distinctive and special contribution to make that would actually transform the public world, if only they were allowed to participate fully in it.

Victorian ideology had assigned to women particular moral capacities and specific responsibilities. They were to be the guardians of virtue; the 'civilisers' of society. Some women came to feminism by taking these responsibilities and capacities seriously. Through philanthropic work they came face-to-face with the evils of industrial capitalism. They witnessed the poverty, brutality and despair that accompanied industrialisation. Many middle-class women became involved in campaigns to alleviate the plight of the poor and the dispossessed but found themselves powerless to eradicate the evils that they saw. To such women it became increasingly obvious that women must be allowed a voice in public affairs if they were effectively to carry out their collective responsibilities and 'civilise' the world. Opposition to war was for many of these feminists part and parcel of introducing what might be termed 'feminine' values into public affairs. These highly 'moral' feminists vigorously denied that granting equal rights to women would, or should entail that women would behave like men. Their voice would be different and would be used to bring peace and harmony into the world. Jane Addams, American moral reformer, feminist and pacifist, pointed to this view of feminism and a strictly equal rights feminism when she said: 'It would be absurd for women even to suggest equal rights in a world governed solely by physical force, and feminism must necessarily assert the ultimate supremacy of moral agencies. Inevitably the two are in eternal opposition.'[1] It was these 'high minded' women who, after war broke out in 1914, began to organise themselves to put pressure on the governments of Europe and the United States to listen to the voice of women, and who in 1919 founded the Women's International League for Peace and Freedom. Committed to internationalism, social justice and constitutional democratic methods of working, they placed their faith in the rationality of their arguments and the development of international institutions to prevent wars and create conditions for lasting peace and co-operation between states. In the interwar period the League flourished and grew with members in towns and cities all over Europe and the US, giving women a voice in international affairs which they used to support the League of Nations, the development of international law and to encourage international disarmament initiatives.

Alongside the League there were many socialist women also committed to peace and disarmament. The Independent Labour Party (ILP) with its pacifist traditions and its adherence to an ethical rather than narrowly economistic vision of socialism attracted many women who also saw themselves as feminist. There were women like Alice and Hettie Wheeldon who were both suffragettes and supporters of the ILP who worked courageously and at great personal risk to protect and support conscientious objectors. Socialist women in the ILP and other socialist organisations were also

1. Jane Addams, quoted in Carolyn Stephenson, 'Pacifism and the Roots of Feminism in the USA 1830–1930', PRIO Report, *Women, Militarism and Disarmament*, Oslo, June 1986.

prominent in the 'No Conscription Fellowship' which was founded in late 1914 and brought together feminists and pacifists, as well as ethical and revolutionary socialists to campaign against the war. Suffragists like Catherine Marshall and Helena Swanwick were involved in both the formation of the Women's International League for Peace and Freedom (WILPF) and the No Conscription Fellowship. They also were instrumental in forming the Women's Peace Crusade of 1917–18 in which socialist and feminist women were active together in pressurising the government to bring the war to an end.

The most important organisation of women socialists involved in peace was probably the Women's Co-operative Guild. The Guild, which was formed as early as 1883, was until 1914 concerned primarily with promoting working-class women's interests in the domestic sphere. As the war progressed, however, the Guild became increasingly appalled by what it saw as the senseless slaughter and resolved to make peace one of its central issues. In the interwar period it became the major organisation through which working-class socialist women organised in opposition to war and re-armament. Like WILPF the Guild strongly supported the development of international institutions and initiatives for disarmament. However, the Guild's commitment to pacifism derived essentially from its vision of socialism. Peace, both within and between nations, could, they believed, only be achieved through the development of a socialist co-operative commonwealth. In an important sense their commitment to peace was not derived from an explicitly feminist perspective. At the same time, however, the Guild was an organisation of women, founded to articulate and promote the interests of working-class women within the co-operative movement, and their arguments concerning peace were intimately linked with this aim of furthering what they saw as women's interests. Most of the Guild's members were wives and mothers and it was from their experience that Guild members derived their major argument for a 'special' women's interest in furthering the cause of peace. They argued that women suffered enormously from the war; it had destroyed the very life that women had created; the life which they as women had a duty to protect and preserve. In so arguing they articulated the experience of a whole generation of women who had suffered the loss of husbands, sons and lovers in the First World War and who, in consequence, were resolved to do all in their power to prevent such a catastrophe occurring again. In an important sense their arguments were not that different from those of women in the WILPF. Both stressed the importance of female experience and the introduction of a 'feminine' ethic of care and compassion into the practices of international relations and public policymaking if war were to be avoided in the future.

What is particularly interesting about these arguments as they were voiced in the 1920s and 1930s was that although they asserted a difference in orientation between the sexes to issues of 'war' and 'peace', this did not appear to result in any antagonism on the part of women peace activists towards men, either in the peace movement itself or in the wider society. Many women were active in mixed organisations like the Peace Pledge Union and both the Guild and WILPF also worked closely with those mixed organisations. Though women in the Guild campaigned against war toys and films which glorified war, these campaigns against militarism and militaristic values were never linked to a critique of 'men' in the way in which they have been today. The reasons for this are complex, but in part I think it was due to the fact that once they had obtained the formal rights of citizenship many women felt very optimistic about the ability of women to influence and even transform politics; that governments would be forced to heed the voice of women. While it was recognised that women lacked experience of, and confidence in acting politically, it was thought that as they became more organised and gained political experience, then their power to influence public decision-making would increase. Only much later did it become apparent that formal equality did not necessarily result in a substantive equality of citizenship, and that the reason for this may have something to do with 'men' and the nature of the inequalities of power between the sexes, which has become a dominant theme for exploration in what has been called the 'second wave' of the feminist movement that emerged in the late 1960s. Secondly, the development of feminism itself in the interwar period made a direct criticism of men unlikely. Few women of this period directly challenged the sexual division of labour in the home, or the assumption that women's role was primarily that of wife and mother. Equal rights, it was argued, were necessary in order to give women a choice: either marriage and family life or a career outside the home. However, it was assumed that most women would continue to opt for marriage and family life when they had such a choice. (The question of whether such a mutually exclusive choice was necessary was rarely raised before the 1960s.) Thus, when women obtained the vote, the majority of feminists were primarily concerned to use it to improve the material conditions of life of women and children. Their major political activities centred around issues such as health, nurseries, education and welfare provision: issues which were seen as directly affecting women's lives. In so doing they tended to conserve and strengthen the idea of 'separate spheres' for men and women which left men unaffected and unchallenged.

Feminism in the 1970s

The contemporary feminist movement grew out of very different circumstances from those which had produced the 'first' women's movement. To a significant extent women had achieved formal or legal equality with men; they were no longer debarred from participating in politics or from entering the universities and the professions. No 'marriage bar' prevented them from continuing to take paid employment after marriage. However, this formal equality had not resulted in any real or substantive equality, and sexual divisions remained entrenched throughout society. Women were grossly under-represented in positions of power and authority. Despite the increasing participation of women in the labour market, and improved educational opportunities for girls, their labour continued to be undervalued and highly concentrated in a few areas of employment. All women, regardless of class, were subject to an ideology of sexual difference which served to define them primarily as wives and mothers, whose major duties lay in the sphere of the home and domestic life.

Changes since the Second World War served to intensify contradictions between a society which proclaimed a commitment to equality of opportunity for all, and the actual reality of women's lives, which was to result in an explosion of a renewed feminist consciousness in the late 1960s. On the one hand, the development, and widespread availability of cheap and relatively reliable forms of contraception, along with the trend towards smaller planned families, meant that the burden of child-bearing and child-rearing was noticeably lighter than it had been in the past. The post-war economic boom and the expansion of state-provided services created more job opportunities for married women. An increasing number of married women began to combine domestic work with regular paid employment. A rapid expansion of higher and further education meant that more and more women were not only well qualified but had high expectations of pursuing satisfying and rewarding careers. On the other hand, there were other factors at work which prevented women taking advantage of these new opportunities. The same period witnessed an intensification of an ideology of domesticity and 'women's place' which placed an enormous psychological and physical strain on many women who were torn between their domestic and employment commitments. Further, both the state welfare system and the practice and policies of employers and trade unions treated women as though they were economic dependents of men, and a marginal workforce.

Several catalysts served to ignite a growing discontent on the part of women and fuse it into a movement for radical social change. In Britain an extremely important factor was the failure of the male-dominated labour and socialist movement to acknowledge the deep sense of grievance that many women felt at the way they were being treated and defined. The trade unions and the Labour Party ignored the stark sexual division of labour in paid employment, and did little to help women achieve equal pay or to combat discrimination based on sex. The New Left, ostensibly involved in constructing a 'politics of liberation', not only denied women's experiences of oppression but actively derided those women who attempted to articulate such feelings. The anger that many women experienced at this rejection convinced them of the need to organise autonomously if they were to build a politics that reflected the needs and aspirations of women.

Neither Liberalism nor Socialism appeared to offer these new feminists an adequate analysis of women's oppression, or a satisfactory strategy for social and personal change. Liberalism, with its stress on equal rights, seriously underestimated the institutional and structural causes of sexual inequalities. Few of these women had the old liberal faith in the ability of reasoned argument and rational persuasion to effect a radical restructuring of power and responsibilities between men and women. Although Marxism had an analysis of women's oppression it rather crudely collapsed the 'problem of women' into its class analysis, the result of which was to marginalise gender issues or to relegate them to some future date when the 'primary' contradiction between Labour and Capital had been resolved. Further, the experience of women in socialist and 'liberationist' politics had convinced many that both the theory and practice of socialism had little to offer women; that on the contrary socialist organisations had the effect of silencing women and rendering them invisible in such movements.

In an important sense then, the women's movement of the 1970s rejected existing parties and movements for change, and consciously set out to build its own style of politics and develop its own analysis of women's oppression, which it was hoped would articulate women's experiences and meet their needs in a way that pre-existing movements did not. The movement, as it emerged, was determined to be rigorously democratic. It eschewed both the social democratic and democratic centralist forms of organisation of the left, arguing that bureaucratic organisations with their consequent division between leaders and led were methods of organisation that disempowered their membership and had been used to 'silence' women very effectively in the past. If women were to be empowered to think and act for themselves, to free themselves from the dominant assumptions of a deeply sexist society, then they must not be dictated to from above, but should decide for themselves how the movement should progress and what strategies and priorities should serve as a basis for action. This radically democratic and decentralised form of organisation developed primarily through what has become known as consciousness-raising (CR) groups. Small groups of women all over Britain began to meet and explore together their experiences of being women in the world. The process was for many women politically very powerful and dynamic. They began to discover that what had appeared previously to be individual and personal feelings of inadequacy, inferiority and powerlessness, were experiences that other women shared. They began to perceive that these experiences were not random and idiosyncratic, but were systematic and socially constructed. Many found being in a CR group extraordinarily therapeutic. For the first time their experiences were being revealed, listened to, respected and valued. The discovery of the systematic nature of women's oppression served to reveal the world in a new light. Women began to discover how deep and all-pervasive were sexist assumptions. Institutions and practices which had previously been perceived as natural (or to the more political as perhaps serving class or race interests) were seen as patriarchal in the sense that they operated through assumptions of sexual difference and assigned to women inferior positions *vis-à-vis* men.

This discovery raised crucial questions about the 'patriarchal' nature of society; how it was produced and reproduced and in whose interest it operated. Though different and competing theories of patriarchy were constructed, it was difficult for feminists to avoid the conclusion that men played some part in the reproduction of patriarchal relationships, and that in consequence the struggle for change and a redistribution of power between the sexes must involve a struggle against men. Through a series of campaigns women began to construct a sexual politics which aimed at exposing the political nature of institutions and practices hitherto considered as 'private' and non-political. The family, sexuality and the cultural representation of women all came under attack from feminists, who saw them as crucial sites of female oppression.

Feminist theory in the early 1970s made a crucial distinction between sex as a biological concept, and gender as a set of socially constructed traits, characteristics and roles which were differently ascribed to men and women in particular societies. Male dominance, it was argued, maintained itself by collapsing these two categories together and claiming gender to be rooted in fundamental biological differences between the sexes. Writers like Kate Millett argued that the concept of 'the feminine', was, in an important sense a myth; a creation of 'man' serving his own interests.[2] The task of feminism was to expose the fallacious nature of this argument, in order to eliminate all gender distinctions, seeing them as a major source of the domination of women by men. Feminists, eager to reject all arguments about 'natural' difference that had been used to silence and confine women, began to reject wholesale everything associated with the 'feminine'. Women, they argued, were not necessarily carers, or naturally homemakers. Neither were they peacemakers! They could be tough, aggressive and independent. With a determination to throw off the domestic responsibilities assigned to them in a patriarchal society, they called for the abolition of 'the family', for the provision of twenty-four-hour nurseries and abortion on demand. The ultimate aim of feminists was the destruction of male power and the institution of an androgynous society where no specific male or female roles would exist. At this stage the feminist argument was not at all amenable to the claim that women had some special contribution to make to peace. Such a claim would have been (and in fact has been) met with scorn and derision, as a dangerous and reactionary argument.

However, more recent developments in feminist theory have provided a more propitious basis for links to be made between feminism and peace. If 'woman' were literally created by 'man' in

---

2. Kate Millett, *Sexual Politics*, New York, 1971.

male-dominated societies, what was her 'true' nature? Were women really like men, or were they different? As women came together, such issues were urgently explored and discussed. Many were critical of a conception of sexual equality that was male defined. They did not feel like men and they did not want to be like them either. For some, denying everything traditionally associated with the feminine was rather like 'throwing the baby out with the bath water'. They felt uncomfortable denying the value of traditional female concerns, such as nurturing and caring. Gradually a shift in feminist thinking began to take place. Rather than seeing all gender distinctions as necessarily disabling, some writers, such as Adrienne Rich and Jean Baker Miller began to stress the positive side of female experience.[3] Rich, for example, argued in *Of Woman Born* that motherhood was potentially an enriching and valuable experience which was only distorted and devalued in a patriarchal culture. This shift in thinking was to result in a positive re-evaluation of 'femininity' and a celebration of what became called 'women's culture', and 'women-centred' values. Rather than seeing woman as 'other' in relation to some male-defined norm, some feminists began to explore the opposite: that femaleness and female experience was potentially a source of strength and ought to serve as a basis for dominant social values. Being a woman was no longer the 'problem'; the 'problem' was men, or more accurately, the gendered male.

This was to lead to a critique of masculinity. Male ways of thinking and acting came under sustained attack. Early radical feminist thinkers like Kate Millett and Shulamith Firestone had already pointed to what they saw as the degeneracy of male-dominated culture.[4] According to Millett, it was sadistic, power-orientated, manipulative and misogynist. This critique was extended and developed. Links were made between male violence towards women and the propensity of men to build weapons of mass destruction and wage senseless and aggressive wars. Female philosophers of science like Jessica Benjamin went on to argue that the male monopoly of 'authoritative' knowledge, namely science, has had profoundly disturbing consequences, not just for women but

---

3. Adrienne Rich, *Of Woman Born*, New York, 1976; Jean Baker Miller, *Towards a New Psychology of Women*, Harmondsworth, 1973.
4. Millett, *Sexual Politics*; Shulamith Firestone, *The Dialectics of Sex*, New York, 1970.

for the survival of the planet itself.[5] They argued that 'scientific' knowledge epitomised the 'male' stance towards the world; scientific ideals such as objective detachment and instrumental rationality have led to a disregard for the natural world and its resources. Scientific progress, rather than leading to harmony and co-operation between peoples has fostered violence, poverty and domination.

Not all feminists were happy with this shift in feminist thinking. Although there had always been important differences amongst feminists, by the end of the 1970s fundamental and opposing conceptions of feminism had emerged which made it increasingly difficult to speak of feminism in an unproblematic way. These fundamental disagreements have become clearly apparent in the attitude of different feminists to the women's peace movement and will be explored in the following section.

The Women's Peace Movement in the 1980s

The 1950s saw a resurgence in the peace movement in response to the Cold War and the development and testing of nuclear weapons. The pre-war women's peace organisations played a not insignificant part in that resurgence. The Women's Co-operative Guild, for example, was one of the first groups to protest at the testing of nuclear weapons, organising large rallies in 1955 and 1956 as well as playing a prominent part in the 'Women's Peace Caravan' in 1958. Yet it would be misleading to suggest that the peace movement of the 1950s and early 1960s 'had an obvious women's' presence as such. Both WILPF and the Women's Co-operative Guild were, for various reasons, losing members and were failing to recruit younger women into their ranks. Many young women saw no reason for joining a women's organisation and viewed feminism as something old fashioned and irrelevant to their lives in post-war Britain. Though many women were involved in peace activities at this time, they tended to be involved in mixed organisations, especially the Campaign for Nuclear Disarmament (CND) and joined as Christians, pacifists, socialists or as concerned individuals rather than

5. Jessica Benjamin, 'The Bonds of Love: Rational Violence and Erotic Domination', in Z. R. Eisenstein and L. Jardine (eds.), *The Future of Difference*, Boston, 1980.

specifically as women. By the mid-1960s, the peace movement and CND had declined in importance as a mass movement. It was not to become a mass movement again until the late 1970s, with the decision of NATO to 'update' its nuclear weapons.

The contemporary women's movement had been, by this time, in existence for a decade and was to be a crucial factor in the development of a distinctive women's peace movement. During the 1970s, partly because the peace movement was at a low ebb, and partly because feminists had other priorities, there was little debate amongst feminists on peace. However, as we have seen, by the late 1970s some feminists had already begun to make crucial connections between the patriarchial oppression of women and militarism which had direct relevance to the emerging peace movement, and it was not long before feminist voices were heard within peace organisations as they developed in the early 1980s. In Britain one of the first signs of a new-style women's peace movement came in 1981 when a group of women (and a few men) calling themselves 'women for life on earth' marched from Cardiff to Greenham Common in Berkshire to protest at NATO's decision to base cruise missiles in Britain. It was not, however, the first women's action. In 1980 there had been an explicitly feminist-inspired anti-militarist march in the USA which produced the 'Women's Pentagon Action Unity Statement' outlining a feminist analysis of the linkages between patriarchy, militarism and violence and which proffered an alternative vision of future possibilities based on peace and justice.

It was Greenham, however, that became the symbol and inspiration for the development of the women's peace movement both in Britain and abroad. Whilst not all the women initially involved for example, in Greenham, defined themselves as feminist, the specific style, organisation and methods of working demonstrate very clearly how much the women's peace movement has been influenced by feminism. Greenham can be seen as an 'ideal type' of feminist organisation, in the ways in which it has changed and developed over time. Its beginnings were rooted in the fear and desperation some women felt at the deterioration of East–West relations and the alarming escalation of the arms race. The original march from Cardiff to Greenham, with its aim of voicing the concerns of 'ordinary' women, especially mothers, was not in itself new. As we have seen there had been many such marches in the past. What made this initiative different was first of all the decision to set up camp at Greenham in order to draw public attention to their cause (some of the women chained themselves to the perimeter fence which was reminiscent of earlier suffragette actions), and perhaps more importantly the decision to make Greenham a women-only camp. The debate over whether Greenham should become women-only is interesting in that many of the arguments used to justify the decision were ones that feminists had earlier used to organise autonomously from the socialist left. Similar criticisms were levelled at CND that had earlier been directed at the male-dominated labour and socialist movements. It was argued that CND was bureaucratic, effectively silencing women and their fears through the 'routinisation' of political activity. Rather than empowering their membership, many women said that they experienced CND meetings as remote and stupefying. Many of the women at Greenham also accepted the feminist argument about the value and necessity of a women-only space if they were to discover their own voice and become effective peace activists. They accepted that the presence of men, however well meaning, might well inhibit that process. In the words of one of the Greenham women: 'I want to say very strongly that having women-only actions in my view has nothing to do with excluding men. It has to do for once with giving women a chance.'[6] The decision to organise separately was also a decision to adopt the methods of organisation of the feminist movement. It was to be ultra-democratic, non-hierarchical, with no leaders, committees or official spokespersons. Every woman was to be included and all were to take responsibility for deciding what initiatives and actions should be taken. For many of the women at Greenham, the camp was not just a protest against nuclear weapons but was a place where women could learn to take responsibility for themselves and for others, and stop seeing themselves as powerless victims of either the military might of the state or patriarchal authority. The accounts by women at Greenham frequently refer to the extraordinary strength and energy they gained by participating in the activities of the camp. These accounts are very reminiscent of the ways in which feminists had earlier described the effects of consciousness-raising groups.

If in style and organisation the women's peace movement has been clearly feminist-inspired there are certain aspects of the movement which have received criticisms from groups of feminists. In

---

6. Quoted in Alice Cook and Gwyn Kirk, *Greenham Women Everywhere*, London 1983, p. 80.

1983 a group of radical feminists published a collection of articles entitled *Breaching the Peace*, in which they questioned the assumption that Greenham and the women's peace movement was feminist at all, and argued that just because a movement is women-only is not enough to make it feminist.[7] If feminism is about destroying male power, they asked, how was the women's peace movement contributing to this? Several of the writers accused the movement of diverting women away from the struggle to overthrow patriarchy, in the name of some supposedly 'higher' cause. Others questioned the 'peace' that the women's peace movement thought it was trying to preserve, suggesting that there can be no 'peace' as long as men continue to rape, batter and in other ways dominate and control women. Above all, the articles expressed a real unease at the ways in which the women's peace movement played upon, and utilised particular traditional stereotypes of women and femininity in the cause of peace: 'Whatever the differing motives of the women involved in Greenham, some women must share some anxiety in operating under the media constructed banner of the "public image" of Greenham with its emphasis on traditional feminine values and its obvious reactionary reinforcement of the stereotyping of women.'[8] They went on to argue that just to equate militarism and nuclear weapons with masculinity was not enough to make it a feminist issue. Not only did it suggest the obverse, that 'femininity' was naturally associated with peace and conserving life, but that if male power were at the root of 'unpeacefulness' then what was required was a strategy for attacking male power where it operated most effectively by undermining the sexual division of labour in the family and at work.

Some of these criticisms, it seems to me, were not particularly well founded. Women in the peace movement have been well aware, for example, that 'peace' is a complex concept and that organising for 'peace' requires more than just ridding the world of nuclear weapons – in fact they have criticised CND for its narrow conception of peace. As the women who wrote 'Piecing it Together: Feminism and Non-Violence' wrote: 'We cannot fight for peace and ignore the violence on the streets and in our own homes; we cannot successfully control the violence of our everyday lives without

7. *Breaching the Peace*, London, 1983.
8. Linda Bellos, *et al.*, 'Is Greenham Feminist?', in *Breaching the Peace*, London, 1983.

struggling for total change.'⁹ Secondly, the women's peace movement has often stressed the relationship between militarism, violence and male power. The writers of *Breaching the Peace* may be mistaken in suggesting that the women's peace movement is necessarily a diversion from the struggle against male power. It is possible to struggle and organise at different levels of male power simultaneously. However, in one very important respect, it does seem to me that the authors of *Breaching the Peace* do raise a fundamental issue that lies at the heart of feminist theory and practice, which has to do with the nature of sexual difference.

The Argument Over Difference

Within feminist theory there appears to be an enduring and fundamental contradiction between those who either deny or minimise differences between the sexes, and who explain difference by reference to the structure and practice of particular patriarchal societies, and those who stress the importance of sexual difference and whose critique of patriarchal societies centres upon the ways in which such societies suppress and undervalue something called 'the feminine'. The former have tended to denigrate the 'traditional' sphere of women, the latter to celebrate it. The theoretical perspectives and arguments found in the women's peace movement on the relationship between women and peace has developed out of, and contributed to, the second perspective and has tended to emphasise rather than deny difference. The literature of the women's peace movement is replete with references to 'male structures', 'male' ways of behaving, and its converse, 'women's' ways of working, 'feminine' perspectives and 'female' values.

It seems to me that both these perspectives are open to criticism. The first because it denies aspects of human experience and operates primarily through a particular conception of 'human' nature which reflects male rather than female experience, as historically constituted. The idea of equality commonly found in the perspective which denies difference tends to appeal to some 'universal' ideal of human nature, which on close inspection turns out to be 'man' in a particular historically determined society. Denying difference has

9. Feminist and Non-Violence Study Group, *Piecing it Together: Feminism and Non-Violence*, Devon and London, 1983, p. 18.

also been associated, particularly in the 1960s and early 1970s, with the view that equality for women can only be achieved if they break free of all their domestic (and in some cases even their reproductive) functions and responsibilities. Implicit in the writings of certain influential feminists like Simone de Beauvoir and Shulamith Firestone is the view that the responsibilities traditionally assigned to women in advanced capitalist societies are not only debilitating for women but are intrinsically worthless.[10] This view clearly denies the experience of vast numbers of women for whom child-rearing and caring for others is of fundamental importance. Not surprisingly, many women, both feminist and non-feminist, responded by arguing that if this was the price equality demanded then they wanted none of it!

The second view, which emphasises difference, is open to a very different set of criticisms. Whilst writers who stress difference utilise a variety of explanations, they normally end up by postulating a false 'universal' picture of fundamental differences between all men and all women in a totally unhistorical manner (an argument, of course, normally associated with anti-feminism). Sometimes the argument is based upon biology, as in Susan Brownmiller's *Against Our Will*, where she appears to suggest that men rape women because they are biologically capable of rape.[11] Most feminists emphasising difference have denied that it is rooted in biology, but some of the most influential writers within this perspective have actually contradicted this denial by the thrust of their arguments. Andrea Dworkin and Mary Daly, for example, both deny biological explanations but go on to postulate some universal 'male need' to dominate and violate women throughout all known history.[12] Daly writes, 'Women are the objects of male terror, the projected personifications of "the enemy", the real objects under attack in all wars of patriarchy',[13] and Dworkin, in similar vein, states: 'Terror issues forth from the male, illuminates his essential nature and basic purpose.'[14] In both cases they deny vehemently that there are, or can be exceptions to this 'universal' view of mankind. There cannot be any pacifist men! The converse of this argument has been to

10. Simone de Beauvoir, *The Second Sex*, New York, 1955; Firestone, *Dialectics*.
11. Susan Brownmiller, *Against Our Will*, New York, 1975.
12. Andrea Dworkin, *Pornography: Men Possessing Women*, New York, 1981; Mary Daly, *Gyn-Ecology*, Boston, 1978.
13. Daly, *Gyn-Ecology*, p. 39.
14. Dworkin, *Pornography*, p. 16.

represent female nature as the repository of 'the good'; loving, nurturant and caring. Dworkin, Daly and others depict the world in a curiously Manichaean fashion, as though it were utterly and irrevocably divided between an essential and eternal 'feminine' within which resides all truth and goodness and a 'masculinity' which is identified with everything bestial, evil and corrupt.

This view, it seems to me, is not only false, but is dangerously threatening both to feminism and to the construction of more peaceful social relationships. First of all, it seems to imply that men are irredeemably doomed; if men by their 'nature', whether biological, or not, are driven to dominate and destroy, what chance is there of social change leading to peace and co-operation between individuals or nations? Secondly, it idealises and hence dehumanises women. Anti-feminists in the past have too often put woman on a pedestal; viewed them as 'goddesses', only to silence them and deprive them of power. It interprets all human history as though women have been the innocent, passive 'victims' of male domination and manipulation. Such a view implies that women have never been the 'real' authors of their actions and can never be held responsible for their activities whether good, bad or indifferent. If women really are as 'robot'-like, as Mary Daly suggests, how can they ever become anything different? Even those writers who suggest that sexual differences are socially constructed are often guilty of universalising a particular concept of masculine and feminine. Dinnerstein and Chodorow, for example, accept the view that men fear women and hold them in contempt, and that women are more nurturant, caring and in touch with their feelings, even though they explain this through the effect on the psychic development of children 'mothered' almost exclusively by women.[15] Rich suggests that there is a 'woman's world', based on the common experiences of women as mothers and child-rearers. What all these writers neglect is that concepts of masculine and feminine vary widely from culture to culture and across history. They also vary in important respects within particular societies, according to such factors as class and race. Men and women are never just men and women; they are always determined by their class, race and to some degree by their personal biographies. Similarly, 'mothering', for example, is never

15. Dorothy Dinnerstein, *The Mermaid and the Minotaur: Sexual Arrangements and the Human Malaise*, New York, 1977; Nancy Chodorow, *The Reproduction of Mothering*, Los Angeles, Calif., 1978.

just 'mothering'; it always takes place in specific contexts and its 'meaning' varies accordingly.

Those who hold to some particular, universal concept of the 'feminine', or common 'woman's world?, forget that 'femininity' has historically been defined as that which is 'not masculine', that is, it has been defined as dependent in relation to man. As Genevieve Lloyd says:

> The idea that women have their own distinctive kind of intellectual or moral character has itself been partly formed within the philosophical tradition to which it may now appear as a reaction. Unless the structural features of gender are understood, any emphasis on a supposedly distinctive style of thought or morality is liable to be caught up in a deeper, older structure of male norms and female complementation. The affirmation of the value and importance of the 'feminine' cannot by itself be expected to shake the underlying normative structures, for ironically it will occur in a space already prepared for it by the intellectual tradition it seeks to reject.[16]

One of the greatest dangers of using essentialist arguments of sexual difference for both feminism and the women's peace movement, is the way in which it seems to neglect the materiality of male power and the way in which it is embedded in the sexual division of labour. To argue that for whatever reason women are more caring or that men are more warlike ironically places all the burden for care and compassion back on to women, and denies men the possibility of participating in that responsibility. At this point the contemporary feminist argument seems to have come dangerously close to defending what it had once vehemently denied – to legitimising separate spheres.

Finally, to 'celebrate' women as carers, nurturers and preservers of life is to fail to remember the way in which those supposed traits or abilities have been used to undermine any sense of autonomy and any concern for the self on the part of women. An ethic of care has been used time and again against women, to prevent them from making choices or acting independently. Further, by stressing the value of the traditional sphere of women such feminists are in danger of idealising the 'private' domestic arena and forgetting what other feminists have so clearly pointed out – that it can also be, and often is, a place where violence, brutality and impoverishment flourish.

16. Genevieve Lloyd, *The Man of Reason*, London, 1984, p. 105.

320

Rethinking Difference

In societies like our own, where sexual divisions are entrenched, it should not surprise us that there are certain significant differences between 'real' men and women in their behaviour, attitudes and understanding of the world, just as there are differences amongst wage-labourers and owners of capital, people of colour and whites in a society divided by class or race.

Empirical research, much of it carried out by feminists, has demonstrated that although there are differences between men and women these differences are often much smaller than had been thought. Many supposed differences have been shown to be myths based upon untested stereotypical assumptions. Within the literature of political science, for example, it was common to find references to women as more conservative, more moralistic, more influenced by personalities than policies, and so on. When political scientists (usually women) took the trouble to investigate these assumptions they discovered they were either fallacious or misleading as statements of fact.

Granted, however, that there are differences it is another matter to claim that they apply to all women and all men in some generalised ahistorical manner, or merely to reverse the evaluations made by sexist anti-feminists by claiming that difference where it exists implies female superiority. Many feminist theorists have (along with other radical social theorists) been extremely critical of the dualism that dominates Western political thought, between theory and practice, subject and object, facts and values, and have argued for the need to transcend and transform such dichotomies in the interest of a more 'complete', more 'whole' form of knowledge. Yet recent feminist thought is in danger of replicating such polarities by their use of 'masculine' and 'feminine' as though they were universal essentialist categories of human existence.

Our understanding of the world, the values and beliefs we hold and the way in which we interpret 'reality' are rooted in our material circumstances. If women do have a different ethic, as Carol Gilligan suggests,[17] if they do have different priorities or a different stance towards the world, then this is clearly a result of the sex–gender division of labour and the sharp division between the

17. Carol Gilligan, *In a Different Voice: Psychological Theory and Women's Development*, Cambridge, Mass., 1982.

'public' and the 'private' that exists in the social world in which we live.

One of the most fundamental advances of the 'second wave' of feminism was to question critically the sex–gender division of labour, and to begin to devise strategies for transforming those divisions, and this is precisely where it seems to me the issue of peace and feminism coincide. Entrenched sexual divisions may well encourage war, militarism and the use of violence to settle conflicts. Conversely, peace may well be enhanced in societies where sex–gender divisions are at a minimum. Overcoming, rather than conserving the divisions between men and women should be the objective of feminists interested in peace and the creation of peaceful social relationships.

17

Peace as a Way of Life: The Life and Ideas of Wilfred Wellock (1879–1972)

Andrew Rigby

I first met Adam Curle during 1968–9 when we were working at the Richardson Institute for Conflict and Peace Research in London. Adam was working on *Making Peace* and its companion volume, *Mystics and Militants*. I was working on a study of those 'mystics and militants' who comprised the commune movement in Britain. My interest in this social movement, which sought to create alternative institutions within the confines of the existing society, reflected my own commitment to radical pacifism and non-violence and my unease with the 'demonstration politics' that had been the hallmark of much of the peace and anti-war movement during the 1960s. One of the key features of the critique that was developed in the pages of publications like *Peace News* during this period was the need to widen one's analysis beyond foreign policy issues and nuclear weapons to encompass the whole socio-economic and political structure that gave rise to nuclear states, the arms race and international war. There was a need to establish a link between people's sense of powerlessness in everyday matters and the burgeoning power of the warfare state. Perhaps most importantly of all, there was a need to balance the struggle *against* nuclear weapons with the positive task of articulating a vision of a non-violent, non-exploitative social order and seeking to *embody that positive vision* in our forms of organising and working for change.

With the resurgence of the nuclear disarmament movement of the 1980s I found these concerns reasserting themselves. I had joined the School of Peace Studies at the University of Bradford in the late 1970s, and by the early 1980s the School had become a major source of information for the new disarmament movement. Much of the important research emanating from the School focussed on the nature and threat of the new generation of nuclear weapons and the changes in strategic thinking that had accompanied their development. I needed no convincing of the crucial significance of this work, but I became a little concerned that in concentrating to such a degree upon the immediate threat of nuclear weapons, we were in danger of losing touch with more positive aspects of peace-thinking and peacemaking. I was familiar, of course, with the counterargument that the threat of nuclear holocaust was so immediate that we could not afford the time to engage in considering such questions as 'What would a non-violent society look like? What would it require to achieve a world without war?' However, I remained, and continue to remain, unconvinced by such an admittedly powerful argument. It seems to me that unless we do make time to reflect upon such questions, however remote they might seem from immediate threats and issues, peace researchers are in danger of becoming mere technocrats of the nuclear disarmament movement, unrivalled in their expertise about the threat we are struggling *against*, but lacking the vision to give any positive content to the notion of peace *for* which we are striving.

This tension within the peace research profession reflects the strain that exists within the peace movement itself – between what we might term, in ideal-typical fashion, the 'resistance' and the 'reconstruction' modes of peacemaking, between those who advocate the need actively to campaign against war-making and war-preparation, and those who place greater emphasis upon the longer-term task of working to eradicate the ultimate causes of war, wherever these might be located. It is also a tension which can cause unease within the individual peacemaker and activist. Gandhi, for example, experienced periods of grave doubt concerning the appropriate balance to draw between his 'constructive programme' for village reconstruction and the political struggle for national independence.

Within the British peace movement, this tension between the two modes – resistance and reconstruction – was particularly prominent during the Second World War, especially after the appointment of John Middleton Murry as editor of *Peace News* in 1940. Under the influence of Murry and Wilfred Wellock the paper, as the official organ of the Peace Pledge Union (PPU), began to give increased coverage to the theory and practice of community building by pacifists in wartime. Wellock shared with Murry the belief that the most crucial task of pacifists during this period was to act as a redemptive minority, bearing witness to a higher order of morality and pointing the way towards a new mode of co-operative life. Wellock advocated a 'politics of creative living', an 'integral pacifism', the task of which was to 'envisage the future and seek ways and means of saving and introducing those values without which the human existence ceases to have any meaning'.[1] In advocating what to many appeared as a quietistic, even retreatist, pacifist position, Wellock laid himself open to the charge of failing to provide any immediately practical guides for action and war-resistance. 'Does Mr Wellock contemplate the actual world?' one correspondent to *Peace News* enquired, 'although his writing may be streaked with prophecy, he is no guide to men living in the grim life today'.[2] Roy Walker, a vocal critic of Middleton Murry and Wellock, complained that 'in place of action we have been given moral uplift' when he urged the PPU to adopt a clear policy with regard to peace aims and launch an active campaign for a negotiated peace.[3] He was joined in this demand by Bill Grindlay, who argued that the renunciation of war did not negate the responsibility to provide answers to the immediate problems of concern to the British people, even if that meant 'in the relative sphere of human politics we have, now as always, to choose the lesser of two evils, and honourably to support the bad against the worse. . . . We cannot philosophise out of the obligations to demand the lesser evil of peace negotiations rather than the greater evil of war.'[4]

This preparedness to choose between lesser evils, to be guided in one's political action by a sense of what is realistically possible within the parameters of 'the world-as-it-is' was characterised by Max Weber as the 'ethic of responsibility' – an ethic that accepts the need for compromise with the realities of existing conditions (including the frailty of human nature and the weight of vested interests) if one is to operate effectively in the world of politics. By contrast, the 'ethic of ultimate ends' (or conviction) is the kind of political morality exemplified by Wilfred Wellock, one characterised by an unyielding commitment to an ultimate set of values and

1. *Peace News*, 14 June 1940.
2. A. South, *Peace News*, 22 September 1944.
3. *Peace News*, 30 May 1941.
4. Ibid.

ideals, and a refusal to compromise the purity of that end by the pursuit of 'impure' means.[5] Associated with these two ideal-type ethical systems is a different emphasis in the self-perception and time orientation of the peace activist. For those who adopt the ethic of responsibility, there is a tendency to define themselves as *active instruments* of peacemaking in the *here-and-now*, whilst the votaries of the ethic of ultimate ends such as Wilfred Wellock tend to see themselves as *witnesses* to a higher order of values which they try to exemplify in their own lives, oriented to a vision of an ideal society to be achieved *sometime in the future*.

Given the time orientation of pacifists like Wellock and their relative unconcern with the achievement of immediate goals, there is a natural tendency to dismiss them to the margins of history, in so far as they tend to live their lives very much on the edge of the mainstream of historical development. However, it can be argued that as relative 'outsiders' they have a far firmer understanding of the crises of the age than those who are actively participating in the political events occasioned by such crises. In the remainder of this chapter I will try to justify this claim through a brief examination of the life and ideas of Wilfred Wellock.

The Christian Pacifist

Wellock was born into a working-class family on 2 January 1879 in Nelson, Lancashire. He began work as a 'half-timer' at a local cotton mill at the age of ten, continuing his education at school in the afternoons. As he grew towards maturity, more and more of his time was taken up by his activities with the local Salem Independent Methodist Church. There was a natural affinity in those days between Salem and the Nelson branch of the Independent Labour Party (ILP). Salem was something of a breeding ground for young radicals, with its emphasis on chapel democracy, social involvement, education and mutual improvement. Most of the ILP members in Nelson had first met at Salem, and partly as a consequence of this the politics of the Nelson ILP was predominantly an ethical socialism, a natural extension of the precepts of the New Testament. They sought the creation of Blake's Jerusalem in England's green

---

5. See Max Weber, 'Politics as a Vocation', in H. Gerth and C. W. Mills (eds.), *From Max Weber*, London, 1967, pp. 77–128.

and pleasant land, a socialist Heaven on Earth. The struggle for socialism was akin to a moral crusade, informed by the belief that social change was indivisible from personal change, and the conviction that a 'revolution by consent' was possible if sufficient numbers of people were converted to the new 'faith'.[6]

The picture that emerges of Wellock as he grew up in this milieu is of a serious young man, bent on educational self-improvement, and with a highly developed social and moral conscience that came from his understanding of the ethical principles embodied in the New Testament. He was later to recall the struggle he had as a young man to discover a right way of living which would accord with his ideals:

> My position in the church as a preacher and teacher of Christian truth demanded that I relate the truth to industrial relationships and conditions generally, including wages in relation to profits and the worker's right to responsibility. I battled with that problem for many years, and my efforts to solve it were the beginning of a never ending search for Truth, which at root is the search for the Good Life. . . . I drew from the Christian Gospels all the sayings of Jesus in order to see if they made a pattern that could be followed as a guide to living. What in fact I did find in the end was the essence of a philosophy . . . that self-giving or self-outpouring in some service to humanity, is a law of spiritual growth, of achieving personal wholeness and abundant life.[7]

For others of Wellock's generation and disposition the ILP became the main channel through which they sought to pursue their vision, but Wellock had reservations about the socialist project:

> Most socialists rested their case solely on the economic argument, whereas I saw the basic error of capitalism in certain spiritual deficiencies, and realised that unless these deficiencies were made good little would be gained in the long run, and my unresolved problem was how the socialists would carry the spiritual idealism of their prophets into the new social order. . . . I began to feel that the most urgent need of our time was knowledge of how to live, in every section of the community, capitalists and workers alike, and that it might be my duty to take part in spreading this knowledge of the art of living, by word, by pen, and by living.[8]

6. See S. Yeo, 'A New Life: The Religion of Socialism in Britain, 1883–1896', *History Workshop Journal*, Autumn 1977, pp. 5–56
7. W. Wellock, *Off the Beaten Track*, Tanjore, 1961, pp. 15, 21–2.
8. Ibid., p. 27.

He reached this decision at the age of twenty-one. To equip himself for this new-found vocation, he saved sufficient money to finance himself for three years at Edinburgh University. Returning to Nelson in 1907, at the age of twenty-eight, he resumed his activities as a lay preacher and teacher at Salem and began to contribute articles to the local press and other publications.

The outbreak of war in 1914 found the established peace organisations in a state of decline, and it was the socialists who were first into the field with an active campaign against militarism in the shape of the No-Conscription Fellowship, founded in November 1914 by Fenner Brockway on the promptings of his wife. The Nelson branch had about forty-five members, the bulk of them members of the ILP but including religious pacifists like Wellock, who was branch secretary. Early in 1916 he began to publish a four-page broadsheet under the title of *The New Crusader*. The main feature of each issue was an article by Wellock on Christian pacifism as an alternative to war, in one of which he confessed that his pacifist commitment sprang from his 'insuppressible admiration for Christ's beautiful and courageous romanticism'.[9] Wellock's own source of courage was tested early in 1917 when he was imprisoned as a conscientious objector. He was released finally in April 1919.

During his time in prison, the publication of *The New Crusader* had been taken over by the Quaker novelist Theodora Wilson-Wilson, and on his release Wellock was invited to join the editorial team of the paper, retitled *The Crusader*. The group saw its main purpose as developing a synthesis of Christian pacifism and socialism, a goal with which Wellock identified unreservedly. At the core of his philosophy was a belief in the need for a change of heart on the part of individuals – workers as well as capitalists. In his novel, *A Modern Idealist*, published in 1917, the main character defends his decision to establish a profit-sharing scheme in his cotton mill against the criticisms of local socialists, emphasising the significance of the 'spiritual factor':

> If you cannot convert men to a finer social idealism now you will not be any more likely to do so when you have got your socialist state. But then if you only get men with the right spirit in them you will have no need for socialism, but will then proceed on the more simple lines of

9. W. Wellock, *Pacifism*, Manchester, 1916, p. 17.

cooperation. . . . In the last analysis all social evil is moral evil. . . . It can only be eradicated by the diffusion of finer ideals.[10]

According to Wellock's view of things, the workers, denied their right to human dignity and self-fulfilment through work, had become slave-like in their mentality, seeking solace in drink, gambling and 'picture palaces'. The capitalists, in their turn, were enslaved and spiritually distorted by their desire for riches, power and status. It was not the capitalists who were the enemy, so much as the spirit of materialism which they worshipped and propagated. Likewise, the source of the workers' discontent was not so much material want as the denial of their right to self-expression through worthwhile and creative work. There was, Wellock maintained, 'a universal desire for a more humane, self-expressive existence'.[11] For this to be realised it was necessary for people to become 'social idealists'. It could not be imposed from above; the processes of self-change and social transformation were indivisibly linked.

Consequently, there was a need for a general process of social education and training during which the true spirit of social consciousness might be cultivated. He placed his faith in so arousing the public conscience that the capitalists would be converted by the social idealism underlying the demands for change, see the error of their ways, and begin to co-operate in the process of social transformation. If they failed in this challenge, then bloody class warfare was the likely outcome – and Wellock was convinced that violence could never bring the New Jerusalem. Rather, he sought a 'revolution through reconciliation', the final outcome of a moral crusade led by those enlightened souls who possessed a clear vision of the new life: 'We must concentrate upon the ideal, preach and teach it everywhere . . . compel the people to see life anew, and in the light of a finer ideal to recreate the world . . . organise a spiritual movement for the overthrow of Capitalism and the establishment of Communism which will be positively irresistible.'[12]

Wellock had begun to describe himself as a Christian communist, and the passage quoted above is typical of his writing during *The Crusader* period – full of moral exhortations, eulogies on the spiritual flowering of self-realised individuals that would ac-

10. W. Wellock, *A Modern Idealist*, London, 1917, pp. 220–3.
11. *The Crusader*, 5 September 1919.
12. W. Wellock, *Christian Communism*, Manchester, 1921, p. 48.

company communism, stirring images of the new age to be achieved. In adumbrating his vision of this new age Wellock freely acknowledged his debt to people like William Morris, Edward Carpenter and Peter Kropotkin. He advocated the radical decentralisation of control of industry to the level of the workplace along guild socialist lines. However, nothing could overcome the monotony of factory work so long as industrial production remained mechanised and with a highly specialised division of labour. He put forward, therefore, the idea of what can perhaps best be depicted as a dual economy, similar to that advanced by Kropotkin.[13] The transformation of industry along co-operative lines would eliminate much waste and would require less labour-hours for production purposes. This would leave people time for 'secondary occupations'. Wellock anticipated the development of local centres of arts and crafts, co-operatively run horticultural projects and the like. Freed from the materialistic shackles of capitalism, there would be a blossoming of all kinds of creative activity, with people migrating to the countryside to revitalise village communities, leaving the cities as centres of large-scale industry to which people commuted to do their share of routine labour.

An attractive vision – but how was the necessary social transformation to be brought about? Wellock placed particular emphasis on the establishment of practical experiments in co-operation: 'the freeing of a few men will provide a practical demonstration of what can be done, and thus begin a movement that none will be able to suppress'.[14] Underpinning his approach was a faith in the power of ideas, articulated and practised by those moral crusaders who had the courage to dedicate their lives to a higher morality, and were prepared to lead others by their personal example along the path towards a true Christian commonwealth: 'the springs of action are in the mind and heart, and to these we must direct our attention if we would attain the kingdom of Heaven'.[15]

His belief in the possibility of a non-violent transformation of society informed by Christian principles of fellowship, service and love, was profoundly shaken in 1920 during a six-month tour of Germany. He had set out in the hope of spreading the idealist message of *The Crusader*. He found material want, starvation and

---

13. See P. Kropotkin, *Fields, Factories and Workshops Tomorrow*, London, 1977.
14. *The Crusader*, 26 September 1919.
15. Ibid., 3 October 1919.

despair. The German working class were being sucked dry by the international capitalist class and their 'merciless, soulless peace, that like a swamp-mist breathed death over everything'.[16] The gulf between the classes was becoming too wide, the conflict too intense, to be bridged through non-violence. 'Three months close touch with hungering folk has burned into my soul,' he was to write, 'How can people trust in ideas, when they are prevented from working and from buying food?'[17] A revolution was imminent, the only question was whether it would be of the right or the left. In June 1920 he confessed: 'For months I have been working in the belief that it were possible to create a public opinion with sufficient spiritual dynamic to effect a social revolution without the shedding of blood. I no longer believe in that possibility.'[18] Reluctantly he felt obliged to consign to secondary importance the individual change of heart upon which he had placed so much emphasis. A pure Christian life was still an admirable ideal, but it would remain largely ineffectual as a means of change unless it was grounded in a mass movement to change the whole structure of society. By 1921 he had to concede that:

By the hard facts of the time, by the phenomenal growth of selfishness and materialism due to the enormous power of the environment; I am being compelled to believe that a change of environment must precede a change of heart in the fuller and deeper sense. . . . We are all so completely in the grip of circumstances that the only hope of social salvation is in first of all, by means of collective action, transforming the social system.[19]

The Socialist Pacifist

In Britain in the early 1920s the Labour Party could still be considered as an obvious vehicle for the socialist transformation of society. Wellock, however, had profound reservations about the commitment of the party leaders. As far as he could judge, 'providing capitalism could guarantee a decent dinner to every worker there is little in the conduct of many labour leaders to suggest that

16. Ibid., 20 February 1920.
17. Ibid., 26 May and 6 February 1920.
18. Ibid., 11 June 1920.
19. W. Wellock, *The Way Out*, London, 1922, pp. 15–16.

they had not thereby won all that was necessary'.[20] At the same
time he was forced to acknowledge that in the public consciousness
Parliament was seen as the proper locus for political change, and so
he accepted that this should be the main area of struggle. His hope
was that a body of committed socialist Members of Parliament
might inspire the Labour Party with sufficient vision and courage to
lead the country towards a new social order. He looked to the ILP
to fulfil this role, observing that:

> As I moved about the country after 1920 it was next to impossible to
> secure a response to any kind of spiritual appeal. . . . The only organis-
> ation that appeared to be advancing was the Independent Labour Party. . . .
> The ILP inherited the spiritual idealism of the early Christian Socialists
> and of the artist-poet-craftmanship school of William Morris. . . . This
> was the only kind of socialism that appealed to me.[21]

He joined the ILP and was soon adopted as the parliamentary
candidate for the Stourbridge constituency in the 1923 election. He
was unsuccessful, but he was elected as Stourbridge's first socialist
MP in 1927, only to lose the seat in the 1931 rout of the Labour
Party. He was later to describe his years in Parliament as the most
frustrating period of his life, serving to convince him that the
peaceful parliamentary road to socialism could only succeed in the
context of a powerful and assertive extra-parliamentary movement
for change. In this he drew inspiration from Gandhi's anti-
imperialist struggle in India, particularly after the Salt Tax *satya-
graha* of 1930. According to Wellock, in their exploration of
methods of non-violent struggle, Gandhi and his followers had
forged 'a new weapon of freedom, developed and proved a new
technique of revolt which ere long will supersede in every part of
the world the old technique of violence, with its barricades, shoot-
ings and guillotines'.[22]

In Britain, the major agency of pacifist anti-militarist activity in
the 1920s and the first half of the 1930s was the No More War
Movement (NMWM), which Wellock had helped to found in 1921.
Most of the leading figures in the NMWM were also involved in the
ILP, and their socialist commitment was reflected in the two-part
membership pledge – which combined an absolute refusal to partici-

20. Ibid., pp. 12–13.
21. Wellock, *Off the Beaten Track*, pp. 57–8.
22. *New World*, vol. 1, no. 2, April 1931.

pate in any kind of war or assist in war preparations with the positive obligation 'to strive for the removal of the causes of war and to work for the establishment of a new social order based on cooperation for the common good'. Dismissive of 'bourgeois pacifists' who believed that international peace could be achieved without socialism, the left wing of the NMWM saw the fight against capitalism and against international war as part and parcel of the same struggle. Thus, according to Fenner Brockway, 'War is an incidental denial of pacifism; capitalism is the permanent denial', whilst for Reginald Reynolds, 'the war against war is also the war against hunger and oppression'.[23] Addressing a meeting in Cologne in the summer of 1932, Wellock argued that,

> War is the logical and inevitable outcome of a social system which is based on greed, on class and sectional rights instead of upon cooperation and human rights. In the deepest sense, to fight for peace and disarmament of the world is to fight for a change in the base of society.... Across the world today we see spreading the class war; from it there may spring international wars or revolution. It can only be removed by the creation of a new social order. Thus every sincere worker must devote himself to the realisation of that great end.... The times lay upon us the task of thinking out and establishing new forms of social and international life.[24]

For Wellock, international war was the final and most decisive manifestation of imperialism. Capitalism was incapable of dealing with the recurring crises of over-production created by the increased productivity of the privately owned and controlled means of production on the one hand, and on the other, the limited purchasing power of the impoverished working class. Increasingly totalitarian measures were therefore required to control class conflict at home, whilst capitalist states sought to extend their domination over wider areas of the globe in their attempt to secure captive markets for goods and sources of cheap raw materials. This inevitably brought about international rivalry and, eventually, war. In a similar vein, Wellock explained the arms race in terms of the need of capital to find ways of absorbing surplus productive capacity that would still ensure a continuation of the private accumulation of profit. As he addressed meetings up and down the country, Wellock

23. *New World*, vol. 3, no. 4, September 1932.
24. Ibid.

repeatedly emphasised the economic causes of war and the consequent need for people to engage in collective political action to effect not only total disarmament but also the establishment of democratic socialism. And yet he still retained his faith in the possibility of a peaceful revolution, a belief that through the generation of a sufficiently powerful movement for change, the hearts and minds of capitalists might be swayed, that those vested interests whose existence he condemned might be persuaded to divest themselves of their privileges for their own and the wider community's sake. Underlying his orthodox socialist analysis of the causes of war there was still the conviction that fundamental change required a spiritual change.

The rise of fascism in Europe and its growing influence within Britain severely tested this faith in the possibility of non-violent revolutionary change. During the 1930s the NMWM was wracked by division and dilemmas: How was it possible to reconcile the pacifist commitment to non-violence with the need to oppose fascism? The Japanese invasion of Manchuria in 1932, the rise of Hitler to power in 1933, the final failure of the Geneva Disarmament Conference to produce any results in 1934, the rearmament of Germany and Britain, and the Italian invasion of Abyssinia in 1935 – all went to confirm the thesis that war was inevitable under capitalism, but what practical programme of action did socialist pacifists have to offer other than rhetorical calls for mass war-resistance and revolution? There was some interest in the ideas of the Dutch anarcho-pacifist Bart de Ligt, who advocated a programme of mobilising anti-war forces into a general strike if war threatened, which could then be developed into a full-grown non-violent social revolution.[25] Richard Gregg's *The Power of Nonviolence*, published in 1934, also began to exert some influence over those seeking a pacifist response to armed violence in domestic and international relations. But it all remained very much in the realm of theory and, as the gulf between the mass of the labour movement and the increasingly small minority of socialist pacifists widened, that was where it remained.

The relative isolation of socialist pacifists like Wellock was highlighted even further in the summer of 1936 when, shortly after Abyssinia was finally overrun, news came through about the Spanish Civil War. The moral dilemma posed by the events in Spain was

25. B. de. Ligt, *The Conquest of Violence*, London 1937.

particularly acute for the members of the NMWM. What attitude should they adopt, given their socialist sympathies, when a popular left-wing government was threatened by right-wing elements supported by the military? The war triggered off a great wave of anti-fascist feeling in Britain, as it came to symbolise the growing division within Europe – and with this came a new willingness amongst the left to oppose fascism by force of arms. As Buzan has observed: 'Militant anti-fascism displaced peace as the foreign policy preoccupation of the majority left, thereby depriving the peace movement of the broad base of social sympathy on which it had stood for so long. . . . After the Spanish Civil War began, peace was no longer the vital issue of the times: fascism, and what to do about it, was.'[26]

To many it appeared that pacifism had no immediate answer to this evil. Fenner Brockway, a co-founder of the NMWM, came to this conclusion in 1936 after he had visited Catalonia where, he later recalled: 'I came to see that it is not the amount of violence used which determines good or evil results, but the ideas, the sense of human values, and above all the social forces behind its use. With this realisation, although my nature revolted against the killing of human beings just as did the nature of those Catalonian peasants, the fundamental basis of my old philosophy disappeared.'[27] It was the Spanish Civil War that occasioned the final demise of the NMWM, when a core group of activists sought to exclude civil wars from the membership pledge, and threatened to resign if their resolution was not accepted. To avoid what would have been a death-blow to what remained of the organisation, a special meeting was held in February 1937 where it was decided that the NMWM should merge with the PPU. The PPU had experienced a phenomenal rate of growth since Dick Sheppard had published his original Peace Letter in October 1934 requesting those who shared his determination never to support another war to send him a postcard affirming this fact. Although the socialists of the NMWM had been dismissive of the 'bourgeois pacifism' of the PPU's predominantly middle-class membership, their sadness at the death of the NMWM was tinged with anticipation of the possibilities for raising the political consciousness of such a well-meaning but politically naive membership, which numbered over 118,000 at the time of the

26. B. G. Buzan, 'The British Peace Movement from 1919 to 1939', PhD thesis, London School of Economics, 1973, p. 318.
27. F. Brockway, *Inside the Left*, Leicester, 1947, pp. 39–40.

merger. Thus, in one of his earliest contributions to *Peace News*, Wellock proclaimed, in provocative fashion, that 'The sentimental pacifist is a social danger.'[28] It was not enough to pass moral judgement on the horrors of war, announce your refusal to fight, and then do nothing more. Pacifism involved the recognition of injustice and the preparedness to act to change such conditions. Pacifists needed to realise that 'Just as social domination leads to poverty and the class war, so imperialist domination leads to the impoverishment of peoples and to international war.'[29] One can understand the slight trepidation with which the leadership of the PPU admitted Wellock and his NMWM colleagues into their midst – there was a genuine concern that such vocal socialists would estrange those sections of the membership who could appreciate the horrors of war, but could not go along with the demand for a socialist revolution that was apparently necessary if such barbarism was to be avoided.

The PPU failed in its basic aim of preventing war. It came on 3 September 1939. Wellock, who had sought unsuccessfully to mobilise the PPU into an active war-resistance stance against Air Raid Precaution measures and the introduction of conscription, and had urged the economic appeasement of the 'have-not' nations of Germany, Italy and Japan in order to avert war, now began to call for an immediate negotiated peace whilst advocating a policy of 'folded arms and fraternization' in the event of an invasion. However, deep down he must have come close to admitting with Sybil Morrison that: 'There was nothing pacifists could do in 1939 but stand still and say, if allowed to say anything at all, that Hitler might be a worse evil than war but that to try to overcome one evil with another evil was not only morally intolerable but could well lead to even greater evil.'[30]

By the spring of 1940, when the Germans had achieved their military breakthrough in Europe and the period of the 'phoney war' was over, a new sense of despair entered into Wellock's writing. Even he was beginning to see the futility of attempting to mobilise the people against the war, as he was moved to confess that: 'Nothing is left but the moral power of the individual to resist whatever evil may befall.'[31]

28. *Peace News*, 21 November 1936.
29. Ibid., 1 November 1936.
30. *The Pacifist*, September 1977, vol. 10, no. 11, p. 12.
31. *Peace News*, 19 April 1940.

And yet within a few months he was writing in optimistic vein about a new role for pacifists in wartime that went beyond providing a humanitarian relief service for the casualties of the violence. The arch-activist who had consistently urged the PPU to oppose conscription and mobilise a movement of mass war-resistance, the ex-chairperson of the NMWM who had maintained that the only road to peace was through socialism created by means of a mass movement, was now advocating the establishment of small islands of democracy in the form of agriculturally based pacifist communities that might grow as the nurseries of a new civilisation. In an autobiographical essay published in 1941, he charted the change in his thinking. Describing his life as a series of 'conversions', he went on to detail his latest discovery:

> that the materialistically decadent civilisation of today led naturally and with increasing inevitability to that modern monstrosity, the totalitarian state, and that this called for a revolt – the creation of microcosms of democracy, which would eventually absorb the state. Finally, it became clear to me that this creative purpose was the true way to world peace, and should therefore be regarded as the essential mission of pacifism. Hence pacifism was no longer a merely negative policy of non-resistance, but an instrument of creative peace, and incidentally a social revolution.[32]

He was to devote the rest of his life to the advocacy of a politics of creative living and the practice of what he came to term 'integral pacifism'.

The Integral Pacifist

Writing in the early 1920s Wellock had dismissed such a politics of creative living as laudable but largely ineffectual as a means of change – a transformation of the social and economic environment was a necessary precondition for the change of heart and consciousness that he acknowledged to be an essential dimension of true socialism. Two decades later, however, he had become disillusioned with state and party politics. According to him, it had been the depression years of the late 1920s and 1930s that had killed off the idealistic socialism with which he identified:

32. Ibid., 3 January 1941.

It was in the 'thirties' that the 'bread and butter politics' of the new materialism completely overwhelmed the spiritual idealism of the earlier Socialists. The decline of that idealism was quickly followed by the rapid spread of the materialistic values of capitalism among the working classes, including the Trade Unions and the Labour Party. This meant that henceforth Party politics would degenerate into a power struggle for the right to determine which social classes or groups should benefit most from the financial policies of the Government.[33]

When one adds to this loss of faith the sense of frustration and failure that accompanied the outbreak of war, and the influence of his fellow PPU sponsors like Eric Gill, Max Plowman, and Middleton Murry – all of whom emphasised the duty of pacifists to bear witness to an alternative way of life – then the change in his approach becomes more understandable.

The need for a complete transformation of lifestyle became the dominant and recurring theme in Wellock's writing as the war progressed. Depicting the contemporary world as a spiritual desert populated by robot-like people, he came to locate the origins of this state of affairs not so much in capitalism, but in the process of industrialisation itself. By September 1943 he was writing that:

> the real dictator of the modern world is the machine. The power of the dictators who are now harassing mankind is derived from the productive power of the machine, as is also the power of the financial dictators. Until the machine is controlled nothing else can be controlled. The profits derived from machinery led to the worship of the machine, but also to huge surpluses of goods on the world's markets, to economic breakdown, to war and revolution. Revolution brought the dictators, whose faith in machinery exceeded that of the capitalists whom they superseded. Out of that faith came total war.... The first enemy of mankind today is the uncontrolled machine.... It is destroying the human person and the foundations of good living everywhere.[34]

It was the same kind of monocausal analysis as before, but 'pushed back' a step. No longer could he believe that socialism was the pathway to the good society and world peace, for socialism itself had fallen victim to the materialism of the machine age. Whereas capitalism was based on the premise of material plenty for the few, socialism had come to mean material plenty for all. The conse-

33. Wellock, *Off the Beaten Track*, p. 65.
34. *Peace News*, September 1943.

quences of such a socialism, the vision of the Webbs updated by Beveridge, would be disastrous. There would be an ever-more desperate search for raw materials to feed the machines, an ever-more intense competitive struggle for markets to absorb the surplus produced by the machines, an ever-deeper spiritual debasement of the people as tools of mass production and ever-greater depletion of the world's finite resources. By the summer of 1944 he was depicting the ideal world of modern socialists as 'little better than a glorified zoo', offering the worker an 'El Dorado consisting of a regular job on the workline, fur-coat-and-car surburbias and ample money by which to escape from them'.[35] Modern capitalism and modern socialism were both of a piece – mechanistic, 'quantitative' civilisations producing uniform commodities and uniform individuals. The pacifist task was to break free in order to lay the foundations of an alternative 'qualitative' civilisation, one recreated from the grass-roots and characterised by greater national and regional self-sufficiency, a breaking down of large-scale industrial plant in the direction of small craft workshops co-ordinated on a guild basis, and the regeneration of an organic social life on the basis of self-supporting and relatively autonomous communities. Whereas he had once believed that wars would cease when people refused to fight, he was now convinced that war would disappear only when people had learnt how to live. The task of the pacifist was to demonstrate such a way of life through propaganda of the deed: 'if peace is to be secured, truth must be lived collectively by way of politics and individually in simpler, friendlier and more neighbourly aims and relations. We have to learn the art of localising, nationalising, and internationalising neighbourliness'.[36]

In developing such views Wellock gave expression to a paradox that characterised much of his thinking. On the one hand, in his reading of history he was prone to emphasise the determining impact of apparently impersonal forces – thus industrialism and the materialistic values to which industrialism gave rise were seen to lead inevitably to totalitarianism – whilst in identifying counter-forces to such 'inevitable processes' he came to stress the power of individual and group witness to the virtual exclusion of almost everything else. It was an uneasy conjunction of historical determinism and 'revolutionary voluntarism' which many of his associ-

35. Ibid., 14 July 1944.
36. Ibid., 18 May 1945.

ates found hard to swallow. He was also accused of idealising the past with his vision of an arcadian pre-industrial age, criticised for turning his back on progress and trying to reverse the clock of history, charged with devaluing the pursuit of economic justice in a world still characterised by gross material inequality, and castigated for failing to provide any immediately practicable guides for action.

He remained unmoved. A visit to India on the occasion of the World Pacifist Conference (1949–50) served to reaffirm his faith in his own analysis, when he had the opportunity to learn of Gandhi's constructive programme for the creation of a non-violent social order based on relatively self-sufficient village republics. As he recalled later: 'I learnt little about Gandhiji's industrial and economy policy until I came to India in 1949. . . . We learnt that in Gandhiji's view war was simply the outward manifestation of inward contradictions within society and within the individual person. Thus the causes of war had to be sought in the way of life and habits of the people.'[37] As he wrote in his Orchard Lee Papers, 'Peace is a way of life for persons and nations alike; it emanates from society as scent from roses.'[38] He therefore enjoined all those who, like him, had a vision of an alternative social order to do all in their power to mould their lives in accordance with its values 'and try to secure group action in the shaping of new institutions in which those values can be realised'.[39] As for himself, he sought to practise what he preached – seeking to limit his wants, engaging in 'bread labour' to produce as much of his food requirements as possible, practising organic agriculture, joining with Ernest Bader and Harold Farmer in the formation of the Society for the Democratic Integration of Industry (Demintry), which was the forerunner of the Industrial Common Ownership Movement (ICOM), and continuing to write and talk about the need for an integral pacifism and a politics of creative living until age began to take its toll. He died on 27 July 1972 at the age of 93.

Conclusion

In the preface to his autobiography Wellock described his life as a 'perpetual series of experiments in the art of living'. Yet, when one

37. *The Khadi World*, vol. 2, no. 1, July 1952, p. 9.
38. W. Wellock, *New Horizons*, London, 1956, p. 12.
39. Ibid., p. 31.

comes to judge that life by conventional criteria, he (and his contemporaries) achieved relatively little. The threat of mass destruction continues to hang over us, the states of the world continue to amass armaments. The scale of things seems to grow ever larger, individuals become increasingly 'cog-like' in their sense of powerlessness as mere spectators of historical development. The destruction of the environment continues apace. Finite resources are devoured as nature is exploited for the sake of private profit and state power. We seem as far from the co-operative commonwealth as ever. Faced with the realities of the world as it is, it is difficult to avoid sinking into a philosophy of despair. To do so, however, would be to relinquish any possibility of acting in the world to change it. The pessimism that comes from a clear intellectual analysis of the world must be balanced by an optimism of the will, a philosophy of hope.

And there are some hopeful signs. During the last quarter of his life when he was advocating a return to a simpler, more self-reliant, integrated and ecologically sound co-operative way of life as a necessary basis for a peaceful world, Wellock was generally considered to be something of a crank by his contemporaries – a charming person but one who was completely out of step with his times. But, as we look around the contemporary scene it is possible to discern a growing interest in the kinds of ideas and practices that Wellock was promoting. Decentralisation, 'small is beautiful', the limitation of material wants, co-operative production, ecologically sound economic systems and modes of life – all these ideas have started to encroach from the margins into the mainstream of current debate. Ideas only reach people who are ready to hear them, and it would seem as if increasing numbers are becoming receptive to the ideas of those, like Wellock, who question the fundamental values and premises upon which our society and our way of life is based.

In 1968 the radical students of France urged 'Be practical, do the impossible.' In equipping ourselves to attempt the impossible, we could do worse than draw some lessons from Wilfred Wellock. Perhaps the key lesson is that the crisis of the arms race, the ecological crisis, and the general human crisis, have their roots in a social crisis. Our domination and exploitation of nature stems from the domination and exploitation of humans by humans, of women by men, of wage labour by capital, of one country by another. All these inter-related forms of domination have their roots in the basic values and human relationships of our society. If we are to have a future we need to reconstruct these values as they are embodied in our daily lives and institutions. We need to see the whole of our daily life as an arena of struggle. The quest for a new social order needs to focus not just on the workplace but the family, not just on the relationship between classes but on the relationships within classrooms, not just on the material conditions of life but on the spiritual condition of the individual psyche. We need to re-empower ourselves, educate ourselves for the role of active, self-governing citizens capable of creating and maintaining self-governing communities and institutions. This, I believe, was the message at the core of Wellock's integral pacifism: the need for a change in the basic organising principle of our lives – away from a conception of the good life as a high standard of living, and a move towards a new understanding of what it means to live well, defined in qualitative, ethical terms of a balanced, self-sufficient life, based on the limitation of wants and mutuality between all living things.

In sketching the appropriate social context for such a life, Wellock drew upon the traditional libertarian ideal of a society of small societies, where people deal with each other on a face-to-face basis, where decisions are arrived at through the direct involvement of all those who wish to participate, where the emphasis in production is upon quality and permanence rather than planned obsolescence, where work is seen as a realm of freedom and a means of self-expression and self-realisation, where the opposition between town and country is transcended, where narrow egotism is transformed into true individuality, and rampant competitiveness is replaced by the practice of co-operative endeavour. This vision is as relevant today as it ever was.

With regard to the means whereby we might seek to achieve such an impossible ideal, the relevance of Wellock's pacifist concern with the continuity between means and ends cannot be overstated. An organic, non-violent social order can only grow from the seeds that we sow in our everyday lives and actions. To the contemporary generation of peace activists 'direct action' brings to mind the range of tactics and strategies available to obstruct and frustrate the functioning of institutions and instruments of oppression and violence. The life and example of Wellock should remind us that the key to direct action is the expression of our claim to be autonomous, self-managing citizens of our society. As such, it is not something to be confined to occasional demonstrations. The authentic expression of the principle of direct action requires us to practise and exercise our capacity for self-management, creative self-expression, mutual care and concern for others, in all areas of life. Only by seeking to transform ourselves at the same time as we seek to reconstruct our institutions can we hope to achieve the impossible, and thereby avert the unthinkable.

Conclusion

Tom Woodhouse

This book has presented some of the recent debates, insights and applications of peace studies. What of the future? In 1985, Johan Galtung, reflecting on progress made during the twenty-five years which had elapsed since the formation of his International Peace Research Institute (PRIO) in Oslo, identified the major dilemmas in peace research in a review of his own intellectual development during the period. His view is that the basic concern of peace research is the reduction of violence of all kinds, and he defines violence as the result of the denial of four basic areas of human need: for survival, welfare, freedom and identity. The relationships which produce peace or violence are formed in four 'spaces': personal relationships (the human space), the social space of societal constructions (broadly culture, politics, economy), the global space of world systems, and the relationship of people to the planet or to nature (the ecological space). This conceptualisation naturally leads to a holistic approach to peace studies; in other words, peace studies has to be, and has operated as an interdisciplinary exercise. It is Galtung's view that the interdisciplinary base needs to be expanded from the existing use of social sciences in order to take in perspectives from the humanities and natural sciences. This approach would have a double benefit (a) enabling peace research to develop a dimension of its work where it was not only critical of existing conditions, but constructive in offering future-oriented visions and options, (b) allowing peace researchers to move on to explore 'the mental and spiritual dimensions of violence, and of human growth and development'.[1] These developments in turn would facilitate the further understanding of a theory of needs in relation to peace and

---

1. J. Galtung, 'Twenty Five Years of Peace Research: Ten Challenges and Some Responses', *Journal of Peace Research*, vol. 22, no. 2, 1985, p. 156.

violence, particularly the place of freedom and identity needs.

There is a pressing need to examine the more concrete paths by which the findings of peace research may be applied to the very real and violent conflicts which plague the globe. As we take stock in the year 2000, Galtung suggests, 'at that point we should be able to say: our activity has not only resulted in an enormous amount of lectures and talks, in articles and books, but also in less violence, more peace'.[2]

Or, as James O'Connell has put it (after the poet Gerard Manley Hopkins), the academic study of peace should be seen in an applied sense, as 'peace with work to do'. O'Connell, in setting out the priorities of the Bradford department after Curle, has insisted on the urgent necessity of peace research to tackle the nuclear issue:

> The truth is that there is no escaping the problem of peace in our time. Minds have been concentrated on the issue by the technical development of weapons in the nuclear age . . . in these circumstances the nuclear issue and the means needed to resolve it retain for us and our contemporaries an excruciating urgency. For that reason there would be an extraordinary failure by academics – an ultimate *trahison des clercs* – were they not to undertake a systematic study of the conditions of contemporary peace.[3]

Much of the work and reputation of the Bradford department in the late 1970s and through the 1980s has been based on its critical research into nuclear arms and disarmament policy. But this has not been its sole area of concentration, and O'Connell has not restricted his agenda of peace research to the technical–political issues of nuclear and non-nuclear defence. Quite to the contrary he recognises the centrality of the positive dimension of peacemaking: the requirement for co-operation and community in pursuit of the universal aims of security, justice and freedom. He also sees peace studies as an integrative or holistic study, bringing together a range of skills and methodologies for the purpose of reducing violence and building world-political systems and ideas which will support peaceful communities. Peace is a long march, not an instant solution, and O'Connell, looking to the year 2000, suggests that future perspectives on peace will emerge from linking the themes of peace, with development and environmental issues:

2. Ibid., pp. 141–58.
3. James O'Connell and Adam Curle, *Peace With Work to Do: The Academic Study of Peace*, Leamington Spa, 1985, p. 7.

Conclusion

Military technology itself in the shape of atomic and nuclear weapons is only one application of science and engineering. Yet technological innovation has taken place so fast in recent times that we are still using thought forms and value attitudes as well as patterns of social organisation that are linked to earlier stages of the industrial revolution. In consequence we have not yet properly come to terms with contemporary technology. . . . [which has] entered on an even faster phase of innovation and change than anything we have seen since the present century began. For such reasons, the crucial alliance for thinking and acting about peace is also the coalition required in a technological age for thinking and acting about the future of the earth and the care of all its peoples.[4]

The conflicts which emerge from this pace of change provide the key justification for peace studies, and their poor management results in widespread misery. New thinking on global security systems, a just economic world order, and wider use of conflict mediation efforts indicate paths forward for peace studies.

In the United States, G. A. Lopez has surveyed the state of peace studies in the universities, where over the past thirty years or so hundreds of peace studies courses have sprung up, many of them initially in response to the Vietnam War. Lopez offers a useful evaluation of the performance of peace education courses during the 1970s and 1980s, and proceeds to suggest a programme of issues to guide curricula development for the 1990s. He makes six general recommendations, as follows:[5]

1. Innovative work must be undertaken in the area of dispute settlement and conflict resolution, and the possible cross-fertilisation between domestic dispute settlement techniques (race, for example), and the problems of international conflict resolution, should be examined.
2. The dominance of political science and its sub-field international relations must be modified to allow an approach which does not lead to focussing only on 'aggregations' and 'generalisations'. The problem of cross-cultural conflict is becoming increasingly apparent and makes it imperative that culturally specific work is carried out: for example, 'an analysis of how far cultural under-

4. See his *Making the Future: Thinking and Acting About Peace in Contemporary Britain*, Stoke on Trent, 1989, p. 23.
5. G. A. Lopez, 'A University Peace Studies Curriculum for the 1990's', *Journal of Peace Research*, vol. 22, no. 2, 1985, pp. 117–29.

standings of religion, of the rule of law in society, and differing concepts of space and time are relevant both in their own right, and in their impact on our understanding of conflict and conflict management'.[6]

3. There is a need to provide educational opportunities for 'imaging the future', a valuable process which enables some escape from the phenomenon of 'nuclear numbness' and which generally can enhance a future-oriented problem-solving capability.

4. There ought to be continued exploration of the traditions of non-violence.

5. The question of defining national security, and its relationship to peace and justice, and to international security, should be a high priority.

6. The multidimensional approach to peace studies should be vigorously continued, and active and intense discussion of methodology and epistemology pursued (cross-cultural training, future imaging, and the linkage of domestic–international conflict-resolution techniques are suggested by Lopez).

It is clear from this brief speculation about the future of peace studies, that there is general agreement on a central role for refining and developing the theory and practice of conflict resolution and mediation. One writer indeed has argued that the concept of conflict and its resolution should be the primary and determining characteristic of peace studies. M. Banks suggests that peace has been conceptualised through four different approaches (peace as harmony, peace as justice, peace as order, and peace as conflict management). His contention is that peace has been thought of as a fixed condition with different prescriptions (swords into ploughshares, world government, justice for all) being proposed in order to deliver a just or an harmonious or an ordered world. Banks makes the important point that desirable though these values might be they constitute the products of peace, but not necessarily the means to attain it.

The core of peace research, he argues, must be conflict analysis and resolution because it provides the best unifying terrain for the study of peace, and in the study and analysis of actual conflicts peace research can find a key role in clarifying options for people and their decision-makers trapped in conflict situations. This

6. Ibid., p. 126.

analysis by Banks[7] is helpful in emphasising the need for peace research to find the methods by which to implement the results of its findings, so that the basic value-orientation of the study, the reduction of violence and the evolution of peaceful relationships at all social levels, is achieved. However, conflict resolution itself is at a fairly rudimentary state of development and much needs to be done still in the areas of theory formation, and in training and education for the application of theory to the resolution of real conflicts. In a recent review of the state of knowledge Connie Peck has put the position well: 'research into the development of methods for resolving conflict by constructive means has virtually been ignored. What work there is has been done by isolated scholars with little in the way of resources. It is estimated that the annual expenditure for peace research throughout the world totals less than the yearly budget for the US government's military bands.'[8]

In advancing both their theoretical acumen, and in developing their skills, conflict resolvers will need dialogue with and insights from the work of a broader community of peace research and education, which in turn will continue to draw its information from a multidisciplinary and multi-issue base. In 1978 the Consortium on Peace Research, Education and Development (COPRED) identified four particular areas within which peace studies courses might concentrate:

1. A futurist or world order approach.
2. A conflict regulation/management approach (reducing conflict tensions through existing institutions).
3. A non-violent values and lifestyles approach.
4. A war–peace systems approach (which draws on international politics and the structure and operation of the current world situation).

Similar priorities may be found in Curle and O'Connell,[9] and one writer has indeed found that there is a remarkable consistency of concepts and interrelated research in peace studies internationally,

7. See M. Banks, 'Four Conceptions of Peace', in D. Sandole and I. Staroste-Sandole (eds.), *Conflict Management and Problem-Solving: Interpersonal to International Applications*, London and New York, 1987, pp. 259–74.
8. C. Peck 'An Integrative Model for Understanding and Managing Conflict'. *Interdisciplinary Peace Research*, vol. 1, no. 1, May 1989, pp. 7–36.
9. See O'Connell and Curle, *Peace With Work To Do*.

indicating a broadly 'unified field rather than divisive schools'.[10]

This book is dedicated to a man who saw the need for new skills and knowledge through the study of peace, and acted on his vision in a practical and an inspiring fashion.

10. See A. Kemp, 'Images of the Peace Field: An International Survey', *Journal of Peace Research*, vol. 22, no. 2, 1985, pp. 129–40.

Bibliography

Adam Curle and Peace Studies

Curle, A., 'Transitional Communities and Social Reconnection', *Human Relations*, pt 1, vol. 1, no. 1, 1947

——'Incentives to Work: An Anthropological Appraisal', *Human Relations*, vol. 2, no. 1, 1948

——'What Happened to Three Villages', *The Listener*, vol. 48, no. 1242, 1952

——'Some Psychological Factors in Rural Sociology', *Tribus*, nos. 4–5, 1954–5

——'The Psychological Theory of Group Work', in P. Kuenstler (ed.), *Social Group Work in Great Britain*, London, 1955

——'From Student To Teacher Status', *The New Era in Home and School*, vol. 36, no. 2, 1955

——'Tradition, Development, and Planning', *Sociological Review*, vol. 8, no. 2, 1960

——'African Nationalism and Higher Education in Ghana', *Universities Quarterly*, vol. 16, no. 3, 1962

——*Educational Strategy for Developing Societies: A Study of Educational and Social Factors in Relation to Economic Growth*, London, 1963

——*Planning For Education in Pakistan: A Personal Case Study*, London, 1966

——'Educational Planning: The Adviser's Role', *Fundamentals of Educational Planning*, series no. 8, Paris, 1968

——*Making Peace*, London, 1971

——*Mystics and Militants*, London, 1972

——*Education for Liberation*, London, 1973

——*Educational Problems of Developing Societies, with Case Studies of Ghana and Pakistan*, London, 1973

——*The Scope and Dilemmas of Peace Studies*, Inaugural Lecture, University of Bradford, 4 February 1975

——*Peace and Love: The Violin and the Oboe*, London, 1977

——'Reflections On Working In a University, *Studies In Higher Education*, vol. 2, no. 1, 1977

——*Peacemaking: Public and Private*, occasional paper no. 5, Queens

University, Ontario, 1978
——*True Justice: Quaker Peacemakers and Peacemaking*, London 1981
——*Tools for Transformation: A Personal Study*, Stroud, 1990
Curle, A. and James O'Connell, *Peace With Work To Do: The Academic Study of Peace*, Leamington Spa, 1985
Curle, A. and E. L. Trist, 'Transitional Communities and Social Reconnection', *Human Relations*, pt 2, vol. 1, no. 2, 1947

Peace Research and Education

Boulding, E., 'Peace Research: Dialectics and Development', *Journal of Conflict Resolution*, vol. 16, no. 4, 1972, pp. 469–75
Burns, R., 'Continuity and Change in Peace Education', *Bulletin of Peace Proposals*, vol. 2, 1981
Council of Europe, *Violence and Conflict Resolution in Schools*, Strasburg, 1989
Galtung, J., 'Twenty Five Years of Peace Research: Ten Challenges and Some Responses', *Journal of Peace Research*, vol. 22, no. 2, 1985, pp. 141–58
Haavelsrud, M., *Education for Peace: Reflection and Action*, Guildford, 1974
Heater, D., *Education for International Understanding in Britain*, London, 1980
Hicks, D., *Education for Peace: Issues, Dilemmas, and Alternatives*, Lancaster, 1985
Lopez, G., 'A University Peace Studies Curriculum for the 1990s', *Journal of Peace Research*, vol. 22, no. 2, 1985
Mack, A., *Peace Research in the 1980s*, Canberra, 1985
Maslow, A., *Self-Actualisation*, San Fernando, Calif., 1972
Rank, C., 'Peace Studies in American Higher Education: The Emergence of a New Field', PhD Thesis, University of California, Berkeley, 1988
Thomas, D. and M. Klare (eds.) *Peace and World Order Studies: A Curriculum Guide*, 5th edn, Boulder, Colo., 1989
Wiberg, H., 'What Have We Learned about Peace?', *Journal of Peace Research*, vol. 18, no. 2, 1981, pp. 111–48

Defence, Disarmament and Peace

Alternative Defence Commission, *Defence Without the Bomb*, London, 1983

Bibliography

——*The Politics of Alternative Defence*, London, 1987
Gaddis, J. L. 'The Long Peace: Elements of Stability in the Post-War International System', *International Security* vol. 10, no. 4, 1986, pp. 99–142
Kaldor, M. and D. Smith (eds.), *Disarming Europe*, London, 1982
Litherland, J. P. 'Soviet Views of the Arms Race and Disarmament: Arms Control and Foreign Policy Research and the Development of Gorbachev's "New Thinking" on Nuclear Weapons', Ph.D Thesis, University of Bradford, 1987
MccGwire, M. 'Soviet Military Objectives', *World Policy Journal*, vol. 3, no. 4, 1986, pp. 667–95
Osgood, C. E., *An Alternative to War or Surrender*, Urbana, Ill., 1962
Palme, O., *Common Security: A Programme for Disarmament*, London, 1982
Roberts, A., *Nations in Arms*, London, 1976
Rogers, P., and M. Dando, *Directory of Nuclear, Biological and Chemical Weapons 1990*, London, 1990
Smith, D., *Defence of the Realm in the 1980s*, London, 1980

Peace and the Resolution of Conflict

International and General

Azar, E. and J. Burton, *International Conflict Resolution: Theory and Practice*, Brighton, 1986
Banks, M., 'Mediation', *World Encyclopedia of Peace*, vol. 1, 1986, pp. 589–92
Bercovitz, J., 'A Case Study of Mediation as a Method of International Conflict Resolution: The Camp David Experience', *Review of International Studies*, vol. 12, 1986, pp. 43–65
Burton, J., *Conflict and Communication: The Use of Controlled Communication in International Relations*, London, 1969
——*Global Conflict*, Brighton, 1984
——'History of Conflict Resolution', *World Encyclopedia of Peace*, vol. 1, 1986, pp. 174–9
——*Resolving Deep-Rooted Conflict. A Handbook*, Lanham, Md, 1987
Current Research on Peace and Violence, 'Special Issue on Peace and Violence', vol. 9, 1986
Deutsch, M., *The Resolution of Conflict: Constructive and Destructive Processes*, New Haven, Conn., 1973

Dunn, D., 'Peace Studies', *World Encyclopedia of Peace*, vol. 2, 1986, pp. 247–51

Fisher, R. and W. Ury, *Getting to Yes*, London, 1987

Fisher, R. and S. Brown, *Getting Together*, London, 1989

Fogg, R. W., 'Dealing with Conflict: A Repertoire of Creative Peaceful Approaches', *Journal of Conflict Resolution*, vol. 29, no. 2, 1985

Folberg, J. and A. Taylor, *Mediation*, London, 1984

Groom, A. J. R., 'Problem Solving in International Relations', *World Encyclopedia of Peace*, vol. 2, 1986, pp. 298–301

Harbottle, M., 'Confidence Building in International Diplomacy', *World Encyclopedia of Peace*, vol. 1, 1986, pp. 165–9

Hill, B., 'An Analysis of Conflict Resolution Techniques: From Problem Solving Workshops to Theory', *Journal of Conflict Resolution*, vol. 26, no. 1, March 1982, pp. 109–38

Jackson, E., *Meeting of Minds: A Way to Peace Through Mediation*, New York, 1952

Marshall, T., 'Alternative Dispute Resolution', *World Encyclopedia of Peace*, vol. 1, 1986, pp. 15–19

Mitchell, C., *The Structure of International Conflict*, London, 1981
——*Peacemaking and the Consultant's Role*, Farnborough, 1981

Mitchell, C. and K. Webb, *New Approaches to International Mediation*, Westport, Conn., 1988

World Encyclopedia of Peace, ed. L. Pauline, 3 vols., London, 1986

Sullivan, P., 'Peace and Conflict Research: Development', *World Encyclopedia of Peace*, vol. 2, 1986, pp. 176–8

Webb, K., 'Conflict: Inherent and Contingent Theories', *World Encyclopedia of Peace*, vol. 1, 1986, pp. 169–74

White, R., 'International Arbitration', *World Encyclopedia of Peace*, vol. 1, 1986, pp. 53–6

Peace and Change, Special Issue on Conflict Resolution, nos. 2–3, 1982

Peck, C., 'An Integrative Model for Understanding and Managing Conflict', *Interdisciplinary Peace Research*, vol. 1, no. 1, May 1989, pp. 7–36

Pruitt, D. and J. Rubin, *Social Conflict. Escalation, Stalemate and Settlement*, New York, 1985

Rubin, J., 'Some Roles and Functions of a Mediator', in J. Thompson (ed.), *Psychology and the Prevention of Nuclear War*, New York, 1986, pp. 490–510

Sandole, D. and I. Sandole-Staroste, *Conflict Management and Problem Solving: Interpersonal to International Applications*, New York, 1987

Sites, P., *Control, the Basis of Social Order*, New York and London, 1973

Touval, S., *The Peace Brokers: Mediators in the Arab–Israeli Conflict 1948–1979*, Princeton, N. J., 1982

Vickers, G., 'Conflict', *Futures*, vol. 4, no. 2, 1972, pp. 126–41

Wehr, P., *Conflict Regulations*, Boulder, Colo., 1979

Bibliography

Young, O., *The Intermediaries: Third Parties in International Crisis*, Princeton, N. J., 1987

Quakers and Mediation

Bolling, L., 'Quaker Work in the Middle East, following the June 1967 War', in M. Berman and J. Johnson (eds.), *Unofficial Diplomats*, New York, 1977, pp. 80–8

Bailey, S., 'Non-Official Mediation in Disputes: Reflections on Quaker Experience', *International Affairs*, vol. 61, no. 2, 1985

Pettigrew, J., 'Quaker International Conciliation: An Evaluation of its Roots, Character and Development', M. Phil thesis, University of Bradford, 1989

Yarrow, M., *Quaker Experiences in International Conciliation*, New Haven, Conn., 1978

Community and Neighbourhood

Beer, J., *Peacemaking in Your Neighbourhood: Reflections on an Experiment in Community Mediation*, Philadelphia, Pa., 1986

Hope, A. and S. Timmel, *Training for Transformation: A Handbook for Community Workers*, pts 1, 2 and 3, Gweru, Zimbabwe, 1987

Kressel, K. and D. Pruitt, 'Themes in the Mediation of Social Conflict', *Journal of Social Issues*, vol. 42, no. 2, 1985, pp. 179–98

Miller, E. J., 'Conflict and Reconciliation: The Newham Experiment', Tavistock Institute occasional paper no. 9, 1986

Skills and Methods

Burnard, P., *Teaching Interpersonal Skills: A Handbook of Experiential Learning for Health Professionals*, Therapy in Practice 10, London, 1989

Conflict Resolution Network (Helena Cornelius and Shoshana Faise), *Conflict Resolution for the Community: Trainers Manual*, 5th edn, Sydney, 1989

Cormack, D., *Peacing Together: From Conflict to Reconciliation*, Eastbourne, 1989

Davis, H. and M. Dugan, 'Training the Mediator', *Peace and Change*, vol. 8, no. 2–3, 1982, pp. 81–90

Fitzduff, M., *Community Conflict Skills: A Handbook for Anti-Sectarian Work in Northern Ireland*, Community Skills Project, Cookstown, Co. Tyrone, N. Ireland, 1988

Jones, K., *Simulations: A Handbook for Teachers*, London, 1980

Katz, N., and J. Lawyer, *Communication and Conflict Resolution Skills*, Dubuque, Iowa, 1985

Quaker Peace Action, *Speaking Our Peace: Exploring Non-Violence and Conflict Resolution*, London, 1987

Psychology of Conflict

Bronfenbrenner, U., 'The Mirror-image in Soviet–American Relations: A Social Psychologist's Report', *Journal of Social Issues*, vol. 17, no. 3, 1961, pp. 45–56

Crum, T., *The Magic of Conflict: Turning a Life of Work into a Work of Art*, New York, 1987

Frank, J., *Sanity and Survival: Psychological Aspects of War and Peace*, New York, 1967

Janis, I., *Victims of Groupthink: Psychological Studies of Policy Decisions and Fiascoes*, rev. edn, Boston, Mass., 1982

Lifton, J., 'Beyond Psychic Numbing: A Call to Awareness', *American Journal of Orthopsychiatry*, vol. 52, no. 4, 1982, pp. 619–29

Menkes, D., 'Psychological Defence Mechanisms and the Nuclear Arms Race: An Interactive Model', *Medicine and War*, vol. 5, no. 2, 1989, pp. 80–95

Oppenheim, A., 'Psychological Perspectives in Conflict Research', in M. Banks (ed.), *Conflict in World Society*, London, 1984

Thompson, J., *Psychological Aspects of Nuclear War*, Chichester, 1985

White, R. K., *Psychology and the Prevention of Nuclear War: A Book of Readings*, New York, 1986

Case Studies in Conflict Management and Conflict Resolution

Burgess, H. and G. Burgess, ' United States Dispute Handling Systems: Traditions, Alternatives, and Current Issues', unpublished paper presented at JSA Conference, London, 1989

Rupesinghe, K., 'Ethnic Conflicts in South Asia: The Case of Sri Lanka and the Indian Peace Keeping Force', *Journal of Peace Research*, vol. 25, no. 4, 1988, pp. 337–50

Problem-Solving Workshops

Boehringer, G., J. Bayley, *et al.*, 'Stirling: The Destructive Application of Group Techniques to a Conflict', *Journal of Conflict Resolution*, vol. 18, no. 2, 1974, pp. 257–75

Doob, L. and W. Foltz, 'The Belfast Workshop: An Application of Group Techniques to a Destructive Conflict'. *Journal of Conflict Resolution*, vol. 17, no. 3, 1973

Doob, L., 'A Cyprus Workshop: An Exercise in Intervention Methodology', *Journal of Social Psychology*, vol. 94, 1974, pp. 161–78

Bibliography

Fetherston, B., 'Conflict Resolution in International Relations. An Evaluation of the Problem Solving Workshop', MA Thesis, University of Bradford, 1989

Fisher, R., 'Third Party Consultation: A Problem-Solving Approach For De-Escalating International Conflict', in J. Maas and R. Stewart, (eds.), *Toward a World of Peace: People Create Alternatives*, Suva, Fiji, 1986

Kelman, H., 'An Interactional Approach to Conflict Resolution', in R. White, (ed.) *Psychology and the Prevention of Nuclear War*, 1986

Kelman, H. and S. Cohen, 'The Problem-Solving Workshop. A Psychological (Social) Contribution to the Resolution of International Conflicts', *Journal of Peace Research*, vol. 13, no. 2, 1976, pp. 79–90

Professional Applications

Family

Dyer, C., *Mediation in Divorce*, 133 Rosslyn Rd, Twickenham, TW1 2AR, 1989

Erickson, S. and M. Erickson, *Family Mediation Casebook*, New York, 1988

Francis, P., *Family Conciliation and Mediation*, Social Work Monographs, University of East Anglia, Norwich, 1989

Roberts, M., *Mediation in Family Disputes: A Guide to Practice*, Aldershot, 1988

Shaw, M. and W. Phear, *The Parent–Child Mediation Manual*, New York, 1989

Education

Council of Europe, *Violence and Conflict Resolution in Schools*, Strasburg, 1989

Frances, N., *Coping with Conflict: A Resource Book for the Middle School Years*, Learning Development Aids, 1987

Francis, R., 'Accounting for Conflict', MA Thesis, University of Bradford, 1987

Judson, S. (ed.), *A Manual on Nonviolence and Children*, Philadelphia, Pa., 1984

The following three titles can be obtained from the Peace Education Project, 6 Endsleigh Street, London, WC1 HOD:

MASHEDER, M, *Let's Co-operate.*

PEP TALK 7, *Co-operative Games.*

PEP TALK 13, *Coping with Conflict in Schools.*

Crime/Law/Policing/Victim Offender

Forum for Initiatives in Mediation and Reparation (FIRM), 'Repairing the Damage: Proceedings of The First National Symposium on Mediation and Criminal Justice', FIRM occasional paper, 1989
MacKay, R., 'Reparation in Criminal Justice', *Scottish Association for the Care and Resettlement of Offenders*, Edinburgh, 1988
MaGuire, M. and J. Pointing, *Victims of Crime: A New Deal*, Oxford, 1989
Wright, M. and B. Galaway, (eds.), *Mediation and Criminal Justice: Victims, Offenders, and Community*, London, 1989

Race/Religion/Ethnicity

Boucher, J., D. Landis and Arnold Clark, K., *Ethnic Conflict: International Perspectives*, London, 1987
Hewstone, M. and Brown, R., *Contact and Conflict in Intergroup Encounters*, Oxford, 1986
Tajfel, H., *Human Groups and Social Categories: Studies in Social Psychology*, Cambridge, 1981

Environment

Bingham, G., *Resolving Environmental Disputes: A Decade of Experience*, Washington, DC, 1986

Peaceful Relationships

Feminism and Peace

Roach-Pearson, R., *Women and Peace: Theoretical, Historical, and Practical Perspectives*, London and Sydney, 1987
Dworkin, A., *Our Blood*, New York, 1976
Bussey, G. and M. Timms, *Pioneers For Peace: The Women's International League for Peace and Freedom*, London, 1980
Gilligan, C., *In a Different Voice*, Cambridge, Mass., 1982
Jones, L., *Keeping the Peace*, London, 1983
Cook, A. and G. Kirk, *Greenham Women Everywhere*, London, 1983
Segall, L., *Is the Future Female?*, London, 1987
Liddington, J., *The Women's Peace Movement*, London, 1989
Thompson, D., *Over Our Dead Bodies: Women Against the Bomb*, London, 1983

Bibliography

Brock-Utne, B., *Educating for Peace: A Feminist Perspective*, Oxford, 1985

Macdonald, S., P. Holden, and S. Ardener, *Images of Women in Peace and War*, London, 1987

Chester, G., and A. Rigby (eds.), *Articles of Peace*, Bridport, 1986

Pacifism

Addams, J., *The Long Road of Women's Memory*, New York, 1916

——*Peace and Bread in Time of War*, New York, 1922

——*The Excellent Becomes the Permanent*, New York, 1932

Brock, P., *Twentieth Century Pacifism*, New York, 1970

Buber, M., *Between Man and Man*, translated by Ronald Gregor Smith, London, 1947

——*Paths in Utopia*, translated by R. F. C. Hull, London, 1949

Ceadel, M., *Pacifism in Britain 1914–1945: the Defining of a Faith*, Oxford, 1980

Friedman, M. S., *Martin Buber: The Life of Dialogue*, New York, 1960

Ligt, B. de, *The Conquest of Violence*, London, 1937

Rigby, A., *A Life in Peace: A Biography of Wilfred Wellock*, Bridport, 1988

Teilhard de Chardin, P., *The Divine Milieu*, New York, 1960

——*The Future of Man*, translated by N. Denny, New York, 1964

——*Man's Place in Nature*, translated by Rene Hague, New York, 1966

Notes on Contributors

Adam Curle was born in 1916 and began his academic career at the Tavistock Institute in London in the immediate post-war years. This was followed by an appointment at the University of Oxford as a lecturer in social psychology in 1950. He was appointed to the Chair in Education and Psychology at Exeter in 1952. From 1956 to 1959 he served as an adviser to the government of Pakistan, followed by two years (1959–1961) as Professor of Education at the University of Ghana. From 1962 he was Director of the Harvard Center for Studies in Education and Development, where he worked until his decision to return to England in 1973 to take the Chair of Peace Studies at the University of Bradford. He retired from this post in 1978, and has since been very active as a mediator (usually working with the Quakers) in a range of violent conflicts.

Elise Boulding is Professor Emerita of Sociology, Dartmouth College, USA. She has been a leading member of the International Peace Research Association and has served on the UNESCO Peace Prize jury, and on the Council of the United Nations University.

Malcolm Dando is Senior Lecturer in Peace Studies at the University of Bradford. He was a member of the first Alternative Defence Commission, and was formerly secretary of the Conflict Research Society (UK).

A. Betts Fetherston is a graduate of the University of Connecticut, where she took a BA degree in Psychology in 1987. In 1989 she was awarded an MA in Peace Studies at the University of Bradford and is currently undertaking doctoral research into the role of the United Nations in conflict resolution.

Johan Galtung is currently Professor of Peace Studies at the University of Hawaii, Honolulu. He founded the International Peace Research Institute, Oslo (PRIO) in 1959 and was the first editor of its *Journal of Peace Research*. In 1987 he won the Right Livelihood Award for his outstanding contribution to peace research.

Kevin Green is currently Head of English in a secondary school in Lancashire, UK. He was a member of the Peace Studies Working Party of Wakefield Metropolitan Borough Council, and was awarded an M Phil. degree from the Department of Peace Studies, the University of Bradford in 1986 for his study of peace education in the UK from which his chapter is drawn.

Paul Landais-Stamp is a graduate of the Department of Peace Studies, the University of Bradford having been awarded his degree in 1989. He has written, with Paul Rogers, a study of New Zealand's non-nuclear defence policy, *Rocking the Boat: New Zealand, the United States and the Nuclear Free Zone Controversy in the 1980s* (Oxford, 1989). He is currently completing an M Phil. thesis on mediation with special reference to environmental conflicts.

359

Notes on Contributors

Andrew Mack is Head of the Peace Research Centre of the Australian National University. He is the author of *Peace Research in the 1980s* (Canberra, 1985) from which his chapter is derived.

Robert McKinlay is a Quaker and as Pro-Vice-Chancellor and Vice-Principal of the University of Bradford, was the main link between the University and the Society of Friends when the Chair of Peace Studies was established. He was also the instigator of the moves which resulted in Adam Curle's appointment to the Chair.

Chris Mitchell was Professor of International Relations at the City University, London, and is currently Professor of Conflict Resolution and International Relations in the Center for Conflict Analysis and Resolution, George Mason University, Virginia, USA.

James O'Connell is Professor of Peace Studies at the University of Bradford, a post he has held since 1978 when Adam Curle retired. He previously served as Professor and Dean of the Faculty of Arts, Ulster College, Northern Ireland Polytechnic; and as Professor and Head of the Department of Government, Ahmadu Bello University, Nigeria. During his time at Bradford, he has served as Dean of Social Sciences and as Pro-Vice-Chancellor.

Sarah Perrigo is currently a lecturer in Peace Studies, University of Bradford. As well as having a B Phil. from Oxford in 1972, she is a State Registered Nurse and was formerly a tutor with the Open University.

John Pettigrew is a member of the Society of Friends and has for twelve years been chairman of his local branch of the United Nations Association. He has recently been awarded an M.Phil. degree from the Department of Peace Studies at Bradford and his thesis, 'Quaker Mediation: An Evaluation of its Roots, Character and Development', forms the basis for his chapter.

Carol Rank is a graduate of the University of California at Berkeley where she was awarded a BA degree in 1975. She subsequently was awarded a PhD for a study of Peace Education in Higher Education the United States (also from Berkeley). She is currently co-ordinator of the Leeds Mediation Service.

Andrew Rigby is a lecturer in the Department of Peace Studies, University of Bradford, and was formerly lecturer in Sociology, University of Aberdeen. In 1988 he published *A Life in Peace*, a biography of the pacifist Wilfred Wellock from which his chapter is drawn.

Paul Rogers is Senior Lecturer in the Department of Peace Studies, University of Bradford. He was Chairman of the Alternative Defence Commission between 1984–7, and is author of the *Guide to Nuclear Weapons* (Oxford, 1988) and co-author (with Paul Landais-Stamp) of *Rocking the Boat: New Zealand, the United States and the Nuclear-Free Zone Controversy in the 1980s* (Oxford, 1989).

Tom Woodhouse is currently Senior Lecturer and chairman of Postgraduate Studies in the Department of Peace Studies, University of Bradford. He was research assistant to Adam Curle until 1975, when he was appointed as a Lecturer in Peace Studies. He has recently become Director of the Centre for Conflict Resolution at Horsley House, which is a new project of the Department of Peace Studies.

Index

Index

Index

Index

in the US, Quakers
interdisciplinary nature, 7, 41,
99–100, 112–14
peace activism, 121
priorities, 5, 7
problems, 130–6
professionalisation, 135–6
values, 120
Peace Studies, Department of, 1–5,
241, 323–4
creation, 59–70
Quaker Peace Studies Trust, 61,
62
critique, 99, 100, 102
see also Bradford, University of,
Curle, A., peace studies
peace studies in higher education,
107–21, 122, 138
areas of study, 112–16
relevance, 108–9
peace studies in the United States,
122–40
infrastructure, 127
journals, 127–30
see also IPRA, COPRED
perestroika, 8
development, 168–71
external aspects, 167–8, 193–4, 196–8
impact on Western Europe,
183–93, 198–9
trust-building process, 167–8
see also Gorbachev, M., NATO,
Soviet Arms Control Policy,
unilateral initiatives
Perez de Cuellar, Javier, 52
Pike, Graham, 153, 154
polarised thinking, 80–1
definition, 45–6
radical/liberal debate in peace
research, 86
Polemological Institute, 5, 81, 82
see also peace research
power imbalance see ethics in
mediation
PPU see Peace Pledge Union
principled negotiation, 46, 55–6
PRIO see International Peace
Research Institute, Oslo
problem-solving, 255
definition, 252–3
problem-solving workshop see
facilitated problem-solving
PSS(I) see Peace Science Society
(International)

Purnell, David, 243
puzzle-solving, 254–5
definition, 252–3

QCEA see Quaker Council for
European Affairs
QPS see Quaker Peace and Service
Quakers, 3, 5, 249
conflict resolution, 241, 241
methods, 10, 47–8
peace testimony, 4, 47, 62
University of Bradford, 59–62
see also Curle, A., Richardson,
L.F., Quaker mediation
Quaker Council for European Affairs,
242
Quaker mediation, 226–46
current status, 240
development, 226–7
evaluation, 231–9
international conciliation and
mediation, 10, 226–31, 244–6
methods, 10, 47–8, 229, 239, 244
training, 243
Quaker Peace and Service, 242, 243
peace education, 243

Rapaport, Anatol
evaluation of Quaker mediation,
233–4, 236
Rathenow, F., 141–2, 155–6
Reading Mediation Centre, 242
realism
balance of power, 77, 101
'peace through strength'
policies, 80, 102, 103
critique, 96–7
reciprocal escalation spiral, 80
critique, 76–80, 105–6
definition, 76
human nature, 95–6
reconciliation, 49
Religious Society of Friends see
Quakers
Reykjavik Summit, 173, 182–3
Rich, Adrienne, 312, 319
Richardson Institute of Conflict and
Peace Research, 39, 82, 101, 240, 323
see also peace research, Richardson,
L.F.
Richardson, Lewis Fry, 80, 240

St. Augustine, 110–11
Schmid, Herman

366

critique of 'liberal' peace research,
85–6
structuralist definition of conflict,
215–16
see also objective conflict
Scientific Council on Peace and
Disarmament, 170
see also IMEMO, ISKAN
Scruton, Roger
critique of peace studies, 98–102, 142
SDI *see* Strategic Defense Initiative
sensitivity training *see* laboratory
method
SIPRI *see* Stockholm International
Peace Research Institute
Sites, Paul
human needs, 95
theory of power and social control,
53, 254, 255
Smoker, P., 141–2, 155–6
social psychology
peace research, 80–1
see also facilitated problem-solving,
polarised thinking
Soviet Arms Control Policy, 170–1
mutual responsibility, 170
unilateral initiatives, 171, 173–5
Soviet Foreign Policy *see* perestroika
START *see* Strategic Arms Reduction
Treaty
Stevens, Robert, 256
see also Formeda Workshop,
Stirling Workshop
Stirling Workshop, 257–8
see also Doob, L.
Stockholm International Peace
Research Institute, 82, 105
Strategic Arms Reduction Treaty, 174
Strategic Defence Initiative, 8, 181–2
structural violence, 6, 9, 83–4, 91–5
conscientisation, 92
see also Galtung, J., peace
subjective conflict, 9, 46, 209–11
see also conflict, objective conflict
Susskind, Lawrence
environmental mediation, 269
method, 277–81

Tavistock Institute for Human
Relations, 31–2, 33
Tavistock model, 257
T-groups, 256–8
Thatcher, Margaret, 190
British Defence Policy, 200

Thee, Marek, 101, 131
Track II diplomacy, 248

UNESCO *see* United Nations
Educational, Scientific and Cultural
Organisation
unilateral disarmament, 98, 101
unilateral initiatives
definition, 101
theory of, 171–3
see also Osgood, C.
UNITAR *see* United Nations
Institute for Training and Research
United Nations
International Mediation Centre,
56–7, 243
mediation, 52
United Nations University, 301
United Nations Educational, Scientific
and Cultural Organisation, 101, 129,
144, 154–5
United Nations Institute for
Training and Research, 129–30,
160–1
United States Institute of Peace, 2, 126
Ury, William *see* principled negotiation
utopias, 20

verification, 174–5, 176
environmental mediation, 281
Vickers, Geoffrey, 171
violence
human capacity for, 200
transcendence of, 1
see also conflict, peace, structural
violence

war
causes, 17–18
Warsaw Pact, 8–9, 13, 196–9
new Soviet Foreign Policy, 176–7
Wehr, Paul, 240
Weinstein, Alan
environmental mediation, 269
method, 277–81
Wellock, Wilfred, 12
life of, 326–43
values, 325–6, 327, 342–3
see also integral pacifism
Western European Union, 183
WEU *see* Western European Union
Wiberg, Hakan
development of peace research, 138
WILPF *see* Women's International